Promise and Performance
Albanese's First Term

Connor Court Publishing

Published by Connor Court Publishing Pty Ltd, 2025.

CONNOR COURT PUBLISHING PTY LTD
PO Box 7257
Redland Bay QLD 4165
sales@connorcourt.com
www.connorcourtpublishing.com.au

We thank David Clune and Bruce Kingston for their advice and providing editing assistance on different chapters in this volume.

ISBN: 9781923224759

Cover design by Ian James. Photos taken from Wikipedia Commons.

.

Printed in Australia.

"Are we going to embark on a new era of economic reform with productivity growth at the centre?

Are we going to stride forward – or instead are we going to slide back?

Are we going to risk three more wasted years?

It is only ever Labor Governments who do the big reforms, drive the big changes, reshape the economy in the best interests of people".

- Anthony Albanese, Election Speech, 1 May 2022 – Perth

CONTENTS

Promise and Performance: An Introduction – Scott Prasser   7

Part 1: Overview: The Changing Political Environment

1 The Albanese Government's Election Performances
– Malcolm Mackerras   25

2 How Albanese and Chalmers have Created a New Narrative of
Australian Politics
– Greg Melleuish   47

3 Labor's Federal Election Performance in Queensland
– John Mickel   67

4 The Dutton-led Opposition in Labor's First Term
– Peter van Onselen   83

Part 2: Managing the Institutions

5 The Public Service under Albanese
– Paddy Gourley   105

6 Creating a New Standards Regime and a Safer Workplace for
Parliament
– Maria Maley   129

7 The Albanese Government's Public Inquiries: Targeting Political
Opponents?
– Scott Prasser   139

Part 3: Managing the Policies

8 The Australian Economy over the Albanese Government's First
Term
– Gene Tunny   165

9 Fiscal Policy under the Albanese Government, 2022-2025
– Saul Eslake   183

10 Perverse Productivity Policies: Rhetoric vs Reality
– Gary Banks   203

11 The Albanese Government's Industrial Relations Program
– Richard Calver   225

12 Energy and Environment Policy
– Aynsley Kellow   241

13 Aviation Policy: A Reluctance to Reform?
– Peter Forsyth   259

14 Labor's Higher Education Agenda: A La-La-Land Wish List
– Salvatore Babones   283

15 The Voice Debacle
– Gary Johns   303

16 The Drift of Australian Foreign Policy
– Michael Easson   315

17 Defence Policy
– David Lee   343

18 The Albanese Government Record on Government Services and
Digital Transformation
– Mike Kelly   **361**

19 Religious Freedom: Always the Bridesmaid, Never the Bride
– Mark Spencer   393

20 Anyone for Footy? A Policy in Search of a Goal: The Albanese
Government's PNG NRL Initiative
– Andrea Wallace   409

Part 4: Aftermath: Lessons for the Future
21 Lessons for the Future
– Scott Prasser   427

Contributors   434
Index   439

Promise and Performance:
An Introduction

Scott Prasser

Introduction

This volume is a critical assessment of the Albanese Labor Government's first term in office. No doubt later assessments will follow, particularly given Labor's 2025 election win, which seems to have entrenched it in power for some time to come. These assessments will inevitably cover a wider expanse of political history than is possible in this volume. They will have access to more information. Eventfully archives will open and memoirs will flow. All that, however, makes this volume's focus on the Albanese Government's first term even more important before attention shifts to its second term agenda. By being just after the first term is over, this volume possibly better catches the immediacy of events, the nuances of the debates, the roles of key personalities and contemporary views about the first Albanese Government's actions and motivations in the context of the times rather than later from a more distant, perspective. By so doing, this volume seeks to identify what went right and wrong during that first term and also possible insights into what factors led to Labor's large 2025 election win and how Albanese might govern in his second term.

Admittedly, there is a danger of focusing on a new government's first term. Assessments might be too easily affected by the immediacy of debates concerning current issues and the politics of the day. As many policies take time for their full impact to be appreciated it may be too soon to accurately assess their success or failure. Also, as the release of archival material is several decades away, verification as to why certain decisions were made or not made, cannot be completely confirmed. And it is too soon for participants' memoirs – they have yet to come.

At the same time, later assessments are not without flaws. Consideration of government policies distant from the times are often viewed by academics through the narrow lens of rational, evidence-based decision making. This ignores the rushed, reactive, political, short term, and pressured nature of modern decision making. Policy actions by government are driven by a host of factors other than just "solving" a policy problem regardless of the accompanying government rhetoric. Ideology, beating the opposition and winning an election are often just as paramount. Means of achieving political survival, not policy outcomes that are only realised often in the distant future, are the name of the game. There is also the danger of "presentism" – judging the past in terms of what we now know and from current values leading to misinterpretation of events, and motives concerning past actions and actors. While archival information like cabinet documents and minutes are important, they only tell part of any public policy story. Not everything in government is captured in such minutes or turns around specific decisions at distinct points in time by office holders. As for memoirs by past players, while sometimes insightful, they can just present a particular participant's version of events exaggerating their contributions, missing the bigger picture, seeking to shift blame elsewhere or to wreak revenge on the reputations of others, including those in their own party. Memoirs, therefore, must be treated circumspectly unless corroborated thoroughly.

How should governments be reviewed?

All this then raises the obvious question, how do we assess a government, particularly as in this case, one so recent as the Albanese Government that has only completed one term?

There are several ways.

Assessing government by its leader

One way often employed to assess a government is from how its leader, in this case, the prime minister performed and is generally perceived. After all, this volume is about the Albanese Government. Certainly, assessing governments through their leaders has often been done in Australia (Strangio et al 2013; Strangio 2022). Reviews of government are usually framed in this way – the "Morrison Government" (McCaffrie et al 2023), the "Rudd Government", or the "Howard Government", and so forth. The increasing "presidentialisation" and "personalisation" of modern-day politics (Dowding 2013; Webb and Poguntke 2013) makes such approaches understandable and analytically useful. Also, reinforcing these trends is increasing centralisation within government with the growth of prime ministers' departments and expansion of their private offices (Strangio et al 2017) with concomitant extensions of their control over ministers and all aspects of policy including their public presentation. In part the Labor Party won the 2022 election as much on perceptions of Prime Minister Morrison's trustworthiness and alleged flaws in his "character" (Grattan 2023: 12-14), as on his government's policy performance. Similarly, it has been argued Labor's 2025 win has been partly attributed to the negative perceptions of Opposition leader Peter Dutton (see van Onselen, **Chapter 4**).

The issue was whether Albanese as prime minister in his first term was ever seen in quite the same commanding way as other earlier Labor prime ministers like Hawke, Keating and Whitlam? Was Albanese, who was so much a product of Labor's factions, able to assert his authority in his government? After all, as Mackerras points out **(Chapter 1)** he had only secured at the 2022 election a narrow one seat majority and had scored one of Labor's lowest primary votes. Consequently, was his authority within government limited, only rarely asserting his leadership on a small number of policy issues? So, one issue explored in this volume was whether there was any evidence of much prime ministerial policy leadership and intervention by Albanese during this first term? Or did Albanese largely preside over the government dominated as it was by his own "left faction" whose agenda he endorsed. His task, in conjunction with Treasurer Chalmers, was to provide a new overarching political narrative for that agenda — one that has proved successful given the 2025 election results (see **Chapter 2**).

Certainly, in probing this issue, none of the chapters in this volume identify strong prime ministerial leadership or intervention on key policy issues. Treasurer Chalmers and other ministers handling economic related portfolios were rarely overruled by Prime Minister Albanese (see **Chapters 8-10**). Nor were there any of the prime ministerial-treasurer conflicts that characterised the Hawke-Keating and Howard-Costello administrations. The climate change driven energy agenda under the firm control of Minister Chris Bowen remained unchallenged regardless of criticism in terms of its costs and achievability (see **Chapter 12**). Despite Albanese's own previous role as Minister for Transport in the Rudd-Gillard governments, the controversial Qatar Airways issue and the insipidness of the *Aviation White Paper* in this area remained untouched by prime ministerial insights (see **Chapter 13**). On the Voice referendum (see **Chapter 15**) on which Albanese publicly placed such emphasis prior to the 2022 election and after gaining office, Albanese kept to the faction and party script with little attempt to intervene even when the Yes campaign was looking increasingly likely to lose several months prior to the vote. Although Prime Minister Albanese, like his predecessors was necessarily involved in overseas official visits, summits and meetings, foreign policy remained firmly in the hands of key minister Senator Penny Wong as did defence with Minister Marles (see **Chapters 16** and **17**).

Reformist government or just labelling?

Governments are often evaluated in terms of some overall theme. This might reflect how they managed or mismanaged a particular crisis that occurred on their watch which either enhances or taints their reputation. A common approach is for modern governments to proclaim themselves as "reformist" in their policy directions and administrative actions. Such self-labelling, sometimes too easily parroted by the media, is used by governments to imply that their policies are only being made for the wider long-term public interest rather than for any immediate, partisan, political gain. Attaching the "reformist" tag to policies and actions can allow a government to deflect criticism and set the political agenda.

Albanese certainly sought to assert his government's "reformist" credentials when he grandiosely claimed in his 2022 election speech, "It's only ever Labor governments who do the big reforms, drive the big changes, reshape the economy in the best interests of people" and that his government would be in the same tradition of previous Labor "administrations of Hawke, Keating, Rudd and Gillard". He expressed commitment to "a new era of economic reform and productivity growth" (Albanese 2022). How does the Albanese Government's performance measure up to that promise?

Gary Banks, former head of the Productivity Commission, and a contributor to this volume (**Chapter 10**), has long argued that the term "reform is being employed liberally today by the proponents of almost any policy change, whether it is likely to advance the public interest or not. It has accordingly begun to lose meaning in public discourse and, worse, risks giving real reform a bad name" (2012: 106). Banks believes true reform means "change for the better" but identifying and agreeing what that means has been increasingly confused, lost and distorted by more ideological, partisan and short-term interpretations. It is now contended that Australia, once seen as a leader in genuine economic and social reform (Banks 2005), has run out of puff especially since the Rudd-Gillard period (2007-2013). Genuine reform has received little impetus under the nine years of subsequent Coalition governments and consequently productivity has flattened, and real incomes are in decline (Kelly 2024; Productivity Commission 2017; Productivity Commission 2023). Fiscal management has also been out of control for some considerable time in Australia.

These issues of "reform" and how the Albanese Government measures up to the 2022 election speech rhetoric are explored through many chapters in this volume. In Greg Melleuish's review of the Albanese Government's unfolding narrative during its first term (**Chapter 2**) he argues that it has established a new positive narrative underpinning a more expansive role for government, redefining policy desirability and success which is very different to the type of "reform" that marked Australia under both Labor and Coalition governments. It was a narrative which the Dutton led Opposition was unable to match either in terms of a positive cohesive structure to enwrap its polices or in relation to practical measures to address openly admitted national problems (**Chapter 4**). Albanese's "reformist" self-accolades are further tested across most of the different policy areas addressed in this volume. **Chapters 8-10** by Tunny, Eslake and Banks respectively give attention to this claim in relation to economic management, fiscal policy and productivity actions; Calver in **Chapter 11** reviews "reform" concerning the government's industrial relations initiatives; Kellow's **Chapter 12** focusses where "reform" fits in environmental and energy issues; Forsyth in **Chapter 13** reviews domestic and international aviation policy; Babones examines the reviews, programs and changes concerning universities (**Chapter 14**); Kelly gives detailed assessment of achievements concerning digitisation in the first term (**Chapter 18**); and Wallace asks whether establishing a National Rugby League (NRL) team in Papua New Guinea at some considerable cost is indicative of "reform" in overseas aid? Most contributors are less than sanguine about the Albanese Government's claims concerning its "reformist" credentials.

Promises and performance

As the theme of this volume is "promise and performance", checking whether a government has honoured its election promises is another means to assess the Albanese Government's first term. Botterill and Walsh (2024: 846) propose that "Election campaigns provide a concentrated presentation of the policy priorities of parties as they seek to sell themselves and their vision for the nation to the voting public". It has been assessed that policy promises made at the 2022 election "have been important in predicting voting choice" (Biddle and Jackman 2022: 7). They are an intrinsic part of the electoral contest. So, whether the Albanese Government's election promises have been achieved must be a prime means to assess its first term. Many of the authors in this volume give weight to Albanese's 2022 election promises in developing their critiques, some of which are linked to the reform issue discussed above.

Botterill and Walsh (845) noted that the Albanese Opposition had "a traditional Labor focus on social democratic values" and that its overarching theme was to "build a stronger, more productive, more resilient economy" across five priority areas:

- Powering Australia — "drive investment in cheap, renewable energy";
- Building up Australian manufacturing capacity - "A future made right here in Australia";
- Investment in infrastructure "to boost productivity and create jobs";

- Jobs and training including a "fair go at work";
- Care – encompassing Child Care, Medicare and Aged care for a "decent society".

Several contributors to this volume express disappointment at the Albanese Government's failure to deliver certain election promises. Maley (**Chapter 6**) believes several major reforms from the 2021 Jenkins Report on the working culture at the Commonwealth Parliament which Labor was strongly committed to in opposition, have yet to be fully implemented. **Chapters 5** and **7** highlight that while the Albanese Government honoured its promise for a royal commission into its predecessor's Robodebt Scheme, it was more ambivalent as to whether one would be appointed into the pandemic despite Albanese's pre and post 2022 election statements to do so. Saul Eslake (**Chapter 9**) highlights that in fiscal policy, the Albanese Opposition "didn't seek a mandate for long-term budget repair" or "wide-ranging tax reform, reform of federal-state financial relations, or anything else of the kind associated with the Hawke-Keating or Howard-Costello governments". Consequently, he argues that it would "be wrong to judge their first-term performance by those standards". Rather, he, like Tunny (**Chapter 8**), has sought to assess the Albanese Government's large increases in spending, which exceeded even its pre-election policies, by looking "beyond the arithmetic of the major budgetary aggregates to consider the quality of the decisions". Banks (**Chapter 10**) welcomes Albanese's 2022 promise to promote productivity but concludes most of its policies did little to achieve it. Concerning industrial relations, Calver (**Chapter 11**) finds a high level of congruence between promises and implementation but, like others writing on the economy, is negative about their adverse impacts especially concerning productivity. He also argues that the "pivotal" promise for real wage growth subsequently claimed was not, on closer analysis, achieved. Kellow on energy (**Chapter 12**) reminds us of the failed promise to reduce power prices by $275 because of what he regards as misplaced energy policies. Relief has only been achieved by large, unsustainable, costly consumer subsidies. Though the Albanese Government kept its promise to hold a referendum on Aboriginal/Indigenous constitutional standing, as noted above, it was poorly executed and failed (**Chapter 15**). While Easson's assessment of foreign policy is generally positive but not expansive (**Chapter 16**), Lee believes the closely related area of defence policy is "in tatters" (**Chapter 17**). Perhaps the most scathing condemnation of failure to achieve a clear election promise and one repeatedly broken by subsequent reiterations in office by Albanese, concerns the legislation for religious freedom. As Mark Spencer (**Chapter 19**) concludes "Like the Morrison Coalition Government before it, the Albanese Labor Government failed in its first term to deliver its promised protections for religious freedom".

Fixing the predecessor's policy mistakes

Another way to assess a new government is to consider just how different it is from its predecessor especially in addressing its alleged faults in terms of policy and governing style. This is fertile ground in assessing the Albanese Government as it came to power very much on the perceived failures and unpopularity of the preceding Morrison Coalition Government. As Michelle Grattan writes in a largely condemnatory academic volume reviewing the Morrison Government "the … overarching story of this term was … by the end of it Morrison had lost the confidence of the Australian public" (Grattan 2023: 2).

According to the McCaffrie, Grattan and Wallace (2023) review of the Morrison Government, it was found wanting across many areas:

- undermining Commonwealth Parliament and responsible government (Chapter 2)
- undermining public service independence and lack of implementation of the Thodey Review (Chapter 4)
- no reforms to federal financial relations (Chapter 5)

- mismanagement of the pandemic (Chapter 7)
- fiscal ineptitude in failing to deliver budget surpluses and its *volte face* during the pandemic of a decade of Coalition budget promises (Chapter 8)
- aged care failure and poor implementation of the *Royal Commission into Aged Care* (Chapter 9)
- failure to give priority to women and gender issues (Chapter 12)
- lack of genuine support of Aboriginal reconciliation (Chapter 13)
- foreign policy concerning antipathy to China and neglect of the South Pacific (Chapter 14)
- entrenching the domination of the oligopoly in communications policy (Chapter 15)
- limited support and funding for the arts sector (Chapter 16)
- lack of integrity and character – the Robodebt scandal (Chapter 10) and failure to establish a national integrity commission (Chapter 17)
- disaster policy characterised by blame shifting, lack of leadership and symbolic only policy responses in relation to the NSW bushfires (Chapters 1 and 18)
- stalled climate change policy (Chapter 19)

Contributors to this volume were asked to consider these alleged failings within the ambit of their different topics. Some do so directly as it relates to their particular issues, while others do so more tangentially. Kellow looking at climate change and energy (**Chapter 12**) for example, does not agree with the Albanese Government's policy diagnosis and so is less than enthusiastic about the new government's achievements. The Morrison Government's supposed gross failure in responding to the pandemic does not get as enthusiastically endorsed by the Albanese Government's *COVID-19 Response Inquiry* as was expected. This is the inquiry that was promised to be a royal commission but was not (**Chapter 7**). The Robodebt Scheme, however, was considered by the promised royal commission and as a result the Morrison Government's mismanagement of this issue and concerns about its relations with the public service, are fully exposed (see **Chapters, 5, 7, 18**). Concerning the Coalition's overall lack of fiscal discipline (Carling 2024), it has not been brought under control during Albanese's first term with spending accelerating rather than moderating (**Chapters 8** and **9**). This includes, what Eslake (2024) has described the worst decisions by a federal government – the Morrison Government's over-generous GST deal for Western Australia. Eslake laments (**Chapter 9**) how Albanese in both opposition and in government largely endorsed this policy – a problem becoming more difficult to manage as the other states ramp up their demands for compensation. Moreover, there has been no attempt by the Albanese Government to address what Fenna saw as the Morrison Government's lack of "real reform to federal financial relations – such as an increase in the rate of the GST or, more ambitiously, income tax sharing" (2023: 63). In foreign policy, (**Chapter 16**) it could be argued that the Albanese Government has made progress in reversing what was perceived as failures by the Morrison Government in terms of its relations with China and the wider Pacific nations community.

The legacy argument

In seeking to evaluate a government, George Brandis, former Liberal Senator and Attorney-General in the Abbott and Turnbull Coalition governments, framed the issue of assessing government this way:

> Of course, every government ushers in new policies; we have seen plenty during Albanese's time. By 'legacy' I don't mean incremental policy changes, or even fundamental policy shifts which are unwound by future governments. I mean the enduring reforms that stand the test of time – the nation-altering initiatives by which prime ministers cement their place in history. (Brandis 2025)

Care, however, is needed in identifying just what exactly is a "legacy" and accepting too uncritically a government's self-declaratory proclamations about theirs. Indeed, even some of those different "legacies" nominated by Brandis concerning both Labor and Liberal governments are contestable.

This raises the issue as to what "enduring" legacies can be identified from the Albanese Government's first term and is it too soon to expect any to emerge? Is there any cohesive pattern of actions and policies or even some single initiative that distinguishes the Albanese Government's record from the usual activities required for just running the country, maintaining policies and adjusting to meet changing circumstances? Chapter after chapter in this volume fail to identify any particular policy or set of policies that amount to a distinctive, enduring legacy. The Albanese Government's real legacy, if it can be called that, is in resetting the policy agenda and redefining "reform" that is different to previous interpretations but which it has done to its great political advantage. This is discussed in more detail in the final chapter of this volume (**Chapter 21**).

Conclusion

Journalist Phillip Coorey noted after the 2022 election that "for the new government, it has three short years to turn around a series of massive problems, many of them beyond its control" (Coorey 2022). The issue of relevance to this volume is not just whether the Albanese Government tackled problems left by its predecessor, but whether it addressed in an effective way these wider emerging concerns that were growing in severity during its first term? Indeed, while the Albanese Government resoundingly won the 2025 election gaining additional seats even in Queensland (**Chapter 3**), it largely did so by being unwilling to confront the issues where it knew that genuine reform effort was needed. Of course, the Coalition was just as culpable in this regard, matching (and even exceeding in some cases) the Albanese Government's pre-election spending sprees (see **Chapter 4**). It also failed to produce a credible alternative economic policy program. As journalist Peter Hartcher (2025) said, after polling day both parties and leaders "will need to come clean and confront the trouble we're in". In its first term the Albanese Government kicked the policy problems down the road to avoid any difficult decisions so as to win the 2025 election. Now, in its second term, the Albanese Government will have to deal with those very same problems, but will it? It is not a question of whether it is up to the challenge. Rather, reading the chapters in this volume and considering the way the narrative and policy agenda that has been reshaped by the Albanese Government in its first term, it seems it does not even want to and sees no need to alter its current policy projections.

References

Albanese, A., (2022), *Vote for a Better Future: ALP Federal Election Party Launch*, Address, 1 May

Banks, G., (2005), *Structural Reform Australian-Style – Lessons for Others*, Canberra; Commonwealth of Australia, May

Banks, G., (2012), "Successful Reform: Past Lessons, Future Challenges", in *Advancing the Reform Agenda: Selected Speeches*, Canberra: Productivity Commission, Commonwealth of Australia, 103-20

Biddle, N., and Jackman, S., (2022), *Research Note: Policy Priorities and the 2022 Australian Federal Election Result.* Canberra: ANU Centre for Social Research and Methods

Botterill, L.S., and Walsh, M., (2024), "An Examination of the Policy Content of Scott Morrison's and Anthony Albanese's 2022 Federal Election Campaign Materials", *Australian Journal of Politics and History*, 70(4), 838-47.

Brandis, G., (2025), "Is Albo destined to be a one term PM?", *Sydney Morning Herald*, 26 January

Carling, R., (2024), "Economic Policy", in Prasser, S., (ed), *Tragedy without Triumph: The Coalition in Office 2013-2022*, Redland Bay: Connor Court Publishing, 119-41

Coorey, P., (2022), "Labor's Big test", *Australian Financial Review*, 22-24 July

Dowding, K., (2023), "The Prime Ministerialisation of the British Prime Minister", *Parliamentary Affairs*, 66, 617-35

Eslake, S., (2024), "The Worst Public Policy Decision of the 21st Century (thus far) – the Changes to the Distribution of GST revenues by the Morrison Government (with the Support of the then Labor Opposition) at the Behest of Western Australia", Address National Press Club, Canberra, 8 May

Fenna, A., (2023), "The Morrison Government and Australian Federalism", in McCaffrie, B., Grattan, M., and Wallace, C., (eds), *The Morrison Government: Governing through Crisis 2018-2022 – Australian Commonwealth Administration series,* Sydney: UNSW Press, 61-71

Grattan, M., (2023), "The Morrison Government., 2019-2022: A Story of Crisis and Character", in McCaffrie, et al, *The Morrison Government,* 1-17

Hartcher, P., (2025), "After polling day our leaders will come clean about the trouble we're in", *Sydney Morning Herald*, 26 April

Kelly, P., (2024), "2024; The Year Australia lost its way", *The Australian*, 28 December

Productivity Commission, (2017), *Shifting the Dials: 5 year Productivity Review*, Report 84, Canberra; Commonwealth of Australia, 3 August

Productivity Commission, (2023), *5- year Productivity Inquiry: Advancing Prosperity, Inquiry Report – volume 1*, Canberra; Commonwealth of Australia, 7 February

Strangio, P., (2013), "Evaluating Prime Ministerial Performance: The Australian Experience", in Strangio P., 't Hart, P., and Walter, W., (eds), *Understanding Prime Ministerial Performance: Comparative Perspectives,* Oxford: Oxford University Press, 264-90

Strangio P., 't Hart, P., and Walter, W., (2017), *The Pivot of Power: Australian Prime Ministers and Political Leadership,* Carlton: Miegunyah Press

Strangio, P., (2022), "Prime-ministerial leadership ranking: The Australian experience", *Australian Journal of Political Science*, 57(2), 180-98

Webb, P., and Poguntke, T., (2013), "The Presidentialisaton of Politics Thesis Defended", *Parliamentary Affairs*, 66, 646-54

Part 1: Overview

The Changing Political Environment

1

The Albanese Government's Election Performances

Malcolm Mackerras

Introduction

"Electoral history is littered with unexpected landslides." That was the favourite aphorism of my friend, the late Sir David Butler (1924-2022). He was the eminent psephologist of the United Kingdom and that was one of the many perceptive comments he used to make when discussing results produced by systems of single-member electoral districts. It is very true, and I can attest that it is rare to have a very close election preceded by pundit predictions that it would be very close. I learnt as long ago as 1961 that very close elections typically come as a shock as was the case in December that year when Sir Robert Menzies was universally expected to win handsomely his sixth straight election – only to be treated to the shock of a very close result.

The year 1961 was the first year of my entitlement to vote. Federally I voted for the Liberal Party's Senate group and for the sitting Liberal member in Bradfield (NSW), then the safest Liberal seat in Australia to which the description" blue ribbon Liberal" was universally given. The very close Menzies win was essentially caused by the wholly unexpected landslide to Labor in Queensland where Labor increased its lower house representation from three seats in 1958 to eleven in 1961 (of 18). By 2025 the party system had changed to the point of Bradfield producing Australia's closest result with 56,114 votes for the winner, "teal" independent Nicolette Boele, and 56,088 for the Liberal Party's losing candidate Gisele Kapterian, a margin of 26 votes.

The word "landslide" is undefined, but few would disagree with me when I write that in my lifetime there have been three landslide wins by Australian Labor prime ministers. They were in August 1943 when John Curtin was confirmed in office in an unexpected landslide victory, in March 1983 when Bob Hawke won a widely predicted landslide election, and in May 2025 when Anthony Albanese won an election surprisingly like that of 1943. Virtually every newspaper carried the headline "landslide" in the aftermath of the Labor victories of 1943 and 2025. That is now the universal description of those election results.

Consider these similarities. John Curtin was Leader of the Opposition from October 1935 to October 1941 during which period he was able to increase Labor's share of the two-party preferred vote from 46.3 per cent in September 1934, to 49.4 per cent in October 1937 and to 50.3 per cent in September 1940. Effectively he won that election, but the circumstances of the day meant he needed to wait until October 1941 to take office as prime minister. Then in August 1943 he was able to increase Labor's share to 58.2 per cent.

I was a four-year-old toddler in August 1943 which means I have no memory of that great event. However, I have read enough history to know that there was great uncertainty during the campaign as to what the result might be. Like Curtin and Hawke, Albanese led Labor out of Opposition and on to the treasury benches. However, Curtin and Albanese won his landslide as prime minister whereas Hawke, like Menzies and John Howard, won the highest office from the position of Leader of the Opposition. Just as Curtin raised the Labor share from 46.3 per cent to 58.2 per cent (a cumulative swing of 11.9 per cent) so Albanese raised the Labor share from 48.5 per cent to 55.2 per cent (a cumulative swing of 6.7 per cent). See Table 1.

That Albanese statistic of 55.2 per cent is the third highest of any win since Second World War. It is higher than Ben Chifley's 53.8 in September 1946 and Malcolm Fraser's 54.6 in December 1977. The only higher figures have been Harold Holt's 56.9 in November 1966 and Fraser's 55.7 in December 1975. (The statistics given in this chapter for 1934, 1937, 1940, 1943, 1946, 1966, 1972, 1974, 1975 and 1977 are *my estimates*. The practice of fully counting out preferences began in 1983. See Table 1).

The House of Representatives Election 3 May 2025

During the term of 47th Parliament (2022-25) there was a general feeling among pundits that Albanese would win a second term at the 48th general election to be held in the autumn of 2025. During the period up to the Voice referendum of October 2023 it was generally thought that a *majority* second Albanese Labor Government was likely. The comprehensive defeat of the Voice, however, changed pundit expectations. From then on it was not common to find a pundit predicting a second Albanese *majority*. A *minority* Labor government became the conventional forecast. Save only this: from July 2024 to March 2025 the betting odds favoured the view that Peter Dutton would become prime minister! Resignations of politicians from the Liberal Party created three by-elections, of which two were of no interest, with Cook (NSW) and Fadden (Queensland) easily being held by the Liberal Party. However, Labor scored a big win with Aston (Victoria) being gained by Labor from the Liberal Party in April 2023.

The death on 4 December 2023 of the Labor member for Dunkley (Victoria) Ms. Peta Murphy created the by-election for her seat on 2 March 2024. The Dunkley swing of 3.6 per cent against Labor was wholly conventional but Labor's win in Aston was ground-breaking. The last time a government had taken a federal seat from an Opposition was as long ago as December 1920.

My view: Albanese is a very good vote-getter

Albanese enjoys the distinction of being a Labor Prime Minister who won two general elections. However, Andrew Fisher won two general elections, in 1910 and 1914. So too did Gough Whitlam, in 1972 and 1974. Hawke won four, in 1983, 1984, 1987 and 1990. The distinction of Albanese is that his second win was stronger than his first. For Fisher, Whitlam and Hawke, by contrast, his second win was weaker than his first. On the conservative side of politics, each of Joe Lyons, Menzies, Fraser and Howard was Leader of the Opposition before leading his party on to the treasury benches. For each of Lyons in 1934, Menzies in 1951, Fraser in 1977 and Howard in 1998 his second win was weaker than his first in 1931, 1949, 1975 and 1996, respectively.

Albanese has never lost a parliamentary election. If he stays as prime minister until Christmas 2026, he will become the second longest serving Labor prime minister. It is possible that his term will finish up to be longer than Hawke's. So, in terms of winning votes it may be difficult to argue that he is more successful than Hawke or Curtin but very easy to argue that he is more successful than every other federal Labor leader.

A look at my various tables indicates clearly that in terms of winning two-party preferred votes and seats Albanese is the best Labor performer. His 55.2 per cent of the two-party preferred vote eclipses Hawke's 53.2 per cent. Each of Whitlam and Kevin Rudd achieved 52.7 per cent at his first win so Albanese eclipses them also, if not at his first win, then at his second. In seats Hawke's Labor never won more than 86 of 148 whereas Albanese has won 94 of 150.

The 2025 election was preceded by redistributions affecting New South Wales (losing a seat), Victoria (losing a seat), Western Australia (gaining a seat) and the Northern Territory where the sole purpose of the boundary change was to equalise the number of electors in its two electoral divisions. No boundary changes occurred in Queensland, South Australia, Tasmania or the Australian Capital Territory. Given that Tasmania and the Northern Territory enjoy privileged status in redistributions it is not surprising that these were the May 2025 numbers of electors at the bottom end of the scale: Clark (Tasmania) 74,315, Lingiari (NT) 76,836, Solomon (NT) 78,723, Bass (Tasmania) 80,392, Franklin (Tasmania) 83,734, Braddon (Tasmania) 84,278, Lyons (Tasmania) 88,962, Canberra (ACT) 102,980, Fenner (ACT) 105,447 and Moreton (Queensland) 109,284.

With 18,098,797 as the total number of electors for Australia as a whole the average was 120,659 electors per electoral division. Given the lack of redistributions in Queensland and South Australia it is not surprising that these were the numbers of electors at the top of the scale: Longman (Queensland) 142,810, Blair (Queensland) 142,021, Wright (Queensland) 140,302, Fisher (Queensland) 139,123, Spence (SA) 138,902, Mayo (SA) 137,756, Fadden (Queensland) 135,790, Petrie (Queensland) 134,418, Forde (Queensland) 134,066 and Adelaide (SA) 131,466.

In any event those boundary changes made no difference to the notional fortunes of the three main parties, Labor, Liberal and the Nationals. In New South Wales the seat abolished was North Sydney, held by a "teal" independent Kylea Tink. The seat abolished in Victoria was the marginal Labor Higgins, but Labor was compensated by the creation of the new marginal Labor seat of Bullwinkel in Western Australia.

At the election Labor lost no seats but gained these 13 from the Liberal Party. I rank them in order of the percentage swing to Labor in each seat: Braddon (Tasmania) 15.2, Leichhardt (Queensland) 9.5, Bass (Tasmania) 9.4, Bonner (Queensland) 8.4, Dickson (Queensland) 7.7, Sturt (SA) 7.1, Hughes (NSW) 6.5, Forde (Queensland) 6.1, Petrie (Queensland) 5.6, Banks (NSW) 5.1, Moore (WA) 3.8, Deakin (Victoria) 2.8 and Menzies (Victoria) 0.7.

During the campaign my final predictions were published on 17 April in *Switzer Daily* (of which I am the politics expert) in an article titled "Will Anthony Albanese be our PM after May 3?". Having asserted that "At Christmas 2025, Albanese will still be Australia's prime minister in a majority Labor government" I listed the seats I expected Labor to gain from the Liberal Party. The only seat in the above list I predicted correctly was Leichhardt! As in 1961 there was an unexpected Labor landslide in Queensland but, unlike 1961, there was also a landslide to Labor in South Australia and Tasmania.

Did Labor perform badly in any seat? In the sense of losing the seat my answer is in the negative. However, Labor lost significant ground in these seats without the Labor sitting member being defeated: Bean (ACT), Bendigo (Victoria), Fremantle (WA), Solomon (NT) and Wills (Victoria).

Where a Labor member had retired one might have expected a "retirement slump" effect. However, in Barton (NSW), Gorton (Victoria) and Moreton (Queensland) the swing was towards Labor! In Whitlam (NSW) and Maribyrnong (Victoria) the sitting Labor member retired and there were small swings to the Liberal Party. The unusual case was Calwell in Victoria. Labor had secured 62.4 per cent of the two-party preferred vote in 2022 in a contest with a Liberal candidate. In 2025, however, the contest was with an independent, Carly Moore. In the end the succeeding Labor member, Basem Abdo won 49,481 votes (55.1 per cent) and Moore won 40,350 votes (44.9 per cent). One could say that was a poor performance by Labor but only by comparing unlike results.

On the other hand, these Coalition seats saw good swings towards sitting members from the Liberal Party or the Nationals. In order of such swings, they were these percentages: O'Connor (WA) 6.6, Flynn (Queensland) 6.4, Durack (WA) 5.5, Canning (WA) 5.4, Riverina (NSW) 2.9, Herbert (Queensland) 1.6, Casey (Victoria) 1.5, Dawson (Queensland) 1.4 and Hume (NSW) 1.2.

Every state recorded a swing to Labor in the two-party preferred vote, the range being from highs of 9.1, 5.2 and 3.5 per cent in Tasmania, South Australia and Queensland respectively, to a low of just under one per cent in Western Australia. By contrast the Northern Territory recorded a swing against Labor of 1.3 per cent. The big swing in the Apple Isle makes Tasmania Labor's strongest state with a two-party preferred percentage of 63.3. Queensland continues to be Labor's weakest jurisdiction with only 49.4 per cent.

All in all, I think the above information constitutes good evidence to justify my claim that Albanese is a very good vote getter.

The Alternative view: Albanese is a poor vote-getter

Those who disagree with me would argue that all the above information is based on the counting of seats in the House of Representatives and of votes couched in two-party preferred terms. They would then argue that the electoral system is very favourable to Labor both in terms of it creating single-member electoral divisions and in terms of the reality that the system of full preferential voting favours Labor.

To discuss this alternative view, I ask readers to look at Table 9 which shows the extent of the movement of votes from the major parties to minor parties and independents. It can be seen that previous Labor prime ministers winning elections, Whitlam, Hawke, Paul Keating and Rudd were able to win primary vote percentages in the mid to high forties. By contrast, Hawke's last win in 1990 and Julia Gillard's sole win in 2010 saw the Labor primary vote failing to get 40 per cent. Yet both won the election narrowly. On the other hand, Albanese was able to achieve majority government with only 32.6 per cent in 2022 and get a landslide win in 2025 with only 34.6 per cent of the primary vote. How do I explain that?

I begin with the Greens. Their share of the national primary vote was stable at 12.2 per cent. Normally, that would be regarded as a good performance. With that percentage they had won four seats in 2022 so pundits were of the view that they might get roughly that result in 2025. In the *Switzer Daily* article quoted above I predicted that Labor would gain Brisbane, but the Greens would hold the other three seats. Yet this is what happened. In Melbourne there was a substantial change of boundaries disadvantageous to the Greens, the Liberal candidate came third and her preferences gave the seat to Labor's Sarah Witty. The primary votes were 38,457 for Bandt, 30,541 for Witty, 19,267 for Steph Hunt (Liberal) and 9,183 for the combination of all the rest. After preference distribution the votes were 51,663 for Witty and 45,785 for Bandt.

In Griffith the Liberal candidate came third and his preferences gave the seat to Labor. The primary votes were 37,686 for Renee Coffee (Labor), 34,570 for the sitting Greens member Max Chandler-Mather, 29,025 for the Liberal candidate Anthony Bishop and 7,931 for the combination of all the rest. After preference distribution the votes were 66,154 for Coffee and 43,058 for Chandler-Mather.

In Brisbane the sitting Greens member Stephen Bates never really had a chance. His 2022 win had been a fluke. In 2025 the primary votes were 37,951 for the Liberal candidate Trevor Evans, 35,607 for Labor's Madonna Jarrett, 28,663 for Bates, and 8,524 for the combination of all the rest. The final count saw the conventional result with Greens preferences giving the seat to Labor. Jarrett finished with 65,295 votes compared with 45,450 for Evans. Meanwhile, Ryan turned in the same result as in 2022 with Labor preferences giving victory to Elizabeth Watson-Brown of the Greens. The Liberal candidate, Maggie Forrest, led on the primary vote count.

It is important to note that there was no redistribution in Queensland, so Bates, Chandler-Mather and Watson-Brown were each contesting their seats on the same boundaries that had given them wins in 2022. The two men who lost, therefore, could not blame boundary change. By contrast Bandt did, understandably, blame the substantial change to his boundaries for the unexpected defeat he suffered. He had been the representative for Melbourne since 2010 and he was the party leader, so Greens supporters were shocked at his defeat.

From all the above information it can be seen that I underestimated the number of Labor gains by 14 seats of which 12 were gained from the Liberal Party (Banks, Bass, Bonner, Braddon, Deakin, Dickson, Forde, Hughes, Menzies, Moore, Petrie and Sturt) and two were gained from the Greens, Griffith and Melbourne. However, I was not alone in my arithmetic being excessively cautious. Former Labor minister Barry Jones wrote an article in *The Saturday Paper* for 26 April to 2 May titled "The last majority government" in which he wrote: "The likeliest result on May 3, will be a small majority for Labor, but it will almost certainly be the last victory for a hegemonic party". The first part of that sentence reflected my thinking at the time, but certainly not the second part. He went on "All future parliaments will have a three-way split in the House of Representatives, as is already the case in the Senate, except where Labor and the Coalition gang up to pursue their own party interests." I have always rejected that view. I think there will be occasional minority governments, but each hung parliament will be followed by a decisive win for either Labor or the Coalition.

A characteristic of this election was the repeated display of wishful thinking by the personalities on the program jocularly known as "Sky News After Dark". The best example was on the night of Thursday 1 May on the *Sharri* program. The host, Sharri Markson, asked a panel for their predictions, every one of which greatly overstated the number of Coalition seats. Finally, Markson herself concluded by predicting 72 Labor, 66 Coalition and 12 on the cross bench. She understated Labor by 22 seats, overstated the Coalition by 23 and understated the cross bench by one. That she could make so big an error can only be explained by saying that she works in an echo chamber in which Liberal Party polling is taken seriously – even though it clashed with all other polling.

Anyway, on polling day *The Weekend Australian* carried its final Newspoll which recorded a two-party preferred vote for Labor of 52.5 per cent and 47.5 per cent for the Coalition. With the final percentages being 55.2 and 44.8 the error in Newspoll was to underestimate Labor by 2.7 per cent. The difference between Newspoll and Markson, therefore, is that Newspoll picked up some of the swing to Labor caused by the campaign but not all of it. Markson, on the other hand, made a prediction that would have been quite reasonable if made back in March but when made in May indicated that she had not noticed the pro-Labor swing which every other commentator observed. It seems to have been quite big in the last week of the campaign.

The non-Greens cross bench secured 12 wins in 2022. Ten of those (in Clark, Curtin, Fowler, Indi, Kennedy, Kooyong, Mackellar, Mayo, Warringah and Wentworth) won again in 2025. The missing two who won in 2022 but not in 2025 were Tink in North Sydney (whose seat was abolished) and Zoe Daniel whose "blue ribbon Liberal" seat of Goldstein returned to Liberal Tim Wilson in the only gain made by the Liberal Party at the 2025 election. Those two seats were replaced by Nicolette Boele gaining Bradfield and Andrew Gee winning Calare as an independent in 2025 where he had won in 2022 as a National. Therefore, the number of non-Greens crossbench wins was 12 in 2022 and is 12 again in 2025.

All in all, I think the above information constitutes some evidence that Albanese is a poor vote getter, but the operation of a pro-Labor electoral system makes him look better than he really is. The argument, however, does not persuade me.

Debate about the electoral system

We can be sure that this result will spark debate about the electoral system. There will be academics and independent psephologists who point to the disproportionalities produced by the system of single-member electoral divisions. They will be joined by the Greens, but no one else. We won't be getting proportional representation for the House of Representatives any time soon.

More important than the above, however, is that the Liberal Party will be determined to see the system of compulsory preferences replaced by optional preferential voting. Liberals will point out that in Aston, Banks, Brisbane, Deakin, Dickson, Menzies, Petrie and Solomon Liberal candidates led Labor candidates on primary votes, but all the Labor candidates were elected. They will also point out that in Bradfield, Curtin, and Kooyong candidates led "teal" independents on primary votes but in each case the "teal" independent was elected on preferences. Finally, they will point out that in Ryan the Liberal candidate was ahead on the first count but the Greens sitting member won the seat. This is a debate for the future. There will be no change during the 48th Parliament.

The Senate election

Electoral systems of proportional representation (PR) do not produce landslides. Consequently, since PR first operated in 1949 there has been no landslide Senate result. However, two recent prime ministers from the Liberal Party, Fraser and Howard, have been able to perform well enough in the Senate vote at his first House of Representatives win to be in a strong upper house position in his first term. Fraser in 1975 was able to win a Senate majority and in 1977 the Fraser Government's majority position was retained – only to be badly lost at the 1980 election, creating the circumstances for the 1983 double dissolution.

In 1996 Howard was able to win 20 of the 40 Senate seats contested. That combined with Liberal leader John Hewson's respectable Senate result in 1993 to produce a strong position in Howard's first term. He needed to wait, however, until his fourth House of Representatives win in 2004 to be able to claim a Senate majority. The strength of his position meant that he never needed to press the double dissolution trigger.

No Labor prime minister of recent times has been able to repeat the kind of achievement of Fraser and Howard. Even Bob Hawke's 1983 landslide win looks rather poor compared with that of Fraser in 1975 and Howard in 1996. However, there have been two terms for Labor in which the Senate position of the government has looked pretty favourable. The terms are the 43rd Parliament (2010-13) and the forthcoming term, the 48th Parliament (2025-28). Let me explain each case because it should be understood that each of Kevin Rudd and Albanese has needed to deal with a difficult Senate in his first term. In both cases nearly half the senators had been elected when the Liberal Prime Minister, Howard and Scott Morrison respectively, had secured a good Senate result for the Coalition, in 2004 and 2019, respectively.

At the half-Senate election held on 24 November 2007 each of Labor and the Coalition won 16 seats from the 36 long-term senators for the states, and the Greens won three. The 36th place was filled by then Senator Nick Xenophon from South Australia. At the half-Senate election held on 21 August 2010 the Coalition won 18 seats, Labor 15, the Greens six and the Democratic Labor Party one seat, a man by the name John Madigan filling that Victorian seat. Therefore, from 1 July 2011 there were 34 from the Coalition, 31 Labor, nine from the Greens plus Xenophon and Madigan.

From the above numbers it can be seen that the left-hand side of politics had the crucial 40 senators to be a majority. The explanation for that lies in the results in Tasmania in 2007 and 2010. Whereas every mainland state split three each between right and left both in 2007 and 2010 in Tasmania the result at both elections was three Labor, two Liberal and one for the Greens. Therefore, from 1 July 2011 the Tasmanian distribution was six Labor, four Liberal and two for the Greens.

Back in the days of Fraser, Hawke, Keating, Howard, Rudd and Gillard it was always the case that each territory split one for Labor and one for the Coalition. That is no longer the case since the ACT elected two left-wing senators both in 2022 and 2025. Therefore, the Senate position of the Albanese Government in the 48th Parliament will be essentially the same as that of the Gillard Government in the 43rd Parliament – except that the numbers for the Coalition will be 27 where it was 34 back then. The important point is that the combination of Labor and Greens will be 39 seats which is a majority. It will be the most left-wing Senate since PR became the electoral system in 1949. And it will operate alongside a big majority for Labor in the House of Representatives.

Table 1: Aggregate Two-Party Preferred Percentages, House of Representatives, 1980-2025

Election	% Labor	% Lib-Nat	% Swing
18 October1980(a)	49.60	50.40	4.20 to Labor
5 March 1983	53.23	46.77	3.63 to Labor
1 December 1984	51.77	48.23	1.46 to Lib-Nat
11 July 1987	50.83	49.17	0.94 to Lib-Nat
24 March 1990	49.90	50.10	0.93 to Lib-Nat
13 March 1993	51.44	48.56	1.54 to Labor
2 March 1996	46.37	53.63	5.07 to Lib-Nat
3 October 1998	50.98	49.02	4.61 to Labor
10 November 2001	49.05	50.95	1.93 to Lib-Nat
9 October 2004	47.26	52.74	1.79 to Lib-Nat
24 November 2007	52.70	47.30	5.44 to Labor
21 August 2010	50.12	49.88	2.58 to Lib-Nat
7 September 2013	46.51	53.49	3.61 to Lib-Nat
2 July 2016	49.64	50.36	3.13 to Labor
18 May 2019	48.47	51.53	1.17 to Lib-Nat
21 May 2022	52.13	47.87	3.66 to Labor
3 May 2025(b)	55.22	44.78	3.09 to Labor

(a)   The full counting of preferences for the two-party preferred vote began with the March 1983 election. Therefore, the statistics for October 1980 are *my estimates*.

(b)   A unique peculiarity occurred in the May 2025 election. The distribution of the two-party preferred votes was halted by the Australian Electoral Commission's fear of a court challenge to the exceptionally close Bradfield result. As of 31 July 2025, the AEC website showed Labor's two-party preferred share nationally as 55.22 per cent, the number shown here. That is based on the AEC *estimate* that the Bradfield count, when done properly, will be Liberal 61,658 votes and Labor 50,544 votes. Although truly an estimate the AEC website describes that with this sentence: "As such, a mathematical equation was applied to approximate the 2PP for Bradfield."

Table 2: Seats Won in House of Representatives, 24 November 2007: Rudd's Win

State/Territory	Labor	Liberal	Nationals	Independent	Total
New South Wales	28	15	5	1	49
Victoria	21	14	2	-	37
Queensland	15	10	3	1	29
Western Australia	4	11	-	-	15
South Australia	6	5	-	-	11
Tasmania	5	-	-	-	5
Australian Capital Territory	2	-	-	-	2
Northern Territory	2	-	-	-	2
Total	83	55	10	2	150

Table 3: Seats Won in House of Representatives, 21 August 2010: Gillard's Win

State/Territory	Labor	Liberal	Nationals	Greens	Independent	Total
New South Wales	26	16	4	-	2	48
Victoria	22	12	2	1	-	37
Queensland	8	16	5	-	1	30
Western Australia	3	11	1	-	-	15
South Australia	6	5	-	-	-	11
Tasmania	4	-	-	-	1	5
Australian Capital Territory	2	-	-	-	-	2
Northern Territory	1	1	-	-	-	2
Total	72	61	12	1	4	150

Table 4: Seats Won in House of Representatives, 7 September 2013: Abbotts's Win

State/Territory	Labor	Liberal	Nationals	Greens	Independent*	Total
New South Wales	18	23	7	-	-	48
Victoria	19	14	2	1	1	37
Queensland	6	16	6	-	2	30
Western Australia	3	12	-	-	-	15
South Australia	5	6	-	-	-	11
Tasmania	1	3	-	-	1	5
Australian Capital Territory	2	-	-	-	-	2
Northern Territory	1	1	-	-	-	2
Total	55	75	15	1	4	150

*   Including Katter's Australian Party and Palmer United Party, both in Queensland.

Table 5: Seats Won in House of Representatives, 2 July 2016: Turnbull's win

State/Territory	Labor	Liberal	Nationals	Greens	Independent*	Total
New South Wales	24	16	7	-	-	47
Victoria	18	14	3	1	1	37
Queensland	8	15	6	-	1	30
Western Australia	5	11	-	-	-	16
South Australia	6	4	-	-	1	11
Tasmania	4	-	-	-	1	5
Australian Capital Territory	2	-	-	-	-	2
Northern Territory	2	-	-	-	-	2
Total	69	60	16	1	4	150

*Including Katter's Australian Party (Kennedy, Queensland) and Nick Xenophon Team (Rebekha Sharkie, Mayo, SA).

Table 6: Seats Won in House of Representatives, 18 May 2019: Morrison's Win

State/Territory	Labor	Liberal	Nationals	Greens	Independent*	Total
New South Wales	24	15	7	-	1	47
Victoria	21	12	3	1	1	38
Queensland	6	17	6	-	1	30
Western Australia	5	11	-	-	-	16
South Australia	5	4	-	-	1	10
Tasmania	2	2	-	-	1	5
ACT	3	-	-	-	-	3
Northern Territory	2	-	-	-	-	2
Total	68	61	16	1	5	151

*Including Katter's Australian Party (Kennedy, Queensland) and Centre Alliance (Rebekha Sharkie, Mayo, SA).

Table 7: Seats Won in House of Representatives, 21 May 2022: Albanese's First Win

State/Territory	Labor	Liberal	Nationals	Greens	Independent*	Total
New South Wales	26	9	7	-	5	47
Victoria	24	8	3	1	3	39
Queensland	5	15	6	3	1	30
Western Australia	9	5	-	-	1	15
South Australia	6	3	-	-	1	10
Tasmania	2	2	-	-	1	5
ACT	3	-	-	-	-	3
Northern Territory	2	-	-	-	-	2
Total	77	42	16	4	12	151

*Including Katter in Kennedy (Queensland), Haines in Indi (Victoria), Sharkie in Mayo (SA) and Wilkie in Clark (Tasmania). In New South Wales one independent is Dai Le in Fowler but four of the five seats (Mackellar, North Sydney, Warringah and Wentworth) were won by so-called "teal" independents as were two of the three in Victoria (Goldstein and Kooyong). The sole independent in Western Australia is another "teal" (Chaney), elected in Curtin. Indi and Warringah had also elected independents in 2019, with Indi electing an independent in 2013 and 2016.

Table 8: Seats Won in House of Representatives, 3 May 2025: Albanese's Second Win

State/Territory	Labor	Liberal	Nationals	Greens	Independent*	Total
New South Wales	28	6	6	-	6	46
Victoria	27	6	3	-	2	38
Queensland	12	10	6	1	1	30
Western Australia	11	4	-	-	1	16
South Australia	7	2	-	-	1	10
Tasmania	4	-	-	-	1	5
ACT	3	-	-	-	-	3
Northern Territory	2	-	-	-	-	2
Total	94	28	15	1	12	150

*Including Katter in Kennedy (Queensland), Gee in Calare (NSW), Haines in Indi (Victoria), Sharkie in Mayo (SA) and Wilkie in Clark (Tasmania). In New South Wales the other independent is Dai Le in Fowler but four of the six seats (Bradfield, Mackellar, Warringah and Wentworth) were won by so-called "teal" independents as was one in Victoria (Kooyong). The sole independent in Western Australia is another "teal" (Chaney), elected in Curtin.

Table 9: Primary Vote Percentages: House of Representatives Elections won by Labor

Election	% Labor	% Greens	% Other	% Lib-CP-Nat
1972	49.6	a	8.9	41.5
1974	49.3	a	5.8	44.9
1983	49.5	a	6.9	43.6
1984	47.6	a	7.4	45.0
1987	45.8	2.1	6.0	46.1
1990	39.4	2.2	14.9	43.5
1993	44.9	1.8	9.0	44.3
2007	43.4	7.8	6.7	42.1
2010	38.0	11.8	6.6	43.6
2022	32.6	12.2	19.5	35.7
2025	34.6	12.2	21.4	31.8

Note: a means less than one per cent.

Table 10: Half-Senate Election, 2022

Date of Election

21 May

Further Information
Seats filled: 40
Total enrolment: 17,213,433
Formal votes cast:15,040,658 (96.6%)
Informal votes: 532,003 (3.4%)
Total votes: 15,572,661

Party	Votes		Seats		Over-under Representation
	Number	%	Number	%	
Liberal-National	5,148,028	34.2	15	37.5	+3.3
Labor	4,525,598	30.1	15	37.5	+7.4
Greens	1,903,403	12.7	6	15.0	+2.3
Pauline Hanson's One Nation	644,744	4.3	1	2.5	-1.8
United Australian Party	520,520	3.5	1	2.5	-1.0
Jacquie Lambie Network*	31,203	0.2	1	2.5	+2.3
Others	2,267,162	15.0	1	2.5	-12.5
Total Formal	15,040,658	100.0	40	100.0	

The senator elected for the Jacquie Lambie Network was Tammy Tyrrell, now an independent.

Table 11: Half-Senate Election, 2025

Date of Election 3 May

Further Information
Seats filled: 40
Total enrolment: 18,098,797
Formal votes cast:15,871,189 (96.5%)
Informal votes:567,305 (3.5%)
Total votes: 16,438,494

Party	Votes Number	Votes %	Seats Number	Seats %	Over-under Representation
Liberal-National	4,744,578	29.9	13	32.5	+2.6
Labor	5,573,028	35.1	16	40.0	+4.9
Greens	1,859,974	11.7	6	15.0	+3.3
Pauline Hanson's One Nation	899,296	5.7	3	7.5	+1.8
Jacquie Lambie Network	166,085	1.1	1	2.5	+1.4
Others*	2,628,228	16.5	1	2.5	-14.0
Total Formal	15,871,189	100.0	40	100.0	

As with Table 10 the sole "Other" elected was David Pocock.

Table 12: Senators with terms expiring 30 June, 2031

Party	NSW	Vic	Qld	WA	SA	Tas	ACT	NT	Total
Labor	2	3	2	2	3	2	-	-	14
Liberal	2	2	1	2	2	2	-	-	11
National	-	-	1	-	-	-	-	-	1
Greens	1	1	1	1	1	1	-	-	6
One Nation	1	-	1	1	-	-	-	-	3
Jacquie Lambie	-	-	-	-	-	1	-	-	1
Total	6	6	6	6	6	6			36

Table 13: Senators with short terms

Party	NSW	Vic	Qld	WA	SA	Tas	ACT	NT	Total
Labor	2	2	2	3	2	2	1	1	15
Liberal	2	1	1	2	3	2	-	1	12
National	1	1	1	-	-	-	-	-	3
Greens	1	-	1	-	1	1	-	-	4
One Nation	-	-	1	-	-	-	-	-	1
United Australia Party	-	1	-	-	-	-	-	-	1
Lidia Thorpe	-	1	-	-	-	-	-	-	1
Fatima Payman	-	-	-	1	-	-	-	-	1
Tammy Tyrrell	-	-	-	-	-	1	-	-	1
David Pocock	-	-	-	-	-	-	1	-	1
Total	6	6	6	6	6	6	2	2	40

Readers should note the following points regarding Table 13. First, Lidia Thorpe was elected in May 2022 as a Greens Senator. Second, Fatima Payman was elected in May 2022 as a Labor Senator. Third, Jacinta Nampijinpa Price (NT) was elected in May 2025 as a Country Liberal Party Senator who had joined the caucus of the Nationals in the 47th Parliament. No sooner had she been elected on that assumption she jumped ship and joined the Liberal Party caucus for the 48th Parliament. Fourth, the respective Labor and Greens WA numbers reflect the decision (announced on Monday 2 June 2025) of Dorinda Cox to switch from the Greens to Labor.

Table 14: State of Parties in Senate from 1 July, 2025

Party	NSW	Vic	Qld	WA	SA	Tas	ACT	NT	Total
Labor	4	5	4	5	5	4	1	1	29
Liberal	4	3	2	4	5	4	-	1	23
National	1	1	2	-	-	-	-	-	4
Greens	2	1	2	1	2	2	-	-	10
One Nation	1	-	2	1	-	-	-	-	4
United Australia Party	-	1	-	-	-	-	-	-	1
Jacquie Lambie	-	-	-	-	-	1	-	-	1
Lidia Thorpe	-	1	-	-	-	-	-	-	1
Fatima Payman	-	-	-	1	-	-	-	-	1
Tammy Tyrrell	-	-	-	-	-	1	-	-	1
David Pocock	-	-	-	-	-	-	1	-	1
Total	12	12	12	12	12	12	2	2	76

2

How Albanese and Chalmers have Created a New Narrative of Australian Politics

Greg Melleuish

Why Narrative?

Narratives are important in Australian politics because they set out how a government sees its role and frames the way in which it acts. Narratives explain both the past, from where the government has come, and the future where it believes that it is taking the country. The most common narrative used in Australian political life, from both sides of politics, is one of progress and improvement, the idea that the role of government is to facilitate improvements in the well-being of Australians, and to implement policies that will achieve this goal.

One traditional narrative applied to Australian politics, particularly favoured by Labor and the left, has been that of parties of initiative versus parties of resistance (Mayer 1956). The party of "initiative", ie Labor, aids progress while non-Labor resists progress and is consequently conservative in nature. The problem with such a view is that it is rather empty, as the connection between initiative and "progress" is unclear. How does one distinguish between "initiatives" that have a positive effect and enhance the well-being of the country, and those that fail in this regard?

The non-Labor response to this can be described as a narrative that claims the need to assume power to clean up the mess that Labor governments invariably make. Labor governments attempt to be progressive but invariably stuff up, leaving those on the other side of politics to clean up the mess. True progress only occurs under the safe and steady hand of liberals and conservatives. Hence Tony Abbott (2013) stated in his 2013 Campaign Speech, "This election is about making a great country even better; and that starts with changing the worst government in our history".

Both narratives invoke progress and lay claims to owning it. The idea of progress has strong utopian themes underpinning it, and it is rarely appreciated how much Australian politics has been driven by visions of utopia, including the yeoman republic of the nineteenth century Land Acts and the "new province for law and order" of the "Social Laboratory" or "Australian Settlement" (Melleuish 2018). These utopian projects invariably failed but this did not prevent new projects rising up to replace them. Many years ago, I called these utopian projects "packages", including among them multiculturalism, the 'clever country' and the republic (Melleuish 1998). The most recent example is "net zero". They are highly ideological, but also extremely dangerous as they too often promote policies that are destroyed on the rocks of human nature.

The "yeoman republic" foundered in the face of environmental reality and human cupidity, as described by John Hirst (1988). In his classic *Australia* (1930), W.K. Hancock made a critique of the policies of the Social Laboratory, invoking as argued elsewhere (Melleuish 1995), the spirit of Machiavellian realism. Hancock described the exuberant radical spirit of the policies of the first decade of the twentieth century, only then to detail how those policies had perverse and unintended consequences that destroyed what they were attempting to do.

What is largely absent in Australia is a restorationist narrative, such has been expounded by both Trump and Putin. This is a narrative that posits that, for any country, there was some sort of golden age in the past when the country was an embodiment of its true principles.

Subsequently, the country has lost its way, become corrupted, and needs to return to its true nature (Melleuish 2025). Restorationism can be traced back to the late Roman Republic and was used by Augustus to help to justify his rule as he argued that he was restoring the *res publica*. Restorationism makes sense in a polity whose members believe that its constitution has been corrupted, and that was the case in eighteenth century America in the 1760s and 1770s (Bailyn 2017). The problem for restorationism in Australia is that the one candidate for a golden age, the 1890s (Palmer 1963) is now repudiated as a time of racism and sexism.

Normality and Emergencies

There is another useful narrative that can be applied to Australian politics. This is that the governing of the country is always moving between two states, one of which may be termed "normality" and the other a "state of exception" (Lazar 2009). In a normal condition the rules of politics and governance continue as they usually do, as established in the Constitution and the conventions of the Westminster system. For example, new policies are generally developed quite slowly and wide consultation occurs with those affected by the policies. There is a considerable concern for legality and proper procedure.

In a crisis, emergency or "state of exception", some rules may be scrapped temporarily, others bent and/or decision making streamlined to deal with emergency circumstances. The capacity to act in an emergency is established by legislation that enables governments to do things that they would not usually be able to do. This was the case during the recent COVID-19 outbreak when emergency provisions within legislation were invoked by both the Australian and state governments.

The first "state of emergency" in Australia occurred during the First World War when the *War Precautions Act* was enacted to allow the Commonwealth Government to do things, including censorship and the exertion of economic powers, that it did not have under the

Constitution. Billy Hughes, at first Attorney General and later Prime Minister, made use of this legislation to assume what have been described as "semi-dictatorial powers" (Greenwood 1955: 262). The Commonwealth Government assumed similar powers during the Second World War to give it wide ranging powers including the banning of pink icing for wedding cakes (Macintyre 2015: 103).

It is not generally appreciated that all governance involves a rhythm that covers a continuum that moves on a sliding scale between normality and emergency. This happens more often than is generally understood; for example emergency powers can be exercised by state governments during bushfires or floods.

Australian politics does not proceed in a simple one-dimensional fashion but consists of what might be termed 'normality' punctuated by occasional crises and emergencies that test the capacity of governments to deal with them. Clearly, this understanding of Australian politics does not sit well with a narrative of progress; to apply it one needs to judge political action in a different way. In particular, it emphasises, following Machiavelli (1998), the capacity of governments and their leaders to "master fortune", by which is meant the capacity to adapt to new political circumstances; good governments and their leaders will thrive despite changes in political fortune; they will recognise the need to change course and act accordingly. Good leaders, and good governments, are not enslaved to an ideology or to a particular narrative. The best example of "mastering fortune" in Australian political history is the decision by the Hawke Government to ditch much of its ideological baggage in order to deal with the financial crisis that emerged in 1983.

Not all governments face major emergencies, although most will face some sort of crisis. For many of these governments the emergencies become too difficult to handle, leading to their destruction. Looking through Australian political history, after First World War the first government to face a major emergency was the Scullin Labor Government when it assumed power in late 1929. It was an economic emergency, and there were no constitutional powers available to it and it floundered. It would be no exaggeration to say that the Great Depression destroyed the Scullin Government, as well as splitting the Labor Party, thereby keeping it out of office for some ten years.

Similarly, Menzies in 1939 faced a state of emergency with the outbreak of the Second World War. It can be argued that the Menzies Government, already weakened by the death of former Prime Minister Joe Lyons in early 1939, despite having constitutional powers available to it, failed to adapt successfully to the new conditions that wartime conditions created. Again, this led not only to the destruction of Menzies' Government but also the United Australia Party, with Menzies establishing a new entity, the Liberal Party, in 1944.

Many other governments faced major emergencies or crises including the Whitlam Labor Government facing an economic crisis in 1974, and the same was true for the Hawke-Keating Government during the mid to late 1980s. Rudd faced one in 2008 with the Global Financial Crisis. The reaction to COVID-19 led to the creation of one in 2020. In the cases of Scullin, Menzies in 1941, Whitlam, Rudd and Morrison the state of emergency helped to create the conditions that led to the demise of their governments. Morrison in 2019 presented himself to the electorate as a "daggy dad'" with a positive and optimistic outlook that was entirely appropriate for the circumstances that were in place at the time of the election. What destroyed Morrison was that normalcy lasted for a very short time following his election victory. He failed to deal with emergencies, first bushfires, and then COVID-19 in an effective and authoritative way. He came to be seen as tricky and devious. In Machiavellian terms, he both failed to master fortune, especially with regard to the COVID-19 pandemic (Duckett 2023: 87-101) and came to be regarded with contempt by large segments of the Australian population.

If the foregoing analysis is correct, the only government of the last one hundred years that, faced with a significant crisis/emergency, was able to "master fortune" was the Hawke-Keating Government of the 1980s and early 1990s. They were able to do so because they jettisoned ideology and a pre-determined defining narrative in favour of adapting their policies to the circumstances that they faced.

Albanese's Narrative

Albanese presented himself as a return to normalcy after the failures of Morrison and a year marked by crisis and exceptional politics.

There is a clear logic to the narrative that Labor and Albanese developed to justify their actions and policies and that narrative is built around "progress" and the unique capacity of Labor to deliver progress for the Australian people. Hence, Labor under Albanese is largely future oriented; it does not look back to the glorious Labor traditions of the past. This is because Labor, which was once a party rooted in Australian nationalism, including the myth of the 1890s, has been forced by its adoption of progressive values in a whole range of areas, especially relating to race and gender, to discard its old nationalist focus in favour of more universalist and human rights approach combined with a narrative that gives a prominence to Indigenous history. Contemporary Labor consequently has no access to a restorationist narrative because it has nothing that it wishes to retore; the past is written off as lacking any real value. If anything, the past is something at the best to be forgotten and, at worst, expunged from memory as a time of evil. There have been critics since the 1980s who claim that Labor has abandoned its traditional working class focus but these have had little or no effect on the how the new Labor narrative is understood (Thompson 1999).

Hence, for Albanese, unlike Paul Keating a mere thirty years ago, Curtin and Chifley simply no longer matter. The real, though unacknowledged, sources of the narrative of Albanese Labor, and the source of its internationalist progressivism, are Evatt, Whitlam and Rudd. Albanese would be embarrassed by the simple nationalism of Bob Hawke. For Albanese, Labor tradition seems to extend only back as far as his own lifetime and the events encompassed by it. Albanese's Labor narrative begins with his upbringing by his single mother, and the implementation of Medicare occupies a significant place in it. What happened pre-Medicare has very little importance in Albanese's narrative because the reality is that Labor was racist, sexist and embodied all the values of the "bad old Australia". Progress is no longer the "Light on the Hill" offering the working-class dignity and respect but becomes progressivism with a powerful international dimension but lacking few roots in Australia's past.

Moreover, we now live in an age that is defined by two characteristics that did not exist in the past, an exaggerated sense of crisis and a desire to avoid harm and maintain comfort. Christopher Booker and Richard North (2007) discuss the large number of panics in the United Kingdom during the 1980s and 1990s and note how the interaction of ambitious politicians, elements of the media and specialists within the government bureaucracy led to their creation. Many of these crises were concerned with health matters, including salmonella and mad cow disease. It also developed in other areas, including the millennium bug and claims of ritualised child abuse. What Booker and North demonstrate is how common the tactic of creating a mood of crisis, or emergency, is in modern Western countries. And that includes Australia.

These "emergencies" come out of a fear of a threat to the relative comfort of the contemporary way of life in the West. There can be no doubt, as I have argued elsewhere, that we live in an age of comfort, at least in the West (Melleuish 2014). People expect a relatively pleasant life. They would not tolerate, as I did for a time when a child, weekly visits to change the toilet pan.

These two factors help explain the new narrative of Albanese Labor.

Albanese (2022) in his 2022 Election Policy Speech constructed a narrative that expressed the party of initiative/party of resistance paradigm by portraying Labor as a conveyer belt of continuous progress, with him as the latest representative of reforming Labor leaders going back to Hawke and Keating, "It's only ever Labor Governments who do the big reforms, drive the big changes, reshape the economy in the best interests of people".

He also picks up the theme found in "It's Time" of Labor as the party of movement as opposed to the Coalition as the "party of stagnation… Australia," he claimed, "If we stand still, we will be left behind. If we don't shape the future, the future will shape us". He also promised an almost idyllic future that will leave behind the unpleasantness of COVID-19 and the

Coalition Government. There will be gain but no pain. All we need to do is spend.

This future oriented narrative was still around in early 2025. Hence, Albanese's comment in January 2025 (Jervis-Brady 2025) that "this election is a choice between building Australia's future or taking Australia backwards". Backwards is bad, because the past is inferior, by definition, to the present and to what is coming in the future. It is something of which we should be ashamed. The important thing here is that Albanese's future has no relationship to the ideals of the extended history of the Labor Party, such as one might have found in most Labor leaders prior to Kevin Rudd.

Rather, the Labor narrative, as understood by Albanese, is a bringing together of the conceptual apparatus of the old "party of initiative" theme, (or has it become a meme?), and a grab bag of contemporary progressive policies that may have only a tangential connection to the real world; they certainly do no connect to many past "initiatives" advocated by Labor.

Hence Albanese (2022) in 2022 set out the plan in this way:

It can be seen in phases.
We've been through the pandemic response.
We are in the middle of the recovery.
And reform will be the key to renewal.

From response and recovery – to reform and renewal.

Albanese continues, by claiming that there are a number of "foundations of economic success". These are:

- Affordable and reliable clean energy
- A better and fairer education system
- Skilled workers, secure jobs, fair wages
- Modern infrastructure
- Shared ambition with business and private capital
- And a positive regulatory environment.

There sounds as if it could have been penned by Dr Pangloss from

Voltaire's famous novel *Candide* and his faith that we live in the best of all possible worlds; all progress requires is an Australia led and coordinated by a Labor government so that everyone is heading in the same direction down the same river together. The key elements would appear to be the use of renewables, a focus on education, an economic environment in which business works together with, and is directed by, government, and the creation of local industry. It is as much a utopian vision as many previous projects in Australia, such as the attempt to create Yeoman republics in the 1860s through the various colonial Land Acts, and the fantasy that a combination of protection and regulated industry would create a "new province for law and order", leading to a unified and prosperous Australia in the early twentieth century. All utopian projects are eventually dashed on the rocks of human nature.

It may be the case that Albanese is trapped by his own narrative. The narrative is one of progress and improvement, of delivering for the Australian people, all under the care and direction of the government. It is a narrative driven by the ideas of "normality" and "reform" with "normality" being understood as a time that is largely crisis free, if only because governments can control those crises. Therefore, it is a time when governments and the people should work together in the cause of progress. This, I believe, was the logic behind the campaign for "The Voice". Albanese understood it as part of the fabric of progressive evolution; the government would lead and the country would fall in behind him. He had no real explanation for the failure of "The Voice" other than to blame that failure on misinformation and disinformation, and to bide his time while he looked for other ways of implementing it.

His attitude to "The Voice" is mirrored by that of his response to other policy issues. In a time of normalcy, and with crises under control, there is no need to change one's path, even if the policies may have disastrous consequences. The path to a progressive future has been determined and the imperative is to remain on it. This can be seen in a whole range of policies, including the race for net zero, including such fantasies as "green hydrogen", the development of new Australian industries, again linked to a green agenda, and the belief that the government is a "magic pudding" for funding all sorts of things, regardless of whether it can afford them or not. If government leads the way and we all work together with it on its agenda we will advance and come to live in the "best of all possible worlds".

Therefore, there can be no turning back, no Machiavellian attempt to consider the brute reality that certain policies might impose on the country. There are no failures, no real obstacles; reality can be made to bend to the utopian dreams of a government leading its people into the promised land. And, if reality refuses to bend to the progressive ideal, the solution is to redefine reality in terms of the ideal so that any evidence that might undermine the ideal is classified as disinformation or misinformation.

Chalmers' Narrative

The Treasurer Jim Chalmers has a similar attitude to Albanese but is far more explicit in his exposition of the "new" Labor narrative of progress, and the role of Labor in shepherding the country to a brave new world of unity and harmony, especially as set out in his 2023 *Monthly* article. This is also illustrated by this account (Keheo and Mizen 2025):

> At a press conference in Canberra last year, the *Australia Financial Review* put to Chalmers that the former Productivity Commission and Treasury officials had raised concerns about him ditching the free market model and reforms that delivered prosperity. Chalmers responded by saying the world had changed and the past "is not necessarily the right economic orthodoxy for the big turning points". 'I genuinely believe in some of those people who I greatly admire from the '80s and '90s ... the vast achievements of those incredible performing governments under Bob and Paul', Chalmers said. 'But we have to recognise that the world moves on, and we need to move with it. Because if we get stuck in the past, this country will be poorer'.

In other words, for Chalmers, even the 1980s and 1990s are to be expunged from the Labor heritage which is now clearly focused on the

21st Century and the new world that has been created in those years. What exactly is this new world that has come into being since the time of "Bob and Paul'+"?

These passages from Chalmers' article in *The Monthly* (2023) article gives us a clue: "Now, once again, the world is entering a stream full of perilous white water. But each crisis is different, and each time, the people and country are different as well".

Unlike Albanese, Chalmers builds his case on the idea that the contemporary world is characterised by being a time of "crises". Crises are thus the new "normal" but crises are redefined. One can argue that the idea that we are living in an "age of crises" that is somehow unique, especially in the case of Australia, is a fabrication, as the country has had a relatively good passage economically over the past thirty years. What has changed is our perception of crises and a tendency to turn everything into a crisis. There were influenza pandemics in Australia in the 1950s and 1960s, with large numbers of deaths, but they left no imprint on the public memory because there was no attempt to turn them into "crises". One simply lived through them:

> The crises are defined by their differences but have a common thread: vulnerability. In each case our communities, economies, budgets, environment, financial and energy markets, international relationships, and our politics – already fragile enough – became more so. (Chalmers 2023)

This passage is very interesting because of the use of the words "vulnerability" and "fragile". Our age is characterised by the fragility of the people living through it. This is in stark contrast to what might be considered to be the traditional Australian, and Labor, view of the world and the people who compose it. Consider what former Labor leader Billy Hughes (1948: 87) wrote about the 1890s: "I have always rated initiative and resource amongst the most valuable qualities of a man's character; along with courage, tenacity of purpose, and vision, they go to make up the ideal man".

In *The Case for Labor*, written during the first decade of the twentieth century, Hughes (1970 [1910]: 59-65) also expressed his admiration of John Stuart Mill's *On Liberty* and opposed the idea of the state directing how people should live their lives. The original Labor ideal emphasised resilience and Australian workers during the Depression were not enthusiastic about receiving assistance. Consider this statement by Labor Prime Minister from 1945 to 1949 Ben Chifley (1952: 33): "Self-respect is born in people who have the opportunity to work and that benefits the community of which they are members". Chifley (1952: 37) represented a traditional Labor viewpoint that the role of government was to enable individuals to develop their self-respect so that they would not have to go "to a police station to get a six shillings a week dole".

If the world creates people who are fragile and vulnerable, then the case for the state to protect and guide the people becomes all that much stronger. In an age of continuous crises, as envisioned by Chalmers, government must play a leading role ensuring that individuals do not come to harm. The primary function of government is alleviate, and hopefully eliminate, harm, including harm of a psychological nature. In fact, the idea of a government engaging in therapeutic practices to ensure the well-being of the people, goes hand in hand with the idea, promoted by Chalmers, that the role of government in an age of crises is to prevent harm from occurring, ie of protecting the people from possible crises.

This is quite different from the social liberal view of the state where it is assumed that the state can be used to create the conditions that allow individuals to enhance the capacities and capabilities. It is also a long way from the ancient Greek ideal that suffering is necessary for wisdom. In an age of uncertainty and vulnerability the people need the government to provide guidance for them (Chalmers: 2023):

> Successive leaders failed to find their way conclusively or convincingly past the neoliberalism of the pre-crises period. In other words, while the world was getting more uncertain, we had been growing more vulnerable. Domestic policies – and policy vacuums – accelerated rather than alleviated this problem.
>
> Our mission is to redefine and reform our economy and insti-

tutions in ways that make our people and communities more resilient, and our society and democracy stronger as well.

Neoliberalism is defined as belonging to a previous "pre-crises period" but no longer has any use because the world has changed; it has become both more "uncertain" and more "vulnerable". This makes a number of assumptions. One is that there were no crises before 2008 and the other is that "neoliberalism" only worked when times were good. This is odd as it would be difficult to argue that the 1980s, leading to the "recession that we had to have" were the good times. At that stage neoliberalism was seen as the solution to economic problems, not their cause:

> Below, where ministers sat, there was no thought for the potential of the fourth industrial revolution, or changing work patterns, no understanding that the COVID recession hurt women disproportionately, and, of course, a denial of the economics and opportunities of cleaner energy. (Chalmers 2023)

This is an interesting passage where Chalmers invokes Klaus Schwab and the WEF and argues that a "new" economic age is emerging. Note how he links together economics and "cleaner energy". Chalmers here creates what has been termed in the past as a "package" (Melleuish 1998) bringing together things that have no real connection, such as the "fourth industrial revolution", whatever that might mean, COVID and women and so-called "clean energy". There is no real logic in this linkage beyond ideology.

What it does justify is a doctrine of governance that gives governments the central role in the contemporary world as they come to coordinate the "fragile" and "vulnerable" society and economy that we inhabit:

> Here, government has a leadership role to play: defining priorities, challenges and missions – not 'picking winners'. This is critical to guide how we design markets, facilitate flows of capital into priority areas, and ultimately make progress on our collective problems and purpose.

> Our success also depends on market design and disclosure to

ensure our private markets create public value.

> The clean energy sector is a perfect example of how greater
> levels of private investment are achieved when the government
> ensures the flow of first-class information. Businesses want
> to manage climate risk, but investors don't have a consistent
> framework to compare how businesses are doing this. Investors
> should be able to work out the climate-risk rating of a firm just
> as a lender can work out a credit-risk rating. (Chalmers 2023)

These passages indicate where Chalmers considers that the Australian version of the "great reset" will take the country. In a dangerous age marked by the need to "protect" a "vulnerable" and "fragile" people, the government won't "pick winners" but it will "design markets" (how is it even possible to "design markets"?) such that markets become tools of government policy. This can be seen quite clearly in what Chalmers writes about the "clean energy sector". Governments and businesses will work together to take the country down a particular managed route that accords with a goal that will be determined by government.

It is somewhat unclear as to what that goal, that "light on the hill", actually is. It is not socialism. Consider this serving of word salad by Chalmers:

> My optimism doesn't just come from the beginning of a new
> year, it comes from believing that, amid all the difficulties, 2023
> will be the year we build a better capitalism, uniquely Australian
> – more confident and forward-thinking; more aligned with our
> values; based more on evidence and integrity; more capable of
> building resilience, not just building buffers. (Chalmers 2023)

A new type of narrative with some resonances from the past

It doesn't actually say anything much about what the outcome will be: what values? Based on what evidence? Its very vagueness means that it can be incorporated into the traditional Labor idea of "party of initiative". The narrative would seem to indicate that if a Labor government wished to continue along the road of progress in an age of vulnerability and fragility then it should take a leading hand in ensuring that the actions of its citizens conform to the goals and objectives of the government.

Potentially, it is a model for a form of soft authoritarianism where the bars limiting the activities of the citizenry are made of gossamer, not iron. Although Chalmers appears to have taken at least some of the inspiration for his narrative from the World Economic Forum, the older source of influence is the 'third way' philosophy espoused by figures such as Tony Blair. The new normal is not a return from the crises of the past few years; rather it seeks to absorb aspects of crisis management, including a concern for "vulnerability", an extended use of soft coercion and increased government oversight of the activities of the citizenry into that "normal". Even worse, governments increasingly possess the technology to use those gossamer bars in an effective fashion.

Once launched, this narrative, which sees itself as the answer to the crises of the age, has no mechanisms to deal with the crises that it, itself, might cause. The only way forward is forward, regardless of where that leads. The important thing is that it leaves no room for what might be termed a "Machiavellian manoeuvre" when it is discovered that the rigidity of the narrative may be leading the country into a black hole. If one is going to be an effective political leader it is crucial that one is able to escape the narrative that brought one to power and to adapt accordingly.

The Labor narrative builds on a nation of crisis and the need to return the country from crisis to normality. The clear message is that although we live in an age of crises the government can act in such a fashion as create normality, or at least its façade. This can only be achieved if Labor, the party of progress, is allowed to implement its policies. These policies, however, are not those that Labor followed successfully in the 1980s to deal with what one generally understands to have been a very real, perhaps existential, crisis for Australia. The day of "neoliberalism" is over and a "new" set of policies need to be implemented.

Normality, or perhaps a bubble of normality, has returned and the appropriate course of action is to pursue those policies that will some-how create a better future. The crises are being safely managed, even if they remain ever present.

It needs to be understood that this new narrative might resemble the "party of initiative" narrative, but, in fact it is something quite new and innovative. One key aspect of this new narrative are invocations of vulnerability and fragility, especially in terms of emotion. Tradi-tionally, as we have seen, Labor sought to create the conditions un-der which people could obtain the circumstances that allowed them to exercise self-respect, possess dignity, and exercise control over their lives. It was not really concerned with telling them how they should live, and improve, their lives. That was the territory of the churches and the Wowsers. Hence in the1980s the Hawke/Keating government was willing to take hard decisions, as had many governments before them when faced with a crisis, even though those decisions had an ad-verse effect on many people, including "the recession we had to have" and 13 per cent interest rates.

The new Labor narrative has a much more powerful therapeutic di-mension to it. No one is to be allowed to suffer or to be hurt. Govern-ment policy needs to be made in such a way that any potential harm is minimised; there should only be measures that lead to a win-win out-come. The government acts as a sort of paternalistic body that brings everyone together in pursuit of a common cause, leading to the "best of all possible worlds". Or rather, in a term coined by psychologist Ronald Conway (1978: 30-3), it follows the practices of "matrist in-dulgence", of implementing policies that indulge the populace, rather than asking them to make sacrifices, so that its members do not feel threatened or fearful of the world.

For example, when the road to a green future based purely on renew-ables is sketched out there is no indication of a need for struggle and sacrifice as may have been found in the past, such as can be found in Chifley's speeches of the post Second World War era. Hence Chifley (1952: 168) could write in 1948 in relation to the "sterling crisis" that Australia must "share the burden" of the dollar shortage with Britain. "This is not a mere matter of sentiment, but one of sheer hard neces-sity". For Chifley, necessity demanded that sacrifices needed to be made. This attitude may well have cost Labor the 1949 election. If climate change was such an existential threat, then one would expect that Albanese and Chalmers and Bowen would use a similar sort of language. They clearly do not, instead painting an almost Pollyanna vision of the future in which no pain will occur. Energy prices will fall and there will be a seamless transition to renewable energy and everyone will benefit. As was mentioned earlier, a Panglossian view of the world.

The government will "manage" the transition, bringing together government, business and the wider community in a seamless process that will build an almost utopian future. As there is no struggle or sacrifice, and no true obstacles, there is no need for a more Machiavellian approach to events, no need to take into account the dictates of necessity. Strangely, this excessively optimistic vision of how the world works is eerily reminiscent of W.K. Hancock's description of Australian government behaviour in the last 1920s. If the source of the problem were bad policies, including excessive tariff protection and an over-regulated industrial relations system, then the government response was to go even further down this road and extend tariffs even further. Australians failed to understand the reality of the circumstances in which they were placed; they lacked realism.

The election result demonstrates how powerful different versions of the Albanese/Chalmers narrative have been in Australia. Hancock's assessment of Australian political culture in 1930 seems to be very similar to what is the case in 2025. Australians, like Mulder, want to believe; they are not good at dealing with the harsh realities of the wider world. This may be the result of being an imperial dependency for so long, combined with being the second last bus stop on the planet. They are suckers for a narrative that tells them that all they need to do is follow a certain path and they will arrive at their destination without having to suffer much in the way of pain or harm. In the case of Hancock's analysis, tariffs were destroying the fabric of the economy, so the solution was to impose even more tariffs. In the current circumstances, net zero is doing the same thing, so the answer is even more renewables.

The last two federal election campaigns have been very odd beasts;

they were periods when real time was suspended and the real world ignored, in favour of a talk fest at which were served up endless plates of word salads, when political parties could offer policies that were often very fanciful in nature. In the case of Labor, its narrative and policies offered not only a road to the future that required little in the way of sacrifice by the Australian people but which was also framed in therapeutic terms, as one would expect in the twenty first century. Labor convinced large parts of the electorate that it would look after it and not allow it to suffer, either physically or mentally. It was the caring party. The Coalition lacked any real narrative. In an age of "caring" it would be difficult to go back to Menzies' distinction between leaners and lifters; to call someone a leaner might be to threaten their mental health.

Now the election is over, we re-enter the real world and real time, and all the problems and threats and imperfections that reality entails. The world of 2025, in reality, is a very threatening place that cannot be wished away by fanciful narratives; it remains to be seen how long the Labor narrative will be able to paper over all the very real crises that threaten the world. The Albanese/Chalmers/ Labor narrative still has a long way to run.

References

Abbott, T., (2013), "Liberal Party Election Speech", Liberal Party of Australia https://electionspeeches.moadoph.gov.au/speeches/2013-tony-abbott

Albanese, A., (2022), "Election Speech," https://electionspeeches.moadoph.gov.au/speeches/2022-anthony-albanese

Albanese, A., (2022), "Building for a better future", Address, National Press Club. https://antonyalbanese.com.au/media-centre/building-for-a-better-future-national-press-club

Bailyn, B., (2017), *The Ideological Origins of the French Revolution*, Harvard: Harvard University Press

Booker, C., and North C., (2007), *Scared to Death*, London: Continuum

Chalmers. J., (2023), "Capitalism after the Crises," *The Monthly* https://www.themonthly.com.au/february-2023/essays/capitalism-after-crises

Chifley, J.B., (1952), *Things Worth Fighting For*, in Stargardt, A.W., (ed), Carlton: Melbourne University Press

Conway. R., (1978), *The Land of the Long Weekend,* Melbourne: Sun Books

Duckett, S., (2023), "The (Mis)Management of the COVID-19 Pandemic," in McCaffrie, B., Grattan, M., and Wallace, C., (eds), *The Morrison Government: Governing Through Crisis, 2019-2022,* Sydney: UNSW Press, 87-101

Greenwood, G., (1955), "Australia at War 1914-18" in Greenwood, G., *Australia: A Social and Political History,* Sydney: Angus and Robertson

Hancock, W.K., (1930), *Australia,* London: Benn

Hirst, J.B., (1988), *The Strange Birth of Colonial Democracy,* Sydney: Allen and Unwin

Hughes, W.M., (1948), *Crusts and Crusades,* Sydney: Angus and Robertson

Hughes, W.M., (1970) [1910], *The Case for Labor,* Intr. By Sir Robert Menzies, Sydney: Sydney University Press.

Jervis-Brady, D., (2025), "Anthony Albanese switches to election footing with blitz of three campaigning battlegrounds," *The Guardian*

https://www.theguardian.com/Australia-news/2025/jan/06/Anthony-albanes-switches-to-election-footing-with-blitz-of-three-campaign-battlegrounds

Kehoe, J., and Mizen, R., (2025), "Cold Controlled Anger: Jim Chalmers' Battle to Control the Narrative", *Australian Financial Review,* 28 February

Lazar, N.C., (2009), *States of Emergency in Liberal Democracies,* Cambridge: Cambridge University Press

Machiavelli, N., (1998), *The Prince,* Skinner, Q., and Price, R., (eds), Cambridge: Cambridge University Press

Macintyre, S., (2015), *Australia's Boldest Experiment: War and reconstruction in the 1940s,* Sydney: NewSouth Publishing

Mayer, H., (1956), "Some conceptions of the Australian party system 1910-1950", *Historical Studies, Australia and New Zealand,* 7, (27), 253-7

Melleuish, G., (1995), *Cultural Liberalism in Australia,* Cambridge: Cambridge University Press

Melleuish, G., (1998), *The Packaging of Australia,* Sydney: UNSW Press

Melleuish, G., (2014), "Living in an age of comfort: understanding religion in the twenty first century", *Telos,* 166, 9-24

Melleuish, G., (2018), "The Machiavellian takeover of Australian Universities," *Quadrant,* 62,1-2, 66-74

Melleuish, G., (2025), "Trump and the "Golden Age", *Telos*, 210, Spring, 151-53

Palmer, V., (1963), *The Legend of the Nineties*, Carlton: Melbourne University Press

Thompson, M., (1999), *Labor without class: The gentrification of the ALP*, Annandale: Pluto Press.

Voltaire, (2006), *Candide*, Trans. Cuffe, T., London: Penguin.

3

Labor's Federal Election Performance in Queensland

John Mickel

Introduction

Following the 2025 federal election, Queensland Federal Labor could only nostalgically look on its historical periods of electoral dominance, when it routinely secured the majority of federal seats in the state. However, the 2025 election did not mark a return to those times. Although Labor experienced a modest improvement in its federal seat count, it did not achieve a majority of federal seats in Queensland. The historic national swing towards Labor did not translate into equivalent seat gains within the state.

Labor has not secured a majority of Queensland's federal seats since 2007, which is widely regarded as an outlier in the context of the state's enduring conservative alignment, persisting since 1993 (Williams 2019). In the 2025 election, despite winning the national vote and forming government, Labor secured only 12 of the 30 federal seats in Queensland – an increase of seven seats, including five gained from the Liberal National Party (LNP) and two from the Greens (AEC 2025).

At the national level in 2025, Labor achieved its strongest performance since in terms of both two-party-preferred vote. A notable outcome was the electoral defeat of Federal Opposition Leader Peter Dutton

– the first instance of a sitting opposition leader losing their seat in Australian political history. Nonetheless, the attainment of majority seat status in Queensland remains elusive for Federal Labor.

This chapter presents an historical analysis of Labor's federal electoral performance in Queensland, observing trends within the context of national political dynamics.

Background

Federation to 1929

There are two distinct periods for Labor's performance in Queensland: pre-Second World War and post-war. From federation until the First World War in 1914, Labor dominated federally in Queensland, winning majorities in 4 out of 6 federal elections (1903, 1910, 1913, 1914), with its best effort in 1903, winning 7 out of 9 seats. This was followed by 6 bleak elections from 1917 until 1929 (Sharman and Dodds 2022).

1929 until 1961

Between the Great Depression and Second World War (1929-1946), the Australian Labor Party held a majority of federal seats in Queensland and controlled the state government. However, from 1949 onwards, two major events – the election of the Liberal Menzies Government and the 1957 Queensland Labor split – led to Labor losing its majority in federal seats. The best results for Labor during this period were in 1954 and 1955, winning only five out of 18 seats (Sharman and Dodds 2022).

The 1957 split severely weakened Labor, causing it to lose control of the State government, cabinet ministers, and presence in rural areas (Thornton 1986). The decline in support from rural trade unions, particularly the Australian Workers' Union (AWU), further hurt Labor. Political power in the Queensland Labor Party was mainly based on the rural-oriented AWU, making Labor as much an agrarian party as a labour party (Costar 2013: 6).

Queensland's socio-economic structure during this period posed challenges for Labor. Unlike other Australian states, most of the

"Queensland's population resided outside the capital city, Brisbane" (Ward 1997: 117). Queensland's economy largely depended on agriculture and resources.

Until the 1950s, a significant portion of Queensland's agricultural labour – especially in the sugar, sheep (Pollard 2001) and port industries (Hull 1973) – was carried out by a unionised workforce under the industrial coverage of the Australian Workers' Union (AWU). The disaffiliation of the AWU from the Queensland Labor Party coincided with substantial socio-economic and technological changes across the state (Bowden 2013: 6).

Increased mechanisation in agriculture and urban migration led to the dismantling of shearing shed culture and closure of regional rail networks. The 1957 party split alienated Catholic farmers, weakening Labor's support from ex-Irish Catholic small landholders and eroding its rural sociological and electoral base (Verrall in Costar and Woodward 1985: 22).

As a result, Labor's competitiveness as a political force in regional Queensland was considerably weakened. The disaffiliation of the AWU not only deprived Labor of vital rural organisational infrastructure but also initiated a transformation in the party's identity. For the first time, the Queensland branch of the Labor Party became primarily an organisation representing the urban blue-collar working class (Bowden 2013: 6), thereby limiting its demographic appeal and geographic reach.

From 1957 onward, control of the Queensland branch of the Australian Labor Party (ALP) shifted decisively to a Brisbane-based Trades Hall faction, led by the combative figure of John Alfred Roy Edgerton (Cross 2011). At the time, the full extent of this factional dominance and its adverse effects on the party's broader political fortunes were not fully appreciated. Until then, Queensland Labor had appeared to be the natural party of government at the state level, having been out of office for only three years between 1929 and 1932. This dominance fostered a misplaced confidence that internal divisions would be resolved quickly and that a return to government would occur within a short timeframe.

In the 1961 federal election, Labor showed signs of resurgence, particularly in Queensland. The Menzies Coalition Government narrowly stayed in power as the "credit squeeze" that year had electorally harmed the government. At that election, Queensland Federal Labor secured a majority of the state's seats – 11 out of 18 – but this recovery was shortlived (Sharman and Dodds 2022).

1961–1993: A prolonged electoral decline

During the 1960s and 1970s, Labor struggled to win State government in Queensland and failed to secure a majority of federal seats in the state. The 1963 election saw federal losses, which continued in 1966. Although there was some recovery in 1969, the federal victory under Whitlam in 1972 did not lead to significant gains in Queensland, with Labor winning only eight seats again.

The 1970s were particularly challenging. After the 1975 election (the Fraser Coalition landslide) Labor held just one of Queensland's 18 federal seats, a low point since 1925. Despite poor outcomes and calls for reform, the Queensland ALP branch resisted change. In the 1980 election, Labor won five seats – four more than in 1975 – all in Brisbane's urban areas, matching counts from earlier decades when Queensland had fewer electorates (Sharman and Dodds 2022). Federal Labor leader Bill Hayden struggled to gain support in Queensland when he was opposition leader facing in 1980 his first election in that position. Although a local former police officer, and federal member for the Ipswich based electorate of Oxley for 19 years, his leadership did not connect with voters, despite being respected intellectually.

Organisational reform and recovery in the 1980s

A significant event transpired in the 1980s when the National Executive of the Federal Labor Party intervened in the affairs of its Queensland branch. This intervention dismantled the entrenched power structures that had characterised the party since Edgerton's leadership. Edgerton's political credibility had waned following his acceptance of a knighthood from the Fraser Government in the late 1970s (Moore 2010). The subsequent organisational reforms resulted in a more diverse and representative array of candidates for Federal Labor in Queensland.

On the eve of the 1983 federal election, Opposition Leader Bill Hayden relinquished his leadership for the charismatic, former ACTU President, Bob Hawke. Under Hawke's leadership, Labor saw significant electoral success at the March 1983 election. Between 1983 and 1993, the party consistently secured a considerable number of Queensland federal seats: 10 out of 19 in 1983, 13 out of 24 in 1987, 15 out of 24 in 1990, and 13 out of 25 in 1993. This period marked the peak of Queensland Federal Labor in numbers of seats until 2007 (Sharman and Dodds 2022).

National trends in the 1980s were favourable to Labor, and Queensland Labor reflected this momentum. Labor's gains were also influenced by the unpredictable and increasingly divisive leadership of Queensland Premier Johannes Bjelke-Petersen. Attempting to replicate his earlier success in opposing the Whitlam Government, Bjelke-Petersen launched the "Joh for PM" campaign in 1987, which ultimately failed due to the lack of a federal seat and sufficient financial backing (Davey 2015). The campaign caused fractures within the federal Coalition, weakened the National Party in Queensland, and eventually led to Bjelke-Petersen losing his premiership at the end of 1987. His actions destabilised conservative politics in the state, creating opportunities for Federal Labor.

The National Party had governed Queensland independently from 1983, following a split with its junior coalition partner, the Liberal Party in 1983 and its ability following the subsequent state election to form government in its own right – a rare occurrence in Queensland and Australian politics (Prasser 1984). However, its tenure became increasingly affected by both perceived and actual systemic corruption, (Fitzgerald 1989) leading to the imprisonment of several former Cabinet ministers and significantly undermining public confidence. The decline of the Bjelke-Petersen personality cult, once central to the National Party's dominance, coincided with a notable electoral shift.

This shift enabled Labor to achieve temporary dominance at the federal level in Queensland. The trend of the Nationals holding more

federal seats in Queensland than the Liberals – prevalent throughout
the 1980s – was reversed in the 1990 election and has not reappeared
since. While part of the Nationals' previous success was attributed to
their effective campaign infrastructure, the Liberal Party's decline was
mainly due to Labor's increasing strength in Brisbane's outer northern
and southern suburbs. These gains came largely at the Liberals'
expense and helped Labor achieve its peak Queensland representation
at the 1993 federal election. At that time, the Federal Labor Keating
Government was re-elected contrary to all public polling expectations.
Keating had replaced Bob Hawke after several debilitating leadership
challenges. At no time, did Keating achieve Hawke's popularity and
defeat was assumed. However, Keating's well honed political skills
enabled him to defeat the Liberals in a full-throated policy dominated
campaign.

1996–2022: Fragmentation and Decline

The defeat of the Keating Labor Government in 1996 led to a prolonged
period where federal Labor struggled to win seats in Queensland.
This changed briefly in the 2007 election with Queenslander, Kevin
Rudd's leadership. Rudd had been the federal member for Griffith on
Brisbane's southside from 1998. He had been elected leader of the
Federal Labor Party in December 2006. He had maintained a high
profile whilst opposition spokesman and leader. This combination as
well as his relative youth against the 11-year-old prime ministership
of conservative John Howard had widespread appeal resulting in
Labor securing 13 of Queensland's 25 electorates. (Sharman and
Dodds 2022). However, Labor's success lasted one term. From 2010
Labor's seat presence in Queensland was desultory, and by the 2022
Federal election, they only won five seats. Their support was mainly
in culturally diverse areas south of Brisbane River. Meanwhile, the
Australian Greens gained from urban dissatisfaction, winning three
inner-city Brisbane seats. Labor's continued decline in regional
Queensland and unimpressive Senate results have yet to prompt
significant strategic changes.

Historical context and structural factors

The persistent underperformance of Federal Labor in Queensland cannot be attributed to a single cause. Rather, it reflects a complex interplay of historical, demographic, and structural factors. Electoral dynamics in Queensland have at times mirrored broader trends in federal-state relations. In a federal system, voters may leverage state elections to balance or check federal governments. Conservative parties have governed Queensland for 37 out of the 77 years since the end of the Second World War, including an uninterrupted 32-year period from 1957 to 1989. This prolonged conservative dominance at the state level has undoubtedly influenced federal voting patterns.

From 1946 to 2022, Labor secured a majority of federal seats in Queensland in only seven out of thirty elections. These instances of success typically occurred under specific and exceptional circumstances. One election took place during the immediate postwar period; another during a time of acute economic turmoil. Four victories resulted either from a highly popular Federal Labor leader or a collapse in support for the State Government, usually amid scandal or public dissatisfaction. The success in 2007 was due to both Kevin Rudd's local appeal as a Queenslander and the electorate's weariness with a long-serving Coalition Government.

The ALP secured majority representation in Queensland during seven notable federal elections under various historical and political conditions. In the post-war period under the Chifley Labor Government, Labor won five of ten seats. In 1961, during the Menzies Government's election, Labor obtained eleven of eighteen seats. Under Bob Hawke, Labor captured ten of nineteen seats in 1983 and thirteen of nineteen seats in 1987. In 1990, Labor earned fifteen of twenty-four seats due to backlash against the scandal-plagued National Party Government. The 1993 election saw Labor win thirteen of twenty-five seats, supported by Keating's critique of the Opposition's platform (Sharman and Dodds 2022). Finally, in 2007, Labor gained fifteen of twenty-nine seats driven by a highly regarded state leader and dissatisfaction with the Howard Government.

Incumbency and social conservatism

Queensland has a strong sense of community that enhances the incumbency effect. Notable examples include independent Bob Katter Senior, re-elected since 1993 on a rural populist platform, and Warren Entsch, who consistently wins as a Liberal in a Labor-dominant electorate. In 2022, despite a statewide swing to Labor, Entsch faced less than a 1 per cent swing against him. Incumbency impacts opposition morale and candidate quality, showing resilience against nationwide trends.

Social conservatism is more pronounced further from inner city Brisbane, aiding conservative causes federally when politically exploited. The Marriage Equality Plebiscite saw the highest negative votes in rural and regional areas of Queensland (ABS 2017). Similarly, the 2023 Voice Referendum had Queensland recording the highest "no vote", with metropolitan areas like Brisbane voting "yes" (AEC 2023).

Historical trends echo these outcomes; for instance, the 1999 Republican referendum saw Queensland's highest "no vote," with only the federal metropolitan electorates of Brisbane and Ryan voting "yes" and Maranoa and Kennedy recording the highest 'no votes' (AEC1999).

Distrust of Canberra: Queensland's political exceptionalism

Queensland political culture is marked by scepticism toward central government authority, influenced by populist sentiment and social conservatism. As former Queensland Federal Minister, Sir James Killen noted, "Queensland attitudes to national political endeavour have always been susceptible to suspicion and, at times, open hostility. There is no ready explanation available to explain Queensland's corporate doubt as to the virtue of Canberra's decision making. That it exists is beyond doubt" (Killen, cited in Charlton 1983: 1).

This regional scepticism stems from the state's geographic, cultural, and political diversity, with Dr John Herron describing Queensland as "five states of mind": Far North Queensland, North Queensland, South-East Queensland, Western Queensland, and metropolitan

Queensland and they live in different worlds.

In this 2010 interview, Dr John Herron was enunciating an exhortation that Queensland is different – different from other States (Herron 2010).

Australia's federal system allows voters to evaluate different levels of government. After a 1952 recession, Queensland's Gair Labor Government leveraged this for the 1953 state election, securing 53 per cent of the primary vote and 66 per cent of state seats – the highest post-war state Labor vote. In 1974, Queensland Labor's vote fell to 13.4 per cent. The Goss Government faced voter backlash in 1995 and lost a by-election when the Keating Government called a federal election in 1996, reducing Labor to two seats federally. The Borbidge Coalition Government (1996-98) was defeated following unfavourable decisions by the Howard Federal Liberal Government (eg new guns laws and the coming of the GST) and was succeeded by the Beattie Labor Government that governed through the Howard era. The Rudd-Gillard federal Labor governments (2007-2013) were poorly received in Queensland, with the lowest state Labor vote in 2012 at 26.6 per cent. From 1998 to 2007, Beattie's team governed untroubled alongside the Howard Liberal Government.

From 2015 onwards, state Labor governments returned to power alongside federal Liberal-National governments marked by internal dysfunction. However, federal Liberal Party disunity resulting in three prime ministerial changes between 2013 and 2018 and did not translate into federal success during this period for Labor in Queensland, particularly in regional and rural areas.

The 2019 federal election illustrated this dynamic vividly, with Labor suffering significant losses in Queensland due to southern interference in local affairs. Inner-city Brisbane electorates showed swings towards Labor, highlighting the urban-rural divide in political attitudes. A recurrent Queensland theme occurred in regional Queensland at the 2019 federal election. The election result was fed by a perception that regional and rural Queensland were paying the price in jobs and growth for the ALP looking after Sydney and Melbourne voters (Farr 2019). Former Greens Senator and environmentalist, Dr Bob Brown, led a

"Stop the Adani Convoy" into Queensland – the Adani was the name of a proposed coal mine planned for central Queensland and named after the Indian billionaire proponent, Gautam Adani. Despite ongoing leadership turmoil, Queensland exhibited three distinct voting pattens.

In the regional areas most impacted by the Adani convoy, there were double digit anti-Labor swings in Dawson and Capricornia and the subsequent loss of the north Queensland seat of Herbert. The outer metropolitan areas to the immediate north and south of Brisbane also reacted against Federal Labor's leader and policies, recording huge swings in Forde and Petrie and the loss of the seat of Longman. By contrast, there were notable swings to Labor in the inner-city seats of Griffith, Ryan and Brisbane – illustrating a metropolitan / outer metropolitan/ regional division in Labor's Queensland performance. Overall, in 2019, the Queensland Labor vote varied by -6.9 per cent from the national Labor average (Muller 2020).

Additionally, there may be cultural factors influencing the federal voting patterns between Queensland and the rest of eastern Australia. Political writer George Megalogenis suggests that Queensland's culture is like the American South, due to its strong affinity for religion and firearms –factors less prevalent in New South Wales and Victoria (Megalogenis 2012: 185).

Overall, Queensland's political behaviour reflects a unique blend of regional identity, decentralisation, and historical scepticism of federal authority, making it a politically distinct state.

State and Federal electoral divergences in Queensland

The electoral landscape in Queensland presents a notable challenge for the contemporary Australian Labor Party in securing federal seats, despite its relative strength at the state level. An analysis of federal electoral results alongside the corresponding state electorates underscores this paradox.

For instance, the federal electorate of Leichhardt in Far North Queensland has predominantly been held by the Coalition since

1996, with the exception of a single three-year interlude. Yet, the state electorates entirely contained within Leichhardt – namely Cook, Barron River, Cairns, and Mulgrave – have largely been retained by state Labor. A similar pattern emerges in the federal seat of Herbert, centred around Townsville, which has been predominantly Liberal-held federally since 1996. In contrast, Labor has largely controlled the state electorates of Townsville, Mundingburra, and Thuringowa, all of which fall within the boundaries of Herbert, with only brief interruptions.

This phenomenon is also observable in other federal electorates such as Longman, Dickson, Petrie, Forde, Bonner, and Bowman, where Labor maintains dominance in most of the associated state electorates, yet fails to secure the corresponding federal seats. The crux of this issue appears to be Labor's difficulty in converting its robust state-level support into electoral gains at the federal level.

One plausible explanation is that the federal Liberal Party has benefited from periods of national ascendancy, which have bolstered its hold on Queensland's federal constituencies. Concurrently, Labor's capacity to govern with majorities at the state level reflects its relative strength with service delivery within Queensland. However, this dynamic does not fully account for Labor's notably poor performance in the 2022 federal election, suggesting that additional factors – potentially including differential voter behavior, campaign dynamics, or issue salience—may be influencing electoral outcomes.

2025 Federal election

Following the defeat of the Miles State Labor Government in 2024, Queensland federal Labor entered the federal election unencumbered by the electoral burden of a sitting state Labor government. Nonetheless, despite a record national seat gain and the highest national primary vote for the ALP since 1943, Queensland Labor failed to secure either a majority of votes or a majority of federal seats within the state. The ALP gained seven seats overall – six of which were located in Southeast Queensland. In regional Queensland, Labor holds only one seat: Leichhardt, in the far north. This gain in 2025 was significantly facilitated by the retirement of long-serving Liberal National Party (LNP) member Warren Entsch, and the electorate recorded the largest pro-Labor swing in the state (see Chapter 1 for more detailed 2025 election analysis).

Elsewhere in regional Queensland, electoral outcomes were mixed. In the electorates of Herbert (based on Townsville), Dawson (based on Mackay), and Flynn (around Gladstone), the LNP recorded swings in its favour. Conversely, Capricornia, (Rockhampton) Hinkler (Bundaberg), Wide Bay (Maryborough, Gympie, and Noosa), as well as electorates on the Sunshine Coast and Gold Coast, all experienced swings towards Labor, though not necessarily sufficient to change the seat outcomes.

In Southeast Queensland, Labor performed strongly, securing the seats of Petrie, Dickson, Brisbane, Griffith, Bonner, and Forde, and substantially increasing its vote share in existing strongholds such as Oxley, Moreton, Rankin, Lilley, and Blair (AEC 2025). In the electorates it won within the southeast, Labor's performance closely reflected its previous success in the same region at the state level. Despite its overall loss in the 2024 Queensland state election, Labor had retained a majority of seats in and around Brisbane – a pattern that was replicated federally.

Queensland now mirrors electoral trends evident in states such as Tasmania and South Australia, where the conservative parties hold no metropolitan seats. Across Australia, the conservative vote is increasingly concentrated in rural and regional areas, which continues to limit Labor's ability to convert statewide vote share into a commensurate number of seats in Queensland. This dynamic is particularly pronounced in electorates such as Kennedy, Maranoa, Groom, and Fisher, where Labor finished third behind other parties, underscoring the party's enduring challenge in rural Queensland.

Conclusion

The 2025 federal election marked a significant recovery for the Australian Labor Party in Queensland, particularly in contrast to its disastrous performance in 2019. Following this resurgence, Labor secured four representatives in the federal ministry: Murray Watt and Anthony Chisholm from the Senate, and Dr Jim Chalmers and Anika Wells from the House of Representatives. Additionally, Milton Dick continued in his role as Speaker of the House of Representatives.

However, despite this federal recovery, Labor remains institutionally weak in Queensland across other levels of government. The electoral defeat of the Miles Labor Government in October 2024 left Queensland without a Labor majority at any level of government. Historically, even in its most adverse electoral periods, Labor could rely on controlling the Brisbane City Council, often viewed as a base for rebuilding state-wide support. Yet, this too has become a distant memory; Labor has not held the mayoralty since 2004.

Notably, Prime Minister Albanese chose Queensland as the launch site for his pre-election tour in 2025, a symbolic gesture underscoring the importance of Queensland to Labor's federal ambitions. His effective leadership during a series of natural disasters that struck the state contributed to his political standing. Furthermore, he outperformed Opposition Leader Peter Dutton in his own seat of Dickson, located in Brisbane's outer northern suburbs – an area increasingly representative of Labor's growing strength in metropolitan and peri-urban regions.

Labor's recent gains align with broader demographic shifts that have reshaped electoral patterns nationally. As Kos Samaras of RedBridge Group has noted, these shifts increasingly favour Labor at the federal level. The party's voter base is now concentrated in metropolitan and outer-metropolitan electorates, a trend mirrored in other states. In contrast, the Liberal and National parties have become increasingly reliant on regional and rural constituencies, with more than 80 per cent of their seats situated outside Australia's major capital cities. This evolving urban-regional divide underscores the realignment of party support bases and presents strategic challenges for both major parties moving forward (Samaras 2025). In Queensland, the conservative nature of the electorate means that the Queensland 2025 result reverted to the post war norm whereby Labor underperforms compares with the rest of Australia.

References

Australian Bureau of Statistics, (2017, November 15), Australian Marriage Law Postal Survey 2017: Results, available at: https://www.abs.gov.au/statistics/people/people-and-communities/australian-marriage-law-postal-survey-2017/results

Australian Electoral Commission, (1999), 1999 Referendum Results, available at: https://www.aec.gov.au/Elections/referendums/1999_Referendum_Reports_Results/

Australian Electoral Commission, (2023, October 14), Referendum 2023 Results, available at: https://www.aec.gov.au/referendums/2023-referendum/

Australian Electoral Commission, (2025, June 4), 2025 Federal Election – House of Representatives: Party Representation Leading, Tally Room, available at: https://tallyroom.aec.gov.au/HousePartyRepresentationLeading-31496.htm

Australian Electoral Commission, (2025), Federal Election 2025 Results, available at: https://www.aec.gov.au

Bowden, B., (2013), "Modern Labor in Queensland: Its Rise and Failings, 1978-98", *Australian Society for the Study of Labour History*, 1–26

Charlton, P., (1983), *State of Mind: Why Queensland is Different,* Sydney: Methuen Hayes

Costar, B., cited in Bowden, B., (2013), "Modern Labor in Queensland: Its Rise and Failings, 1978–98"

Cross, M., (2011), [Interview] ORAL TRC 6150/19, National Library of Australia, Canberra 9 July

Davey, P., (2015), *Joh for PM,* Sydney: NewSouth Publishing

Farr, M., (2019), "One word that sums up Labor's election disaster in Queensland", News.com.au, 20 May https://www.news.com.au

Fitzgerald, G.E., (1989), (Chairman), Commission of Inquiry into Possible Illegal Activities and Associated Police Misconduct, *Report*, Brisbane: Queensland Government Printer

Herron, J., (2010), [Interview] ORAL TRC 6100/20, National Library of Australia, 26-27 April

Hull, D., (1973), "Queensland Sugar Ports: Labour and technological change", *Journal of the Australian Political Economy*, 6, 60-72

Killen, D.J., (1983), cited in Charlton, *State of Mind: Why Queensland is Different*

Megalogenis, G., (2012), *The Australian Moment: How We Were Made for These Times*, Melbourne: Penguin Books

Moore, J.C., (2010), [Interview] ORAL TRC 6100/22, National Library of Australia, Canberra. 10 May

Muller, D., (2020), *The 2019 Federal Election, Research Paper Series, 2019–20,* Canberra: Commonwealth Parliament of Australia

Pollard, J., (2001), *Hundred Years of Agriculture: Yearbook 2000,* Australian Bureau of Agricultural and Resource Economics, Canberra: Commonwealth of Australia

Prasser, S., (1984), "The Liberal Party in Queensland," *Current Affairs Bulletin,* 60(10), March, 24-30

Samaras, K., (2025), "The Liberals are fundamentally mismatched with modern Australia", *Australian Financial Review,* 7 May https://www.afr.com/

Sharman, C., and Dodds, A., (2022), The Australian Politics and Elections Archive 1856–2018, available at: https://australianelectionarchive.com/about.php

Thorton, H.J., (1986), *Socialism at Work? Queensland Labor in Office 1915–1957,* Politics Department, Adelaide: University of Adelaide

Verrall, R.J., (1985), cited in Costar, B., and Woodward, D., *Country to National: Australian Rural Politics and Beyond,* Sydney: Allen and Unwin,

Ward, I., (1997), "Queensland: A tale of two elections", in Bean, C., Simms, M., Bennett, S. and Warhurst, J., (eds), T*he Politics of Retribution: The 1996 Federal Election,* Sydney: Allen and Unwin, 117-135

Williams, P., (2019), *State of Play: Queensland Politics since the 1990s,* St Lucia: University of Queensland Press

4

The Dutton-led Opposition in Labor's First Term

Peter van Onselen

Introduction

When Anthony Albanese led Labor to victory in May 2022, few expected the newly formed Dutton-led opposition to offer much resistance. The Coalition, still reeling from its electoral defeat and internal disunity, appeared rudderless and ideologically spent (Coorey 2022). Pundits swiftly wrote Peter Dutton off as unelectable— too divisive to regain the political centre and too anchored to the combative legacy of the Morrison years (Massola 2022). Labor's polling numbers surged during an extended honeymoon, buoyed by perceptions of competence and calm (Essential Report 2022). Yet as the term unfolded, the Dutton-led opposition proved more formidable than forecast. It may not have provided a policy-rich alternative to government, and it ultimately suffered a resounding defeat in 2025, but it succeeded in shaping the political terrain on which Labor was forced to govern. That is, until Treasurer Jim Chalmers' pre-election budget redrew the field once again (Chalmers 2024).

Dutton's opposition drew strength not from bold ideas or a modernising agenda, but from strategic disruption. Through relentless focus on cost-of-living pressures, crime narratives, and cultural flashpoints – most notably the Voice to Parliament referendum – the Coalition capitalised on Labor's vulnerabilities (Murphy 2023; Crowe 2023). A government elected with modest reform ambitions and the promise of stability soon found itself reactive, cautious, and at times panicked. And not always for good reason. Several of Labor's own policy moves – the surprise superannuation tax changes and the eventual backflip on stage three tax cuts – were neither cautious nor consultative (Coorey 2023a; Bagshaw and Crowe 2024). These were the kinds of political surprises it had promised not to spring. In that sense, Labor undermined its own image as a steady, managerial government before the opposition even had the chance to do so.

This chapter examines how the Dutton-led Coalition influenced Labor's first three years in office. Ultimately, not as a credible alternative government, but as a disruptive force capable of narrowing the scope of reform, dictating public narratives, and testing the limits of a governing party's political nerve. In doing so, the chapter also interrogates what this opposition tells us about the state of the political contest in Australia: not simply who wins or loses, but how oppositions can shape governments without returning to power themselves. At the same time, it resists the temptation to frame Labor as a government unjustly stifled by a hostile opposition. This was no government of technocratic saints. Many of its problems – policy confusion, communications failure, and process shortfalls – were entirely self-inflicted. If the opposition made governing harder, it didn't make governing incoherent. Labor managed that on its own (Taylor 2023; Kenny 2023).

From write-off to relevance

When Peter Dutton assumed leadership of the Liberal Party in the wake of the Coalition's 2022 defeat, the consensus from political analysts was that the party had chosen someone unelectable. A former Queensland police officer with a hardline image forged in the portfolios of Home Affairs and Defence, Dutton was cast as the inheritor of a party in retreat – more interested in internal stability than electoral revival (Benson 2022; Crowe 2022a). Many assumed his selection was less a serious bid to recapture the centre ground than a political holding pattern – an interim leadership while the party regrouped and prepared for a post-Dutton future.

Yet that media narrative quickly came undone. Within a year, the Dutton-led opposition was back in the conversation and polling competitively, especially as cost-of-living pressures began to dominate the political landscape (Essential Report 2023). Dutton's style, far from softening, doubled down on combative rhetoric. But this was less alienating than many in the commentariat predicted. He leaned into themes of security, economic anxiety, and cultural division— issues that struck a chord with suburban and regional constituencies (Shanahan 2023). Rather than repositioning himself, Dutton sought to reposition the centre itself, pulling it rightward and forcing Labor to respond.

What helped Dutton regain relevance was not charisma or innovation – it was clarity. In a political climate marked by voter fatigue, cynicism, and post-pandemic volatility, Dutton's bluntness read to some less like political aggression and more like resolve. His critics saw rigidity and a robotic persona lacking warmth or nuance (Savva 2023). Supporters framed it as authenticity. Either way, it contrasted sharply with Anthony Albanese's carefully modulated caution. Dutton's attacks on electricity prices, border protection, and housing may have lacked detailed alternatives, but they cut through. His message was clear, repeated, and aimed squarely at Labor's weak spots.

Crucially, he maintained internal discipline. After a decade of turmoil, culminating in the Morrison-era implosions, Dutton kept both the Liberal and National parties intact. He neutralised dissent, sidelined would-be challengers, and imposed message discipline on a Coalition that had previously struggled to speak with one voice (Crowe 2022b). That unity alone was a political achievement in a party fractured by ideological divisions between moderates, religious conservatives, and populists.

Polling reflected this shift. While the Coalition rarely overtook Labor outright, it narrowed the gap on primary vote and even led in some preferred economic management metrics (Newspoll 2024). In key marginal seats, particularly in Queensland and Western Sydney, Dutton's messaging resonated. Yet this masked a deeper challenge: the Coalition was fighting a war on two fronts—defending outer suburban and regional heartlands from Labor, while also trying (and mostly failing) to win back Teal seats lost to climate-focused independents. That structural dilemma narrowed its electoral pathway considerably (Maley 2023).

Dutton's perceived weaknesses were also overstated by those invested in the idea that the 2022 result marked a cultural realignment. Much of the electorate remained responsive to messages about control, sovereignty, and restraint. Dutton understood that, and he tailored his tone accordingly. He didn't seek to reinvent himself as a centrist because he didn't believe that is where the votes were. On several issues, particularly border policy and law enforcement, he was right – at least in political terms. But his inability to broaden the Coalition's appeal beyond its base would ultimately prove decisive.

Nowhere was this more evident than in the Voice referendum campaign. What began as a modest proposal for constitutional recognition became a polarising fight over identity and trust. Labor's messaging faltered, failing to explain the policy with clarity or conviction. Dutton seized the vacuum, prosecuting a culturally loaded No campaign that spoke to uncertainty, suspicion, and resentment of elite consensus (Benson 2023). The result was decisive: over 60 percent voted No, with majorities in every state. While it would be inaccurate to credit Dutton solely, his role in reframing the debate as a risk to national unity rather than a gesture of reconciliation was pivotal.

More broadly, Dutton benefited from Labor's reluctance – or inability – to define itself. Elected on a small target platform and determined to avoid overreach, Albanese's government struggled to construct a compelling story. Instead, it delivered competent administration with little fanfare, leaving rhetorical space for the opposition to dominate the conversation. Dutton filled that space, not with vision, but with relentless energy.

But that energy did not amount to a governing philosophy. Dutton's leadership did not signal a renewed conservative agenda. There was no modernisation, no comprehensive rethink of Coalition priorities. His was an opposition in the purest sense: obstruction, criticism, disruption. The strategy was effective, but shallow.

Ultimately, Dutton made the Coalition matter again. He revived its competitiveness and returned it to relevance. That his own seat fell at the 2025 election only underscored the contradictions in his leadership. He was able to reassert the Coalition's presence in national politics, but he never convinced enough voters that he could lead the country. The achievement was real, but so too were its limits.

The Opposition Agenda: Disruption as Strategy

Peter Dutton never pretended to be a visionary leader. His lone foray into future-oriented policy—support for nuclear energy—was floated late in the term, and even then lacked detail or implementation pathways (Dziedzic 2023). From the outset, his political approach was tactical, not transformational. The Coalition under Dutton engaged in precision attacks rather than presenting a comprehensive agenda. His team chose their targets carefully: cost-of-living pressures, energy reliability, housing affordability, crime, and border control. In each case, the goal was not to offer a new vision, but to sustain a sense of unease about the government. It was politics of repetition, not reinvention.

This was a deliberate strategy. After nearly a decade in power, the Coalition was intellectually and ideologically fatigued. Dutton's leadership offered little appetite for policy renewal and even less for consensus building across the party's factions. Internally, there was no agreement on what a modern conservative agenda should look like. So, the opposition defaulted to critique. Rather than construct, it deconstructed. The idea was simple: keep the political terrain narrow, and make sure Labor was always playing defence (Crowe 2023a).

The context helped. The optimism that greeted Labor's 2022 victory soon collided with economic realities. Inflation surged, interest rates climbed, and wage growth stagnated. Rather than explaining global inflationary trends or structural headwinds, the opposition simply amplified pain. Dutton didn't need to solve the crisis—he only needed to make sure voters felt it and saw Labor as culpable (Coorey 2023b). The "Labor has no plan" line became a daily refrain. It wasn't true in the literal sense—Jim Chalmers did have a suite of fiscal responses – but it was true emotionally, which mattered more in political terms (Chalmers 2023).

National security also featured prominently. Dutton's background in Defence and Home Affairs gave him a natural platform. He warned of Chinese cyber threats, critiqued foreign policy caution, and styled himself as a leader who "understands the stakes" (Wroe 2023). These interventions rarely came with policy specificity. Instead, they worked by insinuation: Labor was weak, uncertain, insufficiently serious. The Coalition offered a sense of surety—not necessarily better answers, but clearer alarms.

Then came the Voice. Dutton's decision to oppose constitutional recognition of an Indigenous advisory body was the most consequential move of his leadership. It was not simply a case of declining to endorse the proposal; the Coalition actively led the No campaign. Dutton framed the Voice as an unclear and divisive reform that risked entrenching difference rather than reconciliation (Benson 2023). The government's strategy, by contrast, was undercooked. Relying too heavily on moral suasion and assumptions of goodwill, Labor failed to clearly articulate what the Voice would do and why it should be in the Constitution. The campaign misread the electorate and mishandled the messaging (Tingle 2023). While some on the Yes side blamed misinformation, the more plausible explanation is that the case for change was not made with sufficient clarity or urgency. In contrast, Indigenous leaders like Jacinta Nampijinpa Price and Warren Mundine offered punchy, direct arguments that resonated far more deeply than anything coming from government spokespeople (Martin 2023).

Beyond these headline issues, the Coalition's messaging operation remained highly centralised. Dutton was the primary face of opposition; the frontbench was mostly invisible. This was by design. Even when scandals or policy failures invited broader engagement, the opposition stuck to its chosen themes. This wasn't because it lacked capacity—

it was because it prized message discipline above policy creativity. Consistency won over coherence. The daily drumbeat – Labor can't manage money; Labor is soft on crime; Labor is failing on housing— set the tone for media coverage and framed parliamentary debates (Savva 2024).

Tactically, the Liberal Party adapted to this narrowed focus. It avoided major policy announcements that could be picked apart. Instead, it embraced political theatre: press conferences outside supermarkets, rhetorical ambushes during Question Time, viral media moments designed to dominate the evening bulletins. Politics as performance is nothing new, but under Dutton it became the default mode. The goal wasn't persuasion through substance—it was dominance through perception (Murphy 2024).

Critics rightly pointed out the shallowness of this approach. It leaned heavily on grievance and showed little appetite for nation-building. But Dutton's team made a cold calculation: voters weren't looking for inspiration. They were looking for clarity – or, failing that, someone to blame. Disruption wasn't just a fallback. It was the strategy.

Even on climate and energy, areas where the Coalition had been punished electorally, the opposition found traction. Rather than denying the need for emissions reductions, Dutton shifted the conversation to reliability, affordability, and the pace of transition. Labor's energy policies were framed as hasty and economically harmful, a message that resonated in outer-suburban and regional areas already distrustful of "city-first" policies (Crowe 2023b). The aim wasn't to reclaim teal seats. It was to hold or flip lower-income electorates in Queensland, Tasmania, and the outer suburbs. As Liberal MP Tim Wilson noted in a post-election interview, "The path back doesn't go through Wentworth. It goes through Rockingham and Longman" (Wilson 2025).

In this sense, the opposition strategy was about subtraction. The goal was not to build a new Coalition platform. It was to chip away at Labor's support base issue by issue. There was no grand policy offer— no Liberal version of the National Reconstruction Fund or workplace reform. The opposition defined itself by what it opposed: rising costs, constitutional change, soft sentencing, and unreliable energy. Each line of attack was chosen for its ability to erode Labor's momentum, not replace it with an alternative vision.

As the 2025 election approached, that vacuum became harder to ignore. The opposition had spent three years dictating the political agenda, but it struggled to pivot to a governing posture. Its critiques remained sharp. Its policies remained vague. There was no clear alternative economic plan. No comprehensive IR policy. No meaningful proposal for Indigenous recognition. What had worked as disruption failed as aspiration.

Yet judged by opposition standards—especially in today's climate—Dutton was effective. He shaped the national conversation, kept the government under pressure, and ensured that Labor's first term never became a story of confident reform. Whether that added up to a case for government was another matter entirely.

Labor on the defensive

For a government elected on a platform of stability and steady reform, Labor's first term quickly became a case study in political defensiveness. Rather than seizing the opportunity to set the agenda, the Albanese government often found itself reacting to it—sometimes sluggishly, sometimes awkwardly, and not always on its own terms. While some of this dynamic owed to an aggressive and tactically disciplined opposition, much of it was self-inflicted. From communications failures to poor process, Labor undercut its own credibility on multiple fronts.

From the outset, the government sought to define itself by contrast: calm after chaos, competence after crisis. Albanese promised "no surprises, no excuses" (ABC News 2022). But that pledge was soon broken. The superannuation tax changes, announced with limited consultation and framed as modest but unexpected, took even some within Labor's own caucus by surprise (Coorey 2023a). More damaging still was the reversal on the stage three income tax cuts—a shift that contradicted repeated assurances and handed the Coalition an easy narrative of broken promises (Bagshaw and Crowe 2024). These were not the actions of a government governed by cautious incrementalism. They were abrupt, and arguably necessary, but they punctured the trust Labor had sought to build around its economic stewardship.

The cost-of-living crisis underscored Labor's vulnerability. With inflation still elevated and interest rates repeatedly hiked, many households felt no better off than they had under the Morrison government. The Albanese Government's explanation – that global forces were to blame – was technically accurate but politically tone-deaf (Chalmers 2023). Voters wanted urgency. What they got was restraint. The Coalition, meanwhile, did not need a credible plan of its own. Its job was simply to reinforce the perception that Labor was out of touch – and too slow to act (Savva 2024).

Other policy areas followed the same pattern: process breakdown followed by defensive retreat. The rollout of the "Nature Positive" reforms—a proposed overhaul of national environmental laws—descended into confusion and resentment among stakeholders, with critics accusing the government of sidelining proper consultation in favour of headline-driven urgency (Karp 2023). Similarly, a surge in net overseas migration, partly a by-product of pandemic-era visa backlogs and workforce gaps, became politically toxic. Labor was slow to respond, missing early signals that housing pressure and population growth were beginning to merge in the public mind (Dziedzic and Worthington 2023). By the time action was taken, including capping student visas and tightening pathways to permanent residency, the political damage was done.

In many ways, the government was governed by caution—but not always wisely. Anthony Albanese's leadership style, shaped by years in opposition and scar tissue from Labor's internal wars, leaned toward process and consultation. But consultation often became delay, and delay fed into Dutton's narrative of a government unwilling – or unable – to make hard decisions. Ministers were tightly managed, media appearances carefully controlled, and messaging relentlessly polished. Yet in an environment increasingly shaped by social media skirmishes and rolling outrage cycles, that caution read less as prudence than inertia.

The Voice referendum became the clearest expression of this tension. Labor believed the case for constitutional recognition was self-evident. It wasn't. Instead of mounting a clear, forceful, and emotionally resonant campaign, the government relied on appeals to decency and unity – while failing to rebut concerns about legal ambiguity, institutional design, or constitutional risk. Dutton stepped into the vacuum. While some Yes advocates complained about misinformation, it was Labor's own messaging failure that proved decisive (Tingle 2023; Martin 2023). As Price and Mundine sharpened the No case, the government remained reluctant to fight back with equal clarity.

Labor also came under sustained pressure from its left. The Greens, emboldened by their expanded Senate presence and growing House numbers, demanded stronger commitments on housing and climate. Crossbench independents called for integrity reforms and greater transparency. But Labor responded with negotiation, not confrontation. This may have been good parliamentary politics, but it diluted the sense of purpose. The government triangulated—between the opposition's relentless attack lines and a restless progressive flank. What emerged was not bold reform but incrementalism with an apologetic edge.

For all that, Labor did deliver: the National Reconstruction Fund was legislated, emissions reduction targets were codified, and paid parental leave was expanded. But few of these measures cut through. They were policy achievements in search of a narrative. Without a unifying theme or a bold vision, they were easily overshadowed by the politics of grievance and disruption.

The government's media strategy also faltered over time. The early glow of a fresh start dimmed as journalists demanded clearer storylines and more decisive action. Albanese's low-key persona, initially an electoral asset, became a liability. Where Dutton projected certainty – however superficial – Labor too often projected process. Ministers retreated into scripted talking points. Interviews became risk-avoidance exercises. And when substance did emerge, it was rarely defended with vigour. The government looked steady, but also slow, even hesitant.

Nowhere was this more evident than in the final year of the term, when the ground shifted sharply following Labor's backflip on the stage three tax cuts. Initially legislated by the Morrison government and upheld—repeatedly—by Labor as a promise not to be broken, their eventual reversal was framed as necessary economic management. But the political cost was steep (Bagshaw and Crowe 2024). It allowed the opposition to frame Labor not just as reactive but dishonest. It also undermined Labor's claim to economic steadiness—right at the time when cost-of-living concerns were at their peak.

In the end, Labor governed, but it did not dominate. It moved legislation, delivered budgets, and avoided scandal. But it did not project authority. It mistook incumbency for control, and process for strength. That left the field open for Dutton's opposition to define the terms of debate. The government was not overwhelmed by a hostile opposition; it was undermined by its own reluctance to lead forcefully—and its own failure to build trust through clarity.

Opposition without alternatives

For all the noise generated by the Dutton-led Coalition throughout Labor's first term, one feature stood out: the absence of a coherent policy offering. Nuclear energy was floated as a bold idea, but it was policy in silhouette – headline without architecture (Dziedzic 2023). The broader picture was barren. The opposition highlighted Labor's flaws with zeal but offered no compelling vision of its own. This was no accident. It was a deliberate strategy: avoid detail, minimise risk, maximise control.

Dutton and his team concluded early that rolling out substantive reform proposals would invite scrutiny the party was not prepared to absorb. Internal tensions ran deep – between moderates and conservatives, urban liberals and regional traditionalists. To publish a governing manifesto would require resolving those tensions. It was easier, and politically safer, to stay in critique mode. The role of opposition was redefined: not as preparation for government, but as the practice of pressure.

This trend reflects a broader shift in oppositional politics, where critique is elevated over construction. Tony Abbott's 2013 victory is often cited as proof that an opposition doesn't need a sweeping agenda to win. His campaign was anchored in negation - "stop the boats," "axe the tax" – and succeeded in defeating a Labor government already on the ropes (Kelly 2014). Dutton's strategy echoed that playbook. But the contexts were different. Abbott offered disruption with ideological coherence. Dutton offered disruption alone.

The nuclear energy announcement underscored this point. It was the exception that proved the rule: a solitary policy drop in an otherwise policy-light term. It arrived late and without costings or site plans. It generated coverage but little confidence (Dziedzic 2023). That was the point. The Coalition's offering wasn't designed for implementation; it was designed for disruption.

Take housing. The opposition savaged Labor's Housing Australia Future Fund, criticising its delayed delivery and convoluted structure (Crowe 2023a). But it offered no detailed alternative. Vague commitments to cutting red tape and boosting supply were unaccompanied by funding models, zoning strategies, or timelines. The same was true in energy. Dutton accused Labor of rushing the transition and wrecking grid reliability. But the Coalition declined to commit to updated targets, new investment vehicles, or transition support mechanisms. The void was filled with rhetoric about "keeping the lights on" and "protecting the economy" (Taylor 2023).

In industrial relations, the opposition accused Labor of siding with unions and undermining business confidence. But again, the critique came without an alternative model. There was no serious engagement with the issues of insecure work, wage stagnation, or bargaining reform. Dutton revived the old slogans—flexibility, productivity—

but gave no sense of what the Coalition would actually do. Economic policy, in general, was reduced to a hollow invocation: Labor can't manage money; the Coalition can. It made for a solid attack line, but a shallow policy foundation.

Even internally, there were signs of frustration. Post-election, Senator Hollie Hughes criticised the lack of meaningful engagement with the Shadow Expenditure Review Committee (ERC), stating: "We were never really allowed to do the policy work. Everything was driven by media strategy, not by what we might actually do in government" (Hughes 2025). Shadow ministers operated on a short leash. Strategic discipline meant avoiding anything that looked like a target.

This worked – until it didn't. As the 2025 election approached, the Coalition struggled to pivot. It had spent three years defining what it was against but hadn't laid the groundwork for what it was for. Its hastily assembled campaign platform included gestures toward immigration caps, housing supply, and energy affordability, but it read more like a media release than a roadmap. The idea seemed to be that voters would reward disruption and fill in the policy blanks themselves. They didn't.

By then, the opposition had typecast itself: combative, cohesive, but hollow. Its strategy of minimalism turned from strength to liability. Voters were familiar with Dutton's critiques—but unclear on his plans. Editorials began to reflect this unease (Sydney Morning Herald 2025). Interviews with shadow ministers became evasive exercises. And in focus groups, participants echoed the same sentiment: "We know what he's angry about. We don't know what he'd actually do" (Essential Report 2025).

Labor capitalised – cautiously. Its campaign did not promise transformation. It promised certainty. The absence of a credible alternative gave Albanese the space to define the election as a choice between quiet competence and loud ambiguity. After one term in office, it was enough. Dutton had succeeded in weakening Labor's authority – but failed to strengthen his own.

The lack of policy ambition also stifled internal renewal. Younger moderates, particularly those concerned with climate, education, and social policy, found little room to move. Dutton's grip on the frontbench meant that dissent was minimised and innovation discouraged. What remained was a narrow, reactive opposition that appealed to its base but struggled to grow it. Come election day, that strategy proved inadequate.

The paradox of the Dutton opposition

The Dutton opposition never earned the public trust required to return to government after a single term – but it didn't need electoral victory to exert influence. Through disciplined messaging, relentless attack lines, and strategic issue selection, the Coalition reshaped the environment in which Labor governed. This is the paradox: a defeated opposition that still left its mark. It reveals much about the changed role of opposition in modern Australian politics, where the expectation is no longer that oppositions offer a full vision for government, but rather that they destabilise incumbents and frame the political debate.

The effectiveness of Dutton's opposition wasn't measured in legislation or policy shifts. It was measured in tone and reaction. Labor, despite its majority, often governed as if it were on the back foot – narrowing its agenda to avoid controversy, hesitating to act boldly, and frequently explaining rather than leading. On key policy fronts – housing, energy, immigration, Indigenous affairs – the government's room to move was constrained not only by political reality but by an opposition that had successfully redefined what was "risky" (Murphy 2024).

This raises larger questions about the institutional function of opposition. The conventional wisdom is that opposition should both scrutinise the government and present itself as a credible alternative – what some call a "rehearsal for government". But that idea has increasingly come under pressure. Abbott's victory in 2013 – achieved with minimal policy detail and maximum oppositional energy – demonstrates that electoral success does not necessarily depend on offering a governing agenda (Kelly 2014). Dutton followed that logic.

But where Abbott had a few resonant slogans linked to a broader ideological project, Dutton's pitch lacked connective tissue. It was resistance without direction.

The Voice referendum further illustrates the limits of that approach. The Coalition did not just oppose the proposal; it helped define its defeat. But to blame that result solely on Coalition "misinformation" is reductive. Labor's campaign was vague and morally presumptive, assuming consensus that did not exist and failing to rebut legitimate concerns around clarity and constitutional design (Tingle 2023). Figures like Jacinta Nampijinpa Price and Warren Mundine offered sharp, persuasive arguments that cut through far more effectively than Labor's appeals to national unity (Martin 2023). If Dutton capitalised on scepticism, it was because Labor created the space for it to flourish.

As the election approached, the Coalition's failure to shift gears became more apparent. The party had shaped the political debate for much of the term, but it had no blueprint for governing. Voters knew what Dutton stood against – but struggled to identify what he stood for. This vacuum became a liability. Labor, sensing its opportunity, ran a low-risk campaign centred on stability and competent management. It made no grand promises, but it didn't have to. The alternative was too vague to be trusted.

The result was not just a verdict on Dutton, but a reflection of a broader democratic malaise. When oppositions can shape the political climate without presenting a governing vision, accountability suffers. Voters are left adjudicating between a government that acts cautiously and an opposition that critiques endlessly. Neither is compelled to articulate a long-term strategy. The result is a feedback loop of minimalism: governments afraid to lead, and oppositions afraid to plan.

Dutton's tenure embodied that dynamic. He perfected the politics of critique but offered no serious attempt at policy reinvention. His message discipline, media management, and combative style made him a potent force in mid-term skirmishes. But without a forward-looking agenda, he could not convert disruption into leadership.

His legacy is complicated. He restored the Coalition's relevance after a heavy defeat. He prevented further fragmentation. He kept the party intact during a period when ideological fracture seemed inevitable. But he failed to resolve what the Liberal Party should become in the post-Morrison era. Its instincts were conservative, its strategy populist, and its tone unyielding. That mix made for an effective opposition – but not a governing proposition.

There is a broader lesson here for both major parties. For Labor, the warning is clear: don't mistake caution for authority. For the Coalition, the lesson is more confronting: oppositional strength is not enough. Voters may tolerate noise mid-term, but come election time, they want substance. Dutton gave them friction, not direction. That might deliver political oxygen. It does not deliver power.

Conclusion

In the end, Peter Dutton lost – and not simply because of tactical missteps or a weak campaign. The Coalition's failure to return to government in 2025 can be traced, first and foremost, to Dutton himself. His personal unpopularity never shifted, despite his political discipline. For many voters, particularly in urban and outer-metro areas, Dutton remained a rigid and unrelatable figure – a politician more comfortable prosecuting arguments than connecting with the electorate (Savva 2023). However effective he may have been in destabilising Labor's narrative, he could not convince Australians to hand him the prime ministership.

The contradictions of his leadership became clearer as the campaign neared. A party that had spent three years attacking Labor with message discipline and strategic aggression had no comprehensive alternative to offer. "Going nuclear" may have generated headlines, but it was not a platform. On housing, energy, tax, and industrial relations, the Coalition offered talking points, not plans (Dziedzic 2023; Crowe 2023a). Its campaign, when finally released, read like a checklist of grievances repackaged for television grabs. By then, the vacuum had become the message.

And yet, to dismiss Dutton's impact would be a mistake. He helped revive a moribund Coalition, kept it unified, and forced Labor to govern defensively for much of its first term. He ensured the opposition remained relevant, even as it struggled to appear electable. Through cost-of-living attacks, border rhetoric, and targeted disruption, Dutton narrowed Labor's governing bandwidth. He didn't reshape Australian conservatism, but he did recalibrate how oppositions wield power outside of government.

The paradox of Dutton's tenure lies in that very tension: he was a leader of consequence, but not of direction. He shaped the political terrain without mapping a route through it. His opposition was defined not by ideas, but by obstruction. That may have been tactically astute mid-term, but it proved strategically fatal by campaign's end.

More broadly, the 2025 election revealed the narrowing of Australia's political imagination. Labor campaigned on steadiness, not ambition. The Coalition offered critique, not renewal. Neither side proposed a compelling future. It was a contest between technocratic continuity and rhetorical disruption. In the end, continuity won – but only because disruption had no destination.

This is a warning, not a resolution. If oppositions believe they can shape government behaviour without offering an alternative, and if governments believe they can survive by doing just enough, then both sides contribute to a diminished democratic contest. Dutton's defeat does not redeem Labor. Labor's victory does not erase its failures. The cycle of minimalism continues – unless someone breaks it.

References

ABC News, (2022), "Albanese vows 'no surprises, no excuses' as PM", 23 May https://www.abc.net.au/news/2022-05-23/anthony-albanese-sworn-in-as-australian-pm/101089430.

Bagshaw, J., and Crowe, D., (2024), "Stage three tax cuts overhaul: Why Labor changed course", *Sydney Morning Herald*, 24 January https://www.smh.com.au/politics/federal/albanese-s-labor-to-scale-back-stage-3-tax-cuts-20240124-p5f89q.html.

Benson, S., (2022), "Peter Dutton emerges as leader after Morrison", *The Australian,* 30 May

Benson, S., (2023). "Dutton launches Voice No campaign", *The Australian*, 15 August

Chalmers, J., (2023), Economic update: Managing inflation and growth, 6 October https://ministers.treasury.gov.au/ministers/jim-chalmers-2022/speeches/economic-update-october-2023.

Chalmers, J., (2024), Federal Budget 2024-25 Speech. 14 May https://budget.gov.au/2024-25/content/speech.

Coorey, P., (2022), "Coalition in crisis post-election", *Australian Financial Review*", 24 May

Coorey, P., (2023a), "Labor's super tax surprise causes stir", *Australian Financial Review*, 28 February

Coorey, P., (2023b), "Cost-of-living message sticks for Dutton", *Australian Financial Review*, 10 July

Crowe, D., (2022a), "Dutton takes leadership amid internal Liberal divisions", *The Age*, 31 May

Crowe, D., (2022b), "How Dutton imposed party discipline", *The Age*, 15 June

Crowe, D., (2023a), "Coalition's critique of housing policy", *The Age*, 5 September

Crowe, D., (2023b), "Coalition targets energy policy", *The Age*, 12 November

Dziedzic, S., (2023), "Dutton backs nuclear energy plan", *ABC News*, 20 October

Dziedzic, S., and Worthington, B., (2023), "Migration surge sparks housing concern", *ABC News*, 3 December

Essential Report, (2022), "Public opinion polling May–December", 15 December" https://essentialreport.com.au,

Essential Report, (2023), "Opposition gains ground on cost-of-living", 20 November https://essentialreport.com.au.

Essential Report, (2025), "Focus group summary - April 2025", 10 April 2025https://essentialreport.com.au,

Hughes, H., (2025), "Post-election interview on Sky News", *Sky News Australia*. 4 May

Karp, P., (2023), "Nature Positive laws spark backlash", *The Guardian*, 18 July

Kelly, P., (2014), *Triumph and demise: The broken promise of a Labor generation*, Carlton: Melbourne University Press

Kenny, M., (2023), "Labor's own worst enemy on policy delivery", *Canberra Times*, 22 August

Maley, J., (2023), "Coalition's teal seat problem remains", *Sydney Morning Herald*, 14 September

Martin, S., (2023), "Price and Mundine define Voice debate", *The Guardian*, 10 October

Massola, J., (2022), "Why Dutton's leadership is seen as a dead end", *Sydney Morning Herald*, 5 June

Murphy, K., (2023), "Coalition campaigns on cost-of-living", *The Guardian*, 8 November

Murphy, K., (2024), Labor on the defensive as Dutton attacks. *The Guardian*. 12 February 12

Newspoll, (2024), Coalition leads Labor in key marginals, *The Australian*, 18 October

Savva, N., (2023), *Bulldozed: Scott Morrison's fall and Anthony Albanese's rise,* Melbourne: Scribe Publications

Savva, N., (2024), Dutton's hard edge a liability in campaign", *Sydney Morning Herald*, 25 April

Shanahan, D., (2023), "Dutton finds traction on economic message", *The Australian*, 1 December

Sydney Morning Herald, (2025), "Editorial: Coalition still lacks policy depth", *Sydney Morning Herald*, 2 May

Taylor, L., (2023), "Labor's credibility on energy tested. *The Guardian*", 30 September

Tingle, L., (2023), "The Voice: A case never clearly made", *ABC News*, 14 October

Wilson, T., (2025), Interview with Sky News post-election analysis, *Sky News Australia*, 5 May

Wroe, D., (2023), "Dutton presses national security credentials", *Sydney Morning Herald*, 18 November

Part 2: Managing the Institutions

5

The Public Service under Albanese

Paddy Gourley

Introduction

When the Australian Labor Party (ALP) won the 2022 federal election it inherited a public service down on form, lacking match fitness and burdened with an awkward injury list.

The previous Coalition government had a good deal to answer for, but it could share discredit with governments on all sides of politics going back many years. Yet, as might be expected with a large, complex administration, the picture was uneven and some organisations may have been working well.

Indeed, Commonwealth and state government authorities did much good work in the heat of the COVID pandemic. The COVID Response Inquiry Report (Kruk 2024: 5; see Chapter 7) said that Australia "should be proud of what was achieved during the pandemic". Another assessment reckoned that "policy successes outweighed policy failures. Overall, Australia's handling of the pandemic was exceptionally good" (Holden and Hamilton 2024; Shergold 2022).

Nevertheless, generally applicable policies, combined with neglect and bad habits, affected the efficiency and effectiveness of government agencies, if unevenly. For example:

- For more than 30 years governments had applied an annual dividend on almost all agencies regardless of their individual circumstances. This slovenly, invidious way of seeking efficiencies doesn't admit that the financial circumstances of individual agencies are, to a significant degree, the consequence of the power of their Ministers in bidding for budget funds. That is to say, it has most likely excused the strong and punished weak and less politically esteemed. Limited funding for improvements in staff remuneration added to the pressures. Lots of money has been saved although that should not be taken to mean greater efficiency.

- Institutional arrangements supporting the provision of forthright and comprehensive public service advice to Ministers and government had been weakened. Secretaries of departments have no security of tenure and can be sacked at whim and many have been in some cases because of fortuitous association with policies that came to be disliked. Further, ministerial staff, some of whom may know more about politics than policy, appear, in varying degrees, to have reduced the demand for public service advice. Ambiguous remarks by Prime Minister Morrison after the Coalition won the 2019 election were interpreted as signalling that policy should be left to ministers and their offices with the public service left to concentrate on the implementation of government decisions (Morrison 2019).

- Consultants, contractors and labour hire personnel had been increasingly used to perform tasks for government, including to do jobs indistinguishable from those usually performed by public servants. While much of this was legitimate, for example, the selective rather than reflexive use of consultants and the provision of cleaning, grounds maintenance and like services by private companies. Yet the outsourcing of swathes of work to labour contracting firms in particular was dubious and damaging. The constitutional and legal provisions for the employment of staff were worked around and the gates were opened to nepotism and corruption in public employment with consequences for efficiency and effectiveness.

- Appointments to statutory authority positions, where independence from politics is especially critical, were politicised, the former Administrative Appeals Tribunal (AAT) being perhaps the most prominent but not only example (Pelly and McIlroy 2022).

- In the public service proper, that is those agencies covered by the *Public Service Act*, devolved pay and conditions fixing created wide disparities in remuneration between departments based on the fraudulent pretence that improvements were based on agency productivity. This had made a mockery of public service wide classification structures, undermined recruitment by disconnecting remuneration from outside labour markets for comparable work and damaged the internal promotion and transfer of staff system.

- Concerns about "integrity" were not confined to the notorious Robodebt fiasco[1] (see Holmes 2023) but extended to the administration of community grants programs, sly and incompetent handling of contracts, undue secrecy, an apparent lack of concern about conflicts of interest in post separation employment and more.

- The senior level organisational structures of departments had become top heavy drawing work up hierarchies and coagulating management. Thus, while the number of staff in the public service has decreased by around a hundred thousand in the last 50 years and its work has become less complex, the number of deputy secretary positions has increased by around sevenfold with consequent increases in other levels of the Senior Executive Service.

- Political considerations appeared to be more prominent in the organisation of the machinery of government none more so than in the creation of the Home Affairs Department and its associated portfolio that appeared to be designed to fail, did so and continues to. The positioning of arts functions was unduly affected by the personal interests of ministers rather than what was more administratively appropriate. That is to say, the appreciation of sensible principles of the machinery of government appeared to be low in this and other respects.

- It had become increasingly apparent that the central management of the public service as a whole had been weakened over a long period. While the departments of the Prime Minister and Cabinet and Finance remained reasonably strong, the Public Service Commission had little power beyond exhortation and reporting. The Secretaries Board, composed of departmental secretaries and several others – effectively a standing inter-departmental committee of some 18 members – was unaccountable and secretive. Indeed, in advising the government to knock back important recommendations of a major review of the public service, the so-called Thodey Review (Thodey 2021), the Board showed itself to be more of a hindrance than a help (Gourley 2023). As if to prove its insensitivity, the Secretaries Board commissioned one of its former members to review its performance. Needless to say, the subsequent report was extremely complimentarybecause it failed to examine any serious questions about the performance of the Board, matters the reviewer should have been keenly aware of given her intimate, recent association with the organisation.

There is more but this is enough to illustrate that, while not exactly on its knees, there was a good deal to be dissatisfied with in the structures, procedures and operation of the Commonwealth's administration as it stood at the 2022 election.

Transition to the Albanese Government

In his first press conference after the election on 21 May 2022, the new Prime Minister, Mr Albanese, praised the "professionalism" of the public service and said "We won't be sacking public servants…we will be valuing public servants and respecting them" (Burton 2022).

Well one, Simon Atkinson, the Secretary of the Department of Infrastructure, Transport, Regional Development and Communications, and former senior Treasury official was dismissed in unexplained circumstances.

Before the election Albanese alleged that the position of the Secretary of the Department of the Prime Minister and Cabinet, Mr Phil Gaetjens "had been politicised" (Maiden 2022). So, it was not surprising when he left that position on 23 May for while he still had some months before the period of his appointment expired, he did not continue in office to assist with the transition to the new government.

Gaetjens was succeeded by Dr Glyn Davis, an academic who had been head of the Office of Cabinet in the Queensland Goss Labor Government. While he was dismissed from that role in 1996 by the incoming Borbidge Coalition Government, he returned as Director-General of Premier and Cabinet under the Beattie Labor Administration in 1998. He was subsequently Vice Chancellor, first of Griffith, then Melbourne, universities and the CEO of the Paul Ramsay Foundation. Davis was without overt party political affiliation and his appointment seemed to be widely welcomed.

While she was not sacked, Ms Kathryn Campbell, who had been the Secretary of the Department of Foreign Affairs and Trade, was removed from that position in June 2022. Campbell, who had been Secretary of the Department of Human Services and then Social Security in the ten years from 2011, was given a role in the Department of Defence on the AUKUS project, without any apparent checking on her involvement in the Robodebt scheme by the Secretaries of the Department of the Prime Minister and Cabinet (Dr Davis) or Defence (Mr Moriarty) or the Public Service Commissioner (Mr Woolcott).

So, there was no great agitation on account of the sacking of secretaries such as has come with some other changes of government, as occurred in 1996 by John Howard when six secretaries were replaced (Halligan 2000: 58-60). Nevertheless, there were changes at the time of the Albanese Government taking office (Albanese 2022; Dennett 2022). Further departmental secretary changes occurred during the first term as some incumbents retired and their replacements were recruited from the senior ranks of State administrations. Others were replaced because of findings from the *Royal Commission into the Robodebt Scheme* as is discussed below.

Alterations to the machinery of government were minimal.

There were new departments of Climate Change, Energy, the Environment and Water, and Employment and Industrial Relations. And the Department of Infrastructure, Transport, Regional Development and Communications gained responsibility for "the arts" which was signified in its title in accordance with the bizarre notion that as many departmental functions as possible should be listed in departments' titles, a habit signifying an immature and unhelpful sensitivity. The Department of Defence should be on the watch lest it become the Department of Defence, Navy, Army, Airforce, Materiel Acquisition, Estate Management, Intelligence, Strategic Policy and Contract Mismanagement.

In a move that could have gone much further, the Australian Federal Police was transferred from Home Affairs to the Attorney-General's portfolio while later in the government's term the ASIO was likewise sensibly transferred. Unfortunately, the major function of immigration remained submerged in the security obsessed dry gulch of Home Affairs where its effective administration continued to be troubled although in some respects marginally improved (see Nixon 2023; Parkinson et al 2023; Hughes 2025).

In all, however, the transition to the new government seemed to be smooth enough, even-tempered and with refreshing goodwill.

Getting down to it

While in opposition the ALP had made plenty of noise about what it saw as weaknesses and failings in the public service. Like most oppositions it had no embracing pre-election platform for administrative improvement apart, in the main, for a commitment to an anti-corruption commission. It also promised *a* Royal Commission into the Robodebt saga (Dawson 2023; see Chapter 7;) that courts had found to be illegal and for which the Morrison Government had had to pay hundreds of millions of dollars in compensation.

Early in the Albanese Government's term a position of Secretary for Public Service Reform was created in the Department of the Prime Minister and Cabinet. The designation of "Secretary" didn't fit well as the definition of "Secretary" in the *Public Service Act* which indicates it as being secretary of a department – this position was not. Anyway, Dr Gordon de Brouwer, a former departmental secretary, was appointed to it. He, and the real Secretary of the Department of the Prime Minister and Cabinet, Dr Davis, had been members of the

Thodey Review (see Thodey 2019) of the public service that reported to the Morrison Government in 2019 and got pretty short shrift from it. It was not a good report (Gourley 2023), and in some ways deserved its fate, but whatever, Davis and de Brouwer were now in critical positions to be energetic in helping the Albanese Government develop a quality bundle of substantial improvements. The omens were good.

In a speech October 2022, the Minister for Finance and Minister for the Public Service, Senator Gallagher set out a clear analysis of the deficiencies she saw in the system and said that the Prime Minister had "tasked me to develop an ambitious and enduring reform plan for the APS" (Gallagher 2022).

Minister Gallagher said the "priority areas" for the "reform agenda" were a public service that:

- "embodies integrity in everything it does";
- "puts people and business at the centre of everything it does";
- "is a model employer"; and,
- "has the capability to do its job well".

To give meaning and dimension to these imprecise ambitions, the Minister said she wanted, among other things, to:

- establish an anti-corruption commission (the ALP had committed to this and a Royal Commission on the Robodebt Scheme before the election);
- include in law an "inspiring purpose statement" for the public service to give it a "unified vision";
- "enshrine the responsibility of stewardship in the Public Service Act", stewardship having become what Professor Richard Mulgan had called a "term du jour";
- institute "long term insight briefings";
- stress gender equality and diversity in staffing;
- build on "flexible working arrangements" that had been forced by the COVID pandemic;
- have a centralised pay and conditions negotiation for the public service as a whole and in doing so begin to reduce "fragmentation in remuneration";
- conduct an audit of employment to assess the extent of the use

of consultants, contractors and labour hire, and,

- re-establish "capability reviews" of departments and agencies.

Some of this was admirable, some ho-hum and some, like the "inspiring purpose statement", foolish. In all, however, it was not easy to see the scope of the Minister Gallagher's intentions as an "ambitious and enduring reform plan".

What was done

Amending the Public Service Act 1999

In the first half of 2023 the Albanese Government issued a "consultation paper" and an "exposure bill" on proposed amendments to the *Public Service Act*.

The four page "consultation paper" devoted two and a half pages to an outline for five possible amendments to the Public Service to:

- include "stewardship" as a public service "value";
- have an "inspiring APS purpose statement" (a legacy of the 2019 Thodey Report on the public service);
- require capability reviews of agencies and "long term insight briefings"; and,
- publish aggregate results of the public service employee census.

The paper was inadequate in its content and as a vehicle for consultation.

Stewardship is not a value it is a function, and the *Public Service Amendment Act* now defines it curiously as "The APS builds its capability and institutional knowledge and supports the public interest now and into the future, by understanding the long-term impacts of what it does". Putting aside the question of neglecting the short and medium term "impacts", this definition is inadequate. If it means anything, stewardship must involve taking actions necessary to see that the public service has the appropriate, structures, governing procedures and resources to do its job as best it can. That is the responsibility of ministers and senior officials. But by making "stewardship" a "value", all staff are responsible for it as now defined and can be subject to disciplinary action if they fail to understand "the long-term impacts" of what they do. This makes no sense.

Wrestling with the "purpose statement" was a comedic amateur hour. It was proposed that options should be developed by a 40-person committee with one of those options being determined by the Secretaries Board. That is to say, the purpose of the public service was to be determined by subordinate officials over and above what the Parliament has set out in law. Then while the Bill was being considered by the Parliament, the penny dropped and the Secretaries Board and others involved in the development of this twaddle twigged that the *Public Service Act* already had a purpose statement, so the proposed amendment was abandoned without a hint of shame or apology. It was as if those responsible for this diversion hadn't read the Act they were proposing to amend. How the nominal head of the public service and the Chair of the Secretaries Board, Dr Davis and the Public Service Commissioner, Dr de Brouwer, could have allowed the "purpose statement" folly to run away like it did is a mystery.

Of the other amendments:

- Mandating capability reviews has the potential to be useful but those held in the last few years have not obviously been so, they being formula like box-ticking exercises where it has been difficult to relate generalised recommendations to evidence of shortcomings (see Gourley 2024a and Gourley 2024b).
- "Long term insight briefings" however they may be conceived could be useful but the new related provisions in the *Public Service Act* are enabling not mandatory. That is, the new law has added nothing to what could have been done without it.
- Publishing employee census results? This may be worthwhile although it is not of great moment.

An Act to give effect to these amendments and several other minor matters was given assent in June 2024. Further amendments to the Act gave the Public Service Commissioner powers to investigate former officials.

At the margin some of these new laws are useful but they do not address the major weaknesses affecting the public service. Put it another way, if these provisions had been in the *Public Service Act* prior to the initiation of the Robodebt Scheme, they would not have impeded it by an inch. Indeed, the nature of the amendments, their advocacy and their handling were sufficiently bumbling as to raise doubts as to how well the government was being advised about public service reform. The reduced capacity of the public service seemed to have extended to its ability to provide advice on how to improve it.

Politics and the appointment of secretaries of departments and statutory officers

The influence of politics in the appointment of departmental secretaries has been a constant in Commonwealth public administration. The selections of the likes of H.C. Coombs and L.F. Crisp by the Curtin-Chifley governments, Peter Wilenski, James Spigelman and John Menadue by Whitlam to departmental secretary roles, and through to Phil Gaetjens by Morrison have raised hackles like "quills upon the fretful porpentine" pace the ghost of Hamlet's father. The cry of "jobs for the boys" may no longer reverberate as it once did but the sentiment is alive and kicking. For further detail and commentary (see Prasser 2023).

Albanese's selection of Dr Davis to be the head of his department was, as indicated, uncontroversial and it seemed to set the tone for other secretary appointments none of which attracted accusations of political partiality. And Dr Davis appeared frequently to have been more consultative and careful in advising the prime minister on secretary appointments.

Yet to reduce the risk of advice to the prime minister being gamed, there would be advantage in adopting the recommendation of the Thodey Review, of which as indicated both Drs Davis and de Brouwer were members, for the Public Service Commissioner to be the prime adviser on secretary appointments but doing so with the agreement of the Prime Minister and Cabinet Secretary. That is to say, the current roles of these two offices should be reversed. That has not happened. What Secretary of the Department of the Prime Minister and Cabinet would want to reduce the power that derives from this function?

The intrusion of politics into statutory officer appointments is more serious because the very purpose of these positions is to remove functions from the direct influence of governments and other political powers.

Notwithstanding such sensitivities, Commonwealth governments of all political persuasions have allowed politics to outweigh merit in appointments to statutory positions. As noted above (Pelly and McIlroy 2022), it reached a terrible pitch in the Liberal-National party governments in the years before 2022 with appointments to the quasi-judicial Administrative Appeals Tribunal, a body which more than most should be beyond political suasion. The effects on the standing of this Tribunal became dire enough for the Albanese Government successfully to propose legislation to abolish it and replace with a new body, the Administrative Review Tribunal; it began operating in October 2024. Thus, members of the Administrative Appeals Tribunal were set free and fresh appointments were made to the new body, including some from the old one. Unfortunately, procedures for the appointment of members to the new Review Tribunal, while different, remain open to the same kind of manipulation that led to the abolition of its predecessor.

The crux of the problem is that notwithstanding professions of good intent, ministers and governments seem always to want the flexibility to put in "their own people", the only question being how far they're prepared to stretch a point.

In February 2023, the Albanese Government announced a review, to be conducted by Ms Lynelle Briggs, of public sector board appointment processes (henceforth the Briggs Report). It said the object of the review was to "enhance integrity and trust in government" and that the exercise fell "under the priority area of an APS that embraces integrity in everything it does". The announcement said a report could be expected to be released in late 2023.[2] By March 2025, the Briggs Report had still not been released and Minister Gallagher indicated that no decisions had been taken on it. It appears as if good intentions have been hoisted on what has ever bedevilled statutory appointments

– the desire of ministers to have a free hand. For as long as this remains so, the embrace of integrity in everything that is done will continue to wear a sore which will fester in proportion to the extent of political honour or the lack thereof, an unenticing prospect.

Consultants and labour contractors

As the precise extent of the use of consultants, labour contractors and the like was unclear and had never been adequately accounted for, the Department of Finance and the Public Service Commission conducted an audit of agencies staffed under the *Public Service Act*.

The audit said that during 2021-22, the public service had an external labour force of consultants, contractors, labour hire and outsourced service providers equivalent to around 54,000 staff, or 37 per cent more than staff directly employed under the *Public Service Act*. The cost of the external labour force was $20.8 billion a year.

Outsourced service providers accounted for about 50 per cent of this labour force many of whom were heavily concentrated in the Department of Defence providing cleaning, grounds maintenance, catering and like services. That is to say, they represent whole functions outsourced based on better value for money and where there are no questions of injury to inherent public service capability or the existence of an employment relationship between the Commonwealth and the relevant staff.

Of the remainder of the external labour force, 37 per cent were contractors 12 per cent labour hire and 2 per cent consultants. Here again Defence is the major player but Agriculture, Home Affairs, Social Security among others had significant arrangements. Even the Departments of Finance and the Prime Minister and Cabinet had hundreds of such personnel on their books. They were engaged on tasks such as IT and digital, program management, research, service delivery, regulation and compliance and legal and parliamentary functions – that is to say, work usually undertaken by staff employed through the merit recruitment provisions of the *Public Service Act*.

There will always be a legitimate place for consultants to provide advice and assistance. The significant risk however is where contractors and labour hire are used to undertake ongoing work normally the responsibility of public servants.

Of course the question of relative cost is important but not as important as the effects on the long term capacity of the public service which, if it becomes divorced from and ignorant about the particulars of certain functions, its ability even to specify statements of requirements for services it seeks from outside may be compromised to say nothing of its ability effectively to manage related contracts. Serious concerns have been expressed about these consequences, including by the aforementioned Thodey Review of the public service.

Equally there are legitimate questions about how the use of contractors and labour hire engaged effectively in an employment relationship with the Commonwealth fits with related provisions in the Constitution and the *Public Service Act*.

Section 67 of the Constitution provides that public servants should be appointed by the Governor-General "until the Parliament otherwise provides...". For departments and dozens of other agencies the Parliament has only otherwise provided via the *Public Service Act*, these being arrangements to ensure appointments are based on merit and equal opportunity rather than nepotistic associations and corruption. Thus, the use of contractors and labour hire personnel to do work in the public service on the basis of an employment relationship – a contract of service – does not prima facie fit with either the spirit or letter of the Constitution and the *Public Service Act* because they have obtained that employment on the basis of an association with a contracting or labour hire firm rather than being independently assessed in a merit competition in which all eligible citizens have an opportunity to play. To the extent that the best possible people are thus not being engaged, the efficiency and effectiveness of the public service is being impaired.

Whatever, the government has moved to reduce public service reliance on an external labour force. The basis for doing so is outlined in a document produced by the Public Service Commission titled *APS Strategic Commissioning Framework* released in October 2023. This document is hopelessly flawed. It does not even mention Section 67 of the Constitution and its imperatives about avoiding nepotism and corruption of public service appointments, a startling omission for an organisation established in pursuance of the objectives inherent in Section 67. Rather the framework leads agencies into the delusional belief in "core functions", the examples of which it gives could all be performed outside the public service. That is to say, the basis upon which departments are being asked to reduce reliance on consultants and contractors is a house of cards without a rational foundation.

What the Albanese Government should have done, but hasn't, is amend the *Public Service Act* to make it clear that where personnel are engaged in an employment relationship involving a contract of service, those engagements should be made under the *Public Service Act*. That is to say, it has not sandbagged the public service from the kind of abuse from which it has greatly suffered in the more recent past, abuse that has been allowed by previous governments and arranged by departmental secretaries who seem to have been far from the embrace of the so-called "pro-integrity culture".

To ice the cake, increases in the numbers of public servants as a consequence of the reductions in the massive external labour force and its ills became a matter of the cheapest form of politics in the lead up to the 2025 federal election with the Dutton Coalition promising to reduce the number of public servants in Canberra by 41,000.

Integrity

Robodebt was the great cloud over the integrity of federal politics and administration at the beginning of the Albanese Government. The Royal Commission it established, the openness of its proceedings and its compelling final report did much to clear the air. It gave those on the sharp end of the scheme the satisfaction of having its malignity and illegality more fully exposed and those who designed it held more fully to account. It produced sensible recommendations almost all of which were accepted by the Albanese Government, better ensuring honest legal advice to Cabinet, the re-creation of the Administrative Review Council, the bolstering of the capacity of the Ombudsman and more.

It did not, however, come fully to grips with a critical ingredient that bedevilled Robodebt – unrestrained careerism at both the ministerial and public service levels. Morrison and other ministers saw the chance to advance their careers by offering up big budget savings from social welfare. Secretaries of departments, who could be dismissed at a pen's stroke, must have realised all too keenly that their jobs could be at risk if they did anything other than to bow to ministerial ambitions even if that meant not providing comprehensive and honest advice about what was legal and what was not.

These insidious apprehensions seep through to subordinate staff in departments. Their consequences are mixed, of course, and they vary with circumstances and with individual ministers and officials. But they are a real and unhealthy impediment to the provision of full and proper public service advice to ministers and governments.

The Royal Commission did not make recommendations about these malign influences and it failed to endorse relevant recommendations of the Thodey Review that had been shelved by the Morrison Government. Nor has the Albanese Government done anything to clean it up, so the danger remains. It is not difficult to mitigate. Secretaries of departments should be given the same tenure as all other public servants, that is to say, they should only be dismissed for reasons of performance, misbehaviour, incapacity or redundancy without the prospect of being summarily dismissed for any or no reason. Of course, secretaries should be able to be moved where they cannot get on with their ministers but on the basis that every effort would be made to find them commensurate positions. That is to say, the tenure arrangement for secretaries should be returned to that during the Hawke Government, a period that not coincidentally was characterized by sound relations between ministers and the public service.

As a footnote on the tenure of departmental secretaries, in late 2023, Mr Michael Pezzullo, who had been the Secretary of the Department of Home Affairs, was sacked for numerous breaches of the public service code of conduct. At least he had the consolation of being given a reason for the action taken against him, which is more than can be said for many of his fellow "sackees" going back to 1996.

A sealed section of the Robodebt Royal Commission report detailed referrals of several public servants to the new National Anti-Corruption Commission and the Public Service Commission.

The Public Service Commission investigation found that 12 officers, including two identified departmental Secretaries, had breached the code of conduct 97 times. As one of the secretaries had resigned and the other was sacked, they were beyond any disciplinary action. The other officials who were still in the public service, and who were not named, were pinged with one reduction in classification, one reduction in salary, one fine, three reprimands and one written warning. Apart from the seeming lightness of these penalties for what was one of the great policy and administrative scandals for decades, the Public Service Commissioner's (Dr de Brouwer) statement on them was unforthcoming and unsatisfactory.

And so to the National Anti-Corruption Commission, (NACC) ostensibly the major legislative change affecting integrity in Commonwealth administration.

Legislation establishing the NACC was passed by the end of 2022 and it commenced operation in July 2023. Prime Minister Albanese said he wanted a commission "with teeth" although the sharpness of them has been controversial with much debate about the limitation of public hearings to exceptional circumstances. Legislation proposed but not enacted by the Morrison government was criticised on the same grounds.

The NACC fluffed an early test when it refused to consider the cases of six persons referred to it by the Robodebt Royal Commission, a process from which the Commissioner, Judge Brereton, did not adequately recuse himself because he knew one of the people who had been referred. Brereton was subsequently criticised by the NACC's Inspector, Gail Furness, with the NACC agreeing in February 2025 to consider the Robodebt Royal Commission referrals.

With its second birthday in June 2025, it is too early to be definitive about what contribution the National Anti-Corruption Commission might be able to make but it doesn't want for doubters. A former judge, Stephen Charles, who was a keen proponent for such a commission, gives it "a bad fail". Another former judge, Anthony Whaley says "..it's hard to think of anything useful they've done...". It is claimed the Commission has not yet got any court convictions on matters it has initiated (Rice 2025).

Remuneration

In September 2022, the Albanese Government issued "interim" guidance on industrial relations bargaining pending Public Service-wide negotiations. The objectives were to avoid further disparities between agencies and to "support the Government's commitment to take steps towards addressing fragmentation of remuneration and conditions"(see Australian Public Service Commission 2022).

Thus, agencies whose staff had not had a pay increase for 12 months or who were due for one within the next 12 could negotiate a 3 per cent pay increase. Similar arrangements were applied to agencies not staffed under the *Public Service Act*.

In December 2022, the Government issued further advice on principles and policy for remuneration fixing. The principles included a "unified Commonwealth public service", "mobility, attraction and retention" and "administrative efficiency." The document said that "The Government is committed to providing pay increases for Australian Public Service employees which are underpinned by productivity growth..." although what exactly that implied was unspecified and mysterious as the productivity of most public sector agencies cannot be measured. For *Public Service Act* employees, the Public Service Commission was to conduct centralised negotiations (Australian Public Service Commission 2023).

The centralised negotiations began in March 2023, and the dust settled on an 11.2 per cent pay increase over three years. Staff in some low paying agencies received larger adjustments with the Public Service Commission saying that, "Overall, pay fragmentation has been reduced from 25 per cent to 13 per cent", whatever that meant (see Australian Public Service Commission 2024b). The bargaining also involved the settlement of a range of common conditions of service.

The return to common pay scales for *Public Service Act* agencies remains a tremendous labour. It involves the unpicking of more than 30 years of irresponsible and absurd remuneration policy. Meanwhile, the promotion and transfer of staff between agencies and the Service-wide classification system on which it is based will continue to be undermined.

Moreover, the reduction of pay fragmentation will be painful because the current remuneration policy is utterly wrong-headed. The 11.2 per cent increase is a figure plucked from the air that has been based on all sorts of irrelevancies like expected rates of increase in prices, community wage movements and the like. Rationality and good sense will not be restored to remuneration until it is based on rates paid for comparable work in the labour market on an occupational category basis. Until then, all the inane palaver about "employee value proposition" will remain just that.

The efficiency dividend

While the Albanes Government abolished arbitrary limits on the number of staff in each department and agency (so called staff ceilings) it has retained the equally arbitrary efficiency dividend which has more to do with savings than efficiency. While the severity of the dividend has varied over the decades, the idea that for a very long time savings can be a regularly levied on public sector organisations with fixed outputs and not in the entrepreneurial sector beggars reality and the damage it has done in, for example, so-called cultural institutions has been evident enough. It is rather like requiring a symphony orchestra to become more efficient by playing faster. Efficiencies should be expected of public services but they should be sought by way of careful calculation on an agency-by-agency basis rather than by a lazy levy under which ministers evade their responsibilities for making difficult decisions about what functions will be performed by their departments and at what levels of intensity.

A more thoroughgoing and consistent approach to program evaluation would be useful as ineffective programs are a prime source of inefficiency.

The creation of a Centre for Evaluation in the Department of the Treasury to improve the volume, quality and use of evaluation evidence is commendable but modest. In 2025, the Centre published a report titled *The State of Evaluation in Australian Government* (Treasury 2025). The report says that "while there are promising signs of increasing evaluation effort…there is still much to do to achieve a high quality evaluation practice" and that "only 25 per cent of entities have an enterprise level strategy or framework to plan and prioritise evaluations" (Treasury 2025: 1-3).

The evaluation of government programs is, of course, tricky territory as critical evaluations make for bad politics. Nevertheless, the deeper interests of governments and citizens will be better served by rational rather than arbitrary means. Better evaluation offers one way out.

Ministerial staff

In November 2021, the Morrison Government released a report titled "Set the Standard" (2021) (the Jenkins Report) about improving arrangements in parliamentary workplaces. This resulted in a range of useful institutional measures that should help to minimise the chances of a repeats of certain ugly recent events.

These changes include amendments to the *Members of Parliament (Staff) Act* that regulates the employment of staff of parliamentarians including ministers. Unfortunately, these changes do not go far enough. Thus, there is no legislated code of conduct for relevant staff nor are recruitment procedures sufficiently specified in law to minimise the risks of unsuitable people getting into the inner sanctums. Further, the amendments to the Act removed its provisions dealing with ministerial consultants which provided a safety valve against the politicisation of staffing within the public service. This seems to be yet another example of governments being ineptly advised by public servants.

With ministerial staff, the main difficulty may be that there are so many of them. Albanese has around 60 staff, including 42 "senior advisers". Many more than Whitlam or Hawke and more than any other prime minister (see also Dowd and Prasser 2024; Maley 2018).

Round up

From a public service point of view the transition from the Morrison Coalition to the Albanese Labor Government seems to have been smooth enough.

Although the head of the Department of the Prime Minister and Cabinet, Phil Gaetjens, resigned before he could help, there were no mass sackings of his colleagues or other apparent unpleasantness.

Its wounds notwithstanding, the new Albanese Government expressed faith and confidence in the public service and said it would try to patch things up. Setting up a Royal Commission on the Robodebt was a promising sign as was the Government's acceptance of all but one of its recommendations.

The Government has otherwise tried to put things on a more even footing and it has reinvested significantly in the public service including by replacing many consultants and contractors with staff employed under the merit appointment provisions of the *Public Service Act*.

There are reasons for thinking the administration is now in better shape overall if not in all of its parts.

It should have been a lot better.

In December 2024 the Australian Public Service Commission published a report titled *Driving change for a stronger APS – Annual update on APS Reform,* (Australian Public Service Commission 2024b). This document contains a distracting and suspicious level of rhetoric claiming that what has been done is "helping to create a future where public servants are champions of integrity, conscious of community and business needs, practice inclusion and are highly capable." It says that of 59 "reform initiatives…one third are substantially complete" while lauding the "landmark passage of the Public Service Amendment Act".

The Public Service Commission's update overflows with too much self-congratulating rhetoric to be reliable and only a boundless optimist could regard the Amendment Act as a "landmark". Some of its provisions may be helpful but the Act is trivial and it side-steps matters that should be covered in stronger law. For example, including better appointment and tenure for departmental secretaries, protections against the misuse of consultants and contractors, providing stronger support for merit in staffing including provisions that would limit the politicisation of appointments to statutory offices, providing a law based code of conduct for ministerial staff, giving the Public Service Commission powers that would enable it to help control the rampant increase in senior SES positions and providing procedures to avoid conflicts of interest in post-separation employment. These and other matters were outlined in a substantive discussion paper issued by a former Public Service Commissioner, Andrew Podger, in mid-2024 on proposals for further suggested reforms (Podger 2024). There is little sign of any government intention seriously to pursue these matters.

Apart from an apparent lack of ambition, the strategy and tactics for fixing up the public service have been unwise. Rather than trying to bundle proposed improvements into bigger packages, the government has been inclined to consider changes in small bites, or what it sometimes calls "tranches". This incurs the risk that each of the "tranches" gets to be weakened to accommodate interests and pressures at the ministerial and bureaucratic levels. Bigger packages can mitigate those risks so that trade-offs within them can lessen the dilution of their components.

The Hawke Government in the 1980s brought together comprehensive proposals in four substantial white papers dealing with public service and budgetary reform and the better organisation of statutory authorities and government business enterprises (see Keating 2003 for details). It worked and if any new government after the next election retains a desire to continue to improve its public service and wider administration, it could start by trying to draw on this experience, something that does not seem thus far to have been done.

In the meantime, those who want their public services improved must content themselves with small mercies. Hopes should be kept on a short leash as the loss of public service competence appears to have extended to the capacity and willingness to learn of those now responsible for restoring it.

References

Albanese, A., PM, (2022), "Announcement of New Department Secretaries", *Media Statement*, 22 Jume https://www.pm.gov.au/media/announcement-new-department-secretaries

Australian Public Service Commission, (2022), *Public Sector Interim Workplace Arrangements*, Canberra: Commonwealth of Australia

Australian Public Service Commission, (2023), *Public Sector Workplace Relations Policy 2023*, Canberra: Commonwealth of Australia

Australian Public Service Commission, (2024a), *Annual Report 2023-24*, Canberra: Commonwealth of Australia

Australian Public Service Commission, (2024b), *Driving change for a stronger APS – Annual update on APS Reform,* Canberra: Commonwealth of Australia

Burton, T., (2022), "Albanese mulls appointment of Canberra's most powerful bureaucrat", *Australian Financial Review*, 23 May

Dennett, H., (2022), "Anthony Albanese's public service reshuffle bolsters reformers", *Canberra Times*, 23 June

Department of Finance, (2023), *The Australian Government's Report on the Audit of Employment*, Canberra: Commonwealth of Australia

Dawson, E., (2023), "Robodebts and rollercoasters: Social (in)security in the 46th Parliament", in McCaffrie, B., Grattan, M., and Wallace C., (eds), *The Morrison Government: Governing through crisis, 2019-2022 – Australian Commonwealth Administration series*, Sydney: UNSW Press, 128-41

Dowd, L., and Prasser, S., (2024), "The Resources of the Federal Opposition", in Prasser, S., and Clune, D., (eds), *The Art of Opposition*, Redland Bay: Connor Court Publications, 161-80

Gallagher, K., Minister, (2022), "Albanese Government's APS Reform Agenda", 13 October Minister's website

Gourley, P., (2023), "The 2028-19 Thodey Review into the Australian Public Service – A Lost Opportunity", in Prasser, S., (ed), *New Directions in Royal Commissions and Public Inquiries: Do we need them?,* Redland Bay: Connor Court Publishing, 149-70

Gourley, P., (2024a), "No Longer Fit for Purpose", *Inside Story*, 5 February

Gourley, P., (2024b), "Forgetting Robodebt", *Inside Story,* 30 August

Halligan, J., (2000), "Public service reform under Howard", in Singleton, G., (ed), *The Howard Government*, Sydney: UNSW Press, 49-64

Holden R., and Hamilton S., (2024), "How Australia Crushed the COVID Curve and Lost the Race", *Australian Financial Review*, 20 September

Holmes, C., (Chair), (2023), Royal Commission into the Robodebt Scheme, *Report*, Canberra: Commonwealth of Australia

Hughes, P., (2025), "Australian Immigration and the Federal Election", *Pearls and Irritations*, 12 March

Keating, M., (2003), "The public service and the management of the public sector", in Ryan, S., and Bramston, T., (eds), *The Hawke Government: A Critical Retrospective*, North Melbourne: Pluto Press, 367-80

Kruk, R., (2024), (Chair), The COVID-19 Response Inquiry, *Report*, Canberra: Commonwealth of Australia

Maiden, S., (2022) News.com.au website, 23 May

Maley, M., (2018), "Understanding the divergent development of the ministerial office in Australia and the UK", *Australian Journal of Political Science*, 53(3), 320–335

Mulgan, R., (1998), "Politicisation of Senior Appointments in the Australian Public Service", *Australian Journal of Public Administration*, 57(3), September, 3-14

Nixon, C., (Chair), (2023), Rapid Review into the Exploitation of Australia's Visa System, *Report*, Canberra: Department of Home Affairs, Commonwealth of Australia

Parkinson, M., Howe, J., and Azarias, J., (co-chairs) (2023), Review of the Migration System, *Final Report*, Canberra: Department of Home Affairs, Commonwealth of Australia

Pelly, M., and McIlroy, T., (2022), "Dysfunctional AAT abolished for new body", *Australian Financial Review*, 17 December

Podger, A., (2024), *Discussion Paper: Further Reform of the Public*

Service, July

Prasser, S., (2023), *Politicisation – the attack on merit and our way of life*, Sydney: Centre of Independent Studies, Analysis Paper 52, August

Rice, S., (2025), "Waste of Time and Money: Corruption Watchdog under Fire", *The Australian*, 17 March

Shergold, P., (2022), *Fault Line*, Independent review into Australia's response to COVID-19[3]

Thodey, D., (Chair), 2022, *Our Public Service, Our Future – Report of the Independent Review of the Australian Public Service*, Canberra: Department of Prime Minister and Cabinet, Commonwealth of Australia

Treasury, (2025), *The State of Evaluation in Australian Government*, Canberra: Commonwealth of Australia

Endnotes

1 According to the Holmes Royal Commission (2023: v): "The Robodebt Scheme was a proposal developed by the Department of Human Services (DHS), put forward as a budget measure by the Minister for Social Services in 2015 and begun that year (initially in pilot form and expanded in subsequent budgets). It was designed to recover supposed overpayments from welfare recipients going back to the financial year 2010-11 and relied heavily on a process known as 'income averaging' to assess income and entitlement to benefit".

2 This is the Review of Public Sector Board Appointment Processes.

3 Although proclaimed as an "independent review" it was funded by the John and Myriam Wylie Foundation, the Minderoo Foundation and the Paul Ramsay Foundation with research and secretariat support provided by the e61 institute. It had no powers of investigation or authority unlike a royal commission.

6

Creating a New Standards Regime and a Safer Workplace for Parliament

Maria Maley

Introduction

One of the most difficult and significant tasks that faced the Albanese Government in its first term was to respond to the recommendations of the Human Rights Commission's 2021 *Independent Review into Commonwealth Parliamentary Workplaces* (Human Rights Commission 2021), known as the Jenkins Review. While the Review presented parliament with a clear and detailed template for change, implementing the recommendations involved major institutional reform. Consensus was needed across the parliament for the creation of a new standards regime where none had previously existed. Gaining consensus in an adversarial and low trust environment was very difficult. While multi-party parliamentary committees led the implementation, the most significant reforms were designed and driven by one of Labor's most powerful cabinet ministers: Minister for Women, Minister for Finance and Minister for the Public Service, and Manager of Government Business in the Senate, Katy Gallagher.

Background

The #MeToo movement arrived in Australian politics in dramatic fashion in late 2020 and early 2021. Allegations by former Liberal party staffers of sexual assault, bullying and discrimination were aired on national TV, first by Rachelle Miller (on ABCTV's *Four Corners*) and then Brittany Higgins (on Channel 10's *The Project*). As more and more staffers revealed distressing experiences, there was genuine shock and concern amongst politicians, and also the public. In March 2021 women and men demonstrated across the country, expressing their anger and demanding that parliament take action (Gleeson 2021). With the support of the Opposition and crossbench, the Morrison Government tasked the Human Rights Commission to undertake a review and make recommendations "to ensure that Commonwealth parliamentary workplaces are safe and respectful and that the nation's Parliament reflects best practice in the prevention and handling of bullying, sexual harassment and sexual assault". It also established an interim workplace complaints unit and a 24/7 support line for people working within parliament. It extended the *Sex Discrimination Act* to members of parliament and their staff, who had previously not been protected and thus had no legal recourse to take complaints about sexual harassment.

The Human Rights Commission inquiry was led by Sex Discrimination Commissioner Kate Jenkins, who handed her report to parliament on 30 November, the last sitting day in 2021. Titled *Set the Standard: Report on the Independent Review into Commonwealth Parliamentary Workplaces*, but known as the Jenkins Review, the report found unacceptable levels of sexual misconduct and bullying and made 28 recommendations for reform. On 8 February, the first sitting day of 2022, both houses of parliament issued a statement of acknowledgement and apology to staff – Recommendation 1 of the Report – and both major parties committed to implementing all 28 recommendations. The starement said:

> We say sorry. ... This place and its members are committed to bringing about lasting and meaningful change to both culture and practice within our workplaces. We today declare our personal and collective commitment to make the changes required.

Following Recommendation 2 of the Jenkins Report, Parliament established a multi-party committee to lead the implementation in February 2022. This was known as the Parliamentary Leadership Taskforce. It met three times before the announcement of the 2022 election brought the 46th Parliament to a close.

Implementing the Jenkins Review recommendations

While the initial response to the Jenkins Review was led by Liberal Special Minister of State Simon Birmingham, in late May 2022 a Labor government was sworn in and the task of advancing the project fell to members of the 47th Parliament.

The magnitude of the reforms required should not be understated. New rules, new bodies, new powers and accountabilities had to be created, where there were none. Standards reform had long been resisted in the federal parliament and Australia lagged behind other Westminster parliaments in this regard (Sawer and Maley 2024).

The Westminster principle of parliamentary privilege, understood as the right of each house of parliament to regulate its own affairs and the conduct of its members without external interference, had hampered attempts to regulate conduct in parliamentary workplaces. It had also led to a sense of entitlement amongst politicians. The proposed reforms involved parliamentarians agreeing to put restrictions on their conduct which didn't previously exist and giving powers to external bodies to hold them accountable. This meant unsettling power relationships.

In July 2022 a Joint Select Committee on Parliamentary Standards was appointed to develop codes of conduct, chaired by Labor MP and Deputy Speaker Sharon Claydon. In February 2023 three Behaviour Standards and Codes were endorsed by both houses of parliament: one for all who enter the parliament space, one for parliamentarians and one for staff (Parliament of Australia 2024). But these could not take effect until there was a mechanism to enforce the codes. However, the resilience of the idea that parliamentarians should be exempt from external regulation had collapsed.

The Behaviour Standards covering all those who enter parliamentary workplaces stipulates that they must:

- Act respectfully, professionally and with integrity
- Encourage and value diverse perspectives and recognise the importance of a free exchange of ideas
- Recognise your power, influence or authority and do not abuse them.

- Uphold laws that support safe and respectful workplaces, including anti-discrimination, employment, work health and safety and criminal laws.
- Bullying, harassment, sexual harassment or assault, or discrimination in any form, including on the grounds of race, age, sex, sexuality, gender identity, disability, or religion will not be tolerated, condoned or ignored.

In a sign that Australian reformers built on the work of other parliaments, some phrases are drawn directly from codes in New Zealand, the United Kingdom (UK) and Canada. The "Behaviour Code" of conduct for parliamentarians of both houses states they must "treat all those with whom they come into contact in the course of their parliamentary duties and activities with dignity, courtesy, fairness and respect", foster "a healthy, safe, respectful and inclusive environment" and respect diversity in their workplace. This code states that "Bullying and harassment, sexual harassment and assault, discrimination in all its forms including on the grounds of race, age, sex, sexuality, gender identity, disability, or religion is unacceptable. Such behaviour will not be tolerated, condoned or ignored". Staff of parliamentarians and of ministers are bound by a code with similar conduct provisions.

A new Parliamentary Leadership Taskforce was established on 15 August 2022 and recommitted to the implementation of all recommendations from the *Set the Standard* report. There were three Labor members (Senator Katy Gallagher, Sharon Claydon MP, Senator Don Farrell), three Opposition members (Sussan Ley MP, Senator Jane Hume, Senator Perin Davey), Senator Larissa Waters of the Greens, and Zali Steggall MP, representing Independents and crossbenchers. The Taskforce had an independent chair – former senior public servant Kerri Hartland, who was later replaced by Vivienne Thom, former Inspector-General of Intelligence and Security. The Taskforce disbanded two years later, on 12 September 2024.

The Australian federal parliament lacks leadership bodies, compared to other Westminster parliaments. The Taskforce was innovative, being cross-party, cross-chamber, including both ministers and legislators, and having an independent chair (Parliament of Australia

2025). With eight of its nine members being women, it represented an unprecedented vehicle for women's leadership in the parliament. (Notably, and unusually, neither of the presiding officers were members of the Taskforce.)

The Taskforce had two significant pieces of reform to deliver: an independent HR body for parliament and an independent body to enforce the new codes of conduct and investigate complaints about breaches of the codes. This proved to be difficult. On its website the Taskforce described itself as "a cross-party steering group to ensure coordinated and *non-partisan* implementation of the Report's recommendations and embed institutional leadership." [my italics] Yet partisan dynamics were difficult to avoid. It also decided that "The Parliamentary Leadership Taskforce operates by consensus". Requiring consensus for decision-making risks the drag of slow negotiation, delaying tactics and veto players.

After twelve months the Taskforce had agreed to establish an independent human resources body for the parliamentary workplace, known as the Parliamentary Workplace Support Service. An independent statutory agency headed by an independent CEO, it began operations on 1 October 2023. The Albanese Government allocated $51.7 million to establish and operate the new agency. It is innovative: unlike HR units in other parliaments it is entirely independent of parliamentary and executive governance structures. It draws it authority from an Advisory Board and can make some policies and procedures mandatory, under certain conditions (Sawer and Maley 2024). Its remit is to professionalise the workplace and drive culture change, as well as to support parliamentarians and their staff through normal HR functions.

Twelve months later, in September 2024, the Parliamentary Leadership Taskforce presented legislation to create an Independent Parliamentary Standards Commission (IPSC) to receive complaints, investigate and make findings about breaches of the codes of conduct by parliamentarians and staff. There is a Chair and 6-8 other Commissioners, four of whom must be women. They are appointed from outside parliament, and are currently lawyers, former public servants, tribunal members and ex-ombudsmen. The IPSC began operations in October 2024. For the first time, there can be external review of parliamentarians' conduct.

For parliamentarians, a panel of three Commissioners can investigate and make findings about whether they engaged in misconduct. The IPSC will be able to impose less serious actions such as a reprimand, requirement to attend training or a behaviour agreement. If it believes a more serious sanction is warranted, such as a fine, discharge from a committee or suspension from parliament, the IPSC must refer the matter to the Privileges Committee of the relevant house. For staff, a single Commissioner will make findings about whether they have engaged in misconduct and make a recommendation to their employing parliamentarian about an appropriate sanction. Respondents and claimants can request a review of the Commission's findings.

Concerns and criticism

The main criticisms of the implementation of the Jenkins Review recommendations relate to how long they took to put in place and to problems with the design of the IPSC. In her speech to parliament when the IPSC legislation was presented, Greens Senator Larissa Waters lamented that "we are so disappointed that it's taken so long and that it's a lot weaker than it should be." A member of the Parliamentary Leadership Taskforce, Larissa Waters said "We pushed for it to go as far as it could … but we have a fundamental tension here where, by design, the fox is still in charge of the henhouse" (Waters 2024). Getting agreement in the Taskforce on the design of the IPSC was clearly difficult. Taskforce member Sharon Claydon admitted "while there are some people who want to see more … there are some people who don't want this to see the light of day" (Claydon 2024). Liberal Taskforce member Jane Hume said "the process of the development of this legislation has been a cross-party effort, and this is no easy task. It has pushed and pulled each of us from our original positions. We have engaged with respect, not assuming ill intent, we have listened to each other's concerns, and we have found agreement after discussion. It has reminded many, I suspect, of the wisdom that it is better to get 80 per cent of something than to go over a cliff with your colours flying" (Hume 2024).

A point of contention was how the system of external review would interact with the principle of parliamentary privilege. To protect parliament's right to govern the conduct of its members, the IPSC is required to hand its reports to the Privileges Committee in each house. The Privileges Committees are made up of parliamentarians, almost exclusively members of the major parties. It is up to the Privileges Committees to decide on any action to be taken. We won't know if they depart from the Commission's recommendations, as IPSC reports are not public. There is very little transparency about the work of the IPSC. When it is ministers who are found to have breached the codes of conduct by the IPSC, sanctions will be decided by the prime minister, again without transparency about the decisions.

In the UK House of Commons, which represents best practice in this area, independent investigation reports are handed to a parliamentary committee called the Committee on Standards (Sawer and Maley 2024). Half the members of that committee are MPs, but half are "lay members" – appointed members of the community, including lawyers and HR professionals. Committee reports are published online (eg Committee on Standards 2025). The House of Commons established its standards regime in 2018 and has reviewed and improved it over time. Lay members were placed on the committee because it was evident that MPs found it difficult to judge the conduct of their peers and struggled to hold them accountable. Australia's new standards system leaves decisions in the hands of parliamentarians, without the corrective and robustness that lay members would provide, and without the transparency that delivers accountability.

In line with the Jenkins Review recommendations, in October 2024 parliament decided to create a Parliamentary Joint Committee on Parliamentary Standards, whose functions include reviewing the operation of the new codes and the Independent Parliamentary Standards Commission. This committee should play a leadership role on conduct and culture issues, but its membership is tightly restricted. The government dominates positions and all members must be members of the Privileges Committees. Presiding Officers are not permitted to sit on the committee, despite their important leadership roles and responsibilities in parliament. Crossbenchers and independent parliamentarians are largely locked out of the committee (only two positions are reserved for them), despite the fact they have often been the leading voices calling for culture change. It will be difficult for the Parliamentary Joint Committee on Parliamentary Standards to hold the Privileges Committees accountable for their role in the new system, when the committee itself is comprised only of Privileges Committee members.

Parliamentary Leadership Taskforce member Zali Steggall was cautious about the design of the new standards regime, saying. "Is [the new system] going to provide increased scrutiny on conduct? The jury's out" (Steggall 2024). Senator Larissa Waters feared "there will be a perception by the public and by staff … that this will be a protection racket for politicians" (Waters 2024).

Office of Staff Support

After forming government in May 2022, Labor introduced an innovation in its personal staff structure by creating an Office of Staff Support. With a staffing of six, comprising three senior advisers, one adviser and an assistant adviser, the office reports to the Special Minister of State Senator Don Farrell. Its official role is to "provide advice and support to government staff" and in Labor's first term it developed (and delivered) induction and training programs for Labor staffers. This is a Labor initiative and was not a recommendation of the Jenkins Review. However it addresses a core theme of the Review, which was that by professionalising employment practices and better supporting and managing staff, the workplace will be safer and more respectful. It is likely to be an innovation continued by future governments.

Conclusions

When the 47th Parliament came to an end in March 2025, there were still outstanding recommendations of the Jenkins Review, such as agreeing an alcohol policy for parliament. Concerns about improving respectful behaviour in the chambers had not been addressed. However, the architecture of a standards regime had been put in place. This is a huge achievement and represents historic reform.

The changes are both structural and normative, aiming to create a safer and more respectful parliamentary workplace. While these are achievements of parliament as a whole, designing the reforms and driving consensus - in an adversarial environment - was the difficult task of the Labor Government. Whether the reforms will be effective and long lasting remains to be seen. In line with Jenkins' recommendations, the Parliamentary Leadership Taskforce committed to an external independent review of parliament's implementation of the Jenkins Report. The Taskforce's review is due to occur this year (2025).

References

Claydon, S., Member, (2024), *Commonwealth Parliamentary Debates,* House of Representatives, 10 September, 6412

Committee on Standards, (2025), *Second Report of Session 2024-25: Andrew Bridgen* House of Commons, 832   https://committees. parliament.uk/publications/47688/documents/249189/default/

Gleeson, H., (2021), After Women's March 4 Justice, it is clear anger runs deep – so what happens next? *ABC News* 15 March 2021 https://www.abc.net.au/news/2021-03-15/womens-march-4-justice-brittany-higgins-grace-tame/13249746

Human Rights Commission, (2021), *Independent Review into Commonwealth Parliamentary Workplaces* https://humanrights. gov.au/set-standard-2021

Hume, J., Senator, (2024), *Commonwealth Parliamentary Debates*, Senate, 12 September, 3863

Parliament of Australia, (2024), *Standards of behaviour and behaviour codes for Commonwealth Parliamentary Workplaces* https://www. aph.gov.au/Parliamentary_Business/Chamber_documents/Senate_ chamber_documents/standingorders/Standards_of_behaviour_and_ behaviour_codes

Parliament of Australia, (2025), *Parliamentary Leadership Taskforce* https://www.aph.gov.au/About_Parliament/Parliamentary_ Leadership_Taskforce

Sawer, M., and Maley, M., (2024), *Toxic Parliaments And what can be done about them*, London: Palgrave Macmillan

Steggall, Z., Member, (2024), *Commonwealth Parliamentary Debates*, House of Representatives, 10 September, 6420

Waters, L., Senator, (2024), *Commonwealth Parliamentary Debates*, Senate, 12 September, 3865

7

The Albanese Government's Public Inquiries: Targeting Political Opponents?

Scott Prasser

Introduction

This chapter analyses the Albanese Government's deployment of public inquiries during its first term. It does not seek to cover all the public inquiries appointed as some of these are covered elsewhere in this volume.[1] Instead, this chapter gives attention to those inquiries that gained attention and some notoriety, not just because of the controversial nature of their topics, after all, that is par for the course for many public inquiries especially for royal commissions, that are often established to probe scandals, corruption and maladministration (Ransley 2014; Tiffen 1999). Rather, it is that several public inquiries appointed by the Albanese Government during its first term were seen to be driven more to wreak political damage on its predecessor, the Morrison Government and Prime Minister Morrison in particular, than to address issues of legitimate public interest.

The three inquiries under review are:

- *Royal Commission into the Robodebt Scheme*[2] (henceforth the Holmes Royal Commission) – appointed August 2022, reported July 2023;

- *Inquiry into the Appointment of the Former Prime Minister to Administer Multiple Departments* (henceforth the Bell Inquiry) – appointed August 2022, reported November 2022;

- The *COVID-19 Response Inquiry* (henceforth the Kruk Inquiry) – appointed September 2023, reported October 2024.

Two were appointed within the first six months of the Albanese Government coming to office in May 2022; only one was statutorily based, the *Royal Commission into the Robodebt Scheme;* only one inquiry had more than one member – the *COVID-19 Response Inquiry* with three members. Two were chaired by former judges – the Robodebt Royal Commission by the Honourable Catherine Holmes, former Chief Justice of the Queensland Supreme Court and the *Appointment of the Former Prime Minister to Administer Multiple Departments,* by Honourable Virginia Bell previously of the High Court. All had in common the task of reviewing some aspect of the previous Coalition governments but especially the Morrison Government. All involved topics where Scott Morrison was central to the issues under review. Morrison was Minister for Social Security when the Robodebt Scheme was developed and then Treasurer and finally prime minister. Morrison was the prime minister who oversaw Australia's response to COVID-19 and also the instigator of the multiple departmental roles during the Pandemic.

Defining public inquiries and appreciating their history

Just to be clear, public inquiries in this chapter are defined as those temporary, *ad hoc* bodies, appointed by executive government with their members drawn from outside of government, usually having public hearings or some form of public consultation and whose reports are released. This excludes inquiries appointed by permanent bodies like the Productivity Commission, the new National Anti-Corruption Commission (NACC) or those conducted by parliamentary committees. In this case it also excludes the Solicitor General's report into the same issue as the Bell Review.[3]

Public inquiries can be non-statutory without any powers of investigation, usually employing less formal processes. Such inquiries include independent reviews, committees of inquiry, panels, task forces and working parties. Both the Bell and Kruk inquiries were of this type. Alternatively, public inquiries can be statutorily based like royal commissions with their coercive powers of investigation, formal public hearings and ability to protect witnesses. While royal commissions have in the past been appointed to provide advice on a wide range of policy issues, in recent decades they have been primarily of the inquisitorial type, probing controversial issues concerning corruption, maladministration and calamitous events. It is here where their coercive powers of investigation can be effective in procuring information about an issue which existing authorities have been unable to do (Prasser 2021: 66-9).

By way of background, public inquiries have a long history of use in Australia with the states appointing many before federation. The new Commonwealth Government established its first royal commission in 1902 and subsequently quickly passed the *Royal Commission Act 1902* (Cth) to ensure it had powers to conduct its investigations. Since then, the Commonwealth alone has appointed 138 royal commissions and some 600 non-statutory inquiries (Prasser 2021: 61-80). Since 2013 federal Labor and Coalition federal governments have appointed ten royal commissions and numerous non-statutory policy advisory inquiries into a wide variety of topics.

Issues about appointing public inquiries

The perennial question concerning all public inquiries is why governments appoint them especially given their access these days to a large permanent public service and a wide array of advisory bodies. Making this issue intriguing is that appointing an inquiry is done solely at the discretion of executive government. There are, in most cases, no legislative or constitutional triggers requiring a public inquiry be established at certain junctions in the decision-making process or when certain events occur unlike in Nordic countries where they are integrated into the policy process (Pronin 2023). That decisions about the appointment of inquiries are made by executive government behind closed doors means that the exact reasons for the appointment of a public inquiry are never known until possibly much later when cabinet documents are released.

Appointing inquiries for legitimate reasons

A government's public explanation for the appointment of an inquiry is usually made in terms of serving the "public interest". Such legitimate reasons for establishing a public inquiry include: providing "cold" rational independent expert advice; promoting better understanding of an issue; or to investigate alleged scandals or to clarify the facts and to allocate blame and responsibility for some calamitous events like a natural disaster or major accident.

Appointing inquiries for politically expedient reasons

At the same time, it has long been noted that such executive government explanations must not be taken at face value as public inquiries are often being driven by "highly cynical and self-serving" motives (Bulmer 1982: 97) or what has been dubbed "politically expedient reasons" (Prasser 2021: 159-63). These include: delaying decisions; showing public concern about an issue when no action is intended; co-opting critics; promoting pseudo consultation; justifying decisions already made; and as is the focus of this chapter, to wreak "revenge" on the previous administrations by exposing scandals, improprieties, policy fiascos, and administrative mistakes (Prasser 2021: 174-8).

Appointing inquiries for targeting political opponents

Governments sometimes appoint inquiries to expose a previous government's flaws, to damage it politically, to delegitimise its time in office and to undermine the credibility of its former leaders and thus their ability to recover from their recent electoral defeat. Such actions are usually tied to a wider claim by a new incoming government that they have come to office to "clean up" the "corrupt" system, and to restore "integrity" to what they have inherited. Certainly, Albanese (2022a) gave great weight to this approach prior to the 2022 election when he promised to "end the waste and end the rorts". Labor's support for these three reviews – the Robodebt Scheme, the accretion of excessive powers to Morrison and even, the proposed COVID-19 inquiry – all implied that there was something untoward, possibly even "corrupt" about the Morrison Government. While motives may be genuine for those wanting to initiate "clean-ups", they are not made by disinterested players, but by partisan governments fresh from an election win, confident in both their abilities and mission. As Gillespie and Okruhlik (1991: 82) warned such "clean ups" are:

> Political phenomena ... Decisions to initiate them are political, as are their scope and initial targets ... clean-ups are political instruments which may be used ... to delegitimise the previous regime, to purge opposition, to manipulate the political agenda.

There is a fine line between an inquiry appointed to tackle a legitimate public policy problem or scandal, and one whose real purpose is to embarrass a previous government for partisan gain. After all, such inquiries will be wrapped in the same cloak of "reform" and institutional "clean-ups" that surrounds all public inquiries appointed to investigate scandals. What distinguishes such inquiries as being more politically driven, is that the issues being reviewed may have largely been resolved. They have, for instance, already been subject to a robust independent review followed by appropriate actions such as prosecutions or compensation. A formal apology may even have been made by the previous regime. In the light of these occurring, and if no additional findings are produced by the new inquiry, then a government's motives in its appointment of a further inquiry becomes suspect. Such inquiries seek to keep an issue alive and to redefine the issue more broadly than it really warrants. An oversight, an administrative mistake, a bureaucratic bungle, or a lapse of judgement, while all problematic, is enlarged to be more serious and tantamount to being "systemic failure". Often illegality or unconstitutionality is implied but not always proved. Such inquiries inflict further damage to the previous regime undermining its credibility and thus its ability to criticise the new government. Of course, any government seeking to use a public inquiry in this way must ensure the inquiry they appoint is seen as being as independent as any legitimate review in terms of its membership, terms of reference, processes, reporting timeframes and resourcing. They must all be above reproach, otherwise there may be little political gain and possibly even negative consequences for the appointing government.

Previous inquiries targeting political opponents

Both federal and state governments of all political complexions, have over the years appointed or been accused of appointing certain inquiries primarily for the purpose of damaging their opponents and have done so with varying degrees of success. Some have revealed new issues of concern which inevitably must adversely affect political opponents. Others have been mishandled with the wrong chairs, biased terms of reference, flawed processes and contrived recommendations, consequently boomeranging back on the appointing government as such inquiries also probe into unexpected areas and expose damaging revelations (see Prasser 2021: 174-78).

Controversy, for example, has long swirled, especially across Labor Party circles, about the Menzies Government's 1954 *Royal Commission into Espionage* (Petrov Royal Commission) appointed on the eve of a federal election that year. It was seen as being designed to do maximum damage to the then Labor Opposition (Whitlam and Stubbs 1974). Suspicions that there was a conspiracy orchestrated by the Menzies Government have long been disproved (Manne 1987; Martin 1995).

A clearer example perhaps, of a more politically targeted use of a public inquiry is the Howard Government's 2004 *Inquiry into the Centenary House Lease* (Hunt Commission). The issue was whether the Australian National Audit Office's (ANAO) 1993 lease of Centenary House owned by the Labor Party, was inappropriate. The Keating Government had responded to such criticisms by appointing in May 1994 the *Royal Commission of Inquiry into the Leasing by the Commonwealth of Accommodation in Centenary House* (Morling Royal Commission). It found no major issues of concern. This was rejected by the then Coalition Opposition which once in office eventually established the aforementioned Hunt Commission to review both the leasing arrangements and, almost without precedent,[4] the previous Morling Commission's findings. While some flaws were found they were not enough for further action – no new prosecutions occurred, and the controversy faded. The Howard Government gained little kudos from this exercise and if anything attracted adverse reactions.

The Hawke Labor Government's 1984 *Royal Commission into British*

Nuclear Tests to review the effect on Australian personnel of British nuclear tests in Australia during the1950s and 1960s, was seen as a failed attempt to settle old scores on the earlier Menzies Coalition Government. That it was chaired by a former Whitlam Government minister, Jim McClelland, was criticised for its lack of expertise and the partisan public outbursts by its chair, undermined its legitimacy. Also, many of its recommendations were not accepted or even responded to by the Hawke Government (Prasser 2021: 175-6). This royal commission, said Liberal Senator John Carrick (1986: 1001-2), undermined the stature of such bodies and was "conceived in hate, political bias and Anglophobia".

More recently, the Abbott Government's royal commissions into the Rudd Government's home insulation scheme, the *Royal Commission into the Home Insulation Program* (2013), and the *Royal Commission into Trade Union Governance and Corruption* (2014) both had legitimate issues to investigate. The first was into the mismanagement and poor implementation of a major government program. The second into allegations about trade union corruption. Nevertheless, former Liberal prime minister, John Howard thought at the time of their appointment that they had been formed for "narrow targeted political purposes" that was "an abuse of power" and smacked of being a "political vendetta" (Howard 2014). After all, the home insulation program had been subject to "one of the most scrutinised programs in Australian administrative history" (Padula and Francesco 2017: 9) suggesting the royal commission was unnecessary and politically driven. Others, however, have argued otherwise (Sedgwick 2015). While the *Royal Commission into Trade Union Governance* had serious complaints to investigate, it nevertheless appeared as an inquiry primarily targeted to attack the Labor Party given its traditional links to the trade union movement and that then Labor Opposition leader, Bill Shorten, was a former senior trade union official and was called before it and cross-examined. Few prosecutions flowed from the Royal Commission's final report, and controversies over the independence of its chair (Dyson Heydon) certainly undermined its efficacy despite some expert commentators believing it produced useful recommendations (Forsyth 2017).

It is worth noting, as Margaret Simons (2022) has, that the Fraser Coalition, despite winning the landslide 1975 election, partly on the basis of the Whitlam Government's controversial overseas loan attempts (see Reid 1976: 1-29), did not appoint a major inquiry into this issue. This was partly because Fraser kept his undertaking to Governor-General Sir John Kerr not to appoint any such inquiry as a condition for being appointed to replace Whitlam as prime minister on 11 November 1975. It was also, as Simons points out, because of the possibility of other issues becoming public that might have been detrimental to Fraser and his government.

Let's now review the three inquiries appointed by the Albanese Government and assess whether they were appointed to exact political damage on the Morrison Government or were they established to "seek the truth" about major controversial issues?

The Holmes Royal Commission into the Robodebt Scheme

Background

The background to the Holmes Royal Commission is well known. The Robodebt Scheme, or as it was formally known as, the Income Compliance Program, was introduced at the 2015-16 Budget when Scott Morrison was Minister for Social Security. It replaced in July 2016 a manual system with an automated process to check through data matching of welfare payments to Australian Tax Office records and assess if recipients were being overpaid. If so identified, they were sent notices to substantiate their claims and if unable to do so were then issued with demands to repay the assessed overpayment. There were major flaws in this process so consequently many were unfairly required to make repayments. Complaints, appeals to the Administrative Appeals Tribunal (AAT), actions by Victorian Legal Aid and the Labor Opposition, several Senate Committee reports, eventually led to the Morrison Government admitting there were problems concerning both the accuracy and legality of the scheme. It was thus wound up in 2019-20 with the Federal Court approving settlement of $1.8 billion for nearly 400,000 people who had been wrongly required to make repayments (see Dawson 2023; Holmes

2023; Priergaard 2025). Morrison, by then, prime minister, made an apology in 2020.

Issues

Despite the closure of the scheme, the compensation payouts and Morrison's apology, Labor promised a royal commission prior to the 2022 election believing there were more serious issues still to be resolved. and so appointed a royal commission soon after gaining office. The issue is whether this was necessary given the scheme's closure or was the royal commission just an attempt by the new Albanese Government to further destabilise an already beaten Coalition and to besmirch a failed former leader?

There were several issues that warranted a royal commission:

- None of those involved in developing or administering the Robodebt Scheme had faced any disciplinary action or career repercussions – including public servants and ministers;

- It was unclear how such a major technical and innovative project proceeded without any pre-implementation testing;

- How was a scheme developed and implemented that was later found to be illegal and how long did Morrison Government know of this problem?;

- How was it that the many alerts about the increasing number of complaints, court cases, and investigations were not communicated to decision makers?;

- Why did existing oversight bodies not act earlier and more resolutely?

These issues went beyond simple mistakes isolated to a single minister's office or department, or just some minor administrative breakdown. It met all the hallmarks of a policy fiasco and a scandal (Bovens and 't Hart 1996; Tiffen 1999). Rather, the nature and extent of problems pointed to a system wide breakdown in policy and advisory processes, effective implementation, and proper evaluation. These were serious complaints that went to the heart of the Commonwealth Government's decision-making process and the relationships between an elected government and its officials who appeared to be too compliant to the government's demands. Moreover, unlike with the home insulation case, the Morrison Government had not itself instigated any major independent reviews. Further, given the secrecy that had surrounded much of the Robodebt Scheme's development, there was a need to access departmental files, and to call and cross-examine witnesses, including a former prime minister and ministers and staff, and current senior public servants, and those from existing oversight bodies. Only a royal commission with its legislated coercive powers of investigation and its ability to provide legal protection to witnesses, would do. This then, is what the Albanese Government did, ensuring the royal commission had wide terms of reference, and in other like inquiries into scandals where issues of law and legality were to be assessed, appointed, as noted, a former Supreme Court judge, who also gave the inquiry a sense of independence.

Certainly, the Holmes Royal Commission found fundamental flaws in the policy process of the Morrison Government, a breakdown in the public service providing "frank and fearless" advice and failures by key oversight bodies to follow up on issues. Its report revealed information that had not been previously available concerning the inner workings of federal policy development, advice from department secretaries and senior staff, briefings to prime ministers and ministers, but not, as it complained, all necessary cabinet documents (Holmes 656-7). Its findings were supplemented by a commissioned report by former Commonwealth Public Service Commissioner, Andrew Podger (2023) which highlighted the wider, long term, public administration issues that had contributed to some of the underlying causes of the Robodebt scandal. These matters were discussed in some detail by the Holmes Royal Commission (see Section 7: Improving the Australian Public Service) and included issues such as:

- loss of permanent tenure for senior departmental secretaries and use of contracts (since 1994);
- decline/abolition of strong central personnel agencies (ie the Commonwealth Public Service Board 1987);
- growth of ministerial staff, powers and interference;
- over-reliance of non-Australian Public Service advice and delivery mechanisms.

There is no doubt the Holmes Royal Commission was needed. Like other royal commissions that have been appointed into some scandal or some calamitous event it provided: a detailed description of what happened; identified the key decision makers in the issue; and uncovered numerous previously confidential files and various communications between those involved in tendering advice and making decisions. Its direct criticism of Morrison, along with two other Liberal ministers, however, is what some might regard as an inquiry seeking "revenge". Certainly, the Holmes Commission held Morrison responsible for much of the debacle when he was Minister for Social Security and then Prime Minister:

> Mr Morrison allowed cabinet to be misled because he did not make that obvious inquiry. He took the proposal to cabinet without necessary information as to what it actually entailed and without the caveat that it required legislative and policy change to permit the use of the ATO PAYG data in the way proposed in circumstances where: he knew that the proposal still involved income averaging; only a few weeks previously he had been told of that caveat; nothing had changed in the proposal; and he had done nothing to ascertain why the caveat no longer applied. He failed to meet his ministerial responsibility to ensure that Cabinet was properly informed about what the proposal actually entailed and to ensure that it was lawful. (Holmes: 106)

The Royal Commission (Holmes: 102) also stated that it "rejects as untrue Mr Morrison's evidence that he was told that income averaging as contemplated in the Executive Minute was an established practice and a 'foundational way' in which DHS (Department of Human Services) worked". That the Holmes Commission also produced a sealed section whereby certain individuals would be referred for possible civil or criminal action to a range of different authorities including to the new National Anti-Corruption Commission (NACC), tackled the complaint that those responsible for this policy debacle had not yet faced any possible disciplinary action or prosecution. This action, though, was not without some incident.[5]

These findings were rejected by Morrison (2023: 83-85). He believed that media reporting and comments by the Albanese Government "have falsely and disproportionately assigned an overwhelming responsibility for the conduct and operations of the Robodebt Scheme to my role as Minster for Social Security" and thus represented "a further attempt by the government ... to discredit me and my service to our country". Morrison blamed the use of the royal commission instrument when he observed that "this campaign of political lynching has once again included the weaponisation of a quasi-legal process to launder the government's political vindictiveness" (Morrison: 85).

Inquiry into the Appointment of the Former Prime Minister to Administer Multiple Departments (Bell Inquiry)

The Bell Inquiry was very different to the Holmes Royal Commission in terms of powers, focus and level of seriousness.

As its Chair noted, "The Inquiry was not established under statute and did not have the power to summon witnesses to give evidence or to produce documents (Bell 2022: 13). This also meant that it could not give protection to those who may have wanted to come forward to give evidence. Further, unlike a royal commission it had no formal public hearings though it accepted submissions and met with numerous witnesses including, current and former senior public servants, sitting backbenchers, former Liberal ministers and staff, the former prime minister, Scott Morrison and several academic experts.

The Bell Review's focus was narrow. Its concern was whether it was appropriate under sections 64 and 65 of the Australian Constitution for Prime Minister Morrison to have been appointed during the Pandemic to administer five other departments in addition to his own Department of Prime Minister and Cabinet (Bell: 1). That these appointments had not been made public or it seems to even many of his own colleagues and only became known in a book by journalists after the 2022 election (Benson and Chambers 2022) added to the outrage that something was amiss, that Morrison had acted improperly, that it was in fact a "scandal". As noted above, the Bell Review was appointed after the Solicitor General's Opinion on almost the same issue, except it had been confined to review Morrison's administration of just one additional department. The Bell Inquiry under its terms of reference was required to consider the SG's conclusions.

So, what did the SG conclude? According to Prime Minister Albanese's media statement (2022b) the Solicitor General concluded that "Mr Morrison was validly appointed to administer the department (Department of Industry, Science, Energy and Resources) under the Constitution". By not informing his fellow ministers and Parliament was, however, "inconsistent with the conventions and practices of responsible government". In short, according to the SG's opinion, Morrison's actions were constitutional and legal but there were deficiencies in parliamentary procedural reporting of such arrangements that had long been in existence. Hence the SG's recommendations for changes to remedy that problem.

Given this assessment, it seems that appointing a further inquiry, albeit to examine all the departmental roles Morrison held, was unnecessary and possibly seeking to maintain public attention on an issue that was damaging to the former prime minister. Unlike the Holmes Royal Commission, the Bell Review revealed little new information. It came to the same conclusion as the SG – namely the actions of Morrison were neither unconstitutional nor illegal, and so the seriousness of Morrison's actions, although in many ways inexplicable, depends on interpretation of "responsible government". The Bell Report concluded that "that Mr Morrison did not exercise any of the powers he enjoyed by reason of his appointments apart from making the PEP-11 decision, the implications of the appointments are limited" (Bell: 5). Nor did the Bell Report provide, as it admits (Bell: 92), any empirical evidence as to whether public confidence in government was eroded by Morrison's actions. All this drove one commentator to conclude that the Bell Review was "used and abused to fuel the pyre on which Morrison ... is to be incinerated" (Ergas 2022), very much in keeping with what happened in real "witch-hunts" in the past.

COVID-19 Response Inquiry (Kruk Inquiry)

The last inquiry is *COVID-19 Response Inquiry* which was appointed, as noted, in September 2023, some sixteen months after the Albanese Government had come to office, to review Australia's response to the pandemic. There are several issues of interest concerning this inquiry.

Foremost of these was that it was not a royal commission which Albanese at his February pre-2022 election National Club Address had intimated would be appointerd (Coorey 2022). Indeed, expectations that there would be a royal commission had been further reinforced by the Senate Committee on COVID-19, chaired by Labor front bencher, later Finance Minister, Senator Katy Gallagher, that reported in April 2022 when it recommended that a "Royal Commission be established to examine Australia's response to the COVID-19 pandemic" (Senate COVID-19 Committee 2022: xii). Further, in August 2022 Albanese was reported as confirming that his government would be appointing a royal commission "as soon as practicable" (Clennell 2022). There was widespread support for a royal commission from the media, several former Liberal premiers, health professionals and much of the Senate crossbench (see Prasser 2023a: 89-90).

Second, despite promises and ongoing demands for some form of national inquiry into Australia's pandemic response, it took, as noted, the Albanese Government sixteen months to appoint the *COVID-19 Response Inquiry*. Clearly, establishing the Holmes Royal Commission in August 2022 and the Bell Inquiry at the same time into Morrison's ministerial appointment arrangements, had precedence over reviewing the pandemic. This is despite the pandemic having caused: over 20,000 reported deaths; several hundred thousand hospitalisations;[6] closed national and state borders; imposed severe lockdowns and restricted civil liberties; adversely affected the economy, business and many people's livelihoods; huge, unprecedented increases in public expenditure; increased inflation; and raised issues about federal-state relations and national policy processes.

Adding to the Albanese Government's embarrassment in delaying the appointment of a public inquiry to review the pandemic were some state initiatives. The New South Wales Health Department under the then Coalition Government had established a review of its responses under the oversight of Robyn Kruk.[7] The Western Australian Labor Government also launched in January 2023, an independent review of the state's pandemic responses, albeit not one without some criticisms.[8] Further embarrassment arose from the numerous special commissions of inquiry being appointed in other western democracies to review their pandemic responses like: Sweden (2020), Norway (2020), United Kingdom (July 2022), and a royal commission in New Zealand (December 2022) (see Bardosh et al 2025; Christensen and Laegreid 2023). Australia was not alone in not having a national inquiry in place for some time. Neither the United States under Trump or Biden nor Canada under Trudeau, established a national independent pandemic inquiry.[9] All that Australia had at a national level for some time was a review supported by private philanthropy bodies chaired by the former head of the Department of Prime Minister and Cabinet, Dr Peter Shergold, that was released in October 2022 (Shergold 2022). Although the Shergold Review had no investigative powers and limited resources, its report was nevertheless not without considerable merit in highlighting "significant mistakes" in how Australia responded to the pandemic including by the states and territories. Its lack of official status and powers, however, meant it could be easily dismissed by state premiers like Victoria's Dan Andrews, as just a report prepared by a "bunch of academics" (Clarke 2022).

There are several possible reasons for the Albanese Government's failure to appoint a royal commission and its delay in eventually establishing the Kruk Inquiry. One explanation is that given state responsibilities for responding to the pandemic, and the criticisms that some of their actions attracted, it would have to be a joint federal-state commission. Consequently, there would be difficulty in gaining state and territory agreement on the terms of reference and membership. It would also require complementary state and territory legislation and issuing of similar letters patent. Such federal-state royal commissions have been used frequently in Australia, but they have not been on topics that might directly expose and challenge state government policy decisions and administrative actions. As five of the eight states and territories during the pandemic were Labor administrations and that any such royal commission might be politically damaging may also have been a factor. That the Victorian Andrews Labor Government, where some of the severest lockdowns and loss of civil liberties occurred, was facing an election in November 2022 may have been a further consideration in delaying the appointment of any inquiry. Even as late as August 2023 some fifteen months after being elected the Labor Party in the Senate along with the Greens, successfully opposed the motion of urgency by Senator Babet of the United Australia Party (UAP) for a federal-state royal commission (Babet 2023). This included some of those very same Labor and Green senators who had been members of the 2022 Senate Committee that had recommended in April 2022 a royal commission.

Finally, in September 2023 the Albanese Government announced a public inquiry (the Kruk Inquiry) into the pandemic. It was initially widely criticised for not being the expected royal commission and for having terms of reference that excluded it from reviewing "Actions taken unilaterally by state and territory governments". It was seen as letting the states and territories, especially Labor ones, off any proper independent scrutiny (Coorey 2023; Crowe 2023; Prasser 2023b). Also, the three-member inquiry, though having health expertise, was seen as including those too closely aligned with supporting lockdowns during the pandemic – one of the key issues that any proper review would need to consider – or were too connected to the Labor Party (Chambers and Ison 2023; J. Kelly 2024). Thus, the Kruk Inquiry was initially criticised as being a "second rate, cowardly fix" inquiry (Editorial, SMH 2023) and a potential "whitewash" that might indulge in further criticism of the Morrison Government while overlooking the mistakes and draconian measures of the states and territories.

It was, therefore a surprise, that the Kruk Inquiry consulted widely, partly ignored the constraints of its narrow terms of reference and gave attention to some of the adverse impacts of the often unnecessary lockdowns, school closures, vaccine mandates, loss of liberties, and border closures that had been imposed by the states and territories frequently in defiance of decisions made at the National Cabinet. The Kruk Report (2024: 9) noted that "Australia was one of the most successful countries in its pandemic response" but was not adequately prepared in some key areas. It was praiseworthy of Morrison's "courageous" leadership, in taking early steps in forming the National Cabinet, developing the economic stimulus measures while noting the undermining of agreed decisions by the states. As one journalist noted, "It's little surprise the Prime Minister didn't turn up for its release. This wasn't the narrative the government would have been hoping for" (Benson 2024). All this highlights that a public inquiry no matter how selective its membership or tight its terms of reference can still probe deeply, produce valuable insights and make worthwhile recommendations.

Nevertheless, Paul Kelly saw it as a "flawed report" as its narrow government imposed terms of reference gave "political protection" to Labor states and questions aspects of its economic evaluation (P. Kelly 2024; see also Hamilton and Holden 2024). More importantly, though, as a result, Australia has still not had a thorough, independent, review of the nation's overall response to the pandemic. The Albanese Government, it is argued by critics, has put politics, Labor state politics, before national health policy. Nor, for that matter, has the federal Coalition in office or in opposition performed much better. In office, the Morrison Government failed to initiate any independent national review. This was understandable perhaps, given the political pressures it was under prior to the 2022 election. It thought any inquiry would become another vehicle for it to be further attacked. It had been severely criticised by the aforementioned Labor chaired Senate COVID-19 Committee (2022) released on the eve of the election. In opposition, the Coalition hardly pressed the Albanese Government to honour its royal commission promise. While it supported Senator Babet's motion for a royal commission (Ruston 2023a), it was Babet, who moved the motion, not the Coalition. The Coalition was critical, like many others, of the Kruk Inquiry's narrow terms of reference when it was announced (Ruston 2023b) but its follow-up could have been greater. The Coalition however, following that debate did chair the Senate Legal and Constitutional Committee's review of assessing the "appropriate terms of reference for a COVID-19 Royal Commission". Significantly, it was Senator Roberts of the Pauline One Nation Party that had moved the referral to the Senate committee. It reported in April 2024 and recommended a royal commission with more wide-ranging terms of reference than the Kruk Inquiry (Senate Legal and

Constitutional Affairs Committee 2024). It was almost immediately rejected by the Albanese Government. Despite this Coalition support for a royal commission, it did not, as part of its 2025 election platform, promise to appoint a royal commission if elected.

Conclusions

There is no doubt that the Albanese Government used public inquiries in their various forms, as an instrument of executive government, to suit its policy and political purposes. There was nothing unusual in that, as after all, public inquiries only exist at the whim of executive government to meet executive government needs. While all met certain legitimate policy and political demands, the exact emphasis differed from inquiry to inquiry.

The Robodebt scandal threw up many public policy and public administration issues that warranted an inquisitorial royal commission. That the Holmes Royal Commission had adverse impacts on the Morrison Government could not have been otherwise given the behaviours of that government that were subsequently exposed. That the Albananese Government hoped the Holmes Commission would do so and then sought to maximise political gains from the results was expected. It is what governments and parties do in an adversarial democratic political system. In short, the Holmes Royal Commission was not an inquiry established just to seek outright political revenge. It had legitimate complaints to investigate, and it exposed numerous problems that inevitably condemned the previous Coalition government and undoubtedly through the commission's public processes, prolonged the Coalition's exposure to ongoing public criticism.

The story is a little different with the other two inquiries. The Bell Inquiry was a targeted review of Prime Minister Scott Morrison's actions over ministerial powers, but which were not found to be unconstitutional or illegal and were already known as such by the SG's earlier report. They had no adverse impacts on decision making or the allocation of resources. They were found, however, to be secret. That all this was in a formal report, wrapped in legal and constitutional language and was written by a former High Court judge, gave the inquiry and the issues it reported on, considerably more weight than the issue deserved resulting in a further undermining of Morrison. This was not accidental. It was deliberately designed that way by the Albanese Government to inflict maximum political damage on a fallen opponent,

The Kruk Inquiry was different again. Clearly, the Albanese Government failed to appoint a royal commission into the pandemic despite intimations it was going to do so. It also deliberately delayed in appointing the Kruk Inquiry till September 2023 possibly hoping public interest and anger about some aspects of the different responses to the pandemic would have dissipated. This, combined with the Kruk Inquiry's narrow terms of reference, was seeking to let Labor state governments off the hook. Given the Labor Party's attacks on the Morrison Government's handling of the crisis especially during the 2022 election campaign (McCaffrie 2024: 191-94), then surely the Kruk Inquiry was appointed with every hope that it would do further damage to the previous government. That it didn't, except on certain issues, is to the Kruk Inquiry's credit. Nevertheless, there were, as noted deficiencies in its assessment. That Australia still has not had a full, independent, royal commission into the pandemic is to the Albanese Government's discredit.

References

Albanese, A., (2022a) *Australian Labor Party Policy Speech*, 1 May

Albanese, A., (2022b), "Safeguarding against 'Shadow Government' appointments and strengthening Australia's democracy", *Media Statement*, 23 August

Babet, R., Senator, (2023), *Commonwealth Parliamentary Debates, Senate*, 7 August, 60-61

Bardosh, K., Lacour, M., Pronin, K., Correa A., and Koppl, R., (2024), "How Many Democratic Countries Have Conducted Covid-19 Public Inquiries? An Exploratory Study of Government-Led Post-Pandemic Reviews (2020-2024)", 23 December SSRN: https://ssrn.com/abstract=5069344 or http://dx.doi.org/10.2139/ssrn.5069344

Benson, S., (2024), "Hand to unveil verdict that's critical of Labor leaders", *The Australian*, 30 October

Benson, S., and Chambers, G., (2022), *Plagued*, Neutral Bay: Pantera Press

Bell, V., (Chair), (2024), Inquiry into the Appointment of the Former Prime Minister to Administer *Multiple* Departments, *Report*, Canberra: Commonwealth of Australia, 22 November

Bovens, M., and 't Hart, P., (1996), *Understanding Policy Fiascoes*, New Jersey: Transaction Publishers

Bulmer, M., (1982), *The Uses of Social Research: Social Investigation in Public Policy Making*, London: Allen and Unwin

Carrick, J., (1986), *Commonwealth Parliamentary Debates*, Senate, 13 March, 1001-02

Chambers, G. and Ison, S., "Immunity for mates: PM's COVID cop out", *The Australian*, 22 September

Christensen T., and Laegreid, P., (2023), "Assessing the cris management of the COVID-19: a study of inquiry commission reports in Norway sand Sweden", *Policy and Society*, 42(4), 548-63

Clarke, M., (2022), "Why Dan hasn't read damning Covid report", *Herald Sun*, 10 October 2022

Clennell, A., (2022), "Federal government to conduct a royal commission into Australia's response to the COVID-19 pandemic 'as soon as practicable'" *Sky News*, 21 August

Coorey, P., (2022), "Any pandemic probe must also look at the states" *Australian Financial Review*, 28 January

Coorey, P., (2023), "Coronavirus Australia: Australia to announce COVID-19 inquiry but no royal commission", *Australian Financial Review*, 20 September

Crowe, D., (2023), "Singular crisis needs more than inquiry", *Sydney Morning Herald*, 22 September

Dawson, E., (2023), "Robodebts and rollercoasters: Social (in)security in the 46th Parliament", in McCaffrie, B., Grattan, M., and Wallace C., (eds), *The Morrison Government: Governing through crisis, 2019-2022 – Australian Commonwealth Administration series*, Sydney: UNSW Press, 128-41

Editorial SMH, (2023), "COVID-19 inquiry is a second-rate, cowardly fix". *Sydney Morning Herald*, 22 September

Ergas, H., (2022), Pandemic's lessons burn along with Morrison", *The Australian*, 2 December

Forsyth, A., (2017), "Regulatory Responses to the Trade Union Corruption in Australia", *University of New South Wales Law Journal*, 40(4), 1336-65

Gillespie, K., and Okruhlik, G., (1991), "The Political Dimensions of Corruption Cleanups: A Framework for Analysis", *Comparative Politics,* 24(1), October, 77-95

Hamilton, S., and Holden, R., (2024), "Australia's response to the pandemic was a great success overall", *Australian Financial Review,* 30 October

Holmes, C., (Chair), (2023), Royal Commission into the Robodebt Scheme, *Report*, Canberra: Commonwealth of Australia

Howard, J., (2014), "John Howard questions Coalition's two royal commissions", *The Guardian*, 15 September

Kelly, J., (2024), "Doubts over independence of Labor's COVID inquiry", *The Australian,* 11 January

Kelly, P., (2024), "Transparency, trust, lost in pandemic", *The Australian,* 1 November

Kruk, R., (Chair), (2024), COVID-19 Response Inquiry, *Report*, Canberra: Commonwealth of Australia

Manne, R., (1987), *The Petrov Affair: Politics and Espionage*, Sydney: Pergamon

Martin, A.W., (1995), "New Light on the Petrov Affair", *Quadrant*, June, 46-50

McCaffrie, B., (2024), "The Challenge of the COVID-19 Pandemic: Federal Labor in Opposition 2019-22", in Prasser, S., and Clune, D., (eds), *The Art of Opposition,* Redland Bay: Connor Court Publishing, 181-95

Morrison, S., (2023), *Commonwealth Parliamentary Debates*, House of Representatives, Statements on Indulgence – Royal Commission into the Robodebt Scheme, 31 July, 83-85

Padula, M., and Di Francesco, M., (2017), "The Best Laid Plans: Australia's Home Insulation Program (Epilogue)", *ANZSOG Case Program*, Melbourne: ANZSOG

Podger, A., (2023), *Report to the Royal Commission into the Robodebt Scheme*, prepared for the Royal Commission into the Robodebt Scheme

Prasser, S., (2021), *Royal Commissions and Public Inquiries in Australia*, 2nd ed, Sydney: Lexis Nexis

Prasser, S., (2023a), "A royal commission into Australia's response to the pandemic?", *Australasian Parliamentary Review,* 38(1), Autumn/Winter, 89-107

Prasser, S., (2023b), "Labor quarantines states from Covid accountability", *The Australian,* 22 September

Priergaard, J., (2025), "Not my debt: The institutional origins of Robodebt", *Australian Journal of Public Administration,* 54(1), 142-58

Pronin, K., (2023), "Commissions of inquiry in the Nordic countries", in Prasser, S., (ed), *New Directions in Royal Commissions and Public Inquiries: Do we need them?,* Redland Bay: Connor Court Publishing, 267-86

Ransley, J., (2014), "Public inquiries into political wrongdoing", in Prasser, S., and Tracey, H., (eds), *Royal Commissions and Public Inquiries: Practice and Potential,* Ballarat: Connor Court Publishing, 55-76

Reid, A., (1976), *The Whitlam Adventure,* Melbourne: Hill of Content

Ruston, A., (2023a), Commonwealth Parliamentary Debates, Senate, 7 August, 61

Ruston, A., (2023b), "It's not a proper inquiry", *Courier-Mail,* 23 September

Sedgwick, S., (2015), "Still more to learn from 'pink batts'" *Canberra Times*, Public Sector Informant, 4 August

Senate COVID-19 Committee, (2022), *Final Report,* Canberra: Commonwealth Parliament, April

Senate Legal and Constitutional Affairs References Committee, (2024), COVID-19 Royal Commission, Canberra: Commonwealth Parliament, April

Shergold, P., (2022), (Chair), Independent Review into Australia's response to COVID-19. *Fault Lines,* 20 October

Simons, M., (2022), "Was Fraser right?". *Inside Story,* 12 September

Whitlam, N. and Stubbs, J., (1974), Brisbane: *Nest of Traitors: The Petrov Affair*, Brisbane: Jacaranda Press

Endnotes

1   See Chapter 14 on higher education, Chapters 10 and 11 on the economy, and Chapter 5 covers aspects on different areas and also considers the Robodebt issue.

2   The original name of the scheme was the Income Compliance Program that was introduced in the 2015-16 federal Budget. According to the Holmes Royal Commission (2023: v): "The Robodebt Scheme was a proposal developed by the Department of Human Services (DHS), put forward as a budget measure by the Minister for Social Services in 2015 and begun that year (initially in pilot form and expanded in subsequent budgets). It was designed to recover supposed overpayments from welfare recipients going back to the financial year 2010-11 and relied heavily on a process known as 'income averaging' to assess income and entitlement to benefit".

3   This was the Opinion offered by the Solicitor General on request of Prime Minister Albanese, In the Matter of the Validity of the Appointment of Mr Morrison to Adminster the Department of Industry, Science, Energy and Resources.

4   See Frame, T., Where Fate Calls, Sydney: Coronet, 1992, concerning the appointment of a second royal commission to review an earlier royal commission's findings into the 1964 HMAS Voyager disaster.

5   The National Australian Anti-Corruption Commission initially rejected the need to review the referrals from the Holmes Royal Commission and attracted some criticism. Following a review, the NACC then decided to do so.

6   These figures come from the Australian Institute of Health and Welfare see: https://www.aihw.gov.au/reports/australias-health/covid-19

7   Robyn Kruk was Convenor of the NSW Health COVID-19 System Response Brief that was supported by the NSW Health Department and was appointed in 2022 to oversee the review of the NSW Health system's response to the Pandemic by Department Secretary, Susan Pearce.

8   The inquiry lacked any statutory powers of investigation and none of its three members had any health qualifications, but had served as former ministers, public servants or members of government advisory bodies.

9   One explanation is that it is harder for national inquiries to be established in federations. Though Australia has had numerous federal-state royal

commissions including several during the last decade (eg the 2013 *Royal Commission into Institutional Responses to Child Sexual Abuse*). These, however, were not so potentially political damaging to a state government or to partisan interests.

Part 3: Managing the Policies

8

The Australian Economy over the Albanese Government's First Term

Gene Tunny

Introduction

Economic management was central to Labor's pitch for the 2022 election. Under Albanese, Labor promised it would reduce the cost of living, including a promise of a $275 reduction in power bills, and increase real wages. It would also promote Australia as a "renewable energy superpower" and a "manufacturing powerhouse" (Albanese 2021). This chapter reviews how successful the Albanese Government has been in terms of the economy. It explores what it promised, what it has done, how it compares with previous governments, and whether it can be categorised as a success or failure. Of course, it may be too soon to tell, and a final assessment of the Albanese Government's record will need to consider the results of its second term and any beyond that.

What was expected of the Albanese Government?

Inflation was the pressing issue when the Albanese Government came into power in May 2022. Inflation was running at 6.1 per cent annually in the June quarter of 2022.[1] At the same time, there were concerns about climate change among parts of the electorate, supply-chain resilience coming out of the pandemic, and housing affordability. The Albanese Government had plans to address all these concerns.

Significant economic policy changes were expected for industrial relations and the Reserve Bank of Australia (RBA). It proposed to close so-called loopholes regarding labour hire, casual workers, and the gig economy. Its promised review of the Reserve Bank's monetary policy framework was expected to rebalance the RBA's mandate to give more weight to employment growth relative to keeping inflation in the 2-3 per cent target band. Both these expected changes were consistent with Labor's left-of-centre policy positioning.

Regarding tax, the Albanese Government adopted a small-target strategy. It pledged to keep the Morrison Government's legislated Stage 3 tax cuts and not to amend them.[2] It also ruled out changes to negative gearing and capital gains tax relating to investment properties. Its previous proposals to amend the tax treatment of investment properties contributed to the 2019 election loss for Labor. Finally, the Government pledged it would not change superannuation tax arrangements.

What has the Albanese Government done?

Overview

The Albanese Government took power at a time of accelerating inflation. This was partly due to strong monetary and fiscal stimulus measures enacted by the Reserve Bank and the previous federal and state governments in response to the COVID-19 pandemic. Although inflation returned to the 2-3 per cent target band by the end of the Albanese Government's term, its economic record includes relatively high average inflation compared with previous governments of the last few decades, other than the Hawke-Keating Government (Table 1). The other striking feature of the Albanese Government's economic record is the decline in per capita GDP–the "per capita recession"– labour productivity (GDP per hour worked), and real net disposable income per capita that it presided over. I delve into these declines and their causes below, concluding that, while this decline was largely outside of the government's control, its policy settings did not do much to prevent the decline. On the positive side, the Albanese Government's term saw relatively high employment growth. As we will see, however, this was associated with high immigration-led population growth and a surge in health and social welfare jobs that are significantly subsidised by the government.

Table 1: Economic indicators of Australian governments

Government	Party	Real GDP growth	Real GDP per capita growth	Real Net National Disp. Income per capita	GDP per hour worked growth	Employment growth	Unemployment rate	CPI inflation
Hawke-Keating	ALP	3.6	2.2	1.8	1.4	2.2	8.7	5.2
Howard	LNP	3.7	2.4	2.9	1.9	2.1	6.3	2.6
Rudd-Gillard	ALP	2.6	0.9	1.4	1.4	1.4	5.1	2.7
Abbott, Turnbull & Morrison	LNP	2.5	1.2	1.8	1.0	1.9	5.6	2.2
Albanese	ALP	1.5	-0.7	-1.7	-1.2	2.7	3.8	4.1

Source: ABS National Accounts, Labour Force Survey, and CPI Inflation. For the unemployment rate, the seasonally adjusted monthly unemployment rate was averaged over the term of the Government. For the other indicators, the averages are based on averages of quarterly or monthly percentage changes expressed in annualised percentage terms. For the calculations, the terms are assumed to start the month or quarter following the month or quarter of the election. Note: National Accounts data are up to March quarter 2025, CPI data up to March quarter 2025 and Labour Force data up to May 2025 were used.

The Albanese Government is compared only with governments back to the Hawke-Keating Government due to data availability, specifically the modern Labour Force Survey data, which began in 1978, midway through the Fraser Coalition Government. Comparing averages of economic indicators for different governments is imperfect because some governments may have good policies but bad luck (eg global recessions, financial crises, or pandemics), so outside factors must be considered in the assessment. Furthermore, demographic factors such as the Baby Boom bulge may have contributed to high unemployment in the seventies and eighties.

Cost of living

Regarding its promises on the cost of living, the Albanese Government could claim some success. It presided over a deceleration in inflation after inheriting accelerating inflation on its election. The headline annual CPI inflation was 2.4 per cent in the December quarter 2024, although that was partly due to government energy rebates (ie subsidies of $300 from the Commonwealth and $1,000 from the Queensland Government). That said, core inflation measures were heading back to the 2-3 per cent target band (Figure 1) and in quarterly terms were well within it. For instance, both the trimmed mean and weighted median inflation measures were 0.7 per cent in the March quarter of 2025, corresponding to an annualised rate of 2.8 per cent.

Figure 1: Core CPI inflation, annual

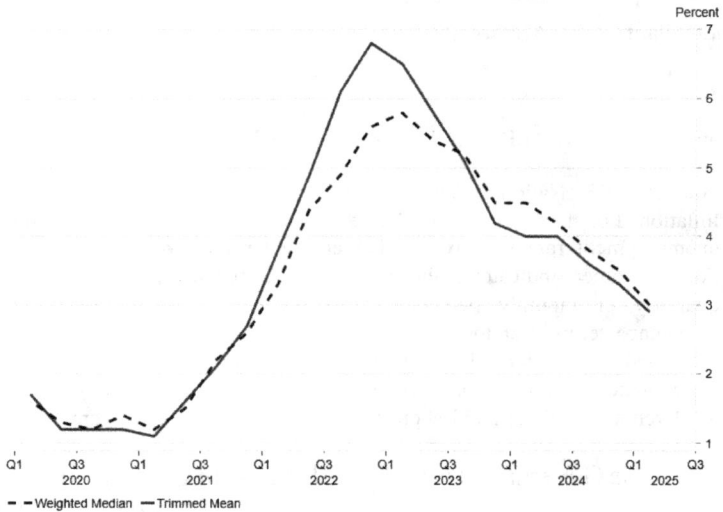

Source: ABS, CPI Inflation, Australia, March quarter 2025.

Broadly speaking, inflation is the responsibility of the RBA because inflation is typically a monetary phenomenon, caused by "too much money chasing too few goods". However, Federal Government fiscal policy can influence the inflation rate by affecting aggregate demand. Treasurer Chalmers deserves credit for delivering two surpluses in 2022-23 and 2023-24, when he would have been pressured to spend more on cost-of-living relief, climate action, housing, or other priorities. However, these surpluses were bolstered by substantial tax revenues associated with high commodity prices related to the global recovery from the pandemic and the Russian invasion of Ukraine. Simply pointing to budget surpluses is insufficient, as it is possible that, given the favourable revenue boost, the government should have run larger surpluses.

The Treasury produces analysis that can allow an estimation of the cyclically-adjusted budget balance and implicitly –the hypothetical budget balance in the absence of cyclical factors–that can inform an assessment of the fiscal impact of the federal budget. If the cyclically-adjusted balance is improving, that suggests a tightening of fiscal policy, while a deterioration in the cyclically-adjusted balance suggests expansionary fiscal policy. Chart 3.13 in the 2025-26 Budget Paper No. 1 reveal the cyclical contributions to the budget were so substantial, at around 2 per cent of GDP in 2022-23 and 1 per cent in 2023-24, that it arguably could have run larger surpluses in those two years and contributed to the inflation fight, bringing inflation down sooner. However, the surpluses were significantly reduced by temporary fiscal measures from the pandemic (eg the boost to the Low and Middle Income Tax Offset) that were still injecting money into the economy, although these were declining considerably in the first two years of the Albanese Government. As a result of the reduction in the temporary fiscal measures, overall fiscal policy was tightening–as evidenced by the underlying cash balance only falling from 0.9% to 0.6% of GDP, even though the contribution of cyclical factors to the balance fell by around 1 percentage point (Australian Government 2025: 88). The previous government largely locked this fiscal policy tightening in, and it was not due to the Albanese Government. It deserves credit merely for not spending all the additional revenue it received due to the surge in commodity prices.

In a way, the Federal Government tried to "hack" the CPI with its $300 electricity subsidy in the 2024-25 Budget. By subsidising electricity, the Albanese Government was directly reducing one price which goes into the calculation of the CPI. This was an unconventional "hack" compared with the conventional policy response to inflation – ie tighter monetary policy from the central bank. This subsidy was enacted around the same time as similar subsidies from state governments, most notably $1,000 provided by the Queensland Labor Government. Economists were largely critical of these measures, and the RBA confirmed it would ignore any temporary reduction in headline CPI inflation due to the subsidies. However, the measures may have had an impact on several "administered" prices (eg child care, fuel and tobacco excise) in the economy that are adjusted in line with headline inflation (van Onselen 2024). Hence, the hack may have contributed to reducing inflation. However, by easing household budget constraints, it will likely mean higher aggregate demand than otherwise, which could put upward pressure on inflation.

Furthermore, once the rebates end, electricity prices will spike and temporarily at least push CPI inflation back up, possibly above the target band. For example, in the RBA's February 2025 *Statement on Monetary Policy*, released prior to the Government's announced an extension to the electricity rebate until the end of 2025, the RBA forecast the removal of rebates would largely be responsible for pushing inflation above 3 per cent temporarily (RBA 2025: 33). To summarise, energy rebates are having a range of impacts with different timings, and these impacts operate in different directions, which will offset each other at least in part. Determining which impact is dominant is beyond the scope of this chapter.

The significant reduction in electricity prices over the term of the Albanese Government was only due to the rebates. Between June quarter 2022 and June quarter 2024, just before the rebates came in, electricity prices increased by around 20 per cent. The failure to address the underlying high cost of electricity, along with gas, has significant cost implications for Australian industry and households. The inability to reduce energy costs beyond subsidies that cost the budget was a substantial failure of the Albanese Government.

Productivity, wages and living standards

One significant criticism of the Albanese Government on economic management is it presided over seven consecutive quarters of negative growth in per capita GDP, the so-called "per capita recession", over March quarter 2023 to September quarter 2024. Real GDP per capita was 1.7 per cent lower in March quarter 2025 than it was in June quarter 2022 when the Albanese Government assumed office. There was an even larger decline over this period, of around 4.7 per cent, in real net national disposable income per capita. Moreover, OECD data (Figure 2) reveal Australia had the largest decline in living standards in the OECD since 2019 (Read 2024). This also takes into account reductions in real disposable income associated with higher mortgage interest payments (Figure 2). These figures illustrate why the cost-of-living was a major political issue for the Albanese Government and why it responded with various forms of cost-of-living support.

Figure 2: Real gross disposable income per capita, Australia and OECD, Index (2007 Q1=100)

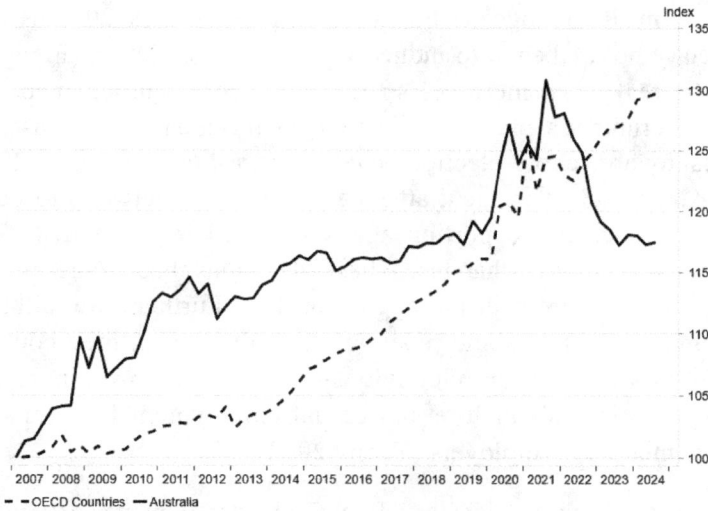

Source: OECD, Household indicators dashboard, quarter 3, 2024, via Macrobond.

The reductions in GDP per capita and real disposable income per capita are related to weak productivity growth alongside high population growth due to immigration. Australia's labour productivity is likely suffering due to strong growth in services sector jobs, which are challenging or impossible to realise productivity gains in, and because many immigrants, particularly those on student visas, are working in low-skilled services sector jobs, many in the gig economy of Uber, Uber Eats, *et cetera*.

The decline in living standards is closely related to declining real wages (ie wages growth less CPI inflation). Declining real wages set in during the Morrison Government and continued under the Albanese Government. The decline in real wages was related to both the surge in CPI inflation associated with COVID-related stimulus and supply-chain disruptions, but also likely related to the large labour supply shock from immigration as it resumed post-COVID in 2022. The real wage decline was mainly out of the Albanese Government's control. As stressed above, however, the government could have done more in fiscal policy terms to contribute to the fight against inflation. Also, as I argue below, it could have done more to significantly reduce the very high immigration rate early in its term. Real wages only started recovering over 2024 as RBA monetary policy began to induce significant disinflation (Figure 3), and the real wage increases so far have been insufficient to meet the Government's pre-2022 election commitment to increase real wages to above pre-election levels (Algra-Maschio et al 2025). The Albanese Government attributes real wage increases to policy decisions such as supporting aged care worker pay and its 2024 *Closing Loopholes* changes. These decisions had some impact, probably only minor in the aggregate data. Furthermore, although they may have had some positive effect on wages, they could be counterproductive for productivity and economic growth in the long run by making labour hire and casual employment less attractive arrangements for employers (Tunny 2023).

Overall, as discussed in Gary Banks' chapter (Chapter 10) in this volume, the Albanese Government appears to be going about raising real wages, which ultimately requires higher productivity, the wrong way. It has shown a preference for a dubious "picking winners" industry policy, its Future Made in Australia agenda, and has shown a willingness to financial subsidise businesses such as the Whyalla steelworks, rather than addressing the underlying cause of their distress – including high energy costs due to flawed energy policies and high labour costs partly due to significant labour market regulations, which the Albanese Government tightened over its first term via the Closing Loopholes amendments. Treasurer Jim Chalmers has promised to make productivity the focus of the Government's second term. But the Albanese Government's first term agenda does not inspire much confidence that the government can boost productivity.

Figure 3: Real wages growth, annual Wage Price Index (WPI) less CPI inflation, Australia

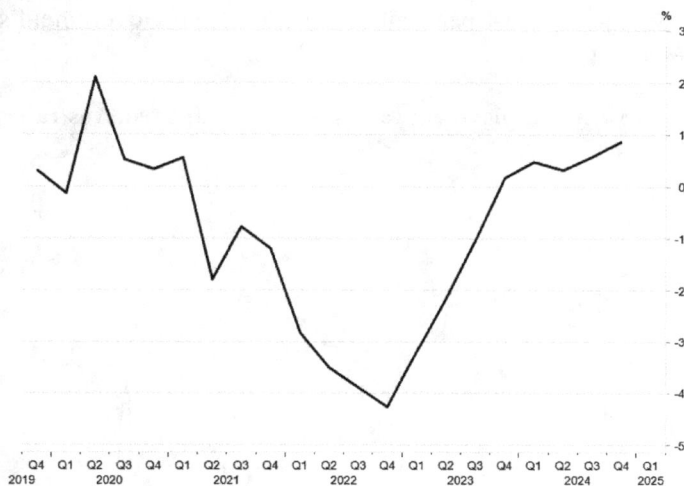

Source: ABS, Wage Price Index, Australia, December 2024 and Consumer Price Index, Australia, March quarter 2025.

Employment growth

The employment statistics for the Albanese Government are very favourable. However, again, monetary policy is the primary macroeconomic policy tool and the degree of credit the Government deserves is debatable. Treasurer Chalmers considered directing the RBA to weigh up inflation and employment equally in its decision-making but wisely backed off from doing that in the new *Monetary Policy Agreement* released in December 2023 (Read 2023). One of the big questions was how much the labour market would need to slow down and how much unemployment would need to increase for disinflation to occur. As of May 2025, the answer is not much. The RBA has been successful. As noted above, by at least running surpluses over 2022-23 and 2023-24, the Albanese Government did not make the RBA's job harder, although it probably could have done more to help it. Furthermore, there is a risk of rising inflation once electricity rebates finally end, as noted above.

Despite the RBA raising the cash rate from 0.35 per cent when the

Albanese Government assumed office to a peak 4.35 per cent, before rate cuts began in February 2025, the unemployment rate remained very low at just over 4 per cent at the end of the Government's first term (Figure 4).

Figure 4: Unemployment rate, seasonally adjusted, Australia

Source: ABS, Labour Force, Australia, May 2025.

Partly, the strong jobs market was due to government-subsidised jobs, either jobs in the public sector itself or in the private sector but funded by the government (eg jobs at private hospitals with public patients, at service National Disability Insurance Scheme (NDIS) providers, at aged care providers, etc.). Health Care and Social Assistance was the fastest growing sector for job creation since the Albanese Government was elected (Table 2). The rapidly increasing NDIS is a significant reason. More broadly, between May 2022 and February 2025, nearly one in every two additional employed persons had a job in a sector that received substantial support from the government: Health Care and Social Assistance, Education and Training, and Public Administration and Safety. As noted above, this could be one reason for low productivity growth. Services sectors are less suitable for productivity improvements than manufacturing or mining, for example, and hence they can weigh on aggregate productivity figures. The manufacturing sector is expanding, but at a lower rate than total employment, and there is no sign of a resurgence of Australian manufacturing that the Albanese Government would like to see.

Table 2: Employment growth by industry, seasonally adjusted, Australia

	Employed (Thousands)	Employed (Thousands)	Change	Change	Contribution
	May-2022	Feb-2025	%	Thousands	% of total
Agriculture, Forestry and Fishing	286.6	290.7	1.4%	4.1	0.4%
Mining	320.9	331.7	3.4%	10.8	1.1%
Manufacturing	834.5	887.4	6.3%	52.9	5.3%
Electricity, Gas, Water and Waste Services	166.4	182.2	9.5%	15.8	1.6%
Construction	1,180.0	1,389.1	17.7%	209.1	20.9%
Wholesale Trade	365.8	349.8	-4.4%	-16.1	-1.6%
Retail Trade	1,302.8	1,332.0	2.2%	29.2	2.9%
Accommodation and Food Services	902.2	967.1	7.2%	64.9	6.5%
Transport, Postal and Warehousing	689.7	729.0	5.7%	39.3	3.9%
Information Media and Telecommunications	197.5	193.7	-1.9%	-3.9	-0.4%
Financial and Insurance Services	559.1	564.4	1.0%	5.3	0.5%
Rental, Hiring and Real Estate Services	226.7	247.0	8.9%	20.3	2.0%
Professional, Scientific and Technical Services	1,261.8	1,267.1	0.4%	5.3	0.5%
Administrative and Support Services	424.5	434.1	2.3%	9.6	1.0%
Public Administration and Safety	912.6	988.1	8.3%	75.5	7.6%
Education and Training	1,129.7	1,260.6	11.6%	130.9	13.1%
Health Care and Social Assistance	2,019.4	2,301.1	13.9%	281.6	28.2%
Arts and Recreation Services	230.4	277.7	20.5%	47.3	4.7%
Other Services	538.9	539.7	0.2%	0.9	0.1%
Employed total	13,528.9	14,527.5	7.4%	998.5	100.0%

Source: ABS, Labour Force, Australia, Detailed, February 2025.

Immigration and housing

As noted above how one contributor to the GDP per capita recession is the surge in immigration, which has seen the addition of many young and low-skilled workers, many of whom have gained employment in the gig economy. Net overseas migration reached a record high of over half a million in 2022-23. Arguably, on its election, the Albanese Government failed to grasp the urgency of controlling immigration. Indeed, it appeared favourably disposed toward higher levels of immigration. For instance, Prime Minister Albanese and Indian Prime Minister Narendra Modi signed the Migration and Mobility Partnership Agreement (MMPA) in May 2023. This agreement expanded opportunities for Indian immigration to Australia. From mid-2023 net overseas migration started to trend down, but it still appears above pre-pandemic levels (Figure 5). Partly the surge in migration post-COVID was expected as students returned to Australia, and hence some reduction from the peak in 2022-23 was expected. The Albanese Government has made some contribution to reducing immigration since late 2023 when it started tightening visa rules, particularly those relating to international students, and hence deserves some credit for the decline in immigration since 2022-23. That said, the 2025-26 federal budget forecasts net overseas migration at 260,000 in 2025-26 and 225,000 (Australian Government 2025: 43), which, while much lower than in 2022-23, are still high levels in historical terms. For example, net overseas migration averaged around 80,000 yearly in the 1990s and 166,000 in the 2000s.[3]

The high level of immigration has contributed to rising housing costs across Australia. In capital cities, vacancy rates have been very low, at 1.1 per cent in March 2025 compared with a healthy range of 2.5-3.5 per cent, suggesting tight rental markets, and capital city rents have increased at high rates.[4] The supply side has been unable to respond sufficiently. Indeed, dwelling completions are below levels before the pandemic and well below the 240,000 annually or 60,000 per quarter needed to meet the national housing target of 1.2 million new homes over the five years from mid-2024 (Figure 6).

Figure 5: Net overseas migration, Australia (not seasonally adjusted), quarterly

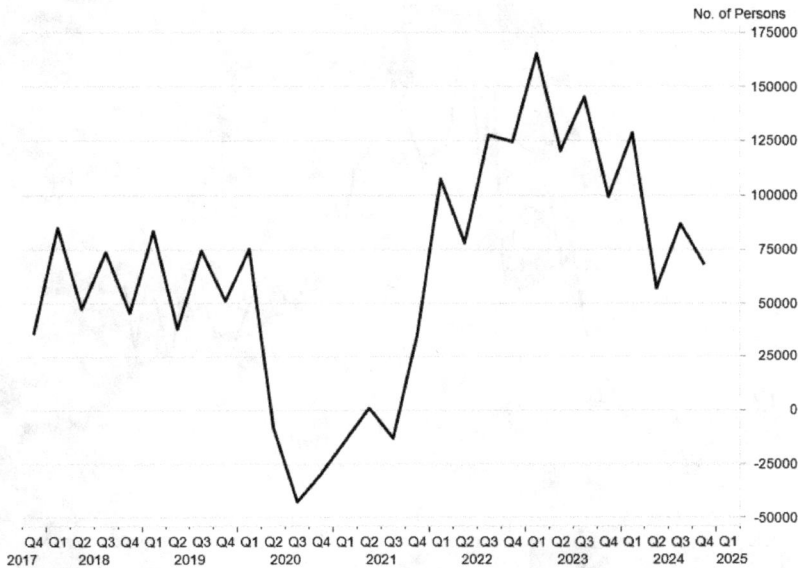

Source: ABS, National, state and territory population, December 2024.

The Albanese Government has offered an inadequate policy response to the housing crisis. Its signature initiative is the Housing Australia Future Fund (HAFF), which is a roundabout and arguably inefficient and ineffective way of boosting housing supply (Murray 2023). The HAFF is a $10 billion investment vehicle that has a mandate to invest in social and community housing projects. This is related to the current approach to delivering social housing as Public Private Partnerships. Whatever its merits, the approach has not made any significant difference in new dwelling completions across Australia as of May 2025. It will likely have a marginal if any impact on improving housing affordability, given it is only designed to support the delivery of 30,000 new social and affordable homes over five years (Collins 2023).

Figure 6: Dwelling completions, Australia, seasonally adjusted, quarterly

Source: ABS, Building Activity, Australia, December 2024.

Tax

The Albanese Government has received criticism for being unambitious about tax reform, and incidentally so has the Opposition (Sobeck 2025). Nonetheless, tax policy has proven contentious for the Albanese Government, although its tax policy changes are likely to have had minimal impact on overall economic performance.

The Albanese Government broke at least one of its promises regarding tax policy and arguably broke two. Its commitment not to amend the Morrison Government's stage 3 tax cut was breached. However, shifting the tax cuts to provide greater relief to low and middle-income earners became politically popular. This ignored the fact that the previous two stages delivered much more relief to lower and middle income earners, and the final stage 3 would have helped mitigate a large amount of 'bracket creep' that had occurred (Carling 2022).

The Opposition accused the Albanese Government of breaking its promise regarding superannuation tax. The Government will double the tax rate on earnings for superannuation accounts over $3 million from 2025-26. The Government argues it kept its promise because the changes did not take effect in its first term (Grattan 2023). Given its application to very large super balances, this measure will have minimal macroeconomic impact. However, because the threshold is not indexed to inflation, it will become more significant over the years.

How has Albanese governed?

Unsurprisingly, the Albanese Government is much more interventionist than the preceding Coalition Government. However, it was also much more interventionist than the two previous Labor Governments: Rudd-Gillard and Hawke-Keating. Treasurer Jim Chalmers set out his vision for economic policy in an essay, "Capitalism After the Crises", published in early 2023 in *The Monthly*, in which he called for " a new, values-based capitalism for Australia" (Chalmers 2023). Chalmers' essay was consistent with the Albananese Government's principal policy directions: an attempt to revitalise Australian manufacturing through additional government support, as discussed in Gary Banks' chapter in this volume (Chapter 10), decarbonisation of the economy, and increasing labour market regulation to close so-called loopholes in labour hire, casual employment, and the gig economy.

The editor of this volume asked authors to consider whether the Albanese Government has set its agenda or been reactive. Typically, setting your agenda is preferable to being reactive. But if a government has set the wrong or an inadequate agenda, it needs to react to circumstances and change its agenda. Arguably, the Albanese Government has not responded sufficiently to the circumstances regarding the interrelated issues of immigration and housing, as discussed above. It has been too slow in bringing down net overseas migration, making housing less affordable and Australia's cities more congested than otherwise.

Conclusions

Overall, the Albanese Government's economic management record was, at best, mixed over its first term. It could even be considered below average or poor, given its failures in major policy areas, as discussed below.

To its credit, the Albanese Government resisted what must have been significant pressure to spend a large proportion of the additional revenue resulting from higher commodity prices in its first two years. Inflation has returned to the RBA's 2-3 per cent target band, with some assistance from tightening fiscal policy as temporary pandemic-related fiscal measures were reduced in magnitude over 2022-23 and 2023-24. One qualification is that inflation and interest rates did not fall as rapidly as in other advanced economies. Still, Australia's recent disinflation appears to have been successful, and the unemployment rate has remained low.

The Albanese Government's most significant failures were those concerning the need to bring power prices down (apart from offering a $300 rebate); its failure to manage immigration and improve housing affordability; and the embedding of significant deficits into the budget outlook, as discussed in Saul Eslake's chapter in this volume (Chapter 9), which will compromise the ability of future governments to respond to future economic shocks.

Finally, the most concerning development during the Albanese Government's first term may have been its embrace of an interventionist industrial policy rather than free trade and market competition, which the Hawke-Keating and Howard governments strongly supported during Australia's microeconomic reform era. The focus of the Albanese Government's second term will be boosting productivity, but it has not set itself up well to achieve this objective.

References

Albanese, A., (2021), *Labor's Plan for a Better Future*, Speech, 5 December

Algra-Maschio, F.R., Campbell, D., and Waller, L., (2025) "Labor made plenty of promises at the last election. Did they deliver?", *The Conversation*, 10 April

Australian Government, (2025), Budget *2025-26: Budget Strategy and Outlook, Budget Paper No. 1*, Canberra: Commonwealth of Australia

Carling, R., (2022), "Why the government has to make the case for stage 3 tax cuts", *Australian Financial Review*, 5 September

Chalmers, J., (2023), "Capitalism after the crises", *The Monthly*, 1 February

Collins, J., (2023), "Government welcomes new support for $10 billion Housing Australia Future Fund", *Media Release*, Minister for Housing, Minister for Homelessness, Minister for Small Business, 4 May

Grattan, M., (2023), "Albanese government to hike tax on earnings from big super balances – but not until 2025-26", *The Conversation*, 28 February

Murray, C., (2023), "Australia's Housing Future Fund - my Senate hearing opening statement and submission", *Fresh Economic Thinking*, 15 March

Read, M., (2023), "RBA dual mandate tweak could mean higher rates for longer", *Australian Financial Review*, 8 December

Read, M., (2024), "How Australia became the world's biggest cost-of-living loser", *Australian Financial Review*, 25 November

Reserve Bank of Australia, (2025), *Statement on Monetary Policy February 2025*, Sydney: Reserve Bank of Australia

Sobeck, K., (2025), "This budget's tax tinkering isn't the same as meaningful tax reform. Here's why", *The Conversation*, 27 March 2025

Tunny, G., (2023), *Closing Loopholes or Closing Opportunities*, Analysis Paper 58, Sydney: Centre for Independent Studies, November

van Onselen, L., (2024), "Administered price inflation RBA's problem and solution", *Macrobusiness*, 8 November

9

Fiscal Policy under the Albanese Government, 2022-2025

Saul Eslake

Introduction

One of the enduring lessons of the past four decades of Australian political history, as exemplified by the experience of the Coalition under John Hewson in 1993 and Labor under Bill Shorten in 2019 is that oppositions cannot win government on a platform of ambitious economic reforms – because if they try, the government of the day will deploy all the vastly superior resources which it has at its disposal to scare the living daylights out of voters as to what might happen if those reforms were ever to be implemented, as Paul Keating did in 1993 and Scott Morrison did in 2019.

First-term governments which assume office on a platform which contains more promises as to what they won't do than as to what they will then have a choice. They can keep their promises – both as to what they would do and what they wouldn't – and then, if so inclined, seek a more ambitious mandate for a second term, knowing (although of course not saying publicly) that no first term Federal Government has failed to secure a second term since 1931, as John Howard did in 1998 (and as Mike Baird did in New South Wales in 2015). Alternatively, they can choose to do some things that they had, before the election, promised that they wouldn't do, hoping subsequently to persuade voters that it was nonetheless the right thing to do. John Howard got away with that in his first term – in part by drawing a distinction between "core" and "non-core" promises. But Tony Abbott and Joe Hockey did not – and nor, even more spectacularly, did Campbell Newman in Queensland.

So, it is hardly surprising that the Albanese Government came to office after the May 2022 elections on a relatively unambitious platform – at least with regard to economic and fiscal policy. It did not seek a mandate for long-term "budget repair", wide-ranging tax reform, reform of federal-state financial relations, or anything else of the kind associated with the Hawke-Keating or Howard-Costello governments. Thus, it would be wrong to judge their first-term performance by those standards – although they would become more appropriate should the Albanese Government secure a second or third term.

What did Labor promise at the 2022 election?

According to its own costings, Labor's 2022 election commitments would have a net (negative) impact on the "underlying" cash balance of $7.4 billion (less than 0.1 per cent of GDP) over the four years to 2025-26, reflecting $18.9 billion of new spending commitments (of which the largest were "cheaper child care", $5.1 billion, and "fixing" the aged care crisis, $2.5 billion), partly offset by $11.5 billion of "savings measures" (including $3.1 billion from 'extending and boosting ATO programs, $3 billion in "savings from external labour", and $1.9 billion from "ensuring Multinationals Pay Their Fair Share of Tax") (Chalmers and Gallagher 2022a: 8-16).

The Parliamentary Budget Office (PBO) subsequently estimated the net cost of Labor's election commitments as adding $6.9 billion to the "underlying" cash deficit over the four years to 2025-26 (PBO 2022: Appendix Table 2A).

Significantly, however, the PBO also estimated that commitments made by Labor during the election campaign would add a further $33.6 billion to "net investments in financial assets for policy purposes" (which are not included in the "underlying" cash balance) over the four years to 2025-26, of which $10.3 billion was for *Rewiring the Nation*, $10.0 billion for the proposed *Housing Australia Future Fund*, $7.6

billion for Labor's "Help to Buy" (shared equity) scheme, and $5.0 billion for the *National Reconstruction Fund* (PBO 2022: Appendix Table 2C). These were not mentioned in Labor's pre-election costing document.

Thus, the PBO estimated the net impact of Labor's election commitments on the "headline" cash balance – which, despite its name, very rarely attracts 'headlines' – at $40.5 billion over the four years to 2025-26, or nearly six times the impact on the more closely-followed 'underlying' cash balance. And whereas the PBO reckoned that Labor's election commitments would only add a further $2.8 billion to the cash deficits projected over the "medium term" beyond the forward estimates period (ie from 2026-27 through 2032-33), it put the impact on the "headline" cash deficits over this period at an additional $31.9 billion (PBO 2022: Appendix Table 2C).

What did Labor do in its four budgets?

Upon assuming office, Jim Chalmers as Treasurer and Katy Gallagher as Finance Minister were confronted with a fairly bleak picture of the outlook for the Federal budget. The Pre-Election Economic and Fiscal Outlook, prepared as required under the *Charter of Budget Honesty Act* 1998 by the Secretaries to the Treasury and of the Department of Finance independently of any political direction, projected "underlying" cash deficits in each of the ten years to 2032-33 (albeit gradually declining from 3.4 per cent of GDP in 2022-23 to 0.7 per cent of GDP in 2031-32 and 2032-33) and with net debt rising from $714.9 billion as at 30 June 2023 to $1013.8 billion by 30 June 2033 (albeit declining as a percentage of GDP from 2026-27 onwards).

Labor's first Budget, presented on 25 October 2022, was in essence, a reworking of the 2022-23 Budget originally presented by the Coalition twelve days before the 2022 election was called. It contained substantial upward revisions to forward estimates and medium-term projections of spending (by an average of 0.7 per cent of GDP over the ten years to 2032-33, as shown in Chart 1), as a result of "higher-than-expected prices and wages", higher interest rates on outstanding debt, further upward revisions to the cost of the NDIS arising from "an updated actuarial assessment", and "to meet the need for unavoidable and essential assistance, and to resolve legacy issues left behind by the former Government" (Chalmers and Gallagher 2022b: 73, 79, 85 and 91).

These were however more than offset, at least for the forward estimates period in that Budget (2022-23 through 2025-26), by upward revisions to revenues totalling almost $145 billion, arising from more favourable assumptions about commodity prices and forecasts of employment (although longer-term revenue projections were dampened by more realistic assumptions about productivity growth than those made in the Morrison Government's last Budget and in the PEFO – see Chart 2 and Table 1).

These "windfall" revenue gains, combined with forecast additional revenues totalling $13 billion over the four years to 2025-26 from "policy decisions" (mainly extending Tax Office compliance programs) allowed the new government both to fund election commitments costing almost $23 billion, *and* foreshadow budget deficits totalling almost $43 billion less over the four years to 2025-26 than had been indicated in PEFO (Chart 3). But the medium-term projections in that first Labor Budget showed larger deficits after 2025-26, and especially after 2029-30, than had been projected in the PEFO – largely as a consequence of substantial upward revisions to medium-term spending projections.

As a result, despite a substantially-downwardly-revised "starting point", net debt was projected to be higher than had been foreshadowed in the PEFO by 2029-30, and to continue rising over the following four years, in contrast to the decline from 2025-26 onwards which had been projected in PEFO (Chart 4).

Chart 1: Successive estimates of 'underlying' payments

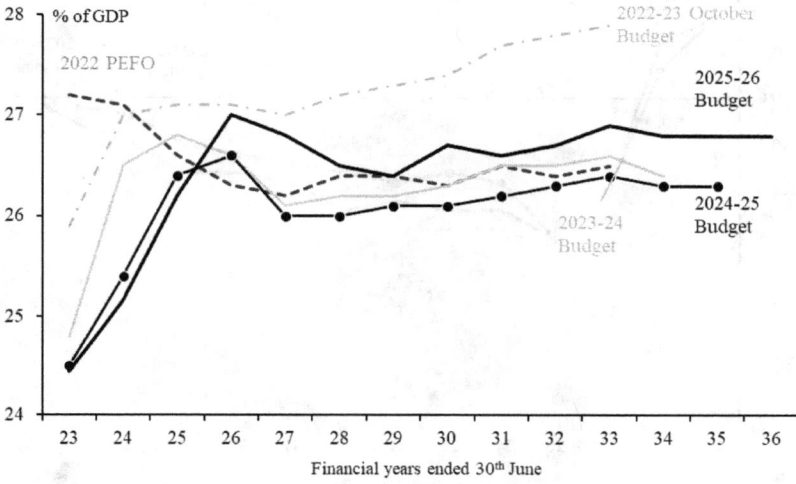

Sources: Chalmers and Gallagher (2022b, 2023, 2024 and 2025a).

Chart 2: Successive estimates of receipts

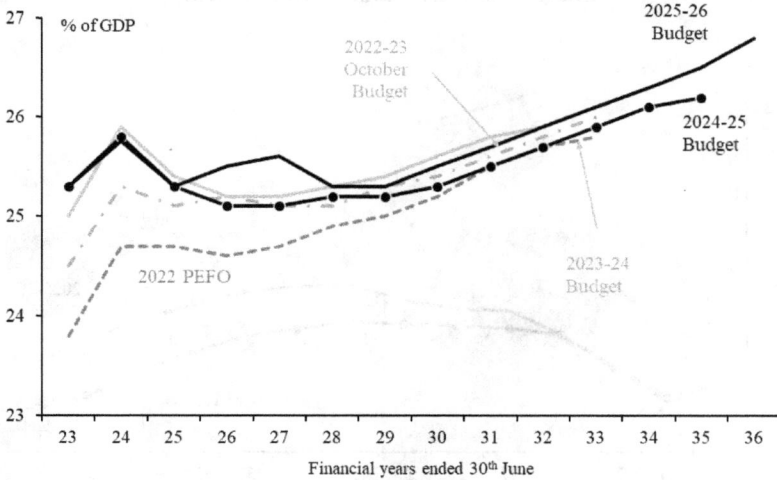

Sources: As for Chart 1.

Chart 3: Successive estimates of the 'underlying' cash balance

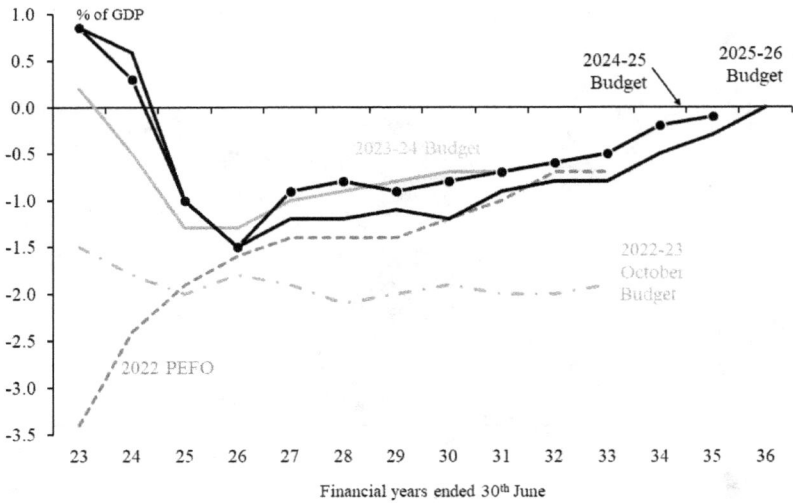

Sources: As for Chart 1.

Chart 4: Successive estimates of net debt

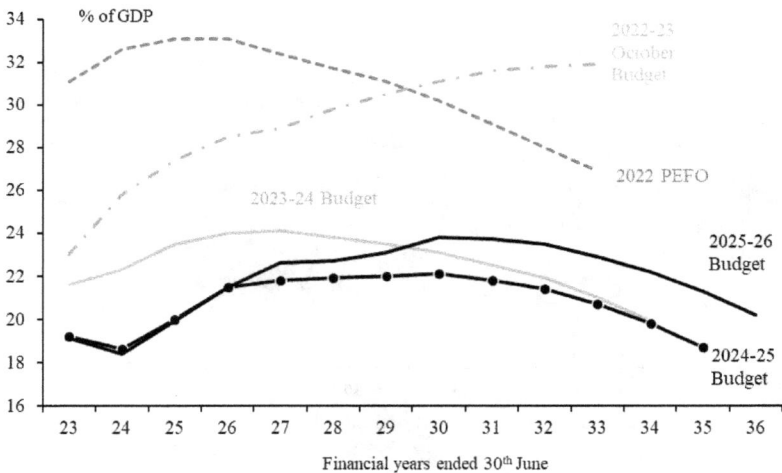

Sources: As for Chart 1.

Much the same – although on a bigger scale – occurred with the 2023-24 Budget, presented on 9 May 2023. Favourable revenue "parameter variations" totalling $131 billion over the four years to 2026-27, this time accompanied by favourable expense "parameter variations" totalling $16 billion, paid more than seven times over for "policy decisions" subtracting almost $21 billion from the "underlying" cash balance over the four years covered by that Budget, allowing it to foreshadow an "underlying" cash surplus for the 2022-23 financial year, and much smaller deficits and lower net debt for the years 2023-24 through 2026-27 than had been projected in the October 2022 Budget.

These two budgets were the basis for Treasurer Chalmers' oft-repeated claim that the Albanese Government had "banked" more than 80 per cent of the "windfall" gains delivered by higher-than-assumed commodity prices and stronger-than-forecast growth in employment (in contrast to the last four Budgets of the Howard Government in which the bulk of "windfall" gains from favourable "parameter variations" were devoted to successive rounds of income tax cuts and increases in cash "bonuses" to pensioners and others).

But things started to change in the 2024-25 Budget, delivered on 14th May 2024. The "windfall" gains from favourable "parameter variations" were smaller, at $57 billion over the five years to 2027-28 – although they were still large enough to "pay for" policy decisions which detracted a total of almost $30 billion from the projected "bottom line" over that period, and resulting in a second consecutive "underlying" cash surplus for the 2023-24 financial year (see Table 1 and Chart 5).

Table 1: The impact of "parameter variations" and "policy decisions" on successive estimates of the "underlying" cash balance, 2022-23 through 2028-29

Budget	'Parameter variations'			'Policy decisions'		
	Revenues	Expenses	Total	Revenues	Expenses	Total
2022-23	144,638	92,173	52,465	13,088	22,870	-9,782
2023-24	130,551	-15,942	146,493	22,055	42,643	-20,588
2024-25	89,858	32,485	57,373	9,264	38,968	-29,704
2025-26	27,189	-5,007	32,196	-12,525	39,824	-52,349
	----------	----------	----------	----------	----------	----------
Totals	392,236	103,709	288,527	31,882	144,305	-112,423

Note: "Parameter variations" are changes in estimates of payments or receipts resulting from changes in economic and other assumptions underpinning the forward estimates; "policy" decisions are changes in estimates of payments or receipts resulting from decisions made by the Government. Figures shown are the totals for the (four or five year) forward estimates period shown in the Budget papers for the year indicated since the 2022 Pre-Election Economic and Fiscal Outlook (for the 2022-23 Budget) or since the preceding Budget (for the other Budgets, including for the 2024-25 and 2025-26 Budgets, the immediately preceding Mid-Year Economic and Fiscal Outlooks). Sources: Chalmers and Gallagher (2022b, 2023, 2024 and 2025a), Statement No. 3.

Put differently, only 52 per cent of the "windfall" gains arising from "parameter variations'"between the 2023-24 and 2024-25 Budgets were "banked".

The 2025-26 Budget – brought down early, on 25 March 2025, after speculation that it might have been deferred until after the election had Cyclone Alfred not disrupted the Albanese Government's reported intention to call the election for 12 April – went even further in this direction.

Chart 5: The impact of 'parameter variations' and 'policy decisions' on successive estimates of the 'underlying' cash balance, 2022-23 through 2028-29

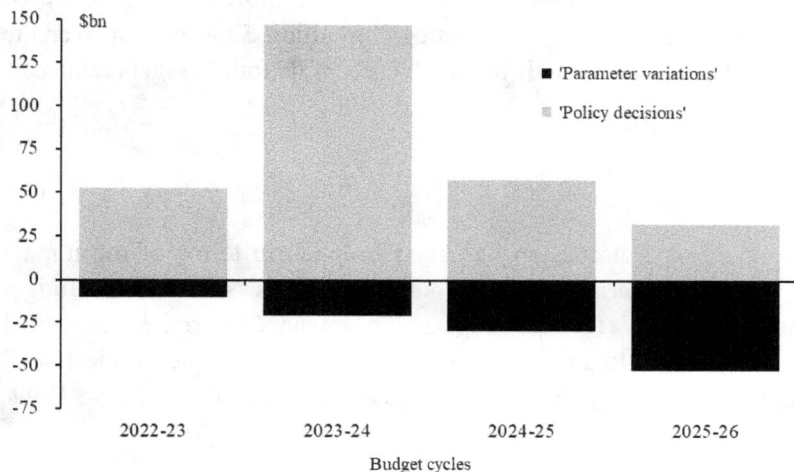

Note: As for Table 1. Sources: as for Table 1.

With commodity prices having fallen from their 2023-24 highs (albeit not as much or as quickly as Treasury's conservative assumptions), "parameter variations"   improved the forward estimates of the "underlying" cash balance for the years 2024-25 through 2028-29 by only $32 billion compared with those in the 2024-25 Budget. But policy decisions taken between those two Budgets (including the income tax cuts announced in the Budget itself) worsened the "bottom lines" for those five years by a total of $53 billion (Table 1 and Chart 5) – resulting in a deterioration in the forward estimates and medium-term projections for both the 'underlying' cash balance (Chart 3) and net debt (Chart 4).

In summary, over the four Budgets delivered during its first term in office, the Albanese Government took policy decisions which increased "underlying" payments by a cumulative total of $144 billion (net of "savings" measures) over the forward estimates periods to which each of those Budgets referred. Of this, $32 billion was "paid for" by policy decisions to increase revenues (net of decisions to cut taxes, including the income tax cuts included in the 2025-26 Budget). On net, therefore, policy decisions taken by the Albanese Government up to and including the 2025-26 Budget worsened the "bottom line" by a total of $112 billion. This was, however, more than fully covered by favourable "parameter variations" totalling $289 billion over the forward estimates periods to which each of its four Budgets related.

That's not all

The foregoing discussion has been couched in terms of the impact of "parameter variations" and "policy decisions" on what the Budget Papers have, since the first budget of the Howard Government presented by Peter Costello in August 1996, referred to as the "underlying" balance (or since the introduction of accrual accounting in the 1999-2000 Budget, the "underlying cash balance").

This concept – which since then has been the principal summary measure of the federal budget's "bottom line" – was intended to avoid the "true" condition of the budget from being flattered or obscured by the proceeds of privatisations, as had occurred under the Hawke and Keating governments (with the sales of Qantas, CSL, Aussat, and part of the Commonwealth Bank) and as the Howard Government proposed with the sale of Telstra (which it subsequently accomplished). And so the proceeds of privatisations, along with what had previously been referred to as "net advances" (loans to state governments and students, and contributions to international financial organisations) were reported and projected in budget documents under the heading "investments in financial assets for policy purposes", which when added to the "underlying" cash balance equalled what became known as the 'headline' cash balance (even though it did not attract "headlines").

For most of the period of the Howard Government, "investments in financial assets for policy purposes" was a positive number – reflecting (for the most part) the sale in three tranches of Telstra – so that the "headline" cash balance was more favourable (ie a smaller deficit or a larger surplus) than the "underlying" cash balance.

But this turned around under the Rudd and Gillard governments, as a result of their strategy of funding the construction of the National Broadband Network (NBN) not by grants from the Department of Communications (which would have been classified in the Budget Papers as "payments") but rather through subscribing equity and making loans to NBN Co (which the Budget Papers classified as "investments" in financial assets for policy purposes) and which, therefore, contributed to what had become 'headline' cash deficits, but not to the "underlying" cash deficits which were the focus of attention. Similarly, decisions to subscribe equity or make loans to NBN Co were not counted as "policy decisions" in the dissections of movements in estimates of the "underlying" cash balance from one budget to the next, presented in the Budget and MYEFO papers.

This was approach was taken to a new level by the Turnbull and Morrison governments, which in addition to continuing to fund the construction of the NBN in this way, did so for a slew of other projects, including Snowy 2.0, WestConnex, Barnaby Joyce's "Northern Australia Infrastructure Facility" and the "Structured Finance Support Fund". "Investments in financial assets for policy purposes" averaged over $10 billion per annum under the Abbott, Turnbull and Morrison governments, compared with just under $6 billion per annum under the Rudd and Gillard governments (Chart 6).

But this category of what has come to be called "off-budget spending" (although it is not really "off-budget") has mushroomed under the Albanese Government – not so much in its first two full years in office, when it averaged just under $5 billion per annum, but in 2024-25 and (as forecast) for the following four years, during which it was forecast (in the 2025-26 Budget) to average almost $12 billion per annum (Chart 6).

This includes, in particular, in addition to the forgiveness of student loans under the HECS and HELP schemes, loans and investments through the Clean Energy Finance Corporation (averaging $4.2 billion per annum over the five years to 2028-29), funding for the National Reconstruction Finance Corporation, one of the vehicles through which subsidies under the Future Made in Australia program will be dispensed ($2.4 billion per annum over the five years to 2028-29),

Housing Australia, through which the Government's social housing construction program is to be funded ($2.5 billion per annum), and the opaque "net other" category, which includes "commercial-in-confidence" items ($2.6 billion per annum over the five years to 2028-29).

Chart 6: Investments in financial assets for policy purposes (aka 'off-budget spending')

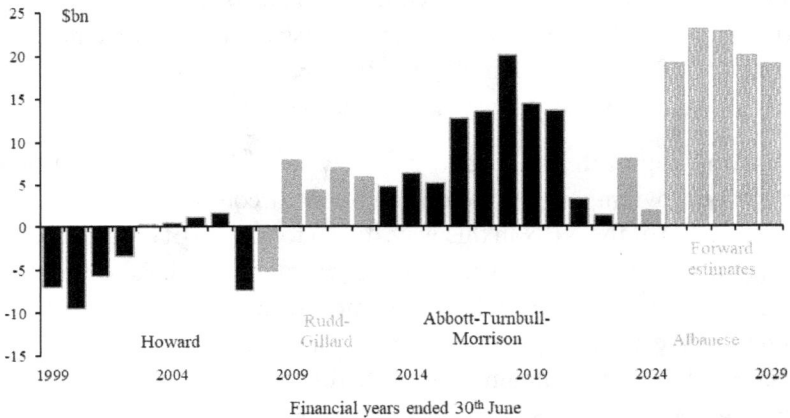

Source: Chalmers and Gallagher (2025a), Statement No 10

As a result, the gap between the "underlying" cash deficit (which has traditionally been the focus of scrutiny of Federal budgets) and the "headline" deficit has widened considerably on the Albanese Government's watch.

In this context, it's important to remember that it is the "headline" deficit (or surplus) which is the principal driver of changes in net debt, not the "underlying" deficit (or surplus). If the "underlying" cash balance is in deficit, then those "investments in financial assets for policy purposes" have to be funded by additional debt. If the "underlying" cash balance is in surplus, the need to finance those "investments in financial assets for policy purposes" necessarily means that less of that surplus is available for paying down debt.

An additional concern is that spending classified as "investments in financial assets for policy purposes" has typically been subject to far less scrutiny than spending included in 'underlying' payments. As noted earlier, it isn't included in the tables in Budget and MYEFO papers showing the sources of changes in the condition of the budget from one set of forward estimates to the next – which means that the totals for spending 'policy decisions' included in the Budget and MYEFO papers (referred to in the previous section) are under-statements.

Moreover, the Treasury does not publish medium-term "projections" for the "headline" balance, for the six years beyond the end of the four-year Forward Estimates period in each Budget, as it does for "underlying" payments, receipts, the "underlying" cash balance and net debt.

That's despite the fact that it would need to have a good idea of the trajectory of the "headline" cash balance in order to make the projections of net debt which it does publish. And the widening gap between the medium-term projections for net debt published in the 2025-26 Budget Papers compared with those published a year earlier (Chart 4 above) contrasted with the narrowing gap between the medium term projections for the "underlying" cash balance, suggests (at least at face value) that the unpublished projections for "net investments in financial assets for policy purposes" show significant increases beyond the end of the Forward Estimates period in 2028-29.

There's more to a final judgement than just the matter of surpluses and deficits

In evaluating the economic management record of the Albanese Government, it is important to look beyond the arithmetic of the major budgetary aggregates to consider the "quality" of the decisions it made both with respect to taxation and government spending, and economic policy more broadly.

The major economic policy challenge confronting the Albanese Government during its first term of office was that of inflation – or, as it was more commonly portrayed (including by the government itself) the "cost of living crisis". Inflation (as measured by the consumer price index) averaged 4.1 per cent per annum under the Albanese Government (up to the December quarter of 2024, the latest available at the time of writing) – the highest under any government since the Hawke-Keating governments' average of 5.3 per cent. Overwhelmingly, that inflation was the result of factors beyond the Albanese Government's control – in particular, the fact that the Reserve Bank left interest rates "too low for too long" (as did every other central bank in the developed world, but the RBA was the second-last central bank in the developed world to start raising interest rates from the record lows instituted during the pandemic), the effects of COVID-related disruptions to global supply chains, and the surge in energy and some food prices which followed Russia's invasion of Ukraine in February 2022.

The Albanese Government can claim some credit for the fact that, after peaking at 7.8 per cent at the end of 2022, "headline" inflation has since fallen to within the Reserve Bank's 2-3 per cent target band, and "underlying" inflation (to which the RBA attaches much greater importance) is likely to have done so during the first half of 2025, allowing the RBA to begin unwinding the series of interest rate hikes it instituted between May 2022 and November 2023, *without* inducing a recession, and *without* a large increase in unemployment – something which has not previously been accomplished in Australia, and something which eluded most of Australia's developed-economy peers during the recent bout of inflation. Of course, most of the credit for that achievement rests with the Reserve Bank – which took a calculated risk not to raise its cash rate by as much as its peers. But the Albanese Government can claim some credit for running budget surpluses in its first two financial years (in marked contrast to, in particular, the United States), and for restructuring the "Stage 3" tax cuts in order to provide some "cost of living relief" to households who would otherwise have "missed out", at zero budgetary cost.

It is a valid criticism that some of the Albanese Government's other "cost of living relief" measures (in particular the electricity bill rebates) were poorly targeted; and there is some truth in the observations by (among others) the Reserve Bank that continued strength in spending by (state and territory as well as the federal) governments to some extent complicated the RBA's efforts to bring aggregate demand into line with aggregate supply through restrictive monetary policy settings (see eg Reserve Bank of Australia 2024: 4, 44 and 50).

Against that, government spending also helped prevent real GDP from contracting in the first three quarters of 2024 (which would have been widely depicted as a "recession") and unemployment from rising by more than it did.

And at least some of the additional spending to which the Albanese Government committed is amply justified, including to ensure the provision of services (such as those to veterans) which had been under-funded by the previous Coalition Government, implementing the recommendations of the Royal Commissions into aged and disability care, increasing the provision of social and affordable housing, and improving access to affordable childcare.

But there were also spending decisions that seem very hard to justify.

Foremost among those is the Albanese Government's ongoing commitment to, and extension of, what this author has called, "Worst Public Policy Decision of the 21st Century Thus Far" – namely, the changes to the principles governing the distribution of revenue from the GST to the states and territories at the behest of Western Australia (Australia's richest state) (Commonwealth Grants Commission 2021, Eslake 2024).

These changes – initially introduced by the Morrison Government (with the support of the then Labor Opposition) in 2018 but maintained and extended by the Albanese Government in November 2023 (Chalmers 2023) – are now expected to cost the Federal Budget $57 billion over eleven years (Chalmers and Gallagher 2025b: 121-123), compared with the original estimate of $9 billion over eight years. That's the "largest blow-out" in the cost of any single "policy decision", ever, with the possible exception of the NDIS.

But whereas the Albanese Government did take steps to rein in the rate of growth in spending on the NDIS – from an average of 41 per cent per annum over the last four years of the Coalition Government to a projected 7 per cent per annum over the four years to 2028-29 – it did absolutely nothing to halt, let alone reverse the extraordinary blow-out in what is the largest single spending program in the Federal Budget. How a Labor Government can reconcile its acquiescence in this extraordinarily bad piece of public policy with its professed commitments to equity and "fiscal prudence" is surely beyond comprehension.

Another major spending decision of dubious merit is the Prime Minister's signature *Future Made in Australia* program (FMIA). This program, announced in the 2024-25 Budget, entails spending of $22.7 billion over ten years to "maximis[e] the economic and industrial benefits of the net zero transformation and secur[e] Australia's place in a changing global economic and strategic landscape" (Chalmers and Gallagher 2024: 14-21).

While a credible rationale can be mounted for the "net zero" component of FMIA (on the grounds that the investment required to ensure that Australia meets its commitments under the Paris Climate Accords won't occur within the required time horizon without at least some form of government involvement and support), the same cannot be said of the much larger "economic security" component. That was supposedly modelled on the Biden Administration's misnamed *Inflation Reduction Act*, and similar "industrial policy" programs in other countries, authorizing massive subsidies and tax breaks for the manufacturing of ostensibly "strategic" products such as solar panels and lithium batteries. The Albanese Government's principal justification for emulating such programs in Australia has been that "other countries are doing it" – even though, unlike most of those other countries, Australia has very little if any comparative advantage in these areas. As the International Monetary Fund has warned, "History shows that industrial policy is prone to policy mistakes", even in "countries with strong institutions", noting that "subsidies may be diverted to politically connected sectors instead of being solely driven by social returns" (IMF 2024: xii and 27-28). The fact that most of the subsidies thus far announced under the "economic security" stream of FMIA are for projects in Western Australia, Queensland and the Hunter Valley underscores the pertinence in Australia of the IMF's concerns.

The elephant in the budgetary living-room

One very big issue which the Albanese Government did not confront, and which it has shown no indication of any desire to confront in its second term, should it get one, is how all the additional spending to which it has committed over the medium term should be paid for. And to be fair, nor has the Coalition in any serious or credible fashion.

It has been evident since the last Budget of the previous Coalition Government that Federal Government spending was set to be some 1½-2 percentage points of GDP higher, on average, during the 2020s and into the 2030s, than it had been on average between the end of the Whitlam years and the onset of COVID-19. The medium-term projections in the 2025-26 Budget suggest that "underlying" payments will average 26.6 per cent of GDP over the ten years to 2035-36 (Chalmers and Gallagher 2025a: 73). That's only 0.1 percentage point of GDP above the projection for the ten years ended 2032-33 in the last Budget of the previous Coalition Government (Frydenberg and Birmingham 2022: 84). Both figures are well above the average of 24.8 per cent for the years 1975-76 through 2019-20 (Chart 7).

Chart 7: 'Underlying' payments and receipts as a percentage of GDP

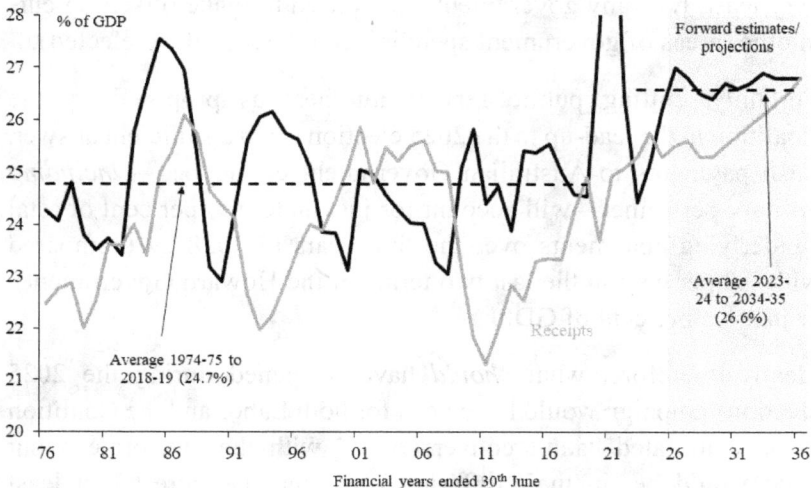

Note: "underlying" payments exclude "investments in financial assets for policy purposes". *Source:* Chalmers and Gallagher (2025a), Statement No. 10.

This sustained increase in Federal Government spending as a proportion of GDP reflects three principal drivers:

- first, the public very clearly wants more spending on health, aged and disability care (unsurprisingly, given that the proportion of the population who are in their 'senior years', and/or living with disability, is rising steadily) and, it would seem, child care;

- second, there is a bi-partisan consensus that, whether the public wants it or not, there will have to be more spending on defence; and

- third, as an unavoidable result of the $851 billion increase in gross debt since the onset of the global financial crisis, and the prospective $940 billion further increase in gross debt over the next decade, there will be (a lot) more spending on interest payments.

And with the exception of some of the bad spending decisions noted earlier – in particular, the "WA GST deal" and the "economic security" component of *Future Made in Australia* – it is difficult to see how other areas of government spending could be cut by enough to offset the increases occurring in the three areas mentioned above (or, at the very least, how any government which tried to make offsetting cuts in other areas of government spending could get itself re-elected).

Certainly, cutting public service numbers as proposed by the Coalition in the lead-up to the 2025 election is not a sufficient answer. Cash payments to Australian Government employees – *including* military personnel – will account for just under 6½ per cent of total "underlying" payments over the five years to 2028-29 (compared with 7.0 per cent in the last two terms of the Howard Government), or just 1.6 per cent of GDP.

Ideally, therefore, what *should* have happened during the 2025 election campaign would have been for both Labor and the Coalition to have initiated "adult conversations" with the electorate about what would be, in their differing opinions, the fairest and least economically damaging ways of raising (say) an additional 1-1½ percentage point of GDP in revenue over the next decade. Because, without some agreement as to how to achieve that, the "default options" are some combination of on-going budget deficits, and increased revenue-raising through "bracket creep", which as Ken Henry has noted, would amount to an "intergenerational tragedy … punishing the young".

Again, ideally, such an "adult conversation" would be led by an incumbent first-term government, seeking election to a second term, as the Howard Government did when seeking a mandate to introduce a GST at the 1998 election. But it wasn't. As noted in the introduction to this chapter, Australian political history dictates that it's far less likely that this challenge would be taken up by an Opposition. And it wasn't.

That represents a tragedy whose consequences will come home to roost – albeit gradually rather than suddenly – over the remainder of this decade.

References

Chalmers, J., (2023), *Extension of 'No Worse Off' deal to help fund essential services*, Canberra: Commonwealth of Australia .6 December

Chalmers, J., and Gallagher, K., (2022a), *Labor's Plan for a Better Future: Better Budget, Better Economy*, Canberra: Commonwealth of Australia. May

_____ (2022b), *Budget Strategy and Outlook - Budget Paper No. 1*, Canberra: Commonwealth of Australia 25 October.

_____ (2023), *Budget Strategy and Outlook - Budget Paper No. 1*, Canberra: Commonwealth of Australia 9 May.

_____ (2024), *Budget Strategy and Outlook - Budget Paper No. 1*, Canberra: Commonwealth of Australia 14 May.

_____ (2025a), *Budget Strategy and Outlook - Budget Paper No. 1*, Canberra: Commonwealth of Australia 25 March.

_____ (2025b), *Budget Paper No. 3: Federal Financial Relations*, Canberra: Commonwealth of Australia 25 March.

Commonwealth Grants Commission (2021), *New Arrangements for distributing GST*, Occasional Paper 4, Canberra: Commonwealth of Australia, 1 September.

Eslake, S., (2024), *Distribution of GST Revenue: the Worst Public Policy Decision of the 21st Century to date*, Hobart, 4 February

Frydenberg, J., and Birmingham, S., (2022), *Budget Strategy and Outlook - Budget Paper No. 1*, Canberra: Commonwealth of Australia, 29 March

Henry, K., (2025), *Keynote Address to the Community Tax Summit*, Percapita, Melbourne, 21 February

International Monetary Fund, (2024), *Fiscal Monitor: Fiscal Policy in the Great Election Year*, Washington DC, 17 April

Parliamentary Budget Office, (2022), *2022 Election Commitments Report: Australian Labor Party*, Canberra: Commonwealth Parliament, 14 July

Reserve Bank of Australia, (2024), *Statement on Monetary Policy*, Sydney: RBA, 6 August

10

Perverse Productivity Policies: Rhetoric vs Reality

Gary Banks

Introduction

In a major speech on the eve of the 2022 election, Anthony Albanese (2022) said:

> Australia must lift the country's productivity, for as the economist Paul Krugman once famously said, 'productivity isn't everything, but in the long run it is almost everything'. ... The economic reforms I am taking to this election will grow the national income and lift productivity. ... What people need from our nation's leaders is what only economic reform and increased productivity can deliver.

One cannot fault these sentiments. Productivity growth is the mainspring of rising living standards. It accounted for over three-quarters of the increase in real per capita incomes in Australia from the middle of last century. And the lack of it has contributed to average per capita incomes declining in recent years, an unusual development at variance with the experience of most OECD countries. As the Reserve Bank has shown, Australia's weak productivity performance has also detracted from the ability to deal with fiscal imbalance, public debt and, not least, price inflation and its impact on "the cost of living" (Plumb 2025).

Policy actions to promote sustained productivity growth therefore have become more important than ever. The problem – and the main theme of this chapter – is that the Albanese Government's reform rhetoric has not been matched by its policy conduct.

That is hardly a novel phenomenon; nor has it been confined to one side of politics. My valedictory "to do list" on leaving the Productivity Commission over a decade ago is testimony to that (Banks 2012). Expectations of the Albanese Government were accordingly never high.

Nevertheless, during its first three years, the Albanese Government managed to surprise even its critics by extending the pre-existing record of poor performance in two key respects:

- *First*, by not just neglecting reforms that would support productivity growth, but taking actions that will *undermine* it.
- *Second*, by repeatedly presenting its anti-productivity initiatives as *solutions* to the country's productivity problem.

Productivity's government connections

Economic theory tells us that productivity growth is in principle limited only by technology and, ultimately, human ingenuity and capability. However, a country's actual productivity performance – where it stands relative to the "frontier" – is conditioned by policy settings and institutional arrangements that influence how organisations make use of technology and resources to create value.

In broad terms, government interventions that promote cost-conscious and innovative behaviour; that facilitate responsiveness to market forces; that enhance access to human capital and efficient infrastructure – and that do not inhibit labour and capital moving to more productive uses – can be labelled "pro-productivity". Those having the opposite effects are "*anti*-productivity".

Many of the latter involve regulations: especially those that distort production decisions, raise risks, stifle innovation or involve excessive costs. Such influences also serve to inhibit private investment, which through "capital deepening" and technology transfer constitutes a key mechanism for productivity improvement, one that has been subdued in recent years.

During what has become known as the "reform era" – roughly, the two decades from 1985 -- governments of both persuasions made a determined effort to reduce regulatory burdens on economic activity. Some of that momentum continued into this century, even if progress slowed. However, "reforms" by the Albanese Government have brought new regulatory impediments and restored others, along with subsidies that divert resources to less productive uses. With external pressures mounting, the undermining of the competitiveness and resilience of Australia's economy could not have come at a worse time.

Among the various anti-productivity policies in reformist garb, those for energy and industrial relations stand out.

A self-inflicted energy crisis

In the case of *energy*, policy failings have been bipartisan in origin. Ambitious targets have been adopted along with an array of opaque interventions, without a proper understanding of their likely cost or even their feasibility.

Contributing to governments' preference for measures that lack transparency is an evident reluctance to be candid with the public about (a) the inevitably high cost of reducing "greenhouse" emissions in Australia, given the low-cost-fossil-fuel foundations of our economy, and (b) the negligible potential impact on global emissions of any measures we do take.

The Coalition Government's ambivalent embrace of "Net Zero" in October 2021 raised the stakes considerably, enabling an incoming Albanese Government to up the ante further and greatly increase the costs, with the Greens and Teals urging them to go even harder.

The new Albanese Government soon moved to embed Net Zero in

legislation, along with a 2030 interim emissions target. It then set its sights on achieving 82 per cent of national electricity capacity from wind and solar by that same year. This new target was originally a projection based on modelling by a consultancy called RepuTex, which also projected the ill-fated $275 reduction in electricity prices that Labor took to the 2022 election (Thomas 2023).

This placed Australia in a virtually unique position internationally. No other government signing up to Net Zero also committed exclusively to a "wind and solar with storage" future for electricity. Most have domestic hydro or nuclear or both, as well as interconnections to other countries' energy grids, which (like our own interstate energy market currently) may also be firmed by coal or gas.

It is now generally accepted, despite ministerial assurances, that the Government's 2030 renewables target is not feasible and probably never was. This reflects the scale of the build, as graphically detailed by Minister Bowen himself in a much-cited press interview, but also the related resource constraints, engineering challenges and "social licence" issues. Securing the net zero emissions target is also increasingly in doubt, both here and internationally (Hilton et al 2024; EIC 2025).

Arguably the more important issue at this point is not whether these targets can or will be met, but the likely impacts on our economy of what the Albanese Government is seeking to achieve and how it has been going about it. In other words, a more fundamental concern is whether the targets *should* be met. The withdrawal of the United States from the Paris Agreement only heightens the need for a reappraisal.

Net Zero means lower (not higher) productivity

That the Albanese Government has pitched its *Powering Australia Plan* and so-called *Rewiring the Nation* policy as forces for productivity improvement is hard to square with reality.

Productivity improvements can usefully be thought of (following Harberger 1998) as reductions in the real costs of production; or fewer inputs being needed to produce the same output. That this could be achieved by requiring no net increase in greenhouse gases is fanciful, at least with current technologies whether or not allowance is made for climate externalities. That the vaunted rise in renewables' market share has depended on substantial and rising government assistance – estimated to have been equivalent to over $16 billion last year (Moran 2025) – is already revealing about the relative costs.

In a nutshell, a "wind and solar with storage" future would require more capital to produce less reliable electricity – or very much more capital to achieve anything like comparable reliability - the antithesis of a pro-productivity outcome. This has as much to do with engineering and physics as economics.

The extra capital includes not only extensive wind and solar assets, and massive new distribution networks for these nationally (not merely "rewiring" as implied), but also the farmland and natural habitat that they displace. Visual amenity is also degraded, as anyone driving on the Hume near Wodonga in Victoria can attest. Distribution costs rise with higher penetration of solar and wind as less 'convenient' sites are utilized.

In addition, there would need to be sufficient storage in the system to meet demand "when the wind don't blow and the sun don't shine". That means potentially satisfying all the demand there is. If reliant on batteries for this, the scale and cost would be prohibitively large (Menton 2022).

Additional costs and complexities that seldom get a mention relate to the machinery needed to achieve grid stability with solar and wind that synchronous coal and gas generators deliver automatically. The larger the presence of asynchronous solar and wind generation, the more challenging and costly that stabilizing function becomes. Having lower inertia, such a system is more prone to failure when "adverse events" occur, as in the Spain-Portugal blackout of April 2025.

In terms of the famous policy "trilemma", lower emissions as currently pursued are putting both affordability and reliability at risk. Prices have been trending upwards and regulatory bodies are warning of looming power failures, with the AEMC stating that "security risks are emerging faster than expected" (Jordan 2025; AEMO 2025).

In 2024, AEMO was obliged to intervene in the market 1800 times, compared to 321 in 2020 and just six in 2016 (Westerman 2025).

The Energy Minister has blamed outages on the unreliability of remaining coal generation plants. However, as would be known, the "deep maintenance" that such plants require has been rendered uneconomic by subsidised renewables, requiring subsidies in turn.

This increasingly fraught situation has been exacerbated by the ban on emissions-free nuclear energy, despite this country's abundant uranium reserves, and regulatory restrictions on the exploitation of our (also abundant) natural gas resources, with gas even excluded from the Capacity Investment Scheme. Gas is ideal for "peaking" purposes and the 'firming' that intermittent renewables require (while also having baseload capability) and emissions-free nuclear is ideal for baseload, with both providing the synchronicity that AC systems depend on. Instead, the Albanese Government only recently conceded a case for gas in the "transition", having mainly pinned its hopes on "green hydrogen" and batteries, notwithstanding lack of evidence that they could do the job.

With the Coalition taking a pro-nuclear policy to the election, a strident debate about its costs relative to an "all renewables" system took centre stage. Assessments by experts (and others) varied greatly, depending on which costs were included, how they were calculated and over what time frames. Naturally, each side cited numbers favourable to its position.

What is clear is that, regardless of the path followed, the pursuit of "Net Zero" will be a costly exercise for our country, with negligible benefits (Hilton et al 2024).

Labour market rigidities restored

Industrial relations regulation has long had "form" as an impediment to productivity at the enterprise level. One might say that an anti-productivity bias was built into the system from its inception, given the centralised, highly prescriptive approach it embodied, and its deeply adversarial nature.

It was not until the Hawke/Keating/Kelty era that the hitherto novel concept of enterprise bargaining began to offer scope for agreements that responded to circumstances "on the ground". Positive results soon followed. As the eminent late Treasury Secretary Ted Evans once observed "the 90s growth in output, in productivity and in employment … owed much to labour market reform" (Evans 2001).

Since then, it has been a case of one step forward, one (or two) steps back; with restrictions falling under Howard, rising in the Rudd-Gillard years and in a holding pattern under the Coalition.

Once again, that changed dramatically with the arrival of the Albanese Government. In short order, successive waves of industrial relations regulation emerged, much of it taking business by surprise. Justified as "getting wages moving" or achieving greater "job security" or "equality", the loss of flexibility entailed in "closing loopholes" reduced firm productivity and competitiveness.

Two reports from the Productivity Commission (PC) underlined the difficulties (PC 2022 2023). To say they displeased the Albanese Government and the ACTU would be an understatement, the latter calling on the former to abolish the organisation. Dismissing the Productivity Commission's recommendations as "scorched earth", the Treasurer ordered his department to conduct reviews of the organisation's "culture" and performance. The former review, by a consultant specialising in the field, contained little to support its many adverse recommendations (De Silva 2023); the latter resulted in a first "Ministerial Statement of Expectations" for the independent organisation (Banks 2024).

The Treasurer's "scorched earth" quip is hard to reconcile with the content of the Productivity Commission's reports themselves, which for the most part would have restored pro-productivity flexibilities consistent with the original Hawke/Keating/Kelty reforms.

For example, with misuse of the "better off overall test" enabling a mutually agreed deal to be blocked by the AIRC if there was potential for even a single "loser", the Commission proposed a pragmatic and fair way of securing workplace agreements (and award amendments) when shown to yield net benefits to an enterprise's workforce as a whole. The report also sensibly sought to amend regulations that, as interpreted by the AIRC, could effectively give unions veto power over productivity-enhancing innovations in the workplace. And it made some useful governance suggestions to improve the functioning of the AIRC itself (PC 2023).

Further anti-productivity provisions identified by the Productivity Commission, included the potential for "industry" deals to be forced on individual firms that were not party to them, and restrictions placed on more "flexible" (but non-unionised) segments of the labour market, such as casuals and the gig economy.

Then there is the "work from home" phenomenon. Commencing as an expedient during the pandemic, the push by unions for it to become a codified "right", combined with new federal regulations constraining managerial contact with staff (the "right to disconnect") obviously pose a significant threat to productivity in both the private and public sectors.

In the lead-up to the election, the draft report of an "independent review" commissioned by the Employment Minister and staffed by his department, was cited as endorsing its "Secure jobs, better pay" legislation (SJBPR 2025). In their report, the two academic reviewers stated that their ability to make useful findings was hampered by participants' "adversarial attitudes" and a lack of reliable data. Their draft findings are accordingly heavily qualified, and they contain little mention of productivity or competitiveness.

In short, while the Albanese Government has labelled its changes to the industrial relations landscape "reforms", few could be said to meet the pro-productivity criteria indicated above. On the contrary, the majority would reduce the ability of enterprises to be adaptable and innovative, while weakening their competitiveness.

Ignoring the elephants in the reform room

For many years, the self-imposed competitive disadvantage of our industrial relations system was partly offset by the advantage of an abundant supply of low-cost energy. Thanks to the policies just described, that is no longer the case.

Yet there has been no discernible recognition of the harm being done. On the contrary, the Treasurer's "five pillars" productivity agenda, which aligns with the headline themes in the Productivity Commission's latest five-yearly report (PC 2023) omits any reference to workplace regulation and essentially posits further subsidized investment in renewables as the sole route to "Net Zero".

Moreover, the Albanese Government has not responded to the many recommendations in the report itself, other than to reject those not "aligned" with its thinking on industrial relations and energy. What's more, with the ink hardly dry on its extensive report, the Treasurer tasked the Commission with conducting inquiries in the same five areas on which it had just reported (Chalmers 2024b).

In an address to the Australian Business Economists, Chalmers opined that the repeat inquiries would be "more targeted, tangible and timely" (Chalmers 2024a). However, to the extent that this can be achieved in broad-brush reviews, the existing report – with its "actionable roadmap" – did remarkably well. Had the Treasurer really wanted 'more targeted and tangible' reporting this time round, he could have commissioned conventional inquiries into specific sectors or issues (like the PC's in-depth report on childcare).

Government achievements

The Treasurer (Chalmers 2024b) remarked in a press release that the Albanese Government had "already progressed significant reforms":

> This agenda includes our $900 million National Productivity Fund to drive competition through states and territories, the biggest reform to our merger system in 50 years, abolishing nearly 500 nuisance tariffs, boosting competition through our

financial system, reforming skills and education, establishing a comprehensive review of R&D, reforming the delivery of aged care, modernising our energy grid and more.

Among the items with stronger claims to being "significant reforms":

- The abolition of 500 "nuisance" tariffs is a bolder initiative than   previous Governments were prepared to contemplate, given the associated loss of revenue. However, while savings in administrative costs are worth having, any allocative or dynamic gains would be very small relative to lowering those tariffs with a protective effect, including those imposed under our increasingly protectionist anti-dumping regime (PC 2016);
- Whether the new mergers law turns out to be a plus for competition and productivity growth will largely depend on how it is administered. The regime is considerably more complex than the one it replaces and will capture many more transactions, with greater uncertainty initially as to outcomes (Downes 2025). Any chilling effect on potentially efficient mergers would be greater if static concentration metrics took precedence over less measurable market dynamics;
- The National Productivity Fund's achievements will depend on what reforms $900 million can "buy" from the states and territories. Much larger "Competition Payments" under the wide-ranging National Competition Policy in the 1990s were only partially successful. And considerable effort was still needed within each jurisdiction to bring the public along. The limited information available to the PC for its modelling of the potential gains, suggests that there is still a way to go to secure agreement on anything tangible, let alone get it implemented (PC 2024a). That said, this stream of work is at least heading in the right direction;
- Then there is the "pro-competition" initiative announced in the Budget to render legally unenforceable "non-compete" clauses for employees earning up to $175,000. This involves trading off potential costs arising from disincentives for training and intangible capital formation, against potential benefits from better job matching and business creation. Modelling by the PC and e61Institute, drawing on US studies, projected productivity gains based on estimated wage increases. (PC 2024, Buckley *et al* 2024) These remain somewhat speculative, however, and there is considerable potential for unintended consequences.

As an aside, it is notable that these four measures have all faced little resistance from the union movement.

Anti-development approval processes

Apart from restrictive workplace regulation and rising energy costs, the most cited impediments to firm productivity are government approval processes for new or expanded resource projects under environmental and heritage laws. These have always had potential to impede productive investment, with a PC study finding "regulatory processes in the resources sector remain unduly complex, duplicated, lengthy and uncertain *and may be becoming more so*" (PC 2020: 2).

This prediction was borne out during the Albanese Government's first term. In several cases, projects that had been cleared at state level, including under Labor Governments, faced the prospect of further protracted delay or rejection at the federal level.

Increasingly, decision-making has been exercised in an untransparent, even secretive, manner. This has served as a magnet for activist organisations with anti-development agendas, such as the Environment Defenders Office (EDO), which the Albanese Government is now funding. "Lawfare" based on dubious claims has become rife.

Unfortunately, given their increasing importance, gas projects have been more afflicted than most. For example, gaining approval to extend the term of Woodside's existing North-West Shelf project took over six years at the State level before facing further delays (and possible rejection) at the Federal level. And a sole indigenous objector, with assistance from EDO, has held up a new $16 billion gas project in Western Australia based on alleged "whale dreaming" mythology.

Potentially more far-reaching has been the attempt to 'reform' the *Environment Protection and Bio-diversity Conservation (EPBC) Act* to assign greater priority to environmental considerations, with the goal of conserving 30 per cent of Australia's total land mass. The so-called Nature Positive Plan, with a new federal Environment Protection Agency to administer it, was essentially developed behind closed doors, following a review commissioned by the previous government. As the legislation stood prior to it being put on hold until after the election, it was set to heighten further the risk of major projects being rejected without a sound rationale or adequate transparency.

Unwarranted regulatory obstacles to new projects result not only in the loss of productive activities and the associated gains in national income; they can have a chilling or diversionary effect on investment generally, including from offshore. As the saying goes, "capital is a coward": all else being the same, it will go where the risks, including regulatory risks, are lowest. Australia is looking less well placed in this respect than it was three years ago.

Pumped up public provision: poor for productivity

A key strand of what the Treasurer called the Albanese Government's "big, broad and ambitious" productivity agenda is to further promote the scale and reach of the burgeoning "care and support economy".

The term covers a range of government-funded services that provide assistance to individuals and families over the life cycle, such as childcare, healthcare, aged care and disability services. In addition to their social role, some of these programs can yield economic benefits by enabling greater participation and/or improved performance in work. Whether these eventuate, however, depends on how well the programs are designed and delivered.

Employment in the care economy and non-market sector more generally has risen sharply, accounting for over three-quarters of the million jobs created last year. While, as the Treasurer has observed, many of these jobs were formally situated in the private/not-for-profit sector, they are underwritten by government programs and paid for out of taxation.

Publicly funded services of this kind tend to have lower measured productivity than other economic activities, as well as slower productivity growth. That reflects not only their greater labour intensity, but also weaker incentives to use resources in cost-effective ways when, as Milton Friedman famously put it, "spending other people's money on other people".

While public spending and jobs surged, labour productivity in the care economy has been stagnant for a decade. Moreover, during the past three years, productivity in the non-market sector as a whole declined to its lowest level this century.

Together with the fact that, in times of relatively full employment, resources will have been drawn from other activities, including those with higher measured productivity, the non-market economy played a key role in Australia's overall productivity slump. It is estimated to have subtracted 0.2 to 0.3 percentage points from annual labour productivity growth in the past three years (PC 2023; Maltman and Rankin 2024; Plumb 2025).

While the need to achieve efficiencies in service provision has been recognised by the Albanese Government, so far there has been little attempt to do so. Indeed, for some services further inefficiencies are being introduced.

A looming example is Albanese's "signature policy", to provide universal childcare at a minimal daily rate regardless of parental income or work status. The PC found in its public inquiry that this would increase outlays by over $8 billion annually, but would make little difference to work participation and almost none to productivity (PC 2024b).

Meanwhile, the Government declared before the election that it will not be addressing what is generally seen as the main driver of the NDIS blow-out; namely eligibility that extends well beyond the life-long profound disabilities it was originally designed for.

"White elephant" parade

At his 2022 campaign launch, Albanese prioritised infrastructure investment as a key mechanism to "boost productivity and create jobs". The provision of new infrastructure can indeed yield significant productivity benefits, by simultaneously reducing real production costs across a range of industries and sectors. Any gains, however, will greatly depend on the type of infrastructure, its demand-side benefits versus its cost, and how well it is managed.

Australian governments have hardly distinguished themselves against such tests and the Albanese Government has been no exception (Banks 2023a).

Within the federal jurisdiction – and energy aside – the National Broadband Network (NBN) is undoubtedly the stand-out example of how *not* to go about infrastructure investment. Described by finance experts as "an economic and productivity albatross around the necks of Australians for generations to come" (Burshtein and Swan 2025), it has turned a $30 billion Government "investment" into a $36 billion loss. The Albanese Government, although late to the party, came up with a further $3 billion for upgrades and extensions that appear to have added to the net losses.

The Albanese Government has also contributed to a variety of state infrastructure projects, some of which are plainly of little merit. Perhaps the worst example is Victoria's Suburban Rail Loop which, like the NBN, was not preceded by a proper business case, let alone cost-benefit analysis, and looks set to cost four times the original "guesstimate". It was nevertheless granted $2.2 billion by the Albanese Government in the lead-up to the last state election. Infrastructure Australia has cautioned against further contributions being made, but this has not been ruled out (Infrastructure Australia 2025).

Public infrastructure spending that fails a cost-benefit test not only does nothing for productivity in its own right, it crowds out projects that could have yielded net benefits to society. The fact that such infrastructure is classified as "off budget" does not in itself lessen the fiscal burden.

The taxation quid pro quo

That much of the dramatic rise in federal government spending over the past three years – up from 24.5 to 27 per cent of GDP, the highest outside crisis years – has done little for productivity is one thing. That it must ultimately require a rise in tax burdens on productive activity is another.

Australia's tax system has notable deficiencies from a productivity perspective. Foremost among these is its reliance on taxing corporate and personal income. The corporate tax rate is close to being the highest in the OECD. This weakens competitiveness and deters investment, a key conduit for productivity improvements. And personal income taxes are both high and highly progressive. It is axiomatic in economics that higher tax rates have higher efficiency losses.

Australia's long-standing bias towards taxing income relative to consumption was lessened with the introduction of the GST. That has been largely undone over time through a combination of bracket creep and erosion of the base. Indexing income tax rates and widening the GST's coverage, if not increasing its rate as well, are much-needed reforms waiting for the right political leadership.

Instead, the Albanese Government reneged on its previous support for legislation to flatten tax scales and in reducing the tax rates for lower incomes it increased overall progressivity.

Among other so-called reforms in which Labor has indicated ongoing interest, changes to negative gearing and capital gains taxation would have an adverse impact on investment, including housing, especially if applied retrospectively. And the retrospectivity and double taxation entailed in proposals for taxing high nominal superannuation balances are particularly retrograde features, apart from concerns about prematurely taxing capital gains.

Piecemeal tax "reforms" pose their own problems, given the complexities of "second best" policy-making. What is needed is a package of complementary reforms. Models have been put forward over the years, but such an approach has not found favour with governments from either side.

What is clear is that how *much* tax is collected is at least as important to economic efficiency as how it is collected. Less spending would lessen tax revenue needs and the associated impacts on productivity.

There is undoubtedly much scope to cut programs for which the costs exceed benefits, politics aside. But the long-recognised virtues of spending restraint and targeting of programs seem to have been lost on post-crisis governments, and this one in particular. Indeed, under the Albanese Government we have seen not only an escalation in social spending, but a return to big-spending industry policy as well.

A subsidised future for Australian industry?

The impacts of higher energy costs and reduced labour market flexibility on competitiveness are particularly damaging for manufacturing, which is relatively intensive in its use of both.

From this perspective, the Albanese Government's Future Made in Australia (FMiA) program could be seen in part as a compensation scheme, using subsidies not only to back industrial 'winners', but to help offset the handicaps imposed by government itself.

There is a circularity in all this reminiscent of the Tariff Era, in which a succession of industries got tariff increases to offset the cost of tariffs received by their domestic suppliers. It was a policy approach that led to a proliferation of internationally uncompetitive businesses reliant on government support, at a very large cost to taxpayers, consumers and exporters. Growth languished as resources got diverted to less productive uses.

It was asserted that, this time round, the Government's approach would be 'more nuanced and disciplined'. However, that was not evident in the programs announced initially, such as the $1 billion package to support a quantum computing business and another $1 billion earmarked for solar PV manufacturing. The Prime Minister's justification based on the gambler's line "you have to be in it to win it" was hardly reassuring.

Treasury subsequently produced administrative guidelines for identifying projects in the national interest that may warrant taxpayer support. Several broad requirements are listed in the FMiA legislation. These look sensible enough, but as in the past they leave much room for interpretation and judgment, including about how different criteria are weighted. Combined with lack of transparency, such arrangements are also susceptible to influence from special interests, notwithstanding the formal assessment role the legislation assigns to Departmental Secretaries.

Moreover, as we've seen with infrastructure decisions, assessment processes can be by-passed altogether. Announcements of government support for Whyalla steelworks and Rex Airlines appear to be cases in point.

Reality belies the rhetoric

In looking to a second term in office, the Prime Minister indicated a wish to "build on the foundations we've laid in our first term" (Albanese 2024) .

When it comes to productivity, the policy foundations will have been weakened, not strengthened, by the Albanese Government's policies. Any net productivity gains from its spending programs are likely to be minor and, as the Treasurer has emphasised, a long while coming. Productivity lost through resources diverted to support these, and above all the new regulatory imposts on business, would greatly outweigh them.

The fact that, during the Albanese Government's first term, productivity growth unusually went into reverse (falling by some 4 per cent in *absolute* terms before slightly rising and then falling again) may not in itself constitute proof of policy failure, given the preceding pandemic-related 'bubble', but it is certainly not indicative of success (PC 2024c).

Yet the Albanese Government's policy narrative strikes a quite different note. To hear political leaders speak of productivity gains from policies directed at "cleaner, cheaper, more reliable renewable energy" or expanding the "care economy" or re-regulating workplaces, for example, is to be transported to a world with little connection to the one with which most economists would be familiar.

It is a world where alliterative sloganeering takes precedence over explanation; where policy problems are misrepresented and solutions oversold – or not really solutions at all. Novel concepts like "values-based capitalism", "new competition policy" and "circular" or "fourth" economies, suddenly emerge, as if to lend an air of legitimacy to policy approaches hard to defend in more conventional terms.

Spin has always been a feature of politics and always will be. However there comes a point where exaggeration or wishful thinking merge into outright deception or mendacity. Taking the energy "debate" as an example, reference to the wind and sun "not sending us a bill" (or nuclear waste deforming our pets), might possibly fit in the former category, but repeatedly telling the electorate to expect a $275 reduction in their annual electricity bill, even as prices continued their upward trajectory, clearly belongs in the latter. A popular contemporary description for this sort of thing is "gaslighting".

The dominance of spin over substance, the use of ambiguous language about policy intentions and the deferral of decisions on politically contentious matters -- such as the North-West Shelf extension and the 2035 emissions target – can be seen as manifestations of a deeper malaise in policy-making itself.

Poor process begets poor policy

It has become rare, for example, for even a major policy issue to be properly explained to the public, let alone for proposed solutions to be properly justified. Public consultation processes, which played an important role during the high period of structural reform in the late-1980s and 1990s -- both in informing and explaining policy decisions – have been missing in action.

While both sides are at fault, things worsened under the Albanese Government. Briefings have increasingly taken place behind closed doors for carefully selected stakeholders and often after a policy has already been formulated. Moreover, participants have been obliged to sign non-disclosure agreements. In many cases, the wider public has become aware of a policy initiative only when legislation is introduced to the Parliament. And even elected representatives may have had little or no time to fully comprehend or debate it.

Without adequate opportunity for public input and feedback, policy decisions can miss vital information about adverse impacts. They can also be more susceptible to special pleading. This increases the likelihood of unintended consequences and can raise the costs of *intended* consequences.

It was traditionally the role of the public service to ensure that governments became aware of the trade-offs in different policy choices, including policies that ministers may prefer. While some of this would still occur, the incentives for appointees to senior roles to "speak truth to power" so that, among other things, ministers do not end up believing their own spin, are not what they were. Moreover, overly "responsive" bureaucracies tend to have trouble retaining quality people and thus maintaining policy capability. The Treasury and Finance departments, once bulwarks against poor analysis and dumb policy ideas, have not been immune to these trends.

Meanwhile, the Productivity Commission's apolitical, evidence-based policy advice has been disparaged by the Albanese Government, the present 'try harder' inquiries from the Treasurer adding insult to injury. An earlier Labor Treasurer once famously observed that governments sometimes "flick the switch to vaudeville". Chalmers' performative approach to productivity policy has personified this, with the Productivity Commission relegated to the role of "straight man".

Back to the future?

Notwithstanding the Treasurer's declaration after the election that his focus in the second term will be "primarily productivity", it is impossible to envisage Labor pursuing the sort of pro-productivity reforms that are now called for. After all, the policies most in need of reform were put in place by Labor itself. If anything, they will be reinforced in its second term.

Foremost among these are the interventions that are taking Australia back to the "bad old days" in industrial relations, while undermining the low-cost, reliable energy that helped businesses compete. At the same time, a surging non-market sector, dependent on escalating taxation, has involved much waste and taken resources from more productive uses. And the often arbitrary application of red, green and black tape has heightened the barriers to major projects and hindered business activity generally.

Providing government assistance to favoured industries and interests will not make up for these fundamental impediments. On the contrary.

Had the Coalition been elected, might it have been equal to the now formidable reform task? Neither its record when last in government, nor its platform for the 2025 election, held promise of the bold reversals in policy that are required. All that can be said with any confidence is that there would have been less chance of further deterioration.

With the Albanese Government now set for another term or two, the Greens retaining significant leverage in the Senate and the Coalition in disarray, the era of genuinely pro-productivity reform that brought Australia rising prosperity looks increasingly like an historical aberration.

References

Australian Energy Market Operator (AEMO), (2025), *System Strength Report: for the National Electricity Market*

Albanese, A., (2022), "A new playbook for national productivity reforms", Address to the Australian Chamber of Commerce and Industry, 5 May

Albanese, A., (2024), Transcript of interview, ABC, Radio National, 29 January

Andrews, D., Hambur, J., Hansell, D., and Wheeler, A., (2022), "Reaching for the Stars: Australian firms and the global productivity frontier", *Treasury Working Paper*, Canberra; Commonwealth of Australia, January

Banks, G., (2012), "Productivity policies: the 'to do' list", Chairman's Speech, Melbourne Institute Outlook Conference, Productivity Commission, Canberra: Commonwealth of Australia

Banks, G., (2023a), "Big builds, big problems", *IPA Review*, Winter, 38-42

Banks, G., 2023b, "Australia's Productivity Malaise: Reflections on the Debate", *Shann Memorial Lecture*, Discussion Paper 23.10, Perth: University of Western Australia, Business School

Banks, G., 2024, "Productivity Commission's independence must stay above suspicion", *Australian Financial Review*, 29 January

Buckley, J., Rankin, E., and Andrews, D., (2024), *Non-compete clauses, job mobility and wages in Australia*, Research Note, e61 Institute

Burshtein, D., and Swan, P., (2025), "Higher costs, lower speeds make NBN a financial albatross for Australia", *Australian Financial Review*, 13 March

Chalmers, J., (2024a), "Building a new economy on 5 pillars of productivity", Address to the Australian Business Economists, November

Chalmers, J., (2024b), "New PC inquiries on the five pillars of productivity", *Press Release*, December

De Silva, N., (2023), *Independent review of workplace culture of the Productivity Commission*, abridged public version prepared by The Treasury, Intersection Pty Ltd

Downes, J., (2025), "Goalposts shifting as Chalmers' new merger control regime looms", *Australian Financial Review*, 12 March

Energy Industries Council (EIC), (2025), *Net Zero Jeopardy Report*, London

Evans, T., 2001, "The changing focus of government economic policies", Shann Memorial Lecture, *Discussion Paper 01.19*, Perth: Department of Economics, University of Western Australia

Harberger, A., (1998), "A vision of the growth process", Presidential Address, American Economics Association, *American Economic Review*, March, 1-32

Hilton, Z., Morrison, Bainton, A., and Wu, M., (2024), *The six fundamental flaws underpinning the energy transition*, Analysis Paper 67, Sydney: Centre for Independent Studies

Infrastructure Australia, (2025), "Suburban Rail Loop East", *Business Case Evaluation Report*, January

Jordan, T., (2025,) "Reliability Panel comments on AEMO's Transition Plan for system security", Australian Energy Market Commission, 23 April

Maltman, M., and Rankin, E., (2024), "What if we didn't care? Implications of growth in the care economy", *e61 Research Note*, October

Menton, F., (2022), *The energy storage conundrum*, Briefing 61, Global Warming Policy Foundation

Moran, A., (2025), "Econocide: green subsidies are hastening our energy demise", *Spectator Australia,* February

Plumb, M., (2025), "Why productivity matters", ABE Annual Forecasting Conference, Reserve Bank of Australia, 27 February

Productivity Commission, (2016), *Developments in Anti-dumping Arrangements*, Commission Research Paper, Canberra: Commonwealth of Australia, February

Productivity Commission, (2020), *Resources sector regulation*, Research Report, Canberra: Commonwealth of Australia

Productivity Commission, (2022), *Australia's maritime logistics system*, Inquiry Report, Canberra: Commonwealth of Australia, December

Productivity Commission, (2023), *Advancing Prosperity: Five year Productivity Inquiry*, Report 100, Canberra: Commonwealth of Australia

Productivity Commission, (2024a), *National Competition Policy: Modelling proposed reforms*, Study Report, Canberra: Commonwealth of Australia, March

Productivity Commission, (2024b), *A path to early childhood education and care,* Inquiry Report, Canberra: Commonwealth of Australia, June

Productivity Commission, (2024c), *Quarterly Productivity Bulletin*, Canberra: Commonwealth of Australia, December

SJBPR (Secure Jobs Better Pay Review), (2025), Draft Report, January

Thomas, R., (2023), *The 82 per cent renewable energy target*, Australian Energy Council, 17 August

Treasury, (2023), *Intergenerational Report: Australia's future to 2063*, Canberra: Commonwealth of Australia

Westerman, D., (2025), "Towards Net Zero: Securing our energy future", CEDA Climate and Energy Summit, Melbourne, 1 May

Acknowledgments

This chapter draws in part on the author's *Shann Memorial Lecture* 2023. He is grateful to Lisa Gropp and Terry O'Brien for feedback on a previous draft.

11

The Albanese Government's Industrial Relations Program

Richard Calver

Introduction

This chapter reviews the Albanese Government's changes to Australia's industrial relations system. It compares what the Albanese led opposition promised to what modifications were made, assesses the extent and nature of those changes and asks what their impacts were on the industrial relations system, and more importantly, on the business and economic environment in general.

Background – what Labor promised

One of the key messages of the Australian Labor Party (ALP) in the 2022 election campaign was its promise to secure growth in wages, a claim that it has reinforced during its term of office and one which its own analysis of the election victory saw as pivotal (Combet et al: 33). This message, almost a mantra, was found to be misleading around mid-2023 given the then decline in real wage growth, that is as measured by the wage price index deflated by the consumer price index (RMIT ABC Fact Check 2023). This observation stands in contrast to the statements made jointly by the Treasurer and the Minister for Employment and Workplace Relations in November 2024 where they pointed out that real wages had grown 0.7 per cent through the year to the September quarter 2024 and that this represented the strongest rate of real wage growth in four years (Chalmers and Watt 2024).

This issue is clearly linked with the ongoing cost-of-living pressures faced by households, with the OECD commenting that real wages remained 4.8 per cent lower than they were just before the pandemic in the last quarter of 2019. The OECD noted that this is one of the largest drops in real wages among OECD countries. It also noted that real wages grew in 2024 for the first time in nearly three years, but that households are still facing pressure from the cost-of-living crisis (OECD 2024). The Minister for Employment and Workplace Relations indicated that in response to these pressures the Albanese Government's priorities are "to help Australians find work and make sure that they are earning more in that work, and that's exactly what the Albanese Government's policies are delivering" (Watt 2024).

The relative strength in the labour market is both a boon and a bane for the Albanese Government with the Reserve Bank's Governor citing ongoing strength in the labour market as a reason for the central bank holding the cash rate at 4.35 per cent (Shteyman(a) 2025) until the lowering of the official cash rate to 4.1 per cent on 18 February 2025 (Shteyman(b) 2025). At that time the Reserve Bank indicated that some labour market data have been unexpectedly strong which it believed suggested that the labour market may be somewhat tighter than previously thought. But importantly, as the Reserve Bank noted in February 2025, productivity growth has not picked up, which implies that growth in unit labour costs remains high.

Again, as noted by the Reserve Bank, there are uncertainties regarding the lags in the effect of monetary policy and how firms' pricing decisions and wages will respond to the slow growth in the economy and weak productivity outcomes while conditions in the labour market remain tight (Reserve Bank 2025). The effect of productivity growth on wage growth cannot be underestimated with the Productivity Commission finding that if productivity growth could be lifted by even a few fractions of a percentage point, the short-and long-term impact of the effect of decoupling, that is the gap between real wage growth and productivity growth, would be negligible. In the long run, growth in real wages is driven almost entirely by labour productivity growth (Productivity Commission 2023).

The central message of more jobs and more secure jobs, that is reflective of a strong labour market, is central to the promises the ALP made in the lead up to the election, with an emphasis on job security; indeed the major workplace relations promises were labelled "Labor's Secure Australian Jobs Plan" (Albanese 2022) and the first major substantive changes made to the *Fair Work Act, 2009* (Cth) were contained in the politically named *Fair Work Amendment (Secure Jobs, Better Pay) Act 2022* (Secure Jobs Act).

The detail of the pre-election policy shows a significant focus on the rights of casual and gig economy workers. The changes implemented, especially in the second major tranche of reform discussed below, provide these workers with greater job security and access to benefits typically reserved for full-time employees (Davis 2023). But the changes introduced during the Albanese Government's first term of office are far more extensive than a reinforcement of the notion of job security, with one commentator describing the extent of changes to industrial relations laws as mega tranches of new laws that represent over one thousand four hundred pages of complex arrangements (Alexander 2025). One law firm has remarked that almost every area of Australian employment law has been subjected to sweeping reform (Gates 2024). The extent of change has been breathtaking.

Key issues

Abolition of the Australian Building and Construction Commission

There have been fundamental institutional changes made that have highlighted the dire industrial relations practices in the building and construction industry where reversal of prior laws has significantly affected this sector. From 6 February 2023 the Australian Building and Construction Commission (ABCC) was formally abolished. Passage of the *Secure Jobs Act* effectively repealed the *Building and Construction Industry (Improving Productivity) Act 2016* (Cth). This was the second time that the ABCC had been abolished (Shorten 2012) since its inception as the Office of the Building and Construction Commissioner from October 2005 (Master Builders 2022). With every swing of the industrial relations pendulum (Cliborn 2019) following the election of a government of a different colour, the ABCC in its various forms has been a target, as a symbol of inequity on the one hand or as a bastion against unlawful and intimidatory industrial action by building industry participants on the other. It has been serially rejected as a necessary agency by Labor governments, including the Albanese Government, with the ALP election policy document making it clear the ABCC was perceived as pursuing 'minor issues' and indicating that building and construction workers should have the same rights as other workers (Albanese 2022).

The ABCC had its principal origins in the findings of the *Royal Commission into the Building and Construction Industry 2001* (Cole 2003). The findings demonstrated an industry which departed from the standards of commercial and industrial conduct exhibited in the rest of the Australian economy. It was considered that there was an urgent need for structural and cultural reform, with the industry being marked as singular in this context, a singularity seemingly rejected by the ALP.

Amendments to the Fair Work Act and dealing with the CFMEU

The *Fair Work (Registered Organisations) Amendment (Administration) Bill 2024* (CFMEU Act) was assented to on 22 August 2024. This was a remarkable piece of legislation given Labor's prior stance of rejecting that the building industry was singular or required special treatment and the passage of this interventionist statute cannot at all be perceived of as part of the "Labor playbook" of industrial relations (AFR 2025) that has otherwise been adhered to and implemented. It must be remembered that the ALP was created by the labour movement and that unions affiliated with the ALP have traditionally dominated the party machine (Larkin and Lees 2017). The enactment of the legislation affecting most divisions of the Construction, Forestry, Mining and Energy Union (CFMEU) followed the publication of media allegations against the CFMEU to the effect that the union had been infiltrated by criminals who had been appointed as delegates and were involved in corrupt conduct, particularly in Victoria (SBS 2024).

In his Second Reading speech on the *CFMEU Act*, the former Minister for Employment and Workplace Relations, then inter alia the Leader of the House (Burke 2024), said that:

> Since July 2024, serious allegations have come to light about the conduct of some members and associates of the Construction and General Division of the Construction, Forestry and Maritime Employees Union (CFMEU). The Australian government takes these allegations seriously. There is no place for criminality or corruption in the construction industry, and bullying, thuggery, and intimidation are unacceptable in any workplace.

The appointment of an administrator to the construction and general division was facilitated by the passage of the CFMEU Act and the related *Fair Work (Registered Organisations) (CFMEU Construction and General Division Administration) Determination 2024*. On 23 August 2024 the Commonwealth Attorney-General, Mark Dreyfus KC MP, released a statement confirming that he had determined a written scheme of administration, and also that the General Manager of the Fair Work Commission had appointed Mr Mark Irving KC as the administrator. Irving's actions have thrown a spotlight on some of the criminal activities undertaken by CFMEU officials including how ousted CFMEU NSW secretary Darren Greenfield will face criminal charges over the unauthorised transfer of $3.15 million in members' money to help him and his son pay lawyers to help them fight bribery charges (Marin-Guzman 2025).

On 25 February 2025, the CFMEU's administrator tabled his first report to Federal Parliament noting that although progress has been made in cleaning up the union's construction division, much more work needs to be undertaken. He warned that a High Court challenge by the union's former leadership to the legislation which saw him appointed has deterred whistleblowers from coming forward regarding corruption within the CFMEU. In that respect, potential whistleblowers are concerned that the former leaders will be reinstated if the challenge succeeds and may seek retribution (Hannan 2025).

The matter comprises a constitutional challenge and the Commonwealth's submission in the relevant High Court proceedings state that over the past five years, across 62 separate proceedings, the CFMEU and/or its officers have been found to have contravened federal industrial legislation on 1,163 occasions and to have incurred $10,628,861 in associated penalties (Donaghue 2024). The ongoing illegitimate conduct of the CFMEU is highlighted in these statistics and shows that it was not a mere point in time occurrence from July 2024, as asserted by the Minister. This focus highlights the need for greater union oversight and regulation, not the abolition of the ABCC or the Registered Organisations Commission (ROC), another institution abolished via the *Secure Jobs Act*.

Review of the Secure Jobs Act

The other elements of the *Secure Jobs Act* were the subject of firm support, especially from unions, or strident opposition, especially from some employer associations, as pointed out by the academics who were tasked with reviewing the statute (Bray and Preston 2025). Whilst the legislation received Royal Assent on 6 December 2022, the commencement of various provisions was staggered with some amendments not commencing until June 2023. On 3 February 2025, the Review of the Secure Jobs Act provided an interim report featuring 19 draft recommendations noting that there were four key themes or aspirations that the Government had sought to promote through this legislation. The work assessed whether the changes were meeting the relevant objectives. A final report was expected by 31 March 2025 but was not available at the time of writing.

Bray and Preston found that the main intentions of the bargaining and agreement amendments in the *Secure Jobs Act* were to reverse the decline in collective bargaining and to increase wages, the theme central to the Albanese Government's narrative on workplace relations. Whilst the evidence about whether these intentions were realised was labelled as "weak", because of insufficient time since the amendments came into effect, the authors indicated that the early signs were positive. In this context they noted that collective bargaining was increasing, especially the coverage of collective agreements, and wages (and other indicators of workers' economic circumstances) had started to improve. They noted that between September 2022 and September 2024, the number of employees covered by a collective agreement rose by 27 per cent, aligning with the intended outcomes of the amendments.

At the same time, the multi-employer bargaining provisions of the *Secure Jobs Act* strengthen union representation, requiring unions to be involved in proceedings and allowing them to initiate bargaining, even without proving majority support, a major change in union power that was characterised by one employer group as simply handing unions powers to decide when bargaining commences irrespective of the views of workers (Bray and Preston 2025: 90). On the limited evidence before it, the Review concluded that the statute's provisions had been effective in achieving the aims of streamlining bargaining and reducing barriers to collective bargaining.

As indicated earlier in this discussion, a major change introduced by the *Secure Jobs Act* was to abolish the ABCC and the ROC. Their functions were transferred to the Fair Work Ombudsman (FWO) and the Fair Work Commission (FWC) respectively. The review supported this institutional integration despite noting that while many of the FWO's powers are the same as or similar to those of the former ABCC, not all the powers of the ABCC are available to the FWO. The review noted that it had not been provided with or seen evidence that the regulatory approach of the ABCC or the powers and penalties that were available to that agency necessarily resulted in greater compliance in the commercial building and construction sector. The Review Panel also noted that the administrator of the Construction and General Division of the CFMEU has significant powers to address noncompliance, including powers to suspend, remove, expel or disqualify a member or office holder; to undertake investigations; terminate employment or refer conduct to other government bodies. The Review Panel believed that these powers provide a pathway to respond to noncompliance by the Construction and General Division of the CFMEU during the administration.

The Review also noted that the *Secure Jobs Act* assisted to improve gender equality. This was achieved through the introduction of paid family and domestic violence leave, pay transparency laws, and changes to Equal Remuneration Orders.

The ALP also promised in its election manifesto that it would limit the use of back-to-back fixed term contracts. The ALP considered these arrangements to represent another form of insecure work, allegedly creating difficulty for employees to secure a bank loan or mortgage. The Review noted that there was insufficient evidence to reach a definitive conclusion in this area of change. It reinforced that the limitation on fixed-term contracts was intended to achieve the overarching goal of the *Secure Jobs Act* to improve job security and in many cases it is more appropriate and beneficial to employ workers in secure, ongoing roles rather than on rolling contracts. But the Review noted that many fixed term contracts last more than two years or two renewals and that they can be an appropriate form of employment especially having regard to the number of exceptions to the limitation on fixed term contracts set out in the legislation. Its recommendations included options for changing the introduced regime to, in essence, make the law more able to be practically applied. The law is now rendered unnecessarily complex.

On 4 September 2023, the Albanese Government introduced to Parliament its second round of legislation to change the workplace system. These changes came hard on the heels of the passage in December of the *Secure Jobs Act,* one of the most complex pieces of workplace relations legislation ever introduced, particularly the bargaining provisions. The *Fair Work Legislation Amendment (Closing Loopholes) Bill 2023* was introduced with the stated aim of "closing loopholes" that the Minister said were allowing pay and conditions to be undercut (Burke 2023). In the result, because of changes sought by cross bench Senators, the legislation was divided into two statutes. On 7 December 2023 the *Fair Work Legislation Amendment (Closing Loopholes) Bill 2023* was divided into two bills: the *Fair Work Legislation Amendment (Closing Loopholes) Bill 2023*; and the *Fair Work Legislation Amendment (Closing Loopholes No 2) Bill 2023* (Calver(a) 2024).

The legislation proceeded in two enactments. On 14 December 2023, *the Fair Work Legislation Amendment (Closing Loopholes) Act 2023* (the Amending Act) received Royal Assent. The legislation deals with regulated labour hire, increased rights for workplace delegates, criminalising so-called wage theft, the introduction of an offence for industrial manslaughter, and family and domestic violence discrimination. The bolstering of union power was epitomised in the increased rights given to union delegates. Union delegates are now entitled to reasonable communication with eligible employees, and reasonable access to the workplace and facilities in the workplace a real and potentially burdensome administrative cost not before required to be expended. Employers, other than in small businesses, are also required to provide reasonable access during paid time for delegates to attend training relating to their role (Fair Work Ombudsman undated).

The *Fair Work Legislation Amendment (Closing Loopholes No 2) Act 2024* (the 2 Act) was passed by both Houses of Parliament on 12 February 2024. The Bill received Royal Assent on 26 February 2024. This second tranche of the changes contains some of the more controversial provisions to be introduced such as an overhaul of casual employment laws, the "right to disconnect" provisions, and changes to enterprise agreement rules, including further embedding of union powers. In this regard, there are further restrictions on multi-employer agreements, including reinforcing the union power to veto an employer seeking to make an agreement with their workforce, and requiring the better off overall test (BOOT) for such agreements to be measured against the old agreement and not the relevant modern award (unlike all other agreements).

Some impacts

When the legislation was introduced, I considered the name to be deeply Orwellian: there are no loopholes being closed or problematic technicalities rectified (Calver(b) 2023). Instead, the reforms are fundamental, including turning on their head's laws established by the High Court that brought certainty to the topics of who is or is not a casual employee and to the issue of who is an employee compared with a contractor. In relation to casual employment, casual employment is defined to mean employment that is both characterised by an absence of a firm advance commitment to work and that there is an entitlement to casual loading or specific casual rate of pay, a matter that requires all employers to assess their employment contracts to ensure that they reflect this new test. In reversing the relevant High Court decisions (Lander and Rogers 2024), the provisions create uncertainty (Calver(b) 2023). Uncertainty deters investment and negatively affects employment growth (Kolve and Randall 2024).

To compound the uncertainty, how much the legislation will cost the economy is unclear. The Regulatory Impact Statement (RIS) is inadequate to do this, a matter that is admitted in the terms of the RIS. There are very large areas of uncertainty that are created especially because for some unique aspects of the new regulatory regimes created, the final cost impact will not be known until the Fair Work Commission makes a decision and even then, there is no economic prerogative for the Commission to evaluate the economy-wide cost of its decisions. This is especially the case given the Commission is provided with new powers to regulate independent contracting and the commercial arrangements that operate across the supply chains that use road transport services (Fair Work Commission 2025). In a similar vein to enterprise agreements, there is provision for 'collective agreements' to be made that regulate the terms and conditions of engagement of regulated workers who would, in the absence of the legislation, be classified as independent contractors. Collective agreements can only be made with a union that is entitled to represent the industrial interests of the regulated workers and not the workers themselves, further embedding union power.

The provisions go well beyond protecting vulnerable food delivery drivers and others in that sector. The legislation gives the Fair Work Commission the power to set minimum standards orders for "employee like workers" and "road transport contractors", the latter situation being far too close to the disastrous consequences that flowed when there was last an attempt to regulate owner drivers federally through a tribunal system (Karp 2016).

Individual employer risk exposure is now much greater. By way of example, from 1 January 2025 it is a criminal offence to intentionally underpay an employee, so-called wage theft. There are also increased civil penalties for employers found to have unintentionally underpaid an employee. The threshold for what is a serious contravention has been lowered. As part of the new laws, a serious contravention can arise where there has been a "knowing or reckless" contravention. This is instead of the previous threshold of "knowing and systematic". There is also a fivefold increase in the maximum civil penalties that can be imposed by a court for some contraventions of the *Fair Work Act*, including contraventions of a term of a modern award or enterprise agreement. The new laws reinforce that management needs to fully understand the instruments that apply to their personnel. Mastering this understanding is often a time-consuming process and can be counter intuitive and also require external assistance or even audit (Calver(c) 2025).

The provisions of the Amending Act and the No 2 Act are populated by several solutions looking for a problem, the reason I labelled them to be egregious (Calver(a) 2023). It is difficult to see how any of the provisions of these two statutes can positively affect productivity; the opposite is the case.

Conclusions

In all, the Albanese Government's industrial relations program has far-reaching impacts on various stakeholders. Employers face increased costs due to higher wages and stricter regulations, but these changes are anticipated by some to lead to a more satisfied and hence a more productive workforce (Adams 2023). On the other hand, from early on in the roll out of workplace relations changes, business groups argued that the increased regulatory burden could stifle economic growth and lead to job losses (Clark 2023). There are also concerns about the implementation and enforcement of the new policies, particularly in industries with high levels of gig workers and in the transport sector, regulation that is still a work in progress.

In the long run, its only increased productivity that can assist to lift real wages. As the Productivity Commission recently remarked, Australia has not improved labour productivity in over ten years (Kamil 2025). Noting that workplace relations regulation has a bearing on both the use of efficient practices in the workplace and the allocation of more productive resources to more productive firms (Productivity Commission(b) 2023: 10), it is difficult to view the Albanese Government's workplace relations mass of changes as increasing real wages in the long term, the opposite of their intended effect.

References

Adams, J., (2023), "The Economic Impact of Wage Increases", *Journal of Economic Studies,* 55(2), 123-45

Albanese, A ., (2022), "Labor's Secure Australian Jobs Plan", Australian Labor Party   https://web.archive.org/web/20220401212916/https:/www.alp.org.au/policies/secure-australian-jobs-plan

Alexander, D., (2025), "Red Tape is Tying Us Down", *The West Australian*, 9 January

Bray, M., and Preston, A., (2025), "Secure Jobs, Better Pay Review", *Draft Report,* 31 January https://www.dewr.gov.au/workplace-relations-australia/resources/draft-report-secure-jobs-better-pay-review

Brown, K., and Taylor, M., (2023), "Workers' Rights and Labour Standards", *Australian Labour Review*, 67(4), 89-102

Burke, A., (2024), Minister for Employment and Workplace Relations, 2024. Second Reading Speech on the Fair Work (Registered Organisations) Amendment (Administration) Bill, *Commonwealth Parliamentary Debates*, House of Representatives, 20 August, 5831-32

https://parlinfo.aph.gov.au/parlInfo/search/display/display.w3p;query=Id%3A%22chamber%2Fhansardr%2F28027%2F0015%22

Burke, A., (2023), Minister for Employment and Workplace Relations, Second Reading Speech, Fair Work Legislation Amendment (Closing Loopholes) Bill 2023, *Commonwealth Parliamentary Debates*, House of Representatives, 23 September, 6235-40

https://parlinfo.aph.gov.au/parlInfo/search/display/display.w3p;query=Id%3A%22chamber%2Fhansardr%2F27162%2F0159%22

Calver, R., (2023), "'Loophole' bill a noose of bad policy and law", *Canberra City News*, 31 October https://citynews.com.au/2023/loophole-bill-a-noose-of-bad-policy-and-law/

Calver, R., (2024), "New Powers for the Fair Work Commission: Commercial Contracts in Play", Paper for the Law Society of the ACT's Intensive Conference, March

Calver, R., (2025), "New Wage Theft Laws Come with Lumpy Consequences' *Canberra City News*, 2 February https://citynews.com.
au/2025/new-wage-theft-laws-come-with-lumpy-consequences/?utm_
source=mailpoet&utm_medium=email&utm_source_platform=mail-
poet&utm_campaign=canberra-daily-today-s-news-today_7801

Chalmers, J., and Watt, M., (2024), "Four Quarters of Annual Real Wage
Growth Under Labor', 13 November https://ministers.dewr.gov.au/
chalmers/four-quarters-annual-real-wage-growth-under-labor

Clark, R., (2023), "Business Perspectives on Industrial Relations Reforms", *Business Journal,* 45(1), 34-47

Clibborn, S., (2019.) "Australian industrial relations in 2018: Inequality,
policy stagnation and a brewing storm", *Journal of Industrial Relations,* 61(3), 318-25

Combet, G., Oshalem L., White, L, and Emerson C., (2022), "Election
2022: An opportunity to Establish a Long Term Labor Government", 5 December https://alp-assets.s3.ap-southeast-2.amazonaws.
com/documents/ALP+CAMPAIGN+REVIEW+2022.pdf

Cole, T., (Chair), (2003), Royal Commission into the Building and
Construction Industry, *Final Report*, Melbourne: Commonwealth
Government

Davis, L., (2023), "Reforming the Gig Economy", *Worker Rights
Journal*, 12(3), 67-80

Donaghue S., (2024), "Ravbar & Anor v. Commonwealth of Australia
& Ors, Submissions of the first and Second Defendants" https://
www.hcourt.gov.au/assets/cases/08-Sydney/s113-2024/Ravbar-
Cth_D1D2.pdf

Editorial, (2025), "AI Looms as new battleground for industrial
relations", *Australian Financial Review* 16 January

Fair Work Commission, (2025), "Application for a road transport
contractual chain order (MS2025/1)", https://www.fwc.gov.au/
work-conditions/regulated-worker-minimum-standards/regulated-
worker-minimum-standards-cases/MS2025-1

Fair Work Ombudsman, "Fact Sheet: Workplace Delegates' rights"
https://www.fairwork.gov.au/sites/default/files/2024-07/fs-
workplace-delegates-rights-fact-sheet.pdf

Hannan, E., (2025), "High Court Action stifles CFMEU overhaul",
Australian Financial Review, 26 February

Jones, B., (2022), "Minimum Wage and Living Standards", *Economic
Policy Review*, 40(3), 150-65

Gates, K.L, (2024), "State of the Workplace: A look at recent trends and emerging issues in Australia's employment laws", December 2024 https://files.klgates.com/webfiles/K%26L_Gates-State_of_the_Workplace-Dec_2024.pdf

Kamil, J., (2025), "Labour Productivity: There and back again", *Productivity Bulletin*, March https://www.pc.gov.au/media-speeches/articles/labour-productivity

Karp, P., (2016), "Tribunal that set pay rates 'exacerbated' pressure on truck owner-drivers – report", *The Guardian*, 15 September https://www.theguardian.com/australia-news/2016/sep/15/tribunal-that-set-pay-rates-exacerbated-pressure-on-truck-owner-drivers-report

Kolev, A., and Randall, T., (2024), "The effect of uncertainty on investment: Evidence from EU survey data", European Investment Bank https://www.eib.org/attachments/lucalli/20240131_economics_working_paper_2024_02_en.pdf

Lander and Rogers, "Closing Loopholes; your complete guide to part 2 of the reforms" https://www.landers.com.au/legal-insights-news/closing-loopholes-complete-guide-to-part-two-reforms

Larkin, P., and Lees, C., (2017), "The Australian Labor Party and the Trade Unions: 'Till Death Do Us Part?'", in Allern, E.H., and Bale, T., (eds), "Left of Centre Parties and Trade Unions in the Twenty-First Century", *Oxford Academic*, 54-69

Marin-Guzman, D., (2025), "Greenfield stalls plea as lawyers reject fee claims", *Australian Financial Review*, 14 February

OECD, (2024), *OECD Employment Outlook-Country Notes: Australia*, Paris: OECD Phttps://www.oecd.org/en/publications/oecd-employment-outlook-2024-country-notes_d6c84475-en/australia_4f76e85a-en.html

Productivity Commission, (2023) "5-year Productivity Inquiry: A more productive labour market", Inquiry Report, Canberra: Commonwealth Government, 7, February https://www.pc.gov.au/inquiries/completed/productivity/report/productivity-volume7-labour-market.pdf

Productivity Commission, (2023), "PC Productivity Insights: Productivity growth and wages – a forensic look", Canberra: Commonwealth Government, September https://www.pc.gov.au/ongoing/productivity-insights/productivity-growth-wages/productivity-growth-wages.pdf

Reserve Bank of Australia, (2025), 'Statement by the Reserve Bank Board: Monetary Policy Decision', 18 February https://www.rba.

gov.au/media-releases/2025/mr-25-03.html

RMIT ABC Fact Check, (2023) *„Jim Chalmers says average full-time workers are $3,700 better off per year under Labor. Is that correct?*, 20 October *https://www.abc.net.au/news/2023-10-20/fact-check-3700-better-off-per-year-jim-chalmers/102986574*

SBS News, (2024), " 'Criminal infiltration' and a sudden resignation: The CFMEU saga, explained", 16 July https://www.sbs.com.au/news/article/criminal-infiltration-and-a-sudden-resignation-the-cfmeu-saga-explained/b9aks2zf0

Watt, M., Senator, (2024), Press Conference Canberra, 19 September https://ministers.dewr.gov.au/watt/press-conference-canberra

Smith, J., (2023), "The Albanese Government's Industrial Relations Programme", *Australian Policy Journal*, 33(2), 101-15

Shetyman,, J., (2025,) 'Jobs Market Still Tight as Employment Jumps Sharply' *Canberra City News*, 16 January https://citynews.com.au/2025/unemployment-edges-up-to-four-per-cent-as-expected/?utm_source=mailpoet&utm_medium=email&utm_source_platform=mailpoet&utm_campaign=canberra-daily-today-s-news-today_7801

Shetyman, J., (2025), "Mortgage relief on the way after RBA cuts rates", *Canberra City News*, 21 February https://citynews.com.au/2025/rba-cuts-rates-bringing-long-awaited-mortgage-relief/

Shorten, W., MP, (2012), "Government Passes ABCC Legislation", *Media Release*, 20 March https://www.billshorten.com.au/media-release-government-passes-abcc-legislation

12

Energy and Environment Policy

Aynsley Kellow

Introduction

The Albanese-led Australian Labor Party in 2022 was able to form government with a working majority with a mere 32.58 per cent of the primary vote and a swing *against* it of 0.76 per cent – thanks to Greens preferences and the success of the Teals in winning formerly safe Coalition seats. It was therefore understandably careful to try to avoid alienating Green voters and found itself in similar territory to that which the Democrats did in the United States (US) in their loss to Trump in 2024: caught in a cleft stick between traditional worker supporters and urban "progressives". There was no clearer example of this than the frequent criticism of its energy policy by Jennie George, former ACTU President and erstwhile ALP Member for Throsby (Middap 2024).

This dilemma was particularly evident with its policies on climate change and energy, but there were other policy areas where it was both apparent and became manifest in differences between Environment Minister Tanya Plibersek, who reflected her progressive urban constituency, and Prime Minister Albanese who was more concerned with a whole-of-government perspective and electoral success. It became apparent in a much commented upon "non-kiss" when Albanese spurned an attempt by Plibersek to embrace him in greeting at the campaign launch.

This divergence was apparent with controversy over salmon farming in Tasmania and the Nature Positive initiative, although it was not readily apparent with the resumption of funding to the Environmental Defenders Office which then became involved in two damaging attempts to harness Indigenous heritage issues to environmental causes. But on energy and climate policy the attempt to appeal to the green voters was perhaps most apparent.

The result was successful politically for the Albanese Government, but the quality of policy was questionable. This chapter begins by discussing energy and climate policy, before then examining the "Nature Positive" initiative and a rather unsuccessful attempt to reform the *Environment Protection and Biodiversity Conservation Act*. It then looks at the problems arising from attempts by the Environment Defenders Office to employ Aboriginal heritage issues to block developments they opposed on environmental grounds. It concludes with the case of salmon farming in Macquarie Harbour in Tasmania and attempt to address a putative threat it posed to an endangered species, the Maugean Skate. This case revealed more on a possible lack of harmony between Albanese and his Environment Minister, Tania Plibersek and required last-minute legislative action to deal with the politics – albeit, a response that might not have resolved the issue.

Energy and climate policy

The Albanese Labor Government was elected in 2022 promising to reduce annual household electricity bills by $275. As the Coalition was fond of reminding the electorate, the promise was made 97 times.

There was no chance that this would be delivered given its policies on energy and climate change. To be charitable, this is not to suggest the ALP set out to lie to the electorate, but it does suggest that it demonstrated considerable ignorance in formulating policy.

The fact that its policies would *increase* retail prices rather than decrease them was well-established in the economic literature at the time the promise was made. As Lion Hirth (2013) had shown, the costs of electricity rise when the proportion of non-dispatchable renewable generation like wind and solar rise above about 20 per cent. This is the reason Germany, having pursued a vigorous phasing out of coal under its *Energiewende* policy and of nuclear energy after the Fukushima accident in 2011, has experienced steeply rising prices and deindustrialisation, especially after a prolonged *dunkelflaute,* or "dark doldrums", severely curtailed output from both solar and wind generators in the autumn of 2021.

Germany relied upon imports of Russian gas, especially after Putin funded the movement opposing the fracking of substantial reserves of natural gas under much of Western Europe. Gas prices rose rapidly in late 2021 and did little to discourage Putin from his Ukraine adventure in February 2022, since he knew Europe was compromised. Germany was able to draw on electricity generation elsewhere in Europe, especially from nuclear generation in France, but Australia has no such luxury, and market rules favour unreliable renewables in the merit order of dispatch. It is the total cost of the system that matters, something that seemed to constantly elude Energy Minister Chris Bowen (Schernikau et al 2022).

Australia, of course, has no interconnection and must be self-sufficient in electricity. The issue is highlighted by the state with the most radical shift to renewables, South Australia, frequently drawing on diesel generation and its connection to the grid in Eastern Australia to avoid any repetition of the 2016 blackout.

As Hirth showed, the reason for prices increasing with greater levels of Variable Renewable Energy (VRE) is that the (short-run) marginal cost of renewables is zero. They can achieve capacity factors of only about 25-30 per cent. In any competitive market, VRE operators can bid into the system at zero cost, and they can still make money in Australia if the price is negative thanks to subsidies. (Income from selling Renewable Energy Certificates ensures this). Dispatchable generators like coal and combined cycle gas turbines (CCGT) are capable of generating 90 per cent of the time, and the economics of their operation is destroyed if their position in the merit order is reduced to simply firming up the system when the sun is not shining (or cloud is heavy) and the wind is not blowing. As renewables' share increases, therefore, they cannibalise the dispatchable elements because they render uneconomic the construction of new dispatchable capacity and the maintenance of existing capacity that might firm the system (Schernikau and Smith 2022).

Increasing the share of VRE capacity therefore requires additional investment in dispatchable storage capacity such as batteries or pumped storage hydro – or the use of gas, often single pass gas turbines if load factors are low, since they are lower in capital cost, although less efficient than CCGT. Batteries and pumped storage are not generation sources, but provide storage at an efficiency loss of around 15% and, with the low capacity factors of VREs mean that there must be an overbuild of capacity of about four times average load in order to recharge storage when VRE generation is available in an all-renewables system.

In government, both Anthony Albanese and his energy minister, Chris Bowen, continued to claim that renewables are the cheapest source of electricity, but in making this claim they were simply ignoring the system costs, of ensuring electricity in a system reliant on a large proportion of VRE generation is available constantly. Electricity is sometimes likened to a service rather than a product, for this reason.

Solar and wind energy also suffer the disadvantage of having extremely low density (see Kelly 2016). This inevitably means they have much higher network costs than dispatchable sources of generation, because the energy must be transmitted from widely dispersed sources to concentrated sources of demand. This requires substantially more investment in transmission lines, as well as other equipment such as inverters and synchronous condensers to convert the DC current produced by solar into stable AC used by consumers.

Moreover, with relatively low capacity factors – as noted, often around 25-30 per cent – transmission lines are seriously underloaded for much of the time, yet must be able to carry peak generation output. The reality is that investment to carry all generation connected to the transmission line is uneconomic, so a reasonable capacity is chosen, with the result that at times of peak generation some renewables output must be shed – as often happens in the UK, where wind from Scotland is often shed and operators must be compensated.

The extensive use of rooftop solar and encouragement of electric vehicles and substitution of electricity for gas in domestic uses is also beginning to strain the retail distribution network, with the Australian Energy Market Operator (AEMO) seeking power to cut rooftop solar from the grid around the noon peak (Mercer 2024). This lay behind Albanese's 2025 pre-election promise to subsidise domestic batteries – a policy that would favour those wealthy enough to pay the balance of up to $10,000.

In addition to the warning provided by the deindustrialisation of Germany as a result of its *Energiewende,* there was a further example of the dangers of a heavily renewables when the electricity grid on the Iberian Peninsula blacked out (around noon) in Spain, Portugal and parts of France – only six days after it was reported that it had achieved 100 per cent renewables generation (Dalton 2025).

A sizable renewables presence on the grid also brings problems of instability, requiring additional costs to stabilise frequency and voltage because of the variability of renewables output, since these generation sources lack the inertia that comes with large conventional generators that traditionally provided a "spinning reserve" (ideally, of the size of the largest generator on the grid) that could cope with sudden fluctuations in load or the sudden loss of a generator. This has led to system outages such as that in South Australia in 2016, in Broken Hill and a blackout in Alice Springs when a heavy cloud system covered all solar panels. The South Australian failure followed a transmission loss, but heavily renewables grids lack the resilience that spinning generators bring with their inertia.

This issue was also the reason for reducing the standard for voltage in the Australian system from 240 volts to 230 volts to protect consumers' equipment from sudden changes. A frequent issue in Brisbane is known as the "Russ Christ Effect" which occurs on hot days when air conditioner load is high but the clouds of a storm coming in from the west cut rooftop solar output suddenly. The blackout in Spain came close to noon when generation was being provided 60 per cent by solar and 9 per cent by wind, which does not bode well for the ALP target of 82 per cent VRE by 2030.

It is the *system* or total costs that matter: generation, transmission, system stability and distribution (Schernikau et al 2022). If the system costs are ignored, a case can be made that wind and solar are the cheapest source of electricity generation, but they cannot be ignored in the real world. Moreover, calculations of generation costs often make heroic assumptions about factors like capital costs, capacity factors and useful life of renewables. On this last point, wind turbines lose efficiency through leading edge erosion from the impact of dust, insects, birds and bats on their blades, and solar panels must be kept clean and lose about 2 per cent efficiency in their first year and 1 per cent thereafter.

Significantly, the report by Reputex (2021) on which the ALP relied for its campaign promise drew on none of the economic literature documenting experience with VRE such as that in Germany, relying entirely on its own modelling and that of consultants' reports and those of green energy lobby groups. Its limitations should have been apparent to the ALP, as it forecast the same 18 per cent reduction in prices by 2025 for all classes of consumer, including both residential and industrial – as well as the wholesale price (Reputex 2021: 9). Generation typically constitutes only about 40 per cent of electricity costs and the relative distribution costs for residential consumers are much higher than those of industrial consumers, so applying the same reduction to both these should have rung alarm bells.

In the September quarter 2023, the abundance of solar generation drove wholesale prices below zero 19 per cent of the time, putting greater pressure on the coal generators, yet default tariffs for households in several states rose by more than 20 per cent on average with some consumers reporting their bills almost doubled (Macdonald-Smith 2023). Coal was still providing about 60 per cent of demand, but losing money, with state governments increasingly having to provide its owners with subsidies to keep them on line to stabilise the system – with renewables generators still making money thanks to the sale of Renewable Energy Certificates. To make matters worse, retailers were having to pay domestic solar providers their contracted feed-in tariffs, and then sell that electricity at negative prices.

The rising retail prices meant by late 2024 130,000 households were on hardship payment plans provided by retailers, with the average owing $1,476 (Packham 2024), making a mockery of Albanese's promise of a $275 annual reduction. Minister Bowen attempted to blame the Russian invasion of Ukraine in February 2022 (despite the bubble in prices having largely passed) and the previous government for not ensuring there was more renewables capacity online. To save at least some face, the government introduced a rebate of $300 per household, with another $150 announced before the 2025 election.

This meant that the Commonwealth Government was subsidising renewable generators, the states were subsidising coal generators to stay afloat and remain in the market and prop up the grid, and the Commonwealth was subsidising consumers and promising to do so for those wishing to install batteries.

At no stage did the Albanese Government reveal the cost of their predominantly VRE policy, while constantly referring to the cost of the Opposition's nuclear option as $600 billion. This figure was the worst-case scenario in analysis by the Smart Energy Council – essentially a solar energy lobby group and hardly a neutral source – but that analysis also gave a lower estimate of $116 billion.

In fact, the SEC conclusion was that "Using data from CSIRO's latest GenCost report and the AEMO Integrated System Plan, the cost of building seven nuclear reactors is at least $116 billion" (SEC 2024). The SEC used all manner of misleading assumptions in its analysis, such as: it is assumed that nuclear plants operate at the same capacity factor as coal plants in 2024, around 60 per cent. In fact, coal plants in Australia had a capacity that low only because of the effects of VRE on the grid discussed above, and nuclear plant is fully capable of achieving 90 per cent. Moreover, both SEC and the AEMO "step change" analysis they quoted erroneously included distributed storage and utility-scale storage as "generation capacity", misrepresenting the fact that storage actually consumes about 15 per cent of the energy it shifts from times when generation is possible to when it is required.

It is to the discredit of the incurious news media that they allowed the ALP to continue to repeat this misleading figure, also ignoring the fact that there is no storage technology yet in existence that will cover "wind droughts" that can last several days, with batteries covering only a few hours and best suited to frequency and voltage regulation. Significantly, the Spanish blackout came in the last week of the campaign and any impact was undoubtedly minimised by the large volume of early voting.

The Albanese Government made much of its *Future Made in Australia* program, but its energy policy was undermining its prospects of success in increasing manufacturing. Plastics resin manufacturer Qenos closed its Altona plant, following on the heels of its Botany plant. This had flow-on effects, with chemicals manufacturer Indorama closing its Sydney plant because of a loss of feedstock from the Botany plant, and the Altona plant causing issues for Exxon as it used ethane, a by-product of gas production, which was transported from Exxon's Long Island gas processing plant. Exxon was reported to be considering having to flare the ethane if an alternative buyer could not be found (Evans 2024; Potter 2024).

Then in January 2025, Oceania Glass, a significant energy user, collapsed. Oceania was one of the approximately 200 companies in Australia covered by the Safeguard Mechanism mandating targets for emissions reductions out to 2030. In addition to rising energy prices, Oceania was also struggling in the face of dumping from China and Thailand (Cameron 2025; England 2025).

The Albanese Government rather painted itself into a corner by rejecting the Coalition's proposal to build seven nuclear generating plants at the sites of retiring coal stations. At COP28 in Dubai Australia declined to endorse the Declaration to Triple Nuclear Energy, endorsed by 25 countries as a response to climate change. Minister Bowen declined to endorse the Declaration on behalf of Australia and rebuffed United Kingdom Minister Ed Miliband, who stated at COP29 at Baku in December 2024 that he expected Australia to join. Bowen suggested "nuclear energy was not a viable option because Australia had more sunshine than the UK" (Shanahan 2024). Dennis Shanahan likened this to "the infantile response of The Simpsons-style cartoon fish with three eyes from Labor to Peter Dutton's initial proposal to look at nuclear energy" (Shanahan 2024). Acting Prime Minister Richard Marles rejected the Miliband overture on the grounds that Australia did not have a civil nuclear industry, ignoring the fact that it had been a member of the Generation IV International Forum developed in 2001 to advance nuclear generation technology.

The Albanese Government's climate and energy policy leaves Australia vulnerable to blackouts and rising costs that will continue to impact what little manufacturing that remains. As it happened, however, it made for good politics with the government was largely insulated from any criticisms by the fact, that as Prime Minister, Scott Morrison had locked the Coalition into pursuing a policy of Net Zero. (Morrison himself had once brandished a lump of coal in parliament to taunt Labor that it was afraid to support it). This left the Coalition to suggest nuclear, which lacked any strong constituency, which support for coal might have attracted (Advanced Ultracritical coal provides emissions reductions of 30-45 per cent). The Australian Manufacturing Workers Union was quick to criticise the nuclear proposal, demonstrating that (together with the Electrical Trades Union) renewables already had a strong constituency.

Nature Positive

A major policy initiative was the *Nature Positive Plan*, released in December 2022 to implement the Kunming Montreal Global Biodiversity Framework and serve as a blueprint for a revision of the *Environment Protection and Biodiversity Conservation Act.* This met with limited success, particularly because of opposition from resources interests and the Western Australian government. Legislation to enact the intended reforms did not enjoy support in the Senate and was delayed, with only the *Nature Repair Market Bill 2023*, establishing a national framework for a voluntary national biodiversity market, passed in December 2023 after a last-minute deal with the Greens.

What was described as Stage 2 of the process saw the introduction in

May 2024 of the *Nature Positive (Environment Protection Australia) Bill,* the *Nature Positive (Environment Information Australia) Bill* and the *Nature Positive (Environment Law Amendments and Transitional Provisions) Bill.* All were opposed by the Coalition, the Greens and two independent senators. A potential deal with the Greens was sunk in mid-September 2024 when Albanese ruled out including a "climate trigger" as part of the reforms.

The proposal to introduce the Nature Positive reforms was brought undone by Western Australian Senator Fatima Hayman, who had been expelled from the ALP over her opposition to Israel. Prolonged negotiations between Adam Bandt, Greens environment spokeswoman Sarah Hanson-Young and independent ACT Senator Pocock had led to a written agreement between the government, the Greens and Senator Pocock. Senator Hanson-Young had progressed the deal by offering to drop demands for a climate trigger in exchange for forest protections and minister Plibersek offered $10 million to establish a dedicated unit inside the proposed EPA to police illegal deforestation.

Senator Hayman killed the proposal, which was very unpopular in her state, indicating she would not support it, depriving the government of the numbers in the Senate. Senator Hayman indicated she would not be backing the reforms following a meeting with Minerals Council of Australia CEO Tania Constable (Greber 2024).

It was reported that the deal was scuppered by Albanese who stepped in and called the Greens Party to say the agreement was off, with Plibersek only finding out subsequently that the deal was cancelled. Western Australia (WA) Minister for Mines and Petroleum, David Michael, informed a Chamber of Minerals and Energy WA event the night the deal was scuppered that Mr Albanese had contacted Premier Cook about the potential deal with the Greens (Lewis, Thompson and Down 2024). Cook stated that he had "received assurances from the highest levels of government" that the EPA bill would not proceed in its current form that week, and that it was going to disadvantage Western Australian industry and risk Western Australian jobs (Lewis, Thompson and Down 2024)

A Global Nature Positive Summit was held in October 2024, intended as a demonstration of Australia's actions under its commitments under the Kunming Montreal Global Biodiversity Framework. It attracted more than 1,000 delegates from around 50 countries including environment and climate ministers, corporate leaders and representatives from environmental groups, Indigenous Peoples, scientists and community leaders.

The Nature Positive Summit did not pass without environmental protests, triggered by Plibersek's approval immediately prior to the summit of the expansion of three coal mines – Whitehaven Coal's Narrabri Underground Extension, MACHEnergy's Mount Pleasant Optimisation Project and Resource Pacific's Ashton-Ravensworth Project. The protests were organised by Move Beyond Coal, XR Drummers and Lock the Gate, angry that she had by then on her watch approved five coal projects and eight gas projects (McIlroy 2024).

In January 2025 it was reported that Environment Minister Plibersek was attempting to again progress the Nature Positive bills, causing concern for the ALP State Government in Western Australia, which faced a March election, but which was also crucial to the Albanese government's electoral prospects. It was reported that Plibersek's staffers had been canvassing miners and the WA Environment Minister, hoping to reach a compromise to create a Commonwealth environment protection agency (Coorey and Rabe 2025). Plibersek was reported to have also been soliciting support from her caucus colleagues to support to legislation to establish the EPA in what was likely to be the last sitting of Parliament before the election.

Environment Minister Tania Plibersek also appeared to be deferring some other crucial decisions until after the election because they required a choice between the traditional ALP constituency of workers and activist green groups. One of these was the decision on salmon farming in Macquarie Harbour on Tasmania's west coast which, it was claimed, was threatening the endangered Maugean Skate (Denholm 2024). This is discussed further below. Also delayed was a decision under the *EPBC Act* on the controversial Robins Island wind farm in northern Tasmania. The Act had required the Minister to make a decision 30 days after receipt of the requested information, but the decision was delayed until 9 December and then again until 2025 (Kaine 2024).

Plibersek was not afraid to jeopardise the renewable energy target by vetoing a Victorian proposal for an offshore wind farm. Citing the commitments to safeguard wetlands under the Ramsar Convention, the minister exercised a veto to protect wetlands from the proposed shore facility which she held stated a "clearly unacceptable" risk (Baxendale 2024).

The Environemtal Defenders Office: Environment and Aboriginal Heritage

Attempting to appeal to the green vote led to some trouble for the Albanese Government. It reversed a 2013 decision by the Abbott Coalition Government to cease funding for the Environmental Defenders Office (EDO), committing to provide $8.2m over four years (Chambers and Garvey 2024). Unfortunately, the EDO then proceeded to engage in somewhat controversial "lawfare" attempting to use Indigenous heritage concerns for environmental purposes, particularly attempting (unsuccessfully) to block Santos's Barossa gas project near the Tiwi Islands, but meeting with greater success in having Minister Plibersek block the McPhillamys gold mine near Bathurst in NSW.

Plibersek approved the Barossa project, but the EDO took legal action in an attempt to overturn her decision. The legal proceedings against the Barossa project revealed that a geoscientist from the University of Western Australia had produced bespoke mapping of songlines drawn so that they would be maximally impacted by the gas pipeline (Chambers and Garvey 2024), for which the EDO was excoriated. Justice Charlesworth stated of the evidence adduced by the EDO, "I have concluded that the cultural mapping exercise and the related opinions expressed about it are so lacking in integrity that no weight can be placed on them" (Cunningham 2024).

Justice Charlesworth subsequently awarded costs of more than $9m against the EDO, which placed it in some considerable financial jeopardy, despite its receipt of substantial overseas funding, including from "pass through" funds supported by interests that would be advantaged by restrictions on gas supply (Kellow 2024).

With the McPhillamys project, a $1 billion gold mine development at Blayney near Bathurst in New South Wales, Plibersek accepted claims that the proposed tailings dam would transgress the songline of the Blue-banded Bee. While the minister claimed she was not denying the project permission to proceed, the proponents stated that they had evaluated all possible sites and no suitable alternative was available. The claim of the bee mythology was rejected by the local Land Council, and the bee turned out to be unknown before 2022, showing every sign of having been created especially for the purpose of halting the mine. Unsurprisingly, the proponents initiated legal action, still ongoing at the time of writing.

Unfortunately, this misuse of Aboriginal heritage claims was undoubtedly harmful, with divisions created between the exponents of the Blue-banded Bee songline and the Land Council, and the dubious nature of both claims probably accentuating scepticism over all such claims by Indigenous activists.

The EDO was also active – though less visibly so – in the campaign against salmon farming in Macquarie Harbour on Tasmania's west coast. Aquaculture was claimed by the Bob Brown Foundation to be causing the extinction of the Maugean Skate, a remnant species from Gondwana 60 million years ago. The skate was only discovered about 30 years previously, and not in Macquarie Harbour, but in Port Davey an inlet off Bathurst Harbour, 100km or more to the south. It was initially named the Port Davey Skate, but it was observed only on three occasions there and not for 30 years, and is presumed to be extinct in that location – in the absence of any aquaculture.

The numbers of the skate population were uncertain, and it was unclear that the bottom-dwelling creature was at risk from aquaculture. Storm surges through Devils Gate, the heads to the harbour, had sometimes displaced water lower in oxygen to higher levels and occasionally caused some salmon mortalities. The skate preferred shallow, brackish water and so was not in direct competition with salmon. Moreover, discharges from the King and Gordon Rivers also complicated the picture, because both were affected by hydroelectric operations, and an oxygenation program and a successful captive breeding initiative appeared to be minimising the risk of extinction.

Nevertheless, the EDO and the Bob Brown Foundation requested that Minister Plibersek reconsider a decade-old approval of salmon farming under the *Environment Protection and Biodiversity Conservation Act*, but no decision was forthcoming before the election was called, and Albanese – keen, no doubt, to maximise his electoral chances in the seat of Braddon – introduced and had passed in the last week before Parliament rose legislation prohibiting the revisiting of permission for established ventures.

The Bob Brown Foundation immediately launched a legal challenge and it was revealed through a Freedom of Information request that the Department still had the case as an active issue, perhaps raising suspicions that Plibersek might still act if re-elected.

Discussion

The Albanese Government at the 2025 election negotiated the shoals of green politics successfully, not only increasing its primary vote to just below 35 per cent, but effectively seeing off the Greens as a party with representation in the House of Representaives. It was assisted only marginally by the Greens' controversial stance on Palestine and a related preferencing the ALP ahead of the Greens by the Coalition., but with Greens preference flows to the ALP that helped turn a little more than a third of the vote into a landside. It has also been suggested that a 20 per cent HECS discount helped lure young voters to Labor.

That was assisted by the Coalition persisting with the commitment Morrison made to Net Zero, which allowed minimal differentiation from the ALP on a crucial issue. Its nuclear policy, unlike coal or construction of renewables, had no extant constituency and it was too slow to counter Labor's blatant lies about its cost. Nor did it make much of Labor's refusal to reveal the cost and risks of its policy or 82 per cent renewables generation by 2030, thus missing the opportunity of making capital from the Spanish blackout with 78 per cent renewables generating in the last week of the election campaign. Moreover, remaining committed to Net Zero meant it could gain nothing from Tony Blair's abandonment of that notion also in the final week.

The ALP's refusal to follow the other Generation IV International Forum nations on nuclear has put the country at risk. Albanese dismissed such a risk in the final week of the campaign by claiming their plan included gas, but he clearly did not understand the importance of the inertia provided by large spinning generators that gas plant on standby could not match sufficiently fast to forestall any threat to the grid.

This points to the rather less impressive *policy* achievements of the Albanese Government on energy and environment policy. The most obvious one is that 82 per cent renewables carries substantial system risks and will continue to drive up prices, which cannot be subsidised forever. It has helped fund a problematic EDO that is likely to continue to cause reputational harm to Aboriginal heritage issues, which have subsequently seen demands by the rebel Bathurst group for heritage listing for Mt Panorama, virtually a sacred site for petrolheads. It has not succeeded in reforming the environmental approvals process, and leaves itself at risk of continued conflict over development approvals.

The fate of the Maugean Skate is not yet finalised, and it is yet to be seen whether the last-minute legislation to stave off the green attack on that will be honoured – or whether the persistence of the issue in Plibersek's department is just a symptom of the extent of the conflict between herself and Albanese. As it happened, she lost the portfolio after the election.

References

Baxendale, R., (2024), "Plibersek ruling on Victoria's offshore wind strategy an ill-wind for ALP energy policy", *The Australian*, 7 January

Chambers, G., and Garvey, P., (2024), "Inside lawfare plot to block Santos's $5.8bn Barossa gas project", *The Australian*, 26 November

Coorey, P., and Rabe, T., (2025), "WA premier warns East Coast latte sippers over 'Nature Positive' laws", *Australian Financial Review,* 29 January

Cunningham, M., (2024), " 'Lacking in integrity': Environmental Defenders Office ordered to pay Santos $9 million over failed attempt to halt gas pipeline project", *Sky News,* 29 November

Dalton, M., (2025) "Spain's blackout is the first of the clean energy era", *The Australian,* 30 April

Denholm, M., (2024), "Confusion over Labor's Tasmanian salmon 'fix'", *The Australian,* 5 December.

England, C., (2025), "Oceania Glass, which collapsed into administration this week, has a huge debt pile", *The Australian,* 6 February

Evans, N., (2024), "Qenos targets September closure of its Altona manufacturing plant in Melbourne", *The Australian,* 16 July

Greber, J., (2024), "Renegade senator Fatima Payman delivers 'oh shit' moment for prime minister on green overhaul", *ABC News*, 29 November

Hirth, L., (2013), "The Market Value of Variable Renewables", *Energy Policy*, 38, 218-36

Kellow, A., (2024), *The Finance Sector and Climate Change: Constraining Credit for Coal*, Newcastle: Cambridge Scholars Publishing

Kelly, M.J., (2016), "Lessons from technology development for energy and sustainability", *MRS Energy and Sustainability*, 3, 1-13

Lewis, R., Thompson, B., and Rhiannon Down, R., (2024), "Anthony Albanese intervenes to stop Labor deal with the Greens, overrides Tanya Plibersek", *The Australian,* 27 November

Macdonald-Smith, A., (2023), "Solar boom unleashes surge of below-zero power prices", *Australian Financial Review,* 23 October

McIlroy, J., (2024), "Protesters outside Nature Positive Summit demand Plibersek take real action", *Green Left*, 1416, 8 October

Mercer, D., (2024), "AEMO says emergency powers to switch off solar needed in every state amid 'system collapse' fears", *ABC News,* 2 December

Middap, C., (2024), "Labor legend Jennie George slams ALP's energy policies", *The Australian,* 15 March

Packham, C., (2024), "Record number of Australians struggling to pay electricity bills", *The Australian,* 2 December

Potter, B., (2024), "Gas costs could sink more manufacturers after Qenos: AIG", *Australian Financial Review*. 18 April

Reputex, (2021), "The economic impact of the ALP's Powering Australia Plan"

Schernikau, L., and Smith, W.H., (2022), "Climate impacts of fossil fuels in today's electricity systems", *Journal of the Southern African Institute of Mining and Metallurgy*, 122(3), 133-45

Schernikau, L., Smith, W. H., and Falcon, R., (2022), "Full Cost of Electricity 'FCOE' and Energy Returns 'eROI'," *Journal of Management and Sustainability*, 12, 96-121

Shanahan, D., (2024), "Richard Marles tangled in a climate mess of Chris Bowen's making", *The Australian,* 20 November

Smart Energy Council, (2024), "Nuclear Fallout: $116-$600 Billion to Build 7 Nuclear Reactors", *Press Release*, 22 June

Thomas, M., (2024), "Australia's Qenos enters administration, to close plants", *Chemical Week,* 26 April

Thompson, B., (2024), "Tanya Plibersek gives green light to four coalmine extensions despite green opposition", *The Australian,* 19 December

13

Aviation Policy:
A Reluctance to Reform?

Peter Forsyth

Introduction

The Albanese Government has been marked by little substantive change in aviation policy, along with one major train wreck (to mix metaphors). In fact, there has not been much change in aviation policy since the turn of the century, and both coalition and Labor governments have been content with leaving things as they are. This is not to say that matters are satisfactory, as the Qatar Airways incident illustrates. Competition in the international sector could be a lot stronger, and performance better, than at present, but governments have been unwilling to reform.

It makes sense to start with a brief background to aviation policy. There is a clear distinction between domestic and international policy. Australia can choose to implement whatever policy it prefers at the domestic level, but it is constrained by its international partners in its international policies. As a result, international aviation policy is more complex and controversial than domestic policy.

The substantive discussion in this chapter covers two topics. First, the Qatar Airways dispute is discussed – this is the most important and controversial issue. Second, in 2024 the Albanian Government released a broad-brush *Aviation White Paper: Towards 2050* (Department of Infrastructure, Transport, Regional Development, Communications and the Arts. The *White Paper* reviewed a wide range of issues and made recommendations, which the government is beginning to implement. The *White Paper* (Department of Infrastructure, Transport, Regional Development, Communications, Sport and the Arts, 2024a) summarises where the Albanese Government stands, except for one important exception – the Qatar Airways incident which was not discussed. It provides a template for the discussion of key issues here such as international aviation policy in general, domestic aviation policy, consumer protection issues, aviation's contribution to climate change, and the allocation of "slots" to airlines at Sydney Airport.

The players and policies

It is sometimes the case that who is involved is a critical determinant of policy outcomes. Such is the case with aviation policy in Australia.

For many years, aviation industry players have been very close to federal governments. Some of the industry players have been very effective in lobbying governments to implement policies to their advantage. Players such as Sir Reginald Ansett dominated policy in the 1950s to the 1970s, and the close relationship between Hawke and Ansett's Sir Peter Abeles from the 1980s and 1990s was instrumental in Australia's move to deregulation. More recently, Qantas's Alan Joyce established a close relationship with Albanese dating back to the time when Albanese was Transport Minister during the Rudd and Gillard governments, and this continued until Joyce retired in 2023 during the Albanese Government (Aston 2024).

This close relationship between the industry and government is not unique to Australia, but Australia has been a classic case study of such relationships. The industry is, almost always, quite oligopolistic, and it is easy for industry players to develop strong connections with governments. It is an industry in which regulation is important, especially for the international aspects. The international markets are such that countries need to negotiate with one and another to establish the rules under which they are going to operate services, which means that there is an essential role for governments and diplomacy. Qantas, in particular, has been effective in lobbying – for example, most members of federal parliament are members of its prestigious Chairman's Lounge (Aston 2024). It is hardly surprising that the industry has a role in influencing government policy.

As mentioned, Albanese was the Minister for Transport during the Rudd and Gillard governments. He had an interest in aviation policy, and during the time, the government produced a *National Aviation Policy White Paper* on the industry (Department of Infrastructure, Transport, Regional Development and Local Government 2009). Albanese has maintained contacts and continued his interest as Prime Minister. The Transport Minister during the Albanese Government's first term (and has continued in that role in the current second term), has been Catherine King (who also has responsibility for surface transport and infrastructure). While Qantas has not always been successful in getting its way in the past, it has been quite successful over the past five years. It has had considerable opportunity to lobby to block Qatar Airway's request for additional flights (Aston 2024). Other airlines have also been able to lobby the government successfully – Regional Express (Rex) has been able to gain considerable help from the government since it went into administration.

Aviation policy has changed very little since the turn of the century. There was a Productivity Commission Review of International Policy in 1998 (Productivity Commission 1998) which recommended more liberalisation, and preferably "open skies" which the then Coalition Government welcomed, however it led to limited change (though there was some extension of open skies). The Labor Rudd and Gillard governments made no significant changes. The Albanese Government issued a new White Paper on aviation in 2024, (Department of Infrastructure, Transport, Regional Development, Communications, Sport and the Arts, 2024a) which suggested several worthwhile improvements (eg to the allocation of Sydney Airport slots).The Albanese Government is implementing some of those changes. Significantly, it did not address the most controversial aviation issue, that of international access to the market, and the problems which airlines such as Qatar Airways have had, nor did it discuss possible policy responses. It is as though the Albanese Government has banished the Qatar issue from its mind as a bad dream, not to be mentioned. Despite this, international aviation is the one area the Albanese Government has the power to influence the current lack of competition – something about which the government professes to be concerned.

The Qatar dispute

By far the most significant event in aviation policy during the Albanese Government's first term has been the Qatar Airways dispute. This is so for several reasons. Up-front there was the dispute itself – a dispute between Qatar and the Australian Government over the latter's refusal to allow Qatar Airways additional flights into Australia. The way in which this was handled led to a Senate Inquiry about the substance of the issue, and the government's handling of this matter (Senate Select Committee 2023). This Senate Inquiry highlighted serious problems with the policy itself. At the same time, the White Paper was being prepared, and a reasonable expectation might be that the policy would be reviewed, to assess whether revisions to the policy, or even whether major changes to the policy were warranted. In the end, the Albananese Government did not even review the policy, and the current policy, under which the Qatar dispute arose, remains in place.

What happened?

In 2022, as international aviation was gradually recovering from the COVID-19 crisis, Qatar Airways applied for approval for an additional 28 flights per week into Australia. Except where countries have an "open skies" agreement (see below), foreign countries must apply for additional flights on a case-by-case basis in Australia (Department of Infrastructure 2024a). Qatar Airways had solid reasons to expect a good reception to its request, given that it had maintained flying to Australia all through the COVID-19 crisis (unlike Qantas), at some cost to itself in terms of profitability (Aston 2024). The only question mark about the airline was that there was an incident at Doha Airport in 2020 in which several Australian women were strip searched at the security check (this was done by the airport security, not the airline). This was a controversial action, and it still has not been satisfactorily resolved.

After a long wait, the request was refused. Initially, no reason for the refusal were given, though as the refusal became more and more controversial, ministers were largely competing with one another to give different reasons, many of where inconsistent with one another. No clear statement was offered. Over time, some of the details for the refusal leaked out. In particular, Qantas, Qatar Airway's competitor, appeared to have had discussions with the Albanese Government (and the CEO of Qantas, was Alan Joyce, a friend of the Prime Minister), but the then CEO of Virgin Australia, Jane Hrdlicka, had had no meaningful discussions. The Albanese Government took the view that the less said the better, and did not discuss the issue further. The Opposition used its numbers in the Senate to set up an inquiry into the matter.

The Senate Inquiry

The Senate Inquiry into Bilateral Air Service Agreements is a good example of the Senate in its role as a house of review (Senate Select Committee, 2023). Given the widespread dissatisfaction with the Albanese Government's handling of the Qatar Airways dispute, the Opposition instituted a Senate Committee inquiry into the matter and related matters. The Senate inquiry was chaired by the Shadow Minister for Infrastructure and Transport, Bridget McKenzie, and included Labor, Green, and independent members. It asked for public submissions and held public hearings. Factual information was provided by the Department of Infrastructure, but no statement of reasons was provided, and ministers did not appear before the Senate Committee. Nor did the CEO of Qantas at the time, Alan Joyce. Dissenting reports were made by the Greens and Labor members.

The Senate Report was predominantly very critical of the government. Not surprisingly, the main support for the government came from Qantas. Even though the Senate inquiry was a quick exercise, some of the submissions did go into the matter in a good deal of depth (for example those of Professor Merkert at Sydney University and Dr Tony Webber, formerly Chief Economist of Qantas). These submissions argued that the Albanese Government's decision to block further

Qatar flights did make an appreciable impact on competition, and thus on benefits to the Australian community.

The Senate Report came up with some straightforward recommendations. These included:

- that the government review its decision, and
- that for future decisions, the government evaluate the costs and benefits of the proposed changes, consult widely with stakeholders such as the ACCC, and publish a statement of reasons. (NB: This is not a new recommendation, since the Productivity Commission and others recommended essentially this at the time of the 1998 Productivity Commission Report, which the Coalition Government of the day accepted as its policy).

In addition, the Senate Report made some further recommendations on related matters, including:

- responding to the Harris Report on Sydney Airport slot management (Harris 2021; Department of Infrastructure, Transport, Regional Development and The Arts, 2024a),
- consumer protection reforms, and
- the need for an Inquiry into potential anti-competitive behaviour in the domestic market.

Some of these were addressed in the Albanese Government's Aviation White Paper.

Given that the Albanese Government was in no mood to respond to the Senate Report, there were few immediate outcomes. Nevertheless, the Senate Report led to some useful outcomes:

- It was useful in information gathering;
- It documented how the government handled a controversial issue;
- It indicated how international aviation negotiations should be conducted consistent with the government's preferred "case by case" approach. This was ignored in the government's Aviation White Paper; and,
- The outcry it generated may have made the government more willing to allow Qatar Airways to buy a 25 per cent state in Virgin Australia.

What is the national interest?

During the Qatar Airways dispute, several ministers justified the government's actions as "being in the national interest" (Aston 2024). However, they did not elaborate what constituted the national interest. The national interest has sometimes been defined in other contexts in economic policy – for example in merger policy. A definition would normally refer to a range of aspects, such as consumer welfare, producer profitability, competition, jobs and environmental aspects. The White Paper says little about the national interest, but it does say that additional flights should not "come at the expense of the sustainability of Australian carriers" (Department of Infrastructure, Transport, Regional Development and The Arts 2024: 204). This is essentially protectionist.

How does this stack up with the decision about Qatar Airways flights? It might seem that these flights could lessen the sustainability of the Australian carriers, principally Qantas. However, most of the flights between Australia and Europe are operated by foreign airlines, such as Emirates, Etihad and Singapore Airlines. These airlines would bear the main brunt of competition from additional flights granted to Qatar Airways. There will be an impact on profits of Qantas which has a strategic alliance with Emirates, which undoubtedly would involve some profit-sharing arrangements. Australian jobs would not be affected except marginally. Qantas is said to have lobbied hard against Qatar Airways being granted extra flights. This is a peculiar case of protection being granted to a foreign, not Australian, business.

What difference to competition would granting Qatar Airways requests have made? At the time of the request the airline industry was recovering from the Covid-19 shock, and many routes were under-provided for. This is especially so for long-haul routes such as Europe – Australia. Demand however was recovering sharply. Flights were relatively scarce, and fares were high, and the additional capacity which Qatar Airways proposed would have made a significant impact. Over time, airlines have been recovering and adding more flights, and fares have been coming down. However, even now, fares have not fallen to their pre Covid level, and flights are below trend. Granting Qatar Airways requests would have made a significant, though diminishing benefit to Australian travellers and the inbound tourism industry.

How was the Crisis Handled?

The entire episode was poorly handled by the government – there were no saving graces. There was a long delay between Qatar Airways seeking approval of additional flights and the response. This does happen from time to time, but it does indicate a flaw in the system since there was no necessary reason for the delay. When the decision was announced, ministers seemed unprepared and proffered a confusing array of conflicting justifications – there was no agreed "party line". What is more, many of the reasons given stretched credulity – for example the claimed need for Qantas to be given freedom from competition from Qatar Airways so that it could invest in new aircraft (when Qantas had little involvement with the European market, having left that to Emirates). No doubt the government was damaged by its failure to get its story right. In spite of this, there were two other opportunities to make amends – the Senate Inquiry into the dispute, and the White Paper on Aviation Policy of 2024. The government took advantage of neither of these two opportunities.

The emerging Qatar/Virgin Link-up

In the past, Qatar Airways have been innovative it the ways they have used the restrictive capacity they have been allowed to operate into Australia. They are continuing to innovate. Having been knocked back on extra flights under their own name, they may be able to achieve their goals using a different route. Qatar Airways been approved to buy 25 per cent of Virgin Australia from Bain Capital. Like other Australian airlines Virgin does have the rights to operate to Qatar, subject to Qatari government approval, and now that it has a commercial interest to do so, it has decided to exercise these rights. Currently, Virgin does not have aircraft suitable for the route, but Qatar can provide them on a "wet" lease basis (ie Qatar will provide the aircraft and crew). This will be almost the same as Qatar operating the flights itself. The Virgin/Qatar Airways tie-up means that there will be more flights on to European destinations via the Doha hub. The government's refusal for additional Qatar Airways flights has been ineffective.

The White Paper and Responses to it

The White Paper (Department of Infrastructure, Transport, Regional Development and The Arts, 2024a) covered a range of aspects to of aviation policy, and five of the more important aspects are covered here.

International policy– Is it a good policy?

Australia has conducted a series of reviews of International Aviation policy, beginning with the International Civil Aviation Policy Review of 1978 (ICAP 1978) and the most recent substantial review was the Productivity Commission Review of 1998. This recommended an "open skies" approach whenever possible, subject to agreement with its bilateral partners. Open skies means that all airlines from the two bilateral partner countries can schedule as many flights to the other country as they wish. The government of the day adopted this recommendation, and there has been some liberalisation since, but actual progress towards the goal has been slow and patchy. Currently Australia has about half its routes covered by open skies agreements, though the actual number of countries with agreements has been small (seven), though they include several important aviation countries such as the US and Singapore. Officially, the Australian policy is to seek open skies agreements with its partners, but this apparently liberal approach is qualified by the requirement that such agreements be in the "national interest", which is defined here as "not at the expense of the sustainability of Australian carriers" amongst other provisos. In other words, the policy is essentially protectionist.

Most of Australia's bilateral agreements (including those with Qatar and the United Arab Emirates) are covered by the "case-by-case" approach. This may seem reasonable, but it masks a number of problems. In principle, countries are allowed sufficient airline capacity or flights to handle expected demand (Department of Infrastructure,

Transport, Regional Development and The Arts 2024a). To obtain more flights, a country, on behalf of its airlines, must apply to the Australian government, which makes an assessment and determines whether to grant the flights, and how many flights to approve. With some countries, the likely need for flights is easy to determine, but for others, this apparently simple rule makes little sense. Several of Australia's aviation long-distance routes are operated by "6th freedom"carriers, which are operated via a hub which is not the final destination for flights. For example, much of the Australian traffic to Singapore is destined for Europe and Asian destinations and airlines exercise rights to fly from Australia to Singapore and from Singapore to other destinations, such as the United Kingdom, to provide a long-haul service (Humphreys 2023). It is hardly clear what the flight capacity needs of Singapore from Australia are (the issue with Singapore was eventually solved by having it as an open skies country). Most of the passengers between Australia and Qatar are flying on to other destinations.

A basic question for the case-by-case approach is – why limit flights at all? It would be feasible to remove the limits even without going to the full extent of open skies. Often, the current system works quite well – until it does not (as the Qatar dispute shows). It is possible to distinguish at least two problems with the system.

1 It is unnecessarily bureaucratic, leading to delays and uncertainties in determining whether flights can be operated, and

2 It is very subject to ministerial intervention, with no clear guidelines as to what will be approved or not. The Qatar case is an excellent case of this.

On the other hand, it is difficult to see what advantages the case-by-case system has. In particular, it is difficult to see any way it contributes to advancing the national interest, with the "national interest" is so poorly defined.

A missed opportunity for reform

The Aviation White Paper mirrored a similar review during the Rudd and Gillard governments, which did not result in much policy change (Department of Infrastructure, Transport, Regional Development and Local Government 2009). One might have expected that the review would have contributed to the international aviation policy discussion – the government response to the Senate review, or a review of how international policy might be improved. As it turned out, there was none of this. The Qatar Airways dispute, the most controversial event during this government's tenure, was not even mentioned. The White Paper in its brief discussion of international policy simply reiterated the implausible claim that Australia was one of the world leaders in progress towards aviation liberalisation. This was a missed opportunity, which did not even set out why the government acted as it did during the dispute.

At the risk of explaining what did not, as opposed to what did, happen, it is worth noting some of the types of policy reforms which could have been advocated. If the government is seeking to continue with a case-by-case approach to international aviation negotiations, it could have suggested ways of making the whole process more rigorous, rather than one depending on the whims of ministers and prime ministers. It could have set out clear criteria for decisions, which has been done for airports. It could have defined the national interest as applied to negotiations. It could have set out processes which decisions could be required to follow, along with timelines. As suggested in the submissions, it could have set up a dispute resolution mechanism under which partner countries could challenge decisions. It could set out which parties should be consulted and which not (many have objected to the preferential access granted to Qantas).

These aspects are all consistent with the government's preferred case-by-case approach. There are other viable alternatives to this, and these most promising is the open skies approach, which is adopted across the board by the US and other countries, and with seven partner countries by Australia. It is an approach which yields maximum overall benefits to the home country in most, but not all cases. Free trade in goods is normally the best policy, but there can be cases where this is not the case. The same is true of open skies in the aviation case. If a country has market power in the provision of airline services on a route, and most passengers are from the foreign partner, open skies may not be the best policy. The Productivity Commission, in its 1998 Report, (Productivity Commission 1998) recommended that Australia adopt where possible, but Australian governments have adopted this policy only sparingly.

A case-by-case approach, when benefits and costs of liberalisation are assessed rigorously, has the potential to be a good policy. However, there is no guarantee that this rigorous assessment will take place. There are no checks and balances to ensure that this happens. As a result, there is a strong likelihood that it will degenerate into an "anything goes" approach, as indeed has happened in Australia. Practical political economy suggests that the better option would be for Australia to seek open skies agreements wherever possible.

Domestic Aviation Policy

Along with most other domestic airline markets, the Australian market was tightly regulated market until 1990. Two airlines, Australian Airlines (now part of Qantas) and Ansett were the two airlines permitted to fly on trunk routes. In 1990 domestic aviation was deregulated, and there were no restrictions on entry by Australian airlines. Occasionally new airlines have attempted to enter, but they failed, and it was not until a low-cost carrier Virgin Blue entered in 2000 that entry was successful. In 2001, however, Ansett failed, and Australia was left with just one major airline. After this, Qantas established a fully owned low-cost airline subsidiary, Jetstar, which remains successful. Over time, Virgin became a full-service carrier and changed its name to Virgin Australia. One significant change was that foreign ownership rules were relaxed, and it by 2000 it became possible for domestic (but not international) airlines to be fully foreign owned.

There has been a burst of activity in domestic aviation since the emergence of the COVD-19 epidemic. Both domestic and international aviation almost ceased very quickly, and both have been moderately slow to recover (partly because of difficulties in getting aircraft and staff). Virgin Australia, as it is now called, collapsed and went into administration soon after the epidemic began. It was bought by (US Owned) Bain Capital with a view to being sold on to longer term owners. Recently, Qatar Airways was permitted to buy 25 per cent of the airline and it was listed on the stock exchange. There have been two attempts at entry into the market. One was by Bonza, a new start-up airline which tried to compete on new and less well served routes. It failed in 2024. The second was an attempt by Regional Express or Rex, a long-established regional airline, to enter the main trunk routes such as Sydney to Melbourne. This also went into administration in 2024, but it still operates its regional network. It might be thought that Rex would be a strong competitor, since it is an established brand. However, when it entered the trunk routes, Qantas responded by entering Rex's regional routes, diluting its profits. In addition, Rex has argued that it had difficulty in securing "slots" at Sydney airport.

Thus, the current situation is that there are two airline groups serving the main trunk routes, and no airline has been able to enter successfully (though Virgin has replaced Ansett). This is a problem which the government and the Australian Competition and Consumer Commission (ACCC) are well aware of, but there are few sustainable solutions to strengthening competition. The Albanese Government in August 2023 has initiated a Competition Review being conducted by Treasury and estimated to take two years. Originally aviation was excluded from this Review, but after considerable criticism, this was reversed. At this stage, no promising suggestions have been made. A suggestion was made, by the Shadow Minister for Transport, Bridget Mackenzie, to vertically separate Qantas and Jetstar. Vertical separation has been a tool used, from time to time, in the United States (US), as a means to lessen market power in various industries, though it is hardly used in Australia, except at times when companies are seeking to merge with other companies operating in a overlapping markets. The coalition did not press ahead with the suggestion.

The aftermath of COVID-19

Two of Australia's three largest airlines have gone into administration since the beginning of the COVID-19 pandemic. Regional Express (Rex) entered administration in 2024 following a misguided attempt to enter main trunk routes. The airline has been provided with loans, but no likely buyer has been found. As a result, the Albanese Government has indicated that it may buy the airline itself (Prasser 2025).

Rex is a regional airline which emerged out of the collapse of Ansett in 2001. It had operated around 60 turboprop aircraft on regional routes moderately successfully. It was the sole supplier on many of these routes. In 2021 it leased Boeing 737s and began operations major trunk routes such as Sydney to Melbourne. Not surprisingly, the major airlines responded by starting operations on Rex's hitherto monopoly routes. This provoked a cash crisis, and the airline failed and went into administration. The first action of the administration was to close the trunk routes, but it has been difficult for the airline to reestablish profitability on its regional routes. Hence the call for drastic action.

The Albanese Government does face a dilemma. The current proposal is to buy out Rex if needed – this would be managerially expensive, as the government is not in the business of running airlines, and restructuring an ailing business would pose lots of challenges. The airline does face several ongoing challenges, such as sourcing and funding newer aircraft. The option has already met with the informal approval of the National Party members, though not yet the Coalition as a whole. Alternatively, it could allow/encourage one of the two main airlines to merge with Rex, allowing the new firm to do what it thinks is necessary to develop a viable regional business. This, however, would lessen competition in what is already a concentrated market. Finally, it could allow Rex to fail – this would mean that for a time, regional centres would have no airline service. Other airlines will step in, but not immediately, and several more marginal routes are likely to miss out.

Improving the traveller experience

The COVID-19 pandemic gave rise to widespread dissatisfaction with the ways airlines were treating their passengers. Prior to COVID, there were occasional issues, but there was no consistent call for reform (though passengers who had been travelling on international flights noted that issues such as delays were handled much more considerately than was the case within Australia). Matters changed when flights were resumed as COVID-19 faded, especially during 2022. Initially, airlines were struggling to bring back aircraft and staff in sufficient numbers to operate services. Cancellations and delays were common, and airlines had to deal with the backlog of commitments they had entered into when they cancelled flights which passengers had paid for. These types of issues were handled relatively smoothly by some airlines, but others including Qantas Group airlines, attracted a lot of criticism for the ways they met their obligations, such as by setting unrealistically short timespans with which to take flights to replace flights which had been cancelled. Other problems included airlines taking bookings to flights which they knew, at the time of booking, had already been cancelled.

The crisis gave rise to many problems which were essentially short term in nature, and which were resolved in one- or two-years' time. The COVID experience, however, highlighted the fact that passengers are treated worse within Australia than they are overseas. In the European Union (EU) and the United Kingdom (UK), Canada and the US, if flights are cancelled or delayed for more than a set time (often three hours), the airline is legally required to pay set compensation within a few weeks. In Australia a passenger delayed five hours might get a $6.50 voucher (if that). (This makes the passenger more prepared to take out membership of a frequent flyer club).

It is not surprising then, that the Albanese Government sought to address this issue. The status quo, of minimal compensation for cancellations and delays was probably not politically feasible, and the government put the matter on the terms of reference for the Aviation White Paper.

The White Paper's solution, which has become government policy, was minimal. It proposed an Aviation Industry Ombuds Scheme which would develop an Aviation Customer Rights Charter, which the ombudsperson would consider "fair and reasonable conduct by the airlines and airports" (Department of Infrastructure 2024a: 55; Department of Infrastructure 2024b). It would set out what delays would be considered unreasonable; it would require timely communication with passengers and require airlines to provide support to passengers in making alternative travel arrangements. Airlines would be required to provide more information about the reasons for delays and cancellations they would be subject to "show cause" for them. And this is all. It should be noted that the scheme is designed to handle day-to-day cancellations and delays, and not the more serious problems which emerged during the Covid crisis, when airlines tried to avoid the responsibility for cancelled flights.

Needless to say, this has not gone down well – consumer groups and the opposition have been very critical. The problem is that it is not a substantial advance on the status quo. The requirements imposed on the airlines and airports are extremely vague – what delays ae "unreasonable". There are no criteria set out. The ombudsperson might make judgments, but there would be no further action about a complaint. The Australian airlines and airports are quite used to being subjected to sharp criticism and then doing nothing about it, especially since the Australian airlines and airports do not, in most cases, face much competition in the market. The Albanese Government's approach was simply announced but not argued for.

As with the government response to the Qatar matter, the consumer protection issue was discussed in another Senate Committee report in March 2025 (Senate Standing Committee Rural and Regional and Transport 2025). This Committee did not have the power to require the government to do anything in particular, but it did have value in teasing out the arguments. Prior to this, the opposition had put forward its own preference for "pay on delay" scheme, whereby airlines would be mandated to compensate passengers for delays or cancellations if they reached a set level. This is similar to the system operating in the EU and in the UK (The US and Canada also have similar systems). The passenger would know just how much compensation they would get if they were delayed, say, five hours.

The Inquiry raised several issues which need to be resolved. These include:

- Who pays for compensation – the airlines or ultimately, the passengers (through higher air fares)? With the oligopolistic or monopolistic markets which characterise most Australian air routes, it is likely to be a combination of both airline and passenger. Airlines typically argue that the passenger ultimately pays (though they oppose the schemes), and consumer groups tend to assume that the airline will pay.

- While cancellations and delays may not be intentionally caused by the airlines, it is in their power to lessen the chance of them coming about. While airlines may not intentionally create delays, if there is no cost to an airline should delays occur, it will face a minimal incentive to avoid them if there is no penalty it faces for having them. Having some penalty will mean that airlines have some "skin in the game", just like regulated rail services in Australia which face penalties for late arrival.

- The causes of airline delays and cancellations are various, (weather, air traffic management congestion etc.) and often they are not the airline's fault. Sorting out who is responsible can be difficult and even lead to litigation.

- If compensation is to be paid, how much should it be? This is not an easy question to answer, and it should be remembered that passengers will be paying for the compensation, at least to some degree. In all sorts of situations, people take out insurance which has a cost to them. In the airline delay and cancellation case, people may be willing to pay more their ticket if there is a compensation scheme in place.

The Albanese Government's approach (which has yet to be finalised) involves minimal change from the status quo. There is considerable dissatisfaction with this by passengers, but the airlines prefer not to change. Ideally, there should be some evaluation of the issues, including those mentioned above. The Productivity Commission would be a logical investigator.

Aviation and climate change

Aviation is a large emitter of greenhouse gases. It accounts for about 2 per cent (and rising) of world CO_2 emissions, and there are other emissions such as NOx (nitrous oxides), methane, and the aircraft contrails also contribute to global warming (Grewe 2020). To make matters worse, Australia is a major user of aviation, particularly for interstate and international travel. A Sydney to London flight will generate at least 2-3 tonnes per economy passenger of CO2. Not only this, is very difficult to abate aviation emissions, unlike most other industries.

The Albanese Government has put a lot of emphasis on reducing Australia's contribution to global emissions – The title of the White Paper is *Aviation White Paper Towards 2050*. It includes some initiatives, but these are modest compared to those of other countries, and especially the UK and the EU. The strongest climate change policies are the EU and UK emissions trading schemes (ETSs) which extend to aviation. The EU scheme effectively imposes a tax of 60 to 100 Euro per tonne of CO2 emitted. By contrast, the strongest policy measure imposed on aviation in Australia is the Safeguards Mechanism, which was strengthened by the Albanese government, and which covers the domestic aviation activities of Qantas and Virgin Australia, but not international flights. This effectively imposes a tax of about $35 per tonne, by requiring the business to purchase offsets (these are not as effective at reducing CO2 as actual reductions in emissions). In addition, Australia has, like most western countries, signed up to the International Civil Aviation Organisation's CORSIA scheme, whereby international airlines are required to purchase offsets for the *growth* in their CO2 emissions (Maertens et al 2020). This is likely to have only a very minor effect in reducing emissions. Like many other airlines, the Australian airlines operate voluntary offset schemes, the effectiveness of which are questionable (Knorr and Eisenkopf 2020)

It is well recognised that aviation is a very difficult industry to decarbonise. As a result, there is much interest in sustainable aviation fuels (SAFs) (Roth 2020). These are low emissions fuels which can be readily used to replace fossil-based jet fuels. There are several limitations with SAF, notably they are in short supply, meaning that the uptake will be slow, and they are expensive, at around three times the price (or more) of jet fuel. Production of SAFs is only just beginning, but the White Paper recommended that the government support production through its Future Made in Australia initiative. This will go a small way towards overcoming the limitations of SAF. There will be a small incentive for airlines serving Australia's international routes through the CORSIA program.

Thus, the Albanese Government has made some steps towards decarbonising aviation, though much more needs to be done. The government has not addressed to the problem of the high cost of SAF – in Europe this has been addressed by imposing mandates on airlines to use increasing proportions of SAFs in their fuel mix. A further issue which the government has not addressed is that of electro fuels, which are even more expensive than SAFs, but which are zero carbon in use (though not zero carbon in production). In the longer-term Australia may have the potential to be one of the main producers of these fuels since they require large amounts of electricity (just as it may be able to produce green steel - see Garnaut et al, 2022).

Reforming Slot Allocation at Sydney Airport

Around the world, when airports are subjected to more demand than they have capacity to service, they normally use a system of allocating slots – to use an airport, the airline must have a "slot" for Each time it lands or takes off. Sydney Airport is the only airport in Australia subject to serious excess demand, and it resolves this by operating a slot system. There have been a number of complaints about the Sydney scheme – for example, airlines asking for more slots than they need, and then cancelling flights. This had the effect of denying slots to other airlines. The previous government commissioned Peter Harris, previously Chair of the Productivity Commission, to suggest reforms. He reported in 2021 (Harris, 2021), and the 2024 *White Paper* recommended that most of his reforms be adopted. The government has followed this recommendation.

One reform which is now in place has been the replacement of the slot coordinator. Until recently, the body which coordinated the slot allocation was a joint venture including the major airlines including Qantas and Virgin Australia. This was a case of the regulator being owned by the bodies which it was supposed to regulate. The government replaced this and conducted a competitive selection process, and has chosen UK based Airport Coordination Limited (ACL), which coordinates major airports such as London Heathrow, to manage the slot system.

Conclusions: An assessment of the Albanese Government's performance

To conclude, it is useful to give an overall summary the Albanese Government's performance in four distinct aspects.

1. *Has the government managed the day-to-day problems well?*
   - Qatar Airways and international aviation: This is a clear no.
   - Domestic competition: The government has responded to the Rex problem using an adequate but expensive option.
   - Consumer issues: Slow to act.
   - Climate change issues: Some progress.
   - Airport Slots: Yes.
2. *Has the government initiated significant reforms?*
   - Qatar Airways and international aviation: This is a clear no. This is the most significant issue in aviation policy, but the government but the government has avoided the issue, claiming that things are just fine. It did not analyse why most observers are dissatisfied with the government's handling of the Qatar Airways issue.
   - Domestic Competition: The government has not done much to explore options to increase domestic competition. It has not (publicly) explored ways of handling the Rex problem.
   - Consumer issues: The government has begun to tackle this.
   - Climate change issues: The government could be much more proactive in addressing the aviation emissions issue, as the UK and EU have been.
   - Airport slots: The solution to the slot problem is good, though it could have gone further.
3. *How independent from industry has the government been?*
   It is often recognised that governments are too dependent on the industries they are regulating when they are developing policies

for them. This is a particular risk for aviation where industry and government are close:

- Qatar Airways and international aviation: This has been a severe problem in both the Qatar Airways case and with international aviation policy generally. The Albanese Government has been excessively dependent on industry input.

- Domestic competition: There is little evidence of independent thinking about the options to solve the Rex Airline problem, or in ways to increase competition in domestic aviation.

- Consumer issues: The government has proposed a very industry friendly approach to the consumer delay and cancellation issue, falling short of the European and North American approaches.

- Climate change issues: Industry involvement is critical, but it should not be dominant.

- Airport slots: There has been evidence of independent thinking on the slots issue, as well as (appropriate) industry input.

4.   *Has the government explained and sold its policies well?*

Often governments are not good at setting out the rationale for their policies. This leads to them being poor at selling or explaining them. This has been an issue with the Albanese Government's aviation policy.

- This has been evident with international aviation policy, particularly as it applies to the Qatar Airways crisis. There was poor decision making and the government did not explain why it was doing what it did. It seemed to be trying to cover up what it was doing, which meant that its explanations were unconvincing. In terms of the broader issue of international policy, something which is of potentially substantial importance, it simply makes Trump-like claims of how well it is doing.

- Domestic Competition: The government has made some decisions, such as how to handle the Rex problem, but it has not explained why it has chosen this option.

- Consumer issues: Here again, there has been little analysis of why the government has chosen the option, which is a minimal change option. This is a matter which is of direct interest to passengers, and it is not surprising that they are disappointed.

- Climate change issues: The government has put a lot of emphasis on developing its climate change policy, and there is significant scope for its aviation climate change policy to be developed further and become a selling point for it.
- Airport Slots: The Sydney Airport slot issue has been explained quite adequately.

The Treasurer, Jim Chalmers, has indicated that a major thrust of the re-elected Albanese Government will be to tackle the productivity problem (on the productivity issue see also Chapters 8, 9, and 10). What does this mean for aviation? With domestic aviation and aviation infrastructure, there has been little by way of assessment of productivity for many years – it may be adequate, but it might not be. Some evaluation is worthwhile. With international aviation, the main issue is that of competition and liberalisation, rather than productivity itself. As indicated in this chapter, there is considerable scope for reforms which can lead to better performance.

References

Aston, J., (2024), *The Chairman's Lounge: The Inside Story of How Qantas Sold Us Out*, Sydney: Scribner Australia

Department of Infrastructure, Transport, Regional Development and Local Government, (2009), *National Aviation Policy White Paper: Flight Path to the Future*, Canberra: Commonwealth of Australia, December

Department of Infrastructure, Transport, Regional Development, Communications and the Arts (henceforth Department of Infrastructure), (2024a), *Aviation White Paper: Towards 2050*, Canberra: Commonwealth of Australia, August

Department of Infrastructure, (2024b), *The Aviation Industry Ombuds Scheme – Consultation Paper*, Canberra: Commonwealth of Australia, August

Garnaut, R., (2022), *The Superpower Transformation -Making Australia's Zero-Carbon Future*, Carlton: La Trobe University Press

Grewe, V., (2020), "Aviation Emissions and Climate Emissions", in Fichert, F., Forsyth, P., and Niemeier, H.M., (eds), *Aviation and Climate Change: Economic Perspectives on Greenhouse Gas Reduction Policies*, London and New York: Routledge, 4-15

Harris, P., (2021), *Review of the Sydney Airport Demand Management Scheme, Independent Review,* Department of Infrastructure and Transport (Australia), Canberra: Commonwealth of Australia

Humphreys, B., (2023), *Regulation of Air Transport: From Protection to Liberalisation and Back Again*, London and New York: Routledge

IPAC, (1978), *Review of Australia's International Civil Aviation Policy, Report of Review Committee*, Canberra: Australian Government Publishing Service

Knorr, A., and Eisenkopf, A., (2020), "Voluntary carbon offset schemes in the airline industry: why did they fail?", in Fichert, Forsyth, and Niemeier, *Aviation and Climate* Change, 130-44

Maertens, S., Grimme, W., and Scheelhaase J., "ICAO's New CORSIA Scheme at a Glance – a Milestone towards Greener Aviation?", in Fichert, Forsyth, and Niemeier, *Aviation and Climate Change*, 117-29

Prasser, S., (2025), "Re-nationalising the airline industry … a sink or soar government decision?" *Canberra Times*, 18 February

Productivity Commission, (1998), *International Air Services: Report No 2*, Canberra: Commonwealth of Australia, September

Roth, A., (2020), "Renewable Fuels for Aviation", in Fichert, Forsyth and Niemeier, *Aviation and Climate Change*, 16-46

Senate Select Committee on Commonwealth Bilateral Air Service Agreements, (2023), *Commonwealth Bilateral Air Service Agreements*, Canberra: Commonwealth of Australia, October

Senate Standing Committee on Rural and Regional and Transport, (2025), *Airline Passenger Protections (Pay on Delay) Bill 2024*, Hearings, Canberra: Commonwealth of Australia, March

14

Labor's Higher Education Agenda: A La-La-Land Wish List

Salvatore Babones

Introduction

Higher education always attracts much more political attention than the sheer size of the "industry" (and university trade groups do routinely call it an "industry") would warrant. Over the last three years, much of that attention has focused on hot-button cultural issues like the conflict in the Middle East, the indigenous Voice campaign, and the ever-shrinking space for viewpoint diversity on campus. Issues like these make the headlines, but most of them affect relatively few students, and in any case the cultural battle-lines are drawn (and shift very little from election to election). The really big changes that occur when governments face the voters have to do with finance and regulation: votes can be won (or lost) when the price of higher education goes up or the quality goes down. Private providers and even public universities also lobby aggressively for their preferred policies. And with international students constituting a substantial portion of the Australian market and workforce, even the business community at large takes an interest in what would otherwise be technocratic decisions about visa processing or student employment. This chapter thus examines the politics of higher education, not with a focus on the culture war headlines, but with a focus on the social and economic issues that really form the higher education agenda for families, institutions – and lobbyists.

From post-election parsimony to pre-election promises

As Australia went to the polls in May 2022, one talismanic issue dominated Labor Party activists' higher education agenda: the future of the Job-Ready Graduates Package. This 2020 Coalition policy (implemented in 2021) substantially reduced subsidies for Commonwealth Supported Places in the humanities and social sciences while simultaneously increasing subsidies for "job-ready" degrees in engineering, nursing, and languages. Notwithstanding the sop to English majors, the Jobs Ready Graduates Package was fiercely denounced by Labor-preferencing arts majors, university student and staff unions, and the intellectual commentariat. The Labor Party itself, however, was strangely silent on the issue.

Three years later, the Job-Ready Graduates Package is still in place. How Labor voters feel about that is unknown, though one might guess. The Greens have consistently condemned the policy ever since 2020, but in Australia's system of preferential voting, it hardly matters. Repealing the policy would be expensive, since it would involve reintroducing subsidies for humanities and social science students – but it would be politically impossible for a Labor government to strip them back from others. Thus, Labor has, perhaps inevitably, kicked the can down the road.

The same might be said for action on overwhelming international student numbers. The entire Australian university system is now oriented toward the admission of ever-increasing numbers of international students, with non-university higher education providers being almost entirely dependent on international enrolments. International students now make up around 3.5 per cent of the entire Australian population, warping rental markets and driving trends in low-wage employment (Babones 2024b). When housing finally transformed international student loads from an education issue into a housing issue, Labor belatedly proposed caps in late 2024, but this initiative was defeated by a lack of cross-party support. Even the proposed caps, however, would likely have limited future growth, not turned back the clock on student numbers.

Having spent its first two years in office cautiously maintaining the status quo, the Albanese Government shifted gears in the runup to the 2025 election. In November 2024, Labor announced a flat 20 per cent reduction in all existing student debts incurred under the Higher Education Loan Program (HELP), resulting in an immediate economic transfer of $16 billion from the general taxpayer to indebted university graduates. When combined with concurrent changes to HELP loan indexation, the cost rises to $20 billion – to be reflected in student accounts, serendipitously, in late May 2025 (Department of Education 2024d). This debt write-off, which was announced out of the blue six months before the end of the current Labor term, is enough to notionally wipe out the government's entire 2023-2024 budget surplus (Treasury Portfolio 2024). And unless the HELP load indexation changes are later reversed, their $4 billion immediate cost will continue to recur for decades to come.

Labor's impulsive HELP debt reduction announcement reflects the general trend of the party's higher education policy: it was unsystematic, fiscally irresponsible, and profoundly unfair. Parents who paid cash for their children's education and debt-averse students who worked hard to pay down their HELP loans would be right to be furious to see their financial caution insulted. The highly contentious student debt relief program of the Joe Biden Administration in the United States was capped and means-tested; Labor's Australian plan is neither. It is an untargeted, unlimited rebate that will reward those who took on the most HELP debt regardless of need or merit. Almost certainly, it will benefit the better-off: those who were financially able to study the longest, taking multiple degrees before joining the workforce. But with no analysis having been offered on the distribution of benefits, no one will ever know.

Zooming out to the wider policy landscape, Labor's actual higher education reform agenda has been stalled in a years-long policy formation process. Six months after taking office, Labor initiated a wide-ranging review of university funding, the Australian Universities Accord. It was anticipated that the Accord would recommend restoring subsidies for the humanities and social sciences, as indeed it did (Department of Education 2023a: 25). But this reform was not to be accomplished immediately. The Accord recommended that a new higher education bureaucracy be created, the Australian Tertiary Education Commission (ATEC). This new commission could then sweep aside Job-Ready Graduates, and a host of other sins along with it. Going into the 2022 elections, the establishment of ATEC is on Labor's agenda for a second term; the Coalition would likely consign it to the dustbin of disregarded university review recommendations (Ross 2025).

The Universities Accord advocates a laundry list of give-aways to core Labor constituencies including universities, unions, students, and recent graduates, with no limits or costings attached. The key to the Accord is the proposed creation of the new universities super-administrator ATEC, which would remove financial constraints on higher education spending from the Treasury by empowering an independent commission to set fees and subsidies for the entire sector. The creation of ATEC, were Labor to follow through as promised, would ensure that all future surpluses are redirected to higher education, whether through grants to universities or fee reductions for students. But the fantastical policies proposed by the Accord go beyond mere finances. They represent a data-free picture of the future of university education in Australia, completely divorced from the reality of future workforce needs, or even of student desires. When it comes to Labor's higher education policies, it really does seem as if the adults have simply left the room.

Labor's big plan: The Universities Accord

The Australian Universities Accord was a 12-month review of Australia's universities that kicked off in November 2022 with a mandate to "drive lasting reform in Australia's higher education system" (Department of Education 2022: 1). The use of the term "accord" to describe the review is both unusual and telling. The term is generally used to describe a non-binding agreement or treaty agreed among equal parties. It is often used in the context of industry agreements on common standards or respect for human rights. It has also been used in reference to a series of Arab-Israeli agreements. It has not historically been used to describe government reviews that are designed to impose accountability on highly regulated institutions like universities. The very word 'accord' implies a mutual agreement among partners, not an evaluation conducted by an overseer. By labelling its latest review of Australia's universities an "accord" the government implicitly telegraphed that the review would be non-confrontational, and indeed cooperative.

Some might consider this conciliatory approach appropriate; others less so. Either way, the Australian Universities Accord's final report reflects the spirit of accord with which the review was initiated. Universities, university associations, academic unions, student unions, indigenous organisations, and the international education industry were all duly consulted (as of course they should have been), and the final report seems to cater to each of their special interests uncritically. This catering is so obvious that the Accord's final report reads more like a special interest wish list than a careful weighing of competing demands. Its 47 recommendations recommend more of everything, for everyone, without any recognition whatsoever of the costs involved. In fact, the only "costs" mentioned are a litany of costs unfairly (the report implies) imposed on universities and their students by the government itself (Department of Education 2023a: 4).

It is no secret that the groups consulted by the Accord are all core Labor constituencies, that the Department of Education is itself, dominated by bureaucrats who are sympathetic to the Labor agenda, and that the broader Labor Party has a general ideological bias toward greater government funding for public services. The 2008 *Bradley Review of Higher Education* was also conducted under a Labor Government (Rudd Government) and reflected similar biases. But the Bradley Review included costings for its proposed reforms and recommended a variety of fee increases to partially offset the expenses. It also pushed back against special interests, particularly regarding to expanding international student numbers (Department of Education 2008: 95 and 97). The Accord's final report, by contrast, endorses university interests to the point of self-contradiction. For example, the report repeatedly recommends increased government funding to "reduce the currently excessive pressure on universities to secure international student revenue" while at the same time quietly advocating for even higher numbers of international students, in particular urging the government "to support the growth of international education in regional and remote areas" (Department of Education 2023a: 6 and 27).

The Australian Universities Accord's final report is, in short, "little more than a la-la-land wish list drawn up by vice chancellors, campaigning groups, and the public sector" (Babones 2024a). Its major recommendations, if implemented, would likely be prohibitively expensive. The Accord's recommendations reflect the interests of university administrators, student unions, and indigenous organizations, but fail to engage with the challenges faced by ordinary academics, Australian students, or indigenous people. Tragically, the Accord's final report says almost nothing about education itself, except that it "calls upon the Australian Government and universities to improve the quality of learning and teaching by embracing the full potential of new teaching technologies" (Department of Education 2023a: 6). This is supplemented by a pro forma call for teaching to be "informed by First Nations knowledges" (Department of Education 2023a: 179). A program of online courses prefaced by acknowledgments of country is hardly an inspiring vision for the future of Australian higher education – but it is a vision that lines up well with the priorities of the special interests that seem to have guided the Accord's review of higher education in Australia.

Empty targets: Attainment rates and workforce development

The headline aspiration of the Accord's final report is for Australia to raise the proportion of young people who complete bachelor degrees from 45 per cent today to 55 per cent by 2050 (Department of Education 2023a). This sounds like a noble goal, and in a country with a liberal education system it could be argued that everyone should continue studying through the university level. But Australia's university system is not structured around the Deweyan goal of providing a liberal education for citizenship. It is designed to offer career-relevant qualifications that are intended to boost individual economic productivity and provide for the country's future workforce needs. The Accord's final report is not couched in the idealistic language of education-for-education's-sake. On the contrary: it uses the word "skill" 775 times, or an average of roughly twice per page. The word "training" appears 230 times and the word "workforce'"191 times. By comparison, the words "democracy" and "democratic" appear a combined 11 times, and the word "liberal" does not appear at all.

The ambition to increase bachelor degree attainment from 45 per cent to 55 per cent must thus be read in the context of future industry demand for university-educated workers, not as an aspiration for higher levels of individual self-actualisation. In setting its bachelor degree attainment target, the Accord relied entirely on a consultancy report commissioned from Oxford Economics Australia, which actually recommended 57 per cent – a figure that was arbitrarily scaled back to 55 per cent by the Accord "to recognise that VET will make a growing contribution to tertiary attainment in the future" (Department of Education 2023a: 70). This is a strange fudge, considering that the Oxford Economics modelling separately accounted for VET-sector tertiary qualifications. Somewhat amusingly, the Oxford Economics model predicts that bachelor degree attainment among 25-34 year olds must already reach 56 per cent by 2030 in order to meet industry needs, rising to 57 per cent in 2035 and remaining stable at 57 per cent in 2050 (Oxford Economics Australia 2023: 8 and 32).

It is difficult to imagine how such a massive restructuring of the economy could occur in just the next six years, yet this is the modelling on which the Accord's targets are based. Nonetheless, Oxford Economics predicts that demand for university graduates will decline through 2026, meaning that the wholesale restructuring to an economy that requires greater than 55 per cent of young people to obtain bachelor degrees will have to occur over a period of just four years (2026-2030) (Oxford Economics Australia 2023: 38). And this rapid adjustment will apparently be made from an even lower base level of demand for qualifications than currently exists in 2024.

This is the least of the problems arising from the Oxford Economics modelling. An analysis of data from the Australian Bureau of Statistics reveals that only two-thirds of Australian residents holding bachelor degrees or above work in jobs that are above Skill Level 1, which is as jobs that "have a level of skill commensurate with a bachelor degree or higher qualification" (author analysis of data from Australian Bureau of Statistics 2024). Thus, although 45 per cent of Australian young people obtain university degrees, something on the order of 30 per cent of them actually work in jobs that require university degrees. Although some jobs that nominally require university degrees are filled by people who lack them, this number is not enough to make up for the apparent discrepancy. In fact, only 34 per cent of jobs in Australia today are considered by the ABS to be commensurate with a university education, based on an analysis of Australian Bureau of Statistics data. The proposition that between 2026 and 2030 the proportion of jobs requiring a university degree will increase from 34 per cent to 46 per cent, and that to facilitate that transition, the number of young people obtaining university degrees will have to rise from 45 per cent to 56 per cent, is simply fantastical.

But it gets worse. Incredibly, the Oxford Economics modelling outcomes picked up by the Accord are those that assume zero net skilled migration to Australia through 2050. Obviously, this is a flatly ridiculous scenario. Skilled migration to Australia is currently running at record levels, and although there are some populist pressures for a scaling back of the country's skilled migration program, no political party in Australia advocates even a 50 per cent reduction, to say nothing of a total immigration moratorium. The disregarding of immigration makes a complete mockery of the Accord's base assumptions. As Oxford Economics itself notes, net skilled migration "resulted in a net oversupply of tertiary qualifications of 234,000 qualifications per year [in 2015-2019] ... [and if] current trends in skilled arrivals continue the net surplus is expected to average 329,000 qualifications over the forecast period" of 2025-2050 (Oxford Economics Australia 2023: 39). In other words, even if the outsized projections of future workforce needs presented by Oxford Economics prove correct, Australia would already be awash in "skills" without any increase in domestic student bachelor degree completions.

Rhetoric over reality: Addressing "First Nations" deficits

The higher education attainment targets set by the Accord are nothing if not ambitious. Unfortunately, the same cannot be said for the Accord's targets for indigenous "equity". For non-indigenous Australians, the Accord set targets for "attainment": that is to say, for the acquisition of credentials resulting from the possession of a completed academic degree. But when focusing on indigenous Australians, the final report makes a subtle shift from "attainment" to "participation" (Department of Education 2023a: 17 and 21). Casual readers are unlikely to notice the difference, but professionals (and by implication: the Accord panellists and professional support staff) are very well-aware that "participation" in higher education does not necessarily imply the "attainment" of a degree. It was frankly disingenuous of the Accord not to clearly telegraph the distinction between participation and attainment targets to readers of the final report, and frankly unacceptable of the Accord to seek "equity" for indigenous Australians only in their participation in higher education. True indigenous equity means equality in outcomes, not merely equality in engagement.

The reason for the shift, however, is obvious: increasing indigenous participation in higher education is much easier than supporting indigenous students through to completion. Although many indigenous students start university studies, relatively few finish them. Direct data on completion rates are not published, but rough indications can be estimated. For example, among indigenous Australians age 25-34, fewer than 10 per cent hold a bachelor's degree, based on an analysis of 2021 Census data. This compares very unfavourably with the figure of 45 per cent given for the "young" Australian population as a whole quoted in the final report (Department of Education 2023a:17). Even acknowledging that indigenous participation rates are on the order of one-third lower than that for non-indigenous Australians, a 10 per cent attainment rate is an extremely low figure. If indigenous Australians finished the degree programs they started at the same rate as other Australians, the indigenous attainment rate would be on the order of 30 per cent roughly three times higher than it is today. The Accord's final report does not mention this staggering comparison, never mind address it.

Even the indigenous higher education participation targets set by the Accord are remarkably unambitious. The final report specifies that indigenous students should make up 3.3 per cent of all Australian (domestic) undergraduate students by 2035, up from 2.1 per cent today (Department of Education 2023a: 21). The 3.3 per cent figure is roughly in line with the indigenous proportion of university-age citizens of Australia in 2021 (quoted statistics can vary due to the large number of non-citizen residents of Australia in this age range). Reaching parity by 2035 might sound like a reasonable target, but in fact the number of people in Australia is itself rapidly rising. It rose by 23 per cent in just the five years between the 2016 and 2021 censuses (Australian Institute of Health and Welfare 2024b). It is likely that the 3.3 per cent participation target would be met in the absence of any policy intervention, simply due to the increasing self-identification of students as indigenous.

Upon receipt of the Interim Report in mid-2023, the Albanese Government announced a step toward meeting the Accord's indigenous participation target as one of its five 'priority actions' for immediate implementation (Department of Education 2023b). Effective 2024, indigenous people living in metropolitan areas were granted access to unlimited Commonwealth supported places in all subjects other than medicine. This extended an offer made in 2021 to indigenous students living in remote and regional areas. While not in itself a bad policy, it is indicative of a government intention to meet its indigenous equity targets by harvesting the low-hanging fruit of recruiting (often newly-identifying) metropolitan indigenous people into university education, instead of tackling the much more difficult challenge of providing support and encouragement for regional and remote indigenous students. Already, indigenous people living in metropolitan areas experience relatively modest disadvantage compared to those living in regional and remote areas, with household incomes hovering at around 80% of the non-indigenous average, compared to less than 50 per cent in remote areas (Australian Institute of Health and Welfare 2024a: 61).

With indigenous-identifying populations now growing rapidly in metropolitan areas, the observed university participation gap between indigenous and non-indigenous Australians is almost certain to close rapidly, regardless of the policies pursued by governments. But a genuine effort to raise university participation and (crucially) degree completion would require much more effort. A good start would be the provision of supportive on-campus residential accommodation, the provision of bursaries for living expenses away from home, and the provision of free preparatory (enabling) courses. The Accord final report recommends making preparatory courses free for all students, but this is not one of the recommendations taken up by the government for immediate action. Actions like these would be expensive on a per-student basis but given the relatively small target population of eligible regional and remote indigenous students, they would be much less expensive than (for example) the already-announced changes to HECS indexing. That said, there are few votes to be gained in regional and remote indigenous Australia, and it is much easier to virtue-signal the metropolitan indigenous elite (the Canadian term "First Nations" is used 314 times in the Accord's final report) than to tackle serious indigenous deprivation in regional and remote Australia.

Rationing places: The proposed Managed Growth Funding System

Under the Higher Education Support Act, all Australian universities must enter into 'mission-based compacts' with the Commonwealth as a condition of their funding. These documents are generally as anodyne as one might expect, full of platitudes about community service and research and teaching 'excellence'. In the wake of the Accord, however, this will change – dramatically. Universities' mission-based compacts will become contracts for the delivery of degrees funded by Commonwealth-supported places. Each university will be assigned a "Managed Growth Target" for the number of students it is expected to enrol, with student numbers rationed across the system by a central regulator. According to the New Managed Growth Funding Implementation Consultation, universities will "be able to move places between courses and levels to meet the demand from students and industry" subject to overall system-wide central planning (Department of Education 2024b: 3). In other words, universities will be allowed to pitch for their preferred allocations, as long as they "align with national priorities and university missions" (Department of Education 2024b: 3). A creeping "funding floor" will be established as a safety net for universities experiencing declining enrolments (Department of Education 2024b: 5-6).

Given the government's ambitions for an expanded university sector, individual university enrolment targets will have to increase consistently year-on-year. These targets are for degrees, not for students, and it is very unlikely that the government will restrict students' access to multiple degrees. The system will thus encourage the strongest universities to establish multi-degree pathways that keep the best students enrolled in Commonwealth-supported places for as long as possible. This will likely include the funnelling of completing undergraduate students immediately into postgraduate degree programs. For the strongest universities (primarily capital city Group of Eight universities), the Managed Growth Target system, if unconstrained, would likely result in a Commonwealth funding bonanza. For the weakest universities, it could result in an enrolment death spiral.

If demand for student places were actually increasing in line with the government's ambitions, the Managed Growth Targets would indeed operate as enrolment caps that force students out of the capital cities and into the regional universities in search of available Commonwealth supported places. Buoyed by captive consultancy advice, the Accord final report claims that in the coming decades "many more people in the employed working age population (aged 15 to 64) will need a tertiary qualification". (Department of Education 2023a: 67). But even the Accord's own consultants estimate a future "gross" deficit of only "21,000 qualifications per year" over the next 30 years "when skilled arrivals are not accounted for" (Oxford Economics Australia 2023: 38). This projection must be seen in the context of Australia's skilled immigration program, which in the 2023-2024 financial year admitted more than 40,000 primary permanent migrants a year – in addition to nearly 50,000 temporary skilled immigrants (Australian Bureau of Statistics 2024b).

Moreover, the Accord's own consultants acknowledge that demand for qualifications is currently declining, though they project a rise beginning in 2026 (Oxford Economics Australia 2023: 38). Even more alarmingly, they report that there has been a "a net oversupply of tertiary qualifications of 234,000 qualifications per year" over the last five years, and that qualifications have been or are projected to be in oversupply for all but one of the eleven years 2015-2025 (Oxford Economics Australia 2023: 39). Qualifications are expected to remain in oversupply for all of the next quarter century under the consultants' default immigration projections (Oxford Economics Australia 2023: 40). This implies that a successful expansion of enrolments in Commonwealth supported places will result in some combination of following three outcomes:

- Increasing unemployment among Australian university graduates
- An increasing share of graduates working in jobs that do not require university degrees
- A rise in the average number of degrees held by each graduate

Under any of these scenarios, it is hard to see any path to sustainable domestic enrolment growth for weaker, regional universities that does not involve meaningful enrolment caps on capital city universities. These stronger universities might be persuaded to accept declining domestic enrolment targets as a quid pro quo for permission to enrol even larger numbers of international students. Even if the government accepts that education is good in itself, without any labour market rationale for increasing enrolments, it will be difficult to convince students to take up the increasing number of Commonwealth supported places offered through expanding Managed Growth Targets. The only realistic way to meet the targets will likely be for the same limited pool of students to accumulate even more degrees than they do already.

The Managed Growth Funding System represents an emphatic rejection of the demand-driven principles implemented by the last Labor government in 2012. The demand-driven model was frozen in 2017 by the Coalition, to be restructured with the implementation of the Job-ready Graduates Package in 2020. This ad hoc reform process resulted in an allocation of Commonwealth supported places that broadly reflects late-2010s student preferences under a now-defunct incentive program. This system is certainly ripe for reform. The Accord has arrived at a reform process that seeks to ensure the continued viability of weaker universities through heroic assumptions about future demand that are unlikely to eventuate; this kind of imaginary thinking will not prevent future defaults requiring Commonwealth intervention. A better reform process would courageously engage with the declining attractiveness of regional universities, supporting them in a rededication to community service in lieu of national and international competitiveness, while returning to a reformed demand-driven model for competition among metropolitan universities for student enrolments.

Administrative bloat: The Australian Tertiary Education Commission

If there is one solution that the Universities Accord final report recommended for almost every challenge, it is bureaucracy. The final report recommends that the Albanese Government establish a new Australian Tertiary Education Commission (ATEC) to produce annual State of the Tertiary Education System and Future of the Tertiary Education Sector reports, a new Centre of Excellence in Higher Education and Research to provide the Commission with academic research support, a new First Nations Council to advise the Commission, a new national "Jobs Broker" agency to place students in part-time work, a new National Student Ombudsman, a new Solving Australian Challenges Strategic Fund, and a new Higher Education Future Fund. The Budget Summary continues this administrative growth bias, providing for the creation of a new unit in the Department of Education to administer a National Higher Education Code to Prevent and Respond to Gender-based Violence. No existing state organs have been slated for elimination, consolidation, or retrenchment.

The proposed Australian Tertiary Education Commission (ATEC) sits at the apex of these administrative reforms. The commission will be charged with implementing the proposed Managed Growth Funding System. It was also envisaged in the Accord's final report that ATEC would oversee the proposed Racism Study, but this plan seems to have been overtaken by events. The commission is intended to become "a steward of the tertiary education system", but it is not clear what this means, and universities will apparently be consulted regarding ATEC's powers. (Department of Education 2024a: 1). According to the ATEC consultation paper, "the absence of a sector steward has, over time, created a system characterised by:

- persistent under-representation of some student cohorts and failure to meet equity targets;
- lack of deep thinking and clarity of direction for the sector to be agile to future needs;
- fragmented changes to policy and funding, driven by immediate priorities rather than long-term strategy;
- inadequate coordination and planning of effort and resources for growth areas, for example the outer metropolitan areas of major cities" (Department of Education 2024a: 1).

That seems like quite a lot to pin on the absence of a commission, to be composed of one full-time and three part-time commissioners (one of them indigenous). The functions proposed for ATEC in the Consultation Paper include the administration of "funding for higher education teaching and research programs" (with the exception of funds provided by research councils) and the setting of "institutions' Managed Growth Targets". This will make ATEC very powerful indeed: it will both tell universities how many domestic students they can enrol and decide how much universities will be paid to enrol them. Since the commissioners will inevitably be appointed from within the university sector, there will be a serious risk of regulatory capture. This is not necessarily a problem when a commission performs largely technical functions, as does the Tertiary Education Quality and Standards Agency (TEQSA). It is of much greater concerns where budget-setting and management oversight are involved, as they will be with ATEC.

As of mid-2024, details have yet to be released about the multiple other bureaucracies proposed by the Accord, and funding mechanisms for the proposed Solving Australian Challenges Strategic Fund and Higher Education Future Fund have proved contentious. But the creation of the Australian Tertiary Education Commission – which seems set to go ahead – would by itself represent both a massive step backward for democratic accountability and a massive increase in administrative bloat. While it is entirely appropriate for technical functions to be hived off into specialised corporate Commonwealth entities, it is not appropriate for core functions of government (like budgeting and oversight) to be placed at arm's-length from political control. The government's intention seems to be to solve the problems of "persistent under-representation", lack of "agility", "fragmented" policy, and the concentration of educational resources in the inner capital cities through the blunt instrument of central planning – conducted by representatives of the industry itself.

Conclusion: The need for a more adversarial approach

The most recent official data indicate that 34.6 per cent of Australia's university students were "international" in 2023, as measured by student load – a figure that certainly rose further in the ensuing two years. (author analysis of data from Department of Education 2024c) Moreover, the children of non-citizen permanent residents of Australia (comprising roughly 12 per cent of the Australian resident population, though an unknown proportion of the student population) are counted as "domestic" students. Thus the true international student load is likely upward of 40 per cent of universities' total enrolments. This proportion is truly extraordinary. The Accord's final report flatly asserts that international education is now "a permanent fixture of the economy", and it is difficult to dispute that claim (Department of Education 2023a: 8). The 2008 Bradley Review raised concerns that excessive concentrations of international students might "lessen the value of the educational experience for both international and domestic students" – this, at a time when international students made up less than 20 per cent of Australian university enrolments (Department of Education 2008: 93 and 91). Sixteen years later, the Australian Universities Accord final report raises no such concerns.

Policymakers and the public have been slow to engage with the fact that more than one-third of students at Australian universities are not eligible for Commonwealth support. Moreover, since international student fee income can be managed at the discretion of university administrators with little government regulation or oversight, international students are disproportionately important to those administrators. The presence of so many international students, and their financial importance, had fundamentally changed the character of Australian universities. Once stodgy organisations run in line with public sector norms, many Australian universities are now managed like for-profit companies (albeit highly-regulated for-profit companies with implicit government financial guarantees). In many ways they thus resemble Qantas, Telstra, and the Commonwealth Bank more than they resemble the government departments that regulate them.

Moreover, although Australia's universities may be structured as not-for-profit entities, their managers are now compensated in line with for-profit norms. This is reflected in their pay, with nearly half of Australia's vice chancellors being paid more than a million dollars in 2023 (White and Groch 2024). It is also reflected in their contracts, which now include target-linked incentive bonuses that are considered "commercial-in-confidence" terms to be kept secret from the public (Babones 2021: 113-14). The transformation of Australian universities from public-service organisations into quasi-commercial entities is intimately connected with the rise in international student numbers. On the domestic side, Australian universities are still administered from the standpoint of filling Commonwealth-supported places. Meanwhile on the international side, the language of business – of markets, competition, and surplus-generation (a stand-in for "profit") – prevails.

Yet the Department of Education is ill-equipped to regulate organisations that operate on business principles. While TEQSA oversees the educational aspects of universities, and ATEC will focus on giving them money, no one at the Department of Education is particularly charged with regulating universities' international surplus-generating activities. The Bradley Review had concluded in 2008 "that the regulatory framework for tertiary education is in need of a major overhaul and that the regulation of international education should be considered in a broader context which involves the creation of a national regulatory body", but this recommendation was not taken up by government (Department of Education 2008: 97). It was certainly not revisited in 2024 by the Australian Universities Accord.

When it comes to the commercialisation of its universities and their leadership, it is likely that Australia has already passed the point of no return. Managing international student numbers down to levels that align with the educational missions of Australia's universities would require wrenching institutional change of the kind that is only possible in a cataclysmic depression or world war. It is thus only realistic to accept that most of Australia's universities are now run on commercial terms, with the attraction of fee-paying international students as their primary concern. Governments in essence fund limited places for domestic students to study within these (nominally not-for-profit) global commercial concerns, while providing a financial backstop to preclude university insolvencies. This new reality calls for a more adversarial approach to the regulation Australia's public universities, and a system review that treats the claims of universities and their industry associations with a high degree of scepticism.

References

Australian Bureau of Statistics, (2024a), *Education and Work, Australia*, Canberra: Australian Government, 8 November

Australian Bureau of Statistics, (2024b), *Overseas Migration*, Canberra: Australian Government, 13 December

Australian Institute of Health and Welfare, (2024a), *Aboriginal and Torres Strait Islander Health Performance Framework - Summary Report*, Canberra: Australian Government,

Australian Institute of Health and Welfare, (2024b), *Profile of First Nations People*, Canberra: Australian Government, 2 July

Babones, S., (2021), *Australia's Universities: Can They Reform?* Brisbane: Ocean Reeve

Babones, S., (2024a), "Trouble with the Universities Accord Goes from Ridiculous to Unreal", *Australian Financial Review*, 3 March

Babones, S., (2024b), "International Student Lies, Damn Lies, and Rental Statistics", *Macrobusiness*, 21 May

Department of Education, (2008), *Review of Australian Higher*

Education: Final Report, Canberra: Australian Government (Bradley Review)

Department of Education, (2022), *Review of Australia's Higher Education System: Review Terms of Reference*, Canberra: Australian Government

Department of Education, (2023a,) *Australian Universities Accord: Final Report*, Canberra: Australian Government

Department of Education, (2023b), *Accord Priority Actions*, Canberra: Australian Government

Department of Education, (2024a,) *Australian Tertiary Education Commission: Implementation Consultation Paper*, Canberra: Australian Government

Department of Education, (2024b), *New Managed Growth Funding: Implementation Consultation*, Canberra: Australian Government

Department of Education, (2024c), *Perturbed Student Load Pivot Table 2023*, Canberra: Australian Government

Department of Education, (2024d), *20% Reduction of Student Loan Debt*, Canberra: Australian Government, 3 November

Oxford Economics Australia, (2023), *Tertiary Education Qualification Demand: Report Produced for the Department of Education*, Canberra: Australian Government.

Ross, J., (2025), "Australian Opposition Eyes Fee Review, Grant Veto, V-C Pay Rules", *Times Higher Education*, 26 February

Treasury Portfolio, (2024), *Labor Delivers Biggest Ever Back-to-Back Surpluses*, Canberra: Australian Government, 30 September

White, D., and Groch, S., (2024), "The Uni Rich List: Vice Chancellors on $1 Million Salaries Revealed", *Sydney Morning Herald*, 30 June

302

15

The Voice Debacle

Gary Johns

Introduction

On election day, 21 May 2022, Prime Minister-elect Anthony Albanese was swept up in the emotion of the moment. After acknowledging the elders, he announced his plan to "commit to the Uluru Statement from the Heart in full". Doubting that more than a handful of voters understood his message, he and his ministers dedicated significant time to preparing for a referendum aimed at amending the Constitution, which took place on 14 October 2023. The referendum failed, with a No vote of 60 per cent across every state and the Northern Territory, while only the Australian Capital Territory voted Yes. Just 34 out of 150 federal electorate divisions voted Yes.

Prime Minister Albanese created a significant credibility gap among his base by holding the referendum. Only 14 electorates saw the Yes vote surpass the 2022 two-party preferred Labor vote; TEAL members held six. In stark contrast, the Yes vote fell short of the Labor vote across 136 seats. In some instances, the gap between the Labor and Yes votes reached a staggering 30 per cent (Brand and Burt in Western Australia and Spence and Kingston in South Australia). The Yes vote was lower than the Labor vote in 74 Labor-held seats.

The Prime Minister created the credibility gap by making two mistakes. He asked the Australian people to decide on a matter that was the plaything of elites, giving them a vote in a referendum, which required a majority of people and states. He also promised to commit to a non-referendum matter, the *Uluru Statement* attached to the Explanatory Memorandum and the Minister's Second Reading Speech for the Referendum Bill.[1] The elements of the Uluru statement were the Voice and the Makarrata Commission, which would guide treaty and "truth-telling" processes. It was simple for referendum opponents to remind Australians that a vote for the Voice was for Voice, Treaty, and "Truth".

The Actors

The National Party, persuaded by Northern Territory Senator Jacinta Price, agreed to oppose the referendum as early as late 2022. However, the Liberal Party found it more difficult. Ten Liberal and former Liberal seats (lost to teal independents in 2022) were among the 14 electorates where the Yes vote was greater than the Labor vote. Numerous Liberal state leaders were supporting the Yes case. Nevertheless, in April 2023, the Federal Opposition Liberal leader, Peter Dutton, announced that his party would oppose the referendum.

Recognise a Better Way was the first significant No group to emerge in the campaign, organised by the author and former Keating Government Minister Gary Johns and Wesley Aird.[2] Indigenous businessman Warren Mundine and country liberal senator Jacinta Price joined early, but following negotiations, Price moved to Advance Australia, a long-standing campaign operation that became the dominant arm of the No campaign. Mundine and Johns sat on the overarching No campaign Australians for Unity. Price and Mundine were the face of the No campaign.

The Yes campaign included the Uluru Dialogue, co-chaired by Megan Davis and Pat Anderson, based at the University of New South Wales. Australians for Indigenous Constitutional Recognition was co-chaired by Danny Gilbert, director of the Business Council of Australia, and film-maker Rachel Perkins.

A notable group was Uphold and Recognise, founded by Damien Freeman of the Australian Catholic University and Julian Leeser, the then Coalition spokesperson on Indigenous Australians. Constitutional lawyer and former Vice Chancellor of the Australian Catholic University, Greg Craven was prominent. Uphold and Recognise board members included the former federal Indigenous Australians minister Ken Wyatt and Sean Gordon.[3]

The campaign was a David and Goliath affair. Estimates of donations to respective campaigns were $70 million to Yes committees and $15 million to No committees.[4]

Under Noel Pearson's spell, *The Australian* newspaper referred to Leeser, Craven, and Freeman as constitutional conservatives. They were not. They sought to introduce a race-based set of collective rights into the Australian constitution. Noel Pearson and other Aboriginal leaders used them for their separatist ends. *The Australian* campaigned for the referendum until the very last day. Its readership was solidly No. The last line of its editorial on referendum morning was that it could not support the referendum – having ignored its readers, it relented in the face of the polls.

Noel Pearson (2023) stated during the campaign that "a whole generation of Indigenous leadership will have failed" if the Voice were not successful. It would be more accurate to say that an entire generation of Aboriginal leaders failed by proposing a shadow government for a tiny constituency. This grab for power marked the final act of a leadership that rested on the shoulders of those pioneers among Aboriginal leaders who fought for and achieved equality, once a cherished Labor goal.

Uluru legitimacy – Statement from the Heart

The Uluru Statement featured heavily in Yes advertising during the campaign. Still, it faded quickly when the proponents realised it was a massive agenda that the electorate would not understand or tolerate.

A large part of the referendum story is how Uluru came to be. The 2018 Joint Select Committee of the Australian Parliament on Constitutional Recognition relating to Aboriginal and Torres Strait Islander Peoples was asked to consider the work of several earlier committees – the Gillard Government's *Expert Panel on Constitutional Recognition of Indigenous Australiana* appointed in 2010, the former Joint Select Committee, the Statement from the Heart, and the Referendum Council. The Statement from the Heart alone brought a new element, The Voice, into the debate.

As Senator Pat Dodson (Labor) and Julian Leeser MP (Liberal) wrote in their final report, "The rejection of all previous proposals was a shame because there were previous proposals which would command broad political support; but we acknowledge that at Uluru they seem to have been taken off the table".[5] The Uluru statement threw two significant new political devices – The Voice and Treaty – into the arena.

The official "Yes" case implied that the Statement reflected "many years of work and countless conversations in every part of the country" and carried the imprimatur of "nearly 250 Aboriginal and Torres Strait Islander leaders and elders". The Uluru statement was credited to Noel Pearson, Referendum Council co-chair Pat Anderson, and academic Megan Davis, although Shireen Morris claimed authorship of the Voice component.

The meeting convention was timed to end on the eve of the 50th anniversary of the successful 1967 Referendum. The convention was merely an "endorsement meeting" whose sole purpose was to "bring together the outcomes" from twelve regional dialogues. Before the convention commenced, organisers had already determined that "A Voice to Parliament" was the only option for constitutional change supported by all dialogues. Participants expressed concern that the meeting might conclude without reaching an agreed position. Records from each dialogue, released under freedom of information laws, indicated that support for the Voice was lukewarm and conditional.

The greatest threat to the Voice's endorsement was not any alternative constitutional alteration but a sense among delegates that the Constitution was not the top priority. Davis, an early supporter of the Voice and the dominant dialogue figure, later conceded that participants' insistence on "truth-telling" was "unexpected". Demands for a treaty were less surprising, though this goal, like "truth-telling", had no obvious constitutional dimension.

Davis later claimed that the regional dialogues had "ranked" the various options and that the Voice consistently ranked first. However, the Final Report does not include such rankings, and most meeting records are vague about the support for the Voice relative to other options. The only consensus that seems to have emerged related to treaties, not the Constitution (Stella 2023).

Faced with the possibility that their constitutional convention might decide to leave the Constitution untouched, Pearson and his collaborators needed a form of words that would appear to make the Voice the servant of treaty and truth. They called it "strategic sequencing", though this term is omitted from the Final Report. The concluding paragraphs contain the Statement's demands. The authors knew delegates overwhelmingly supported both treaty and truth-telling, neither of which would require a referendum. The collaborators devised a clever formula: treaty and truth-telling were positioned as "the culmination of our agenda". Though they were acknowledged as more important than the Voice, the Voice still came first.

Machinations of the Voice

In a poll on the Voice referendum, 17 per cent of Yes voters did so because "the idea came directly from Aboriginal and Torres Strait Islander people".[6] There are two versions of the origins of the Voice. Take your pick – either an Indian Fijian academic or some white one: either way, non-Aboriginal descent. Shireen Morris, of Fijian Indian descent, claimed that she and Noel Pearson at the Cape York Institute developed what would eventually be called the "Voice". The version circulated during the campaign commenced with Damien Freeman, who is of non-Aboriginal descent and from Uphold and Recognise. He took it up with non-Aboriginal academic constitutional lawyers Greg Craven and Anne Twomey, who made various drafts.

According to Twomey (2023), the first meeting to design a constitutional amendment based on the Voice idea was held on 19 June 2014 at the Australian Catholic University's North Sydney campus. Morris and Pearson were present, along with Craven and Leeser, Freeman, and Twomey. The aim was to achieve a "stable constitutional protection of Indigenous rights and interests, shielded from short-term political fluctuations". They also wanted not to undermine or transfer power from parliament to judges.

The first draft of a version of The Voice was published by Twomey in 2015.[7] At the 2018 parliamentary committee, several other versions of this type of amendment were proposed. One of those drafts, submitted by Patricia Anderson, Davis, Pearson, and others, was further developed through several workshops run by the Indigenous Law Centre and the Gilbert Tobin Centre of Public Law at UNSW.

Twomey and many academics and practitioners participated in the workshops. The form of the draft amendment varied from time to time. A version was submitted to the Albanese Government. However, the version that Davis, Pearson, and others extolled significantly differed from the UNSW draft. This is where the Yes case and the so-called constitutional conservatives, such as Craven, parted company.

Craven (2023) believed that "various drafts of the voice referred vaguely to representations to the executive", that is, government. Craven claimed that "no conservative believed this could involve the voice going to court". Many disagreed. Craven claimed he had guaranteed the Voice would never get its hands on government. Davis, in contrast, said that the "voice will speak to all parts of government". With the election of the Albanese government, Pearson and other Aboriginal leaders decided constitutional 'conservatives' were no longer necessary, even though they had done most of the drafting and designing.

Pearson agreed to be part of a four-person team to draft the Albanese amendment secretly. No constitutional conservatives were in the room or consulted. When these conservatives saw the draft "with its lackadaisical treatment of executive representations", they were, according to Craven, 'amazed, horrified and furious". Craven blamed Pearson for "the imbroglio over executive government". Craven wrote, "In a state of political hubris, he excluded his conservative friends from the drafting room and devised an amendment he knew they could not wear. He also stood by as activists such as Megan Davis colonised the voice, turning it from a conservative model free of judicial activism into a judges' junket" (Craven 2023).

Prime Minister befuddled

The Prime Minister frequently referred to the Calma-Langton Indigenous Voice Co-design Process Final Report (Calma-Langton Report 2021) as the model likely to be adopted following a referendum. The Report provided an excellent insight into the thinking behind the Voice. The Prime Minister's hesitation in clarifying the model imposed on him by the approximately 20 Aboriginal "shadow cabinet" members who endorsed it was that it was never merely a call for recognition; it was a move towards a new distribution of political power in Australia. Its impact was to create a shadow government equipped with its advisory framework to make demands of both the government and parliament unavailable to any other constituency (see Calma-Langton Report 2021).

The model not only referred to the process of giving advice, which already existed throughout the Commonwealth government and parliament, but also aimed to bind the government and parliament to "consultation standards" applicable to one group selected by race across the entire Commonwealth public policy. These consultation standards would have created political leverage. While the Voice would not have held a veto over legislation or government policy, it would have offered a platform to trade its ability to delay and grandstand for votes in parliament. Politicians could have used the Voice processes to delay or block government legislation. Senators might have brokered deals with the Voice to push their agendas.

The No case was that such power rewards the powerful; it did not resolve issues. It was not merely voices but somewhat different policies that were needed to change the lives of the small group of Aboriginal people (perhaps 20 per cent of the Aboriginal population) requiring government assistance. For instance, the argument was to consider two persistent issues in Aboriginal communities – banning alcohol and the Basics Card. Aboriginal people are divided on both matters, with opinions both for and against banning alcohol, and similarly divided regarding the Basics Card. Adding more voices expressing the same contradictory opinions does not resolve problems.

At a point in time, votes in Parliament would be traded by persuading a majority of the Voice members to join with a Senator or some Senators to vote up or vote down a proposition – in return for programs or other legislative changes favourable to one dominant faction of the Aboriginal Voice. That is how politics works. It is the context within which the Voice model – the Calma-Langton Report (2021) – had to be understood.

The Calma-Langton scheme was to have 24 national members selected by Aboriginal groups formed at a regional level, who would assemble in Canberra permanently. They were not to be elected, and there was no mechanism for a formal ballot in the model. Member selection would result from the endless struggle for preferment within Aboriginal organisations.

Sitting behind this political melee and embedded in the model were numerous assumptions. Two significant ones were:

- That recognition solves needs: There was no evidence that "recognition would solve the problems of those in need or "Close the Gap";
- Aboriginal people often go unheard.

Since the 1920s, Aborigines have established representative organisations. The national voices include the Peaks of Aboriginal organisations and statutory authorities. Numerous land councils, Aboriginal corporations, agreements between traditional owners and governments, and committees of Aboriginal people exist in every state, local government, and major corporations.

The national Voice 24 members were to be "collectively determined" by thirty-five "Local and Regional" Voice groups. There was no formula for how a combination of individuals and scores of different Aboriginal organisations would come together in regions to choose one delegate as a member of the national Voice. As complex as that task was, it could have been simplified by holding an election of all Aboriginal people in a region. A probable reason for not holding elections was the issue of identification, which would require an electoral roll of Aboriginal people.

Proof of identity was a real issue in Aboriginal politics and during the referendum. Nevertheless, the model recommended a delegate selection process in which delegate selection would involve "navigating their way" between two principles: "Inclusive Participation" and "Cultural Leadership", which would be different in every region. A more befuddled formula for selecting members of the Voice could not be imagined.

Traditional ways of selection are male-dominated and secretive. They are not conducive to ultra-progressive ways of inclusion – LGBTIQ and gender and so on. They are not conducive to democratic processes. Because of these rules, there were likely to be countless legal challenges to the selection of members. The No case asked, at what stage would the progressive ideas of inclusion and gender equity make the whole entity and exercise non-Aboriginal?

The model provided for two members from each state, the NT, ACT and the Torres Strait. A further five members were to represent remote areas. The structure suggested that there was an awareness that remote areas had little voice or were at the most disadvantage. If that were so, why was there a need for an entire shadow government when the real problems exist for a tiny part of the Aboriginal electorate? It also highlighted the issue – what if the NT member was against alcohol bans and the 'remote' member was in favour? Whose voice would win?

The Voice was Canberra-centric, and the vote in the ACT mirrored its mindset. It was intended to be a new independent Commonwealth entity backed by its own Office of the National Voice. A set of consultation standards was to be established, guiding when, how, and on what matters the Australian Parliament and government should consult the National Voice. It aimed to impose mechanisms on the Parliament. The Calma-Langton assertion that "the aim would be to support, not disrupt, effective legislative and policy processes" seemed naïve. The claim that "the compliance of the Australian Parliament and Government with these elements could not be challenged in a court" (Calma-Langton 2021: 11) appeared disingenuous. A legal resolution could have taken years and be subject to ongoing scrutiny when the Voice did not achieve its objectives. Consulting on any relevant matter would require the Office of the National Voice to be substantial. The same would hold for the 35 Regional Voices.

The Calma-Langton model maintains that existing bodies, committees, and processes should not be disturbed. Imagine an Aboriginal organisation presenting before a Senate hearing. Would a member of the Voice step in as the genuine representative? Voice members may have overshadowed other Aboriginal voices. The numerous arrangements established between Aboriginal people, governments, and businesses would face a new layer of politics. Any disgruntled Aboriginal person who felt they had lost out would appeal to their national delegate and start the struggle anew.

The Prime Minister attempted to impose a shadow government on Australians based on race. His preferred model for the Voice indicated as much. Elite opinion perceived greatness: the electorate sensed many public servants and special deals at the taxpayers' expense.

Old Labor

In the late 1950s, Arthur Calwell, the leader of the Federal Labor Party, purchased a kerosene refrigerator for the old Balgo Mission in Western Australia for Aboriginal people arriving from the desert. Old Labor was driven by both head and heart. Sixty years later, Labor endorsed a change to the Australian Constitution that would grant Aboriginal PhD holders an additional voice above all other citizens. Under the Albanese government, New Labor proposed a referendum on a reluctant Australian populace, pressuring them to vote for a voice to parliament.

Arthur Calwell was a product of his times; he and Labor were suspicious of foreign labour. As Immigration Minister, in response to a question in the House in 1947, he made the famous statement, "Two Wongs don't make a White". But as racist as old Labor was, it had a soft spot for Aboriginal people. Trade unions actively asserted the rights of Aboriginal workers. In 1963, the North Australian Workers' Union sponsored a test case on equal wages for Northern Territory Aborigines.

By the 1980s, however, only the Left of the Labor Party took much interest in Aboriginal affairs. The Labor Right concentrated on treasury, and just as well as the Left could not be trusted with treasury. The Labor (or Catholic) Right's abandonment of Aboriginal affairs was the start of the rot. The Left and university anthropologists and historians took over the ideological work that resulted in the referendum of 2023.

The referendum debate divided the nation. An Aboriginal, Kerry White from Port Pirie in South Australia, said of it, "A bit over two hundred years ago, they rounded Aboriginal people up and locked them on missions. Then we come forward to now, the Voice, and they're segregating us again. And frankly, it's racist towards our White brothers and sisters that live in this land with us" (White 2023).

As Janetia Knapp of Fremantle said, "The grassroots women who go to the courts, who go to family courts, who are at the forefront of holding families together; I think they would rather the [referendum] money go elsewhere, to dealing with issues like incarceration, rehabilitation, education" (Knapp 2023).

Labor was dripping with Aboriginal politicians. The last two ministers for Indigenous Australians were Aboriginal, but they were still not happy. Parliament House Canberra was teeming with Aboriginal lobbyists, but still, they wanted more.

Arthur Calwell's wife, Elizabeth, was very active in a group of Catholic fundraisers. Arthur Calwell sent a personal cheque for £ 167 each year for many years to Balgo to pay for fencing (see Johns 2023). Old Labor was head and heart. New Labor and its referendum were misplaced heart and no head.

References

Calma, T., and Langton, M., (Co-Chairs), (2021), Indigenous Voice Co-design Process, *Final Report to the Australian Government*, Canberra: Commonwealth of Australia

Craven, G., (2023), "Indigenous voice to parliament referendum rewrite is a tragedy in the making", *The Australian*, 31 March

Johns, G., (2023), "Why Old Labor Should Vote No", *The Telegraph*, 30 May

Pearson, N., (2023), " 'A whole generation of leadership will have failed' if Voice defeated", *National Indigenous Times*, February 21

Stella, J., (2023), "Peering under the rock: a closer look at the 'Uluru Statement from the Heart'", *Recognise a Better Way*, The No Case Committee

Twomey, A., (2023), Submission to the Inquiry into the Aborigine and Torress Strait Islander Voice Referendum, 13 April

White, K., (2023), *A Better Way*, Adelaide Convention Centre, 23 June

16

The Drift of Australian Foreign Policy[1]

Michael Easson

Introduction

The purpose of this chapter is to sketch what happened in foreign policy in the first term of the Albanese-led Labor government, and to provide context and analysis of the bigger picture. The word "drift" conveys direction of policy and action, rather than uncertain navigation.

Initially, I overview theoretical and historical perspectives on the changing policy environment and discuss the deployment of "soft" and "hard" power in the projection of Australian influence. Without that backdrop, this account would only be of events, one thing after another. (My selection of quotes and facts reflects a personal assessment of the arguments).Then follows discussion on Labor's preparation for government and its approach to foreign policy; then onto headline "challenges" on this Government's watch, namely relations with China, the US alliance, the development of AUKUS and the Quad. Australia's relations with South-East Asian countries – particularly Indonesia, Labor's forging of better relations with the Blue Pacific,[1] is followed by reactions and actions in far flung regions, including Ukraine and Israel/Palestine. The latter is the most domestically controversial international conflict during the last few years. Finally, a brief outline of leading critiques of Australian foreign policy, particularly on AUKUS, rounds off the analysis.

Theoretical overview

The first term of the Albanese Labor government will be remembered for the unmooring and shaky erosion of what were once considered firm pillars, and uncertainty about new directions. The longevity of AUKUS, the Quad, and some earlier creations, including the G20 and APEC, require constant attention. As, indeed, the ANZUS (Australian New Zealand US) Treaty arrangements, forged in 1951, do also. During the first Trump presidency, 2017-2021, the doyen of Australian foreign policy strategy, Allan Gyngell, opined: "Multilateralism is in flux: it is unclear which organisations will continue, which will emerge, and which will atrophy" (Gyngell 2017: 362).

The Albanese Government came to power 16-months after the first Trump presidency ended and was re-elected nearly 15 weeks after the second Trump inauguration. President Joe Biden (President 2021-2025), compared to his immediate predecessor and successor, was a benignly sympathetic figure towards Australian interests (Fullilove 2022). So were many State Department figures, notably Kurt M. Campbell, Assistant Secretary of State, and key strategist on China and US-Asia relations. AUKUS was conceived on Biden's watch, with Albanese's predecessor, Scott Morrison, playing the catalysing role. (P. Kelly 2022: 161-92). In Opposition, Labor endorsed the AUKUS option, though with little debate and scarce transparency. (Simons 2023). President Biden insisted that Morrison test the waters with the then Labor Opposition to secure bi-partisan support. Morrison reciprocated to give the ALP a day to respond. He hoped to wedge Labor on the issue. Albanese and colleagues did not take the bait.

The AUKUS Agreement, the trilateral security partnership between Australia, the United Kingdom, and the United States, has two pillars: Pillar 1 is the supply and delivery of a total of 8 nuclear-powered conventional attack submarines under Australian command by the 2040s; and Pillar 2, providing a platform for advanced technology cooperation. The origin and evolution of AUKUS is further addressed below.

The overall strategic landscape is an environment where much is contested and disputed. Wong says: "Long-standing rules are being bent, twisted or broken" (Wong 2024a). Further: "We live in a world of increasing strategic surprise – ever more uncertain and unpredictable" (Wong 2025). The Albanese Government's second term will reveal how well it has considered and mastered such challenging, difficult conditions.

"For the times they are a-changin'", to quote the Bob Dylan song, have been for some time. Thirty years ago, foreign policy thinker Owen Harries predicted: "A realistic assessment ... is that quite early in the next century – say, in fifteen - or twenty-years' time ... Australia will have lost many of the security advantages it has enjoyed until now".

Harries identified three factors that would diminish the strength of Australia's security – the long receding roar of US presence in the Asia-Pacific region; the rise of economic and security competition; and the world "shrinking", with new technologies, to a 'smaller' place. Let's examine each point. First, he said Australia "will no longer enjoy the assured presence of an enormously powerful but unthreatening ally, one that is firmly committed to its protection and to maintaining a balance in the region". He surmised: "There is no longer a compelling mission for the United States in the Asia Pacific region, no cause, no obvious bad guys to frustrate and good guys to support, nothing (and this is important) that can be clearly and readily explained to the American people. The role usually suggested by strategists – that of a balancer, balancer of last resort – is historically and temperamentally uncongenial to Americans – too complicated, too amoral, involving too much shifting and manoeuvring." Arguably, the rise of the Peoples Republic of China (PRC), provided the new 'bad guy' for America to counter. But it took more than 16-years after Harries wrote the above, a period of grand optimism about US-China engagement (Shambaugh 2025: 53-83), before America's "pivot to Asia" occurred in 2011 under President Obama. The 'pivot' suggested a change of focus or renewed focus on Asia. Some Chinese critics asserted that America was pursuing a "bellicose strategy aimed at containing China's rise", whereas a few western academic scholars only saw an anaemic, half-hearted turn (Silove 2016: 45).

The last decade of American pivots, resets, gyrations, and positioning with respect to China specifically and Asia more generally are as dizzying to watch as a dreidel. Some analysts just saw rotation and no landing. For example, this summation: "Trump's 'pivot actions' appear to be erratic, pragmatic short-term actions rather than a meticulously planned long-term strategy similar to Obama's rebalance (which did not materialise). Thus, while Obama failed to transform the pivot into an effective strategy, neither is Trump's effectiveness backed by a coherent Asian strategy" (Kolmas and Kolmasova 2019:1). Feckless or considered or otherwise, America is no longer the supreme hegemon in the region that it once was. That is part of Australia's reckoning.

Back to Harries, whose second prediction was that Australia would "no longer enjoy the strategic and technical advantage of having more sophisticated weaponry than adjacent countries, an advantage that has until now compensated for lack of manpower. Neighbours will be rich enough to afford the best, in some cases in larger bulk than Australia". In 2023, Indonesia's GDP was 80 per cent of Australia's. If demography is destiny, the size of Indonesia's expanding economy should eclipse Australia's by 2030 or shortly thereafter. The PRC is at least ten times the size of Australia's GDP (World Bank Group 2023). Third, Harries suggested the 'tyranny of distance' would disappear and with it "the protective shield of distance. What Australia will gain economically from the revolution in transport and communication, it will lose strategically in terms of the insulation provided by remoteness" (Harries 1995: 17). Complacency left the nation under-prepared for significant global shifts already probable when Harries wrote. The most recent comprehensive foreign policy review was the 2017 *Foreign Policy White Paper*, now out-of-date given current complexities of the rapidly changed international landscape.

Harries' analysis begs the question of what cards Australia must play in the great game of protecting its interests. Hans Morgenthau in his classic study *Politics Among Nations* focuses heavily on diplomacy as a means of avoiding war. (Morgenthau 1973: 517-529). A more nuanced assessment, considering the mix of "hard" and "soft" options, was coined on the eve of the collapse of the Soviet Union by Joseph Nye Jr. He recognised that power not only grows out of the barrel of a gun, but it also happens through influence, cultural and through other indirect means: "Although force may sometimes play a role, traditional instruments of power are rarely sufficient to deal with the new dilemmas of world politics". There in Nye's phrase "new dilemmas", we see a familiar refrain that the new moment is an inflection point. Gyngell once wryly remarked, "Throughout its modern history Australia has known only a globalising world" (Gyngell 2017: 360). Indeed, when has the modern ever been safely predictable, or not constantly changing?

Nye argued that "intangible forms of power [are now] more important. National cohesion, universalistic culture, and international institutions are taking on additional significance". He concluded that this aspect of power "occurs when one country gets other countries to *want* what it wants" and that this "might be called co-optive or soft power in contrast with the hard or command power of *ordering* others to do what it wants". This idea of 'soft' power is useful to ascribing Australia's opportunities for influencing its allies and friends, fence-sitters, and even antagonists. Nye says such power "is the ability of a country to structure a situation so that other countries develop preferences or define their interests in ways consistent with its own. This power tends to arise from such resources as cultural and ideological attraction as well as rules and institutions of international regimes" (Nye 1990: 164; 168). Arguably, the combination of US hard power (military might, nuclear deterrence, NATO, a web of military alliances) and its decisive influences in shaping world economic institutions (World Trade Organisation, World Bank, World Health Organisation, etc) and its superior advantages in culture, technology, and overall economic dynamism, has underpinned the post-Second World War Two political environment. For most of the last 80-years, the western-aligned world was thereby seemingly safe for America and mostly safe in-itself. This, however, we need to remember, is relative. As for Australia's place, the world is never in stasis.

Not for nothing did former Singapore Prime Minister Lee Kuan Yew use the term "America's catchment area" to describe the world's reliance on the United States as a source of innovation, investment, and political stability. A corollary of this concept is that much of the world is drawn to and benefits from American leadership in various aspects of global affairs. This once included free trade and anti-protectionism, as Lee explained in his address to the US Congress forty years ago. (Lee 1985). Another aspect of the idea is that many of the best and brightest are drawn to migrate to the United States. In 1999, Lee remarked: "Silicon Valley has 260 million Americans to pick from, yet nearly half its brains come from Asia, India, Taiwan, China, and other parts of Asia and the world... American banks in New York have growing numbers of Indians and Chinese in their executive ranks" (Lee 1999). This was the zenith of regard for the United States across Asia and elsewhere.

Back to Nye, who wrote: "Power is the ability to get others to do what you want. That can be accomplished by coercion ('sticks'), payment ('carrots') and attraction ('honey'). The first two methods are forms of hard power, whereas attraction is soft power" (Nye 2025). Australia, notably in the Pacific, enjoys advantages, in both senses of hard and soft. Wong in a landmark speech, "Securing Our Future", to the Australian National University's National Security College in April 2024 recognised this point: "Often, security discourses have artificially divided actions to reassure and to deter. The implication being that the role of diplomacy is exclusively soft persuasion, while the hard edge of the military is our only deterrent. But that thinking limits our potency when we have to maximise all the tools of national power" (Wong 2024a). Further, she said: "Without credible military capability, the efficacy of diplomacy and economic integration are invariably diminished. And without ever more investment into diplomacy and engagement, the risk of military capabilities being called upon for conflict increases." (Wong 2024a). Although the promised AUKUS "hard power" of submarines is not be available for another 20 years, this is where the complementary "soft power" of alliances and diplomacy become a vital, an actual strength of AUKUS, hidden behind the "credible military capability".

Preparing for Government & Labor's Style

Clayton argues: "Traditional Labor foreign policy has been described as being more internationalist, characterised by enhanced multilateralism, particularly in the Asia-Pacific region" (Clayton 2023: 325). Too much can be made of the contrast between the two major parties, however, as both have had strong interests in fostering strong relations with neighbours, in Asia and the Pacific. On the latter, climate change and the shifts and changes of the Liberal-National Party governments, from Abbott to Morrison, were sometimes sources of tension, with one Pacific Islands Forum almost coming to grief on the issue due to ambivalent Australian attitudes (Lyons 2019; Ide 2023; Moore 2024).

Interestingly in the lead-up to the May 2022 Australian election, foreign policy issues barely influenced voters. "Polling data showed that less than 1 per cent of Australians ranked [foreign policy] as their major issue for the campaign" (Blackwell 2022: 621). A comprehensive study of polls and election materials of the major parties in 2022 led to the observation that "[i]nternational relations were also prominent throughout the campaign" (Botterill and Walsh 2024). But not as a major vote mover, unlike earlier elections this century when border protection and defence, as aspects of international security, heavily registered with voters.

In opposition, Labor was determined to defuse certain contentious issues. Albanese said a few months before the 2022 election: "Under my leadership, Labor offered bipartisan support for the Defence Strategic Update 2020, and for AUKUS and the acquisition of nuclear-powered submarines" (Albanese 2022). He blended domestic and discrete foreign policy points into this summation of Labor objectives:

1. Supporting a stronger Australian Defence Force.
2. Prioritising better and smarter cybersecurity.
3. Shoring-up our economic self-reliance.
4. Strengthening our communities and institutions.
5. Deepening our partnerships in the region and globally around the world.
6. Taking action on climate change. (Albanese 2022).

Point 3 indicated part of the appeal of AUKUS for Albanese and many of his then Shadow Ministerial colleagues – namely, the potential to build up domestic manufacturing capacity, in this traditionally highly unionised sector of the Australian economy.

Labor in office tends to be more interested in the United Nations and other international bodies. Several early indicative initiatives of the Albanese Government included the appointment of separate Ambassadors for Climate Change and for First Nations. The former appointment indicates that climate change and achieving CoP targets are relatively non-controversial on the Labor side.

Whenever a change of government occurs in Australia, there is always the continuation of pre-existing policies, together with a few innovations: "consistency and innovation are intertwined in policy development" (Easson 2023: 82). "We can do better than the others", whether in eloquence, competence, or both, is the gist of pitches for support.

Throughout the Albanese Government's first term, statements such as this were uncontroversial: "...we want an open and inclusive region, based on agreed rules, where countries of all sizes can choose their own destiny. Countries want a prosperous, connected region, trading together at the epicentre of global economic growth, through a transparent system, where economic interdependence is not misused for political and strategic ends" (Wong 2023). Wong argued that Australia seeks to influence "by being active, by exercising agency, and by contributing our efforts to the balance of power in our region – so no country dominates, and no country is dominated" (Wong 2024a).

Consistently, Wong has stated: "We are investing in our engagement … because diplomacy is always our first line of defence, and key to shaping our region and world in support of our interests" (Wong 2024c). And that "… our collective interest is that we will always be better off in a world where the rules are clear, mutually negotiated and consistently followed" (Wong 2022).

In recent years, Australia's major diplomatic engagements involved major fora including The Quad, AUKUS, the ASEAN Regional Forum (ARF), ANZUS ministerial meetings, APEC, the G20, G7, and the CoP summits. Working closely with the PM and Foreign Minister, the easing of trade tensions with China was driven by careful diplomatic engagement by Trade Minister Senator Don Farrell.

China

Clayton described the challenge of Australia's China policy as defrosting the relationship. (Clayton 2023). Australian Trade Minister Senator Don Farrell was central to the defrosting of the relationship with China. This is one area of success. Yet, overall, with disputes in the South China Sea and Taiwan, "Australia, like the region, is largely hostage to calculation involving the United States and China. Australian diplomacy needs to be geared to conflict avoidance" (P. Kelly 2022: 211). On the military build-up, Wong stated: "It is worrying that large-scale Chinese military operations in the Taiwan Strait have become a routine event. The risk of an accident, and potential escalation, is growing" (Wong 2024a). The Prime Minister emphasised: "Our Government has put dialogue at the heart of our efforts to stabilise our relationship with China. We are not naive about this process, or its limitations" (Albanese 2023b). The rapid, expanded buildup of China's PLA and associated military material, the 'wolf warrior'[3] rhetoric of its diplomats, its militarisation of disputed Islands in the South China Sea, the assertion of sovereignty over vast swathes of water with the revival of the "nine dash" maritime borders,[4] prompted bipartisan support for increasing Australia's hard power capacities. Australian rhetoric sounds realistic about on-going challenges: "China continues to modernise its military at a pace and scale not seen in the world for nearly a century with little transparency or assurance about its strategic intent" (Wong 2023). Rudd in his analysis of contemporary Chinese political thought, and of the outlook of China's most hardline communist leader since Mao, argues that supra nationalism, ideology, and military build-up under Xi Jinping go together (Rudd 2024: 13-16). In this respect, the Foreign Minister has noted "China is going to keep being China" (Wong 2023). She found a neat and compelling formula to express policy: "...the Albanese Government will be calm and consistent and continue to do as we have since coming to office: cooperate where we can, disagree where we must, manage our differences wisely, and above all else, engage in and vigorously pursue our own national interest" (Wong 2023).

United States

Both the Prime Minister and Foreign Minister pledged fidelity to the US alliance. Wong in 2024 said: "… American leadership remains indispensable" (Wong 2024a) and that "…at the heart of our traditional relationships is our alliance with the United States" (Wong 2024c). But she also knows: "America has often been talked of as the indispensable power. It remains so. But the nature of that indispensability has changed" (Wong 2023). This last, ambiguous point refers to the shifts in the balance of power in the Asia Pacific as well as shifts in American attention to the region.

Prime minister Albanese evinces a personal commitment to the alliance of western democracies and to the American alliance in particular. He endured barbs from conservative commentators for many years that he was really at heart an anti-American leftie; but he actually sees himself firmly in the Curtin-Hawke tradition on the US. He thinks former Prime Minister Paul Keating and former Foreign Minister Bob Carr, are wrong on China. Albanese has actively countered internal ALP criticism, notably from Carr and Keating, deploying allies like Assistant Defence Minister Pat Conroy, elevated to Cabinet in 2024, to manage dissent internally and dampen down resistance to AUKUS in the ALP.

With President Trump returning to the White House at the end of Albanese's first term, however, it looks like Trump's personality makes for a foreign policy grittier than pretty. Early into Trump's second term, America is trashing much of its soft power with zig-zag policy shifts, seemingly random tariff imposts, threats to allies (Greenland), and the like. According to a March 2025 poll by the respected Lowy Institute, only 36 per cent of Australians express any level of "trust in the United States" – the lowest level in Lowy's 21 years of annual polling. Most Australians (68 per cent) are pessimistic about the next four years with Donald Trump as US president (Lowy 2025). Naturally, the US pursues its national interest, as all countries do. But as New *York Times* columnist Bret Stephens said: "To cite Forrest Gump: Life under Trump is like a box of chocolates, because you never know what you're going to get. Except that it's a Pandora's box. And they aren't chocolates" (Stephens 2025). Australia lives in more interesting times than it is used to. The conduct of Australian foreign policy with Trump's erraticism makes it impossible to predict where we might be by 2028 – the time of the next Australian general and American presidential elections.

AUKUS

When AUKUS was first unveiled in 2021, most observers were taken by surprise: "In contrast to … continuities, some new developments caught both scholars and analysts off guard. The announcement of a totally unanticipated initiative in the form of the 'AUKUS' … trilateral agreement unveiled a centrepiece deal… And created shockwaves at the existing French deal to provide conventional vessels was unceremoniously jettisoned" (Abbondanza and Wilkins 2022: 264). Prime Minister Morrison dubbed the agreement the "forever partnership" (Abbondanza and Wilkins: 271). Former Labor Prime Minister Paul Keating scoffed at the so-called benefits saying: "eight submarines against China in 20 years' time will be like throwing a handful of toothpicks at the mountain" (cited in Abbondanza and Wilkins: 272). The then head of the Asia Society, Kevin Rudd, critiqued AUKUS as leaving Australia "strategically naked for 20 years" during the wait for submarines (cited, Clayton 2023: 329).

In contrast, former diplomat and past Australian Secretary of the Department of Defence, Dennis Richardson, argued:

> When we have these nuclear-powered submarines, they will be under Australian command and control as is the rest of the ADF. We will make our sovereign decisions about what capability we deploy or don't deploy in any conflict. In acquiring nuclear-powered submarines, we are no more dependent on US technology than when we acquired the Joint Strike Fighter from the US. In that sense, the submarines do not constitute any historic break with the past. At no point in our history have we possessed independent defence industry capability. Therefore, we will always be dependent upon technology from other countries. The submarine is consistent with that history. (cited in P. Kelly

2022: 189).

Historical evidence of nuclear-submarine project overruns in the US and UK, however, underscores the high risks associated with Australia's reliance on timely and cost-effective delivery of AUKUS capabilities.

The sensitivity of the technology shared and developed on a trilateral basis, the complexity of associated logistical requirements, together with the high-level of required strategic trust is part of the challenge. Pillar 1, is the delivery of nuclear submarines. Pillar 2 is the "the still underdeveloped part of the agreement intended to drive cooperation on advanced technologies such as artificial intelligence, hyper-sonics, quantum computing, cyber, unmanned underwater vehicles, and electronic warfare" (Edel 2023). This aspect of AUKUS fits with the Prime Minister's instinct to develop local defence industry capability, but project management is incredibly complex and hard to master.

A potential AUKUS Pillar 3 relates to energy transition. Discussion now is focused on creating this new Pillar, associated with critical minerals, which opens up a whole other discussion.

Interestingly, Wong has argued that rather than standing apart, AUKUS complements other Australian policy: Understanding this "is a powerful corrective to critics of AUKUS who define it in isolation of our broader efforts" (Wong 2024c). In expressing herself this way, Senator Wong alludes to the argument that the original AUKUS announcement by the Coalition was badly handled. In the Indo-Pacific region, Australian diplomatic missions were given zero notice before the announcement: An unfortunate signal as if this was the old Anglo Whities club being perpetuated, instead of an embrace of the critical need to bring more regional partners into a cooperative fan rework. The formal framing of policy matters.

The Quad and its Potential

The Quad is the diplomatic partnership between Australia, India, Japan, and the United States. Days after being sworn-in as Prime

Minister, Albanese attended the second in-person Quad Leaders' Summit in Japan, where for the first time he met his counterparts (Rudd 2021). After this "triumph"[5] Albanese convened the next one in Australia a year later, with President Biden convening in the US the fourth Leaders' Summit in the US in September 2024.

"Although the significance and potential of the Quad as a stabilising force in the Indo-Pacific remains debated, it certainly is an important grouping for Australian foreign policymakers" (Clapton 2021: 548). The Quad, so far, is a discussion forum, tremendously useful to directly canvass opinion, but not a military pact. It has steered clear of aggressive posturing on some issues, notably with respect to the South China Sea. (Bradford and Emmers 2024).

Arguably, besides strengthrning Australia-Japan ties, the most important impact for Australia of the Quad meetings has been the deepening of Australian-Indian relations, two countries which have never quite "hit it off". After Albanese's visit to India in March 2023, Indian Prime Minister Narendra Modi visited Australia in May 2023, both receiving rapturous receptions. Prominent, "rising star" Labor backbencher Andrew Charlton's book *Australia's Pivot to India* (Charlton 2023), launched by Albanese in September 2023, captured some of the optimism about improved relations. India is now the largest source of migrants to Australia, most of them highly skilled.

There has been talk of South Korea and, potentially The Philippines joining, hence the notion of Quad Plus. But this has so far not eventuated.

South-East Asia

Since Whitlam's prime ministership, it is traditional for Australian prime ministers to visit Indonesia at the beginning or early after their election. Because the second Quad leaders conference occurred immediately after he was elected, Prime Minister Albanese visited Japan, where the Quad was held, and later to Indonesia. Early in her period as Foreign Minister, Senator Wong visited her birthplace in Malaysia and travelled to other countries in the region. Arguably, the

Prime Minister Albanese and Foreign Minister Wong have travelled more kilometres to more countries in the region and beyond than any other combination in Australian history. The prominent presence of a woman of Asian heritage as Foreign Minister is tangible evidence of Australia's changing face as a nation, of importance to Australian diplomacy.

There were few if any significant differences expressed at ASEAN Regional Forum meetings or other fora between Australia and South-East Asian countries. Disputes with China over its belligerent stances in the South China Seas have been mostly expressed behind closed doors.

The hosting of the Special ASEAN Regional Forum in Australia in 2024, as well as the commissioning in 2022 of former Macquarie Bank CEO as Special Envoy for Southeast Asia, marked a significant diplomatic initiative, indicating renewed strategic and economic priority to Australia's "near abroad".

Whereas ASEAN countries mostly felt it wise not to "formally" take sides with growing tensions between the US and China – with Cambodia, Brunei and Myanmar more on the Chinese side – the reputation of American reliability is increasingly in question. Whereas Australia drew strength from its closeness to the US, and the leverage this provided as acting as friendly intermediary for Indonesia in particular, this looks more unpredictable under President Trump II.

Potentially, should American credibility continue to be undermined (by itself) regional concerns about the Quad and AUKUS might become more pronounced. But for Albanese's government, so far, so good. Importantly, however, Australians need to understand:

> ... Indonesia does not see the United States in the same way Australia does ... Jakarta does not define an increased US military presence as necessarily benign or reliable for its own security. Indeed, the likelihood of a US-China conflict has led to a resurgent discussion among defence policymakers and analysts about Indonesia developing its own "anti-access" and "area-denial" strategy against both China and the United States to ensure the neutrality of its waterways and airspace during

wartime". (Laksmana 2024: 30)

Indonesia (and India) has a history of "non-alignment", of not choosing "sides" during the cold war, and a prickly need as a nation to be taken seriously. At the time of writing, President Trump's overall, punitive tariffs against Indonesia, threaten to drastically undermine US credibility and regard. This is another challenge for Australian policy: not to be damaged in the 'crossfire'.

The Blue Pacific

In an address to the National Press Club in Canberra, the Foreign Minister Wong stated this truism: "As a member of the Pacific family, our priority is to ensure the Blue Pacific remains peaceful, prosperous and equipped to respond to the challenges of our time" (Wong 2023). Many Blue Pacific nations are only recently independent: For example, the Solomon Islands and Tuvalu in 1978, Kiribati in 1979, and Vanuatu in 1980. In Senator Wong's first six months as minister, she visited Samoa, Tonga, New Zealand, the Solomon Islands Marshall Islands, Niue, Cook Islands, Nauru, French Polynesia, and Fiji twice (Wong 2022).

The Solomon Islands' security arrangements with the PRC remains of concern. (Blackwell 2022: 624). The Albanese Government, however, has been treading cautiously on this issue. In opposition, then Labor Deputy Leader Richard Marles (in the Albanese Government, Deputy Prime Minister and Minister for Defence) wrote: "Our actions in the Pacific denote our place in the world, where we fall on the spectrum of internationally acknowledged leadership…". He urged: "If Australia's renewed interest in the Pacific is interpreted by the region as an attempt to keep China at bay, then it will be seen in a very cynical light". He went on: "Australia has no right to expect a set of exclusive relationships with Pacific nations. They are perfectly free to engage on whatever terms they choose with China or, for that matter, any other country. Disputing this would be resented…" (Marles 2021: 78;79).

Labor has committed resources and targeted aid to the region. This is the projection of soft power. The Prime Minister noted: "In a region where more than one third of people live on less than $1,000 a year, [Pacific Australia Labour Mobility (PALM) scheme] workers send home an average $1,500 a month boosting Pacific economies and lifting families out of poverty and filling urgent gaps in our workforce, including in aged care and regional communities" (Albanese 2023c). The Prime Minister also observed: "That's also the beauty of a team from Papua New Guinea taking part in the National Rugby League" (NRL) (Albanese 2023c). The funds for that came from the Australian Government. Pat Conroy, Minister for Defence Industry and Minister for Pacific Island Affairs, has travelled extensively for the Albanese Government throughout the Blue Pacific [See Chapter 20 for a critical assessment of the NRL program - editor].

Prior to the 2022 election, Labor committed to a First Nations Ambassador and other policies to "embed First Nations perspectives in Australia's international diplomacy" (Australian Labor Party 2022). Wong argued: "Elevating First Nations' perspectives will strengthen our connections across the world and in our region, especially across the Blue Pacific" (Wong 2023). Though "…it may not be unfair to ask, what is a First Nations foreign policy, how do we achieve it, and what benefits does it bring to Australia?" (Blackwell 2022: 627). In sum, First Nation principles and the stand-alone Ambassador are potentially potent in projecting Australia's empathy with other indigenous people, of importance to the Pacific especially, and in emphasising Australia's respectful, multicultural credentials. (Brigg & Graham 2023). The jury is out on the impact and utility of this initiative.

Two "Far Away" conflicts

Worth mentioning briefly are two conflicts which attracted attention in Australia, namely Russia's attempt to conquer Ukraine and the Israel-Gaza- Palestine conflict.

Ukraine

Russia's most recent invasion of Ukraine began in February 2022. Moscow had earlier annexed Crimea from Ukraine and seized parts of the Donbas region in eastern Ukraine, both in 2014. There is bi-partisan consensus that Australia "should" assist the Ukrainian resistance through humanitarian and military aid. The Prime Minister in 2023 boasted: "… We are proudly one of the largest non-NATO contributors to [Ukraine's] military and humanitarian needs" (Albanese 2023c).

During the 2025 election campaign, there was a brief frisson of excitement when Albanese said he would consider limited troop deployment as part of an international peace-keeping force. But as his comments were qualified and vague, this controversy petered out on the campaign trail.

Israel-Gaza-Palestine

On 7 October, 2023, more Jews were killed in a single day since the Holocaust when Hamas terrorists from Gaza crossed over the Israeli border and slaughtered every Jew they could, killing 1,200 (including some foreign nationals), and taking 251 hostages. This led to the Gaza war and a humanitarian crisis both of which, at the time of writing, are ongoing.

Within Australia, rampant incidences of antisemitism, as well as instances of Islamophobia followed. Community stress in parts of Sydney and Melbourne was high. The crisis further exposed sharp divisions within Australian political discourse, with progressive critiques (including the Greens) accusing the government of insufficient condemnation of Israel, and conservatives criticising perceived equivocation on Hamas terror. Holding a "balanced" view, reflecting sympathy for the humanitarian crisis in Gaza, support for Israel's right to self-defence and the release of all hostages, urging the purge of Hamas from the government of Gaza, and dealing with the timely delivery of aid, tested everyone. The Albanese Government was slow in appointing official envoys to fight antisemitism and Islamophobia (in August and October 2024 respectively). The Prime Minister and the Foreign Minister seemed to dissatisfy key sectors of both the Jewish and Muslim communities. With the former, the decision to annul in October 2022 the Morrison Government's decision in December 2018 to eventually (it was no stronger than that) move Australia's Embassy to West Jerusalem from Tel Aviv, was announced without warning.

The designation at the same time of the West Bank as the Occupied Territories also met criticism, but this nomenclature has been long-standing Labor policy and that of most of Australia's allies, with the exception of the United States.

After the Gaza War broke out, Prime Minister Albanese stated: "Australia recognises that Israel has the right to defend itself – and the way it does so matters. Which is why we have called on Israel to respect international humanitarian law" (Albanese 2023c). But this wordy formulation antagonised, as if Israel needed to be cautioned. Wong expressed frustration about the stalled peace process, stating: "The failures of this approach by all parties over decades – as well as the Netanyahu Government's refusal to even engage on the question of a Palestinian state – have caused widespread frustration" (Wong, 2024a). Israel's global standing is damaged by the presence of diehard extremists in its Cabinet.

Wong's most wounding comment came in a newspaper article where she penned: "While some don't hear our condemnation of Israel Defence Forces' attacks on civilians or aid workers, others wrongly claim we enable Hamas by insisting Israel follow the rules of war" (Wong 2024b). Wong's statement – intended as balanced diplomacy – nonetheless inadvertently implied moral equivalence between IDF actions and Hamas terrorism, as if the IDF had the morals of the Wagner Group.[6] Words matter, and a careless formulation should have been better expressed. An investigation by Air Chief Marshal Mark Binskin, as the Special Adviser to the Australian Government on Israel's response to the IDF strikes on the NGO World Central Kitchen (WCK) aid delivery in Gaza and the killing of an Australian, Ms Zomi Frankcom, concluded *inter alia* that that "the IDF strike on the WCK aid workers was not knowingly or deliberately directed against the WCK" (DFAT 2024: 10). This was only one instant of loss of life by an aid worker. Australia and other Governments will press Israel after the war's end for a full investigation of the overall conduct of the war, as Israel has always done subsequent to past conflicts. Labor's vote in the UN in December 2024 for a "immediate, unconditional and permanent ceasefire" was criticised as undermining Israel's effort to destroy Hamas (M. Kelly 2024).

On the eve of the 2025 election, Peter Wertheim, co-chief executive officer of the Executive Council of Australian Jewry, explained the differences between Liberal and Labor: "You can't say that the Labor government has been derelict in its duty to the Jewish community, or that it has been completely oblivious to or uncaring about antisemitism. That would not be true. They've given us funding for security as well as new laws, and they've taken quite a lot of initiative over the past 18 months. But there's always this perception that it's not quite as strong as it should be, and if you compare the responses on foreign policy issues, there are some significant differences between the two main parties" (quoted in Segall and Malta 2025). Albanese and Wong held off implementing ALP policy to "recognise" Palestine, but this cannot be far off in the second term, probably with "riders" that Hamas be excluded from any Palestine government, together with security guarantees. It is likely that, overwhelmingly, Jewish voters in bigger numbers than ever before cast ballots for the Liberals in May 2025.

At the 2025 election, an avowedly Muslim Party, in the electorates they contested, failed to win a majority of the Muslim vote (Rifi 2025). But their votes in the high teens in several electorates in western Sydney indicated frustration with Labor not taking a harsher stand about Israel in Gaza. The Jewish vote was decisively relevant in the federal electorates of Goldstein and Macnamara, both in Victoria. In the former, the Liberal candidate and former MP won against the Teal independent. (Visontay 2025). The outcome in Macnamara was also important in sending the Greens backward and preventing them from taking the seat off Labor (Solomon 2025). This too, as with the next section, merits detailed consideration unavailable in this necessarily short overview chapter.

Key criticisms

Besides debates on Israel-Palestine, the main criticisms of the Albanese Government's foreign policy centre on the government not doing enough in defence preparations (Sheridan 2025) and, from a different direction, concerning AUKUS and scepticism about American intentions associated with the US-Australian alliance (eg White 2022). The subtitle of Shortis' 2021 book *Our Exceptional*

Friend reads "Australia's fatal alliance with the United States". This succinctly states her perspective. She asserts: "We are allowed to demand better, even if we don't know exactly what better looks like. It' is enough to know that it doesn't look like this. And to know that the long, entangled thread of our shared, human histories might point to other possibilities. That, I think is where hope lives – radical, defiant hope" (Shortis 2021: 233; see also Shortis 2025). Such hazy analysis is matched by Behm who writes: "We leave neither footprints nor fingerprints on any of the major issue confronting the regional or global communities". Unhelpfully, he goes on: "Once we have settled on a clear set of interests and values – clarifying who we are and what we stand for – we need to address the four principal pathologies that affect our strategic mindset: racism, misogyny, isolation and insecurity (the principal indicator of which is the cultural cringe)" (Behm 2022: 285). Such critics, White, and Shortis in particular, are significant as they reflect broad, elite sentiment in the academy.

Of more potent and acute import are analyses that regret the lack of scrutiny of and debate about AUKUS's costs and delivery (Dunley 2023), and the risky, inherent uncertainty associated with Australia's 'bet' on American and UK capabilities to deliver on time, within budget. (O'Connor et al 2023). Australia is also gambling that no matter what, America will honour commitments. The America First antics in the first months of the Trump II Presidency give pause. (Curran 2025). Such critiques are worthy of separate and exhaustive analysis.

Conclusion

Watching "what Labor has done" in the past three years yields the conclusion that the Albanese Government has had a thought-out perspective on the utilisation of "soft" and "hard" power. Senator Wong has articulated a coherent perspective. Policy and outcomes were mostly effective and targeted in befriending Blue Pacific countries, though some problem areas, the Solomon Islands notably, remain on "watch". Relations with most Asian countries are strong and mostly warm, with the single exception of Myanmar. The China relationship is out of deep freeze, defrosted, and nearly all trade restrictions are lifted. That is a singular success., The Albanese Government deserves credit here, but so too do successive Australian governments in standing up to bullying. The swearing-in of President of Indonesia, Prabowo Subianto in October 2024, introduces a potentially mercurial figure at the top. But, early days, Australian relations are warm (as they were with President Jokowi) and there are no troubling signs – other than that President Trump's tariff and protectionist policies and ignorance of Indonesian interests which might cause counter-reactions of consequence for Australia.

The contest between China and the US and its associated tensions, together with the fickleness of US policy and personnel is a reminder, as Allan Gyngell once said, that "the world is a messy place" (cited in Albanese 2023c). As mentioned above, the unprecedented decline in public confidence in the United States by Australians and nearly everywhere else in the Indo-Pacific significantly complicates Australia's diplomatic and strategic calculations, making policy formulation for any Australian Government especially fraught with the Trump Administration.

We are a long way from the America Singapore's leader Harry Lee described, as earlier cited. Australia's Department of Foreign Affairs and Trade (DFAT) and the government itself will need to develop stronger and deeper expertise and deployment of clever personnel to match these new challenges. Australia, effectively, seeks to balance the rise of China with an even deeper alliance with the US. This is aimed at avoiding war (Rudd 2022: 1-18). The future of key treaty commitments, particularly AUKUS, require critical attention to delivery of outcomes. A menu of choices is no substitute, especially where there are optimistic, ill-costed assumptions. A ticking danger for Australia is to rely too much on the new-generation nuclear "subs". US and UK experience suggest likely, major cost overruns. Should the shortage of nuclear engineers in all three AUKUS partners persist, for example, design and construction and delivery will languish.

There is further counsel worth heeding: Owen Harries urged Australian analysts to understand that all treaties are conditional. He wrote: "As statesmen as diverse as Bismarck, Gladstone and Teddy Roosevelt had cause to stress, the reserve *rebus sic stantibus* – 'while the same conditions apply' – is always silently understood in every treaty. In other words, no firm and unconditional guarantees are ever available in international politics" (Harries 2007: 101). There are no timeless warranties even if formally inked on archive-quality paper.

A big issue for a Labor government which prioritises multilateralism and the global order as a shield for middle and lower order powers, is the petering demise of the UN. This relates to the alarming rise in the number and strength of authoritarian states, and the impact this has on UN processes, institutions, and agencies. The patent failure and ineffectiveness of Antonio Guterres as UN Secretary-General is a major defect in the diplomatic matrix and stands in marked contrast to someone like Kofi Annan (1938-2018; UN SG, 1997-2006). This significantly complicates Australia's reliance on multilateralism, necessitating a careful calibration of diplomatic strategy in an increasingly fragmented global order, testing Australia's expertise and capabilities.

Allan Gyngell, who died in 2023, wrote at the end of his opus on Australian foreign policy:

> I have argued ... that the motivating force of Australia's international engagement has been fear of abandonment. For some, that will seem too timid and unheroic a motivation for a great country's foreign policy. But it has also been the driver of one of the most consistent and commendable aspects of Australia's worldview – rejection of isolationism; its conviction that Australia needs to be active in the world in order to shape it, and that gathering combinations of allies, friends and *ad hoc* partners is the best way of doing this. That will be a tradition worth defending in the years ahead. (Gyngell 2017: 363).

The job of Australian politicians, diplomats, the whole foreign policy apparatus, is never done – especially where vital interests are at stake, contested, and worth securing. The Albanese Government grasps the point. The question to be resolved in the next term is whether its team is equal to the challenge.

References

Abbondanza, G., and Wilkins, T.S., (2022), "Issues in Australian Foreign Policy July to December 2021", *Australian Journal of Politics and History*, 68(2), June, 264-78

Albanese, A.. (2022), "An address by Opposition Leader Anthony Albanese", The Lowy Institute, , *The Interpreter*, Lowy Institute, 4 March

Albanese, A., (2023a), "Address to the National Press Club", 22 February

Albanese, A., (2023b), "Speech to the International Institute for Strategic Studies (IISS) Shangri-La Dialogue", 3 June

Albanese, A., (2023c), "Australia in the World", 2023 Lowy lecture, 19 December

Australian Labor Party (2022), *Labor's Commitment to First Nations Peoples*, Canberra: ALP

Behm, A., (2022), *No Friends No Enemies. Restoring Australia's Global Relevance*, Perth: Upswell Publishing

Blackwell, J., (2022), "Issues in Australian Foreign Policy January to June 2022", *Australian Journal of Politics and History*, 68(4), December, 612-30.

Botterill, L.C., and Walsh, Michael, J., (2024), "An Examination of the Policy Content of Scott Morrison's and Anthony Albanese's 2022 Federal Election Campaign Materials", *Australian Journal of Politics and History*, 70(4), June, 838-47

Bradford, J.F., Emmers, R.F., (2024), "Why the Quad is Not Squaring Off in the South China Sea: Evaluating Interests, Objectives and Capacity", *Australian Journal of International Affairs*, 78(1), February, 1-21

Brigg, M., and Graham, M., (2023), "Approaching First Nations Diplomacy from the Australian Continent", *Australian Journal of International Affairs*, 77(6), December, 585-89

Charlton, A., (2023), *Australia's Pivot to India*, Melbourne: Black Inc.

Clapton, W., (2021), "Issues in Australian Foreign Policy January to June 2021", *Australian Journal of Politics and History*, 67(3-4), September-December, 544-58

Clayton, K., (2023), "Issues in Australian Foreign Policy July to December 2022", *Australian Journal of Politics and History*, 69(2), June 2023, pp. 325-340

Curran, J., (2025), "Continental Gift; Trump and Australia's Place in the World", *Australian Foreign Affairs*, Iss. 23, March, 6-25

DFAT, (2024), *Special Adviser Public Report on the Government of Israel's Response to the IDF Attack on WCK Aid Workers in Gaza on Monday 1 April 2024*

DFAT, (2025), *Australia in the World. 2025 Snapshot*, Canberra, Department of Foreign Affairs and Trade

Dunley R., (2023), "The End of the 'Lucky Country'? Understanding the Failure of the AUKUS Policy Debate", *Australian Journal of International Affairs*, 77(3), June, 317-24

Easson M., (2023), *Whitlam's Foreign Policy*, Redland Bay: Connor Court Publishing

Edel, C., (2023), "The AUKUS Wager. More Than a Security Pact, the Deal Aims to Transform the Indo-Pacific Order", *Foreign Affairs*, August

Fullilove, M., (2022), "America and Australia Are Back on the Same Page. How Biden Revived the Alliance", *Foreign Affairs*, February

Gyngell, A., (2017), *Fear of Abandonment. Australia in the World Since 1942*, Carlton: Latrobe University Press/Black Inc

Harries, O., (1995), "Realism in a New Era", *Quadrant*, 39(4), April, 39-46

Harries, O., (2007), "Bipolar Nation" [Letter to the Editor], *Quarterly Essay*, Iss. 26, 99-101

Ide, T., (2023), "Climate Change and Australia's National Security", *Australian Journal of International Affairs*, 77(1), February, 26-44

Kelly, M., (2024), Australia's Damning of Israel is Poisonous. I Say that as an Ex-Labor Minister, *Sydney Morning Herald*, 15 December

Kelly, Paul, (2022), *Morrison's Mission. How a Beginner Reshaped Australian Foreign Policy*, Lowy Institute for Foreign Policy Paper, Sydney: Penguin Special

Kolmaš, M., and Kolmašová, Š., (2019), "A 'Pivot' that Never Existed: America's Asian Strategy under Obama and Trump", *Cambridge Review of International Affairs*, 32(1), 61-79

Laksmana, E.A., (2024), "The View from Jakarta: Friends with Benefits, Not Fellow Fighters", *Australian Foreign Affairs*, Iss. 21, June, 28-44

Lee, Kuan Yew (1985), "Speech by Prime Minister Lee Kuan Yew at the Joint Meeting of the United States Congress", 9 October, https://www.nas.gov.sg/archivesonline/speeches/record-details/7857023d-115d-11e3-83d5-0050568939ad, accessed 30 May 2025

Lee, Kuan Yew, (1999), "Speech by Senior Minister Lee Kuan Yew at the Tanjong Pagar 34th National Day Celebrations", 14 August https://www.nas.gov.sg/archivesonline/data/pdfdoc/1999081404. htm, accessed 30 May 2025

Lowy Institute, (2025), *2035 Lowy Institute Poll*, 21st Annual Poll of Australian Opinion, Sydney: Lowy Institute

Lyons, K., (2019), "Revealed: 'Fierce' Pacific Forum Meeting Almost Collapsed Over Climate Crisis", *The Guardian* [Sydney], 16 August

Marles, R., (2021), *Tides that Bind: Australia in the Pacific*, Monash University's In the National Interest Series, Clayton: Monash University Publishing

Moore, L., (2024), "A Dysfunctional Family: Australia's Relationship with Pacific Island States and Climate Change", *Australian Journal of International Affairs*, 79(3), June, 286-305.

Morgenthau, H.J., (1973), *Politics Among Nations. The Struggle for Power and Peace*, 5th ed., New York: Alfred A Knopf

O'Connor, B., Cox, L., and Cooper, D., (2023), "Australia's AUKUS 'Bet' on the United States: Nuclear Powered Submarines and the Future of American Democracy", *Australian Journal of International Affairs*, 77(1), February, 45-64

Napang, M., et. al, (2019), "Contesting Views of the Philippines and China over the Nine-Dash Line in the South China Sea", *Journal of East Asia and International Law*, 12(1), 180-92

Nye, J.S., (1990), "Soft Power", *Foreign Policy*, No. 80, 153-71

Nye, J.S., (2025), "The Future of American Soft Power", *Project Syndicate*, 16 May https://www.project-syndicate.org/commentary/ the-future-of-american-soft-power-by-joseph-s-nye-2025-05, accessed 24 May 2025

Rifi, J., (2025), "Muslim Votes Does Not Care About, Nor Represent, Muslims", *The Australian*, 10 April

Rudd, K., (2021), "Why the Quad Alarms China. Its Success Poses a Major Threat to Beijing's Ambitions", *Foreign Affairs*, August

Rudd, K., (2022), *The Avoidable War. The Danger of a Catastrophic Conflict Between the US and Xi Jinping's China*, New York, Public Affairs [Hachette Book Group]

Rudd, K., (2024), *On Xi Jinping: How Xi's Marxist Nationalism is Shaping China and the World*, Oxford: Oxford University Press

Segall, D., and Maltz, J., (2025), "For These Australian Jews, There Is Only One Issue in Saturday's Election", *Haaretz* [Israel], 1 May

Shambaugh, D., (2025), *Breaking the Engagement. How China Won & Lost America*, Oxford: Oxford University Press

Sheridan, G., (2025), "Albanese Government is One of the Worst in Foreign Policy", *The Australian*, 14 January

Shortis, E., (2021), *Our Exceptional Friend. Australia's Fatal Alliance with the United States*, Richmond [Victoria]: Hardie Grant Books

Shortis, E., (2025), *After America. Australia and the New World Order*, Vantage Point: Big Ideas in Small Packages, Issue 1, Melbourne: Australia Institute Press.

Silove, N., (2016), "The Pivot before the Pivot: U.S. Strategy to Preserve the Power Balance in Asia", *International Security*, 40(4), 45-88

Simons, M., (2023), "No Daylight: Inside Labor's Decision to Back AUKUS", *Australian Foreign Affairs*, Iss. 19, October, 49-70

Solomon, B., (2025), "Race for Macnamara. Why Voting Liberal Could Result in a Greens Win", *Australian Jewish News*, 11 April

Spearin, C., (2024), "Wagner Group: Comparing and Contextualizing the Russian Monster", *Comparative Strategy*, 43(3), 15363

Stephens, B., (2025), "The Conversation [with Gail Collins], All Good Things Come to an End. What About Bad Things?", *New York Times*, 28 April

Visontay, M., (2025), "Facing the Fallout from an Ugly Election", *The Jewish Independent*, 15 May

White, H., (2022), "Sleepwalk to War: Australia's Unthinking Alliance with America", *Quarterly Essay*, No 86, June

Wong, A., (2021), "How Not to Win Allies and Influence Geopolitics. China's Self-Defeating Economic Statecraft", *Foreign Affairs*, May/June

Wong, P., (2022), "The Whitlam Oration", Speech Given at Blacktown, NSW, 13 November

Wong, P., (2023), "Australian Interests in a Regional Balance of Power", Address to the National Press Club, 17 April

Wong P., (2024a), "Securing Our Future", Speech to the ANU National Security College, 9 April

Wong, P., (2024b), "Australians Are Traumatised by Middle East Horrors. They Deserve the Facts", *Sydney Morning Herald*, 5 November

Wong, P., (2024c), "The Hawke Lecture", Delivered at the University of South Australia, 9 December

Wong, P.,(2025), "Foreword" to DFAT (2025), 1

World Bank Group, (2023), Open Data Series, https://data.worldbank. org/indicator/NY.GDP.MKTP.CD?locations=ID, accessed 13 May 2025.

Endnotes

1   I am grateful for comments on earlier drafts from Shane Easson, Luke Foley, Catherine Harding, Mike Kelly, Alex Polson and Daniel Street; and to Anna Oldmeadow of Senator Wong's office for sending certain background material. All statements, conclusions and mistakes, however, are entirely mine.

2   The term Blue Pacific was first used in 2017 at the Pacific Islands Forum, which describes the region of the Pacific Ocean, its island nations, and their collective interests.

3   The term Wolf Warrior arose following the 2015 Chinese war film of the same name and its sequel, Wolf Warrior 2, and became popularly associated with aggressively nationalistic Chinese diplomacy. (A. Wong 2021).

4   The 'nine dash' line, first inscribed on a Chinese map in 1947, is the dotted line denoting China's maritime claims, which stretch to the coasts of Malaysia and Indonesia. The claim was explicitly rejected in July 2016 as of no legal basis by the Permanent Court of Arbitration in the Hague. (Napang et al 2019).

5   Text from the PM to Michael Easson, 25 May 2022.

6   The Wagner Group was a Russian state-funded, quasi-private military company, which was notorious for its cruelty and flouting of international law. The Group, led and controlled until 2023 by Yevgeny Prigozhin, operated in Syria, parts of Africa, the Ukraine, and elsewhere. (Spearin 2024).

342

17

Defence Policy

David Lee

Introduction

The Albanese Government's defence policy represented a marked departure from the defence policies of previous Labor governments. Stretching back to John Curtin's wartime government, all had prioritised continental defence in some form (Lee 1997 and Lee 2023). One of the most influential late twentieth century defence documents was the Hawke Labor Government's 1987 Defence White Paper, which embedded the "Defence of Australia" (DoA) doctrine in Australian strategy. The DoA recommended a shift away from the "forward defence" strategy of the Menzies era to the "self-reliant" defence of the continent. The DoA's defensive posture was to deny Australia's "sea-air" approaches to an adversary. On coming to office in 2022, the Albanese Government decided to maintain the essentials of the defence policies of the Morrison Government. This involved the Albanese Government explicitly moving from the DoA to a strategy it called "National Defence". Rather than directly defending Australia, "National Defence" amounted to the forward defence of Australia and co-operation with the United States in containing the People's Republic of China. Critics from the Right viewed the Labor Government's policy as insufficiently robust in addressing the enhanced threat from China. Others, including many in the Australian Labor Party (ALP), regarded Albanese as moving unhealthily close to the United States and unnecessarily antagonising

China. As the 2025 election approached, there was widespread agreement that the centrepiece of the Albanese Government's defence policy, the AUKUS project to acquire nuclear-powered submarines, was in tatters. In this respect, the defence policy of the Albanese Government was a failure.

Morrison, AUKUS and the Labor Opposition

The Morrison Government announced the trilateral AUKUS partnership between Australia, the United States and the United Kingdom on 15 September 2021. AUKUS involved two lines of effort described as "pillars". The first pillar involved Australia acquiring nuclear-powered attack submarines and rotating United States (US) and United Kingdom (UK) nuclear-powered submarines in Australia. The second focused on collaboration in the development of advanced capabilities in six technological areas (Wintour 2021).

AUKUS had its origins in the perceived failing of an earlier coalition plan to collaborate with the French to acquire conventional submarines. In 2016, Malcolm Turnbull's Coalition Government signed an A$50 billion deal with the majority French-owned company, Naval Group, to design a new generation of submarines, known as the Attack Class, to replace Australia's ageing Collins Class submarines. In 2019, Turnbull's successor, Scott Morrison, clinched a strategic partnership agreement with the Naval Group to design and construct twelve submarines to be built in Australia. But by June 2021, Morrison was expressing concern about delays in the French project. In August of that year, he cancelled the plan to acquire conventional submarines. Australia, Morrison insisted, now required nuclear-powered submarines, which had the advantage of moving at greater speed, staying under water for longer and carrying heavier loads than conventionally powered submarines (Buckley 2021). In the meantime, Morrison and his advisers had worked with the UK Prime Minister, Boris Johnson, and the President of the United States, Joseph Biden, on a plan to cooperate with the United States and the United Kingdom to acquire nuclear-powered submarines at a cost of up to $368 billion between then and the mid-

2050s. By Morrison's admission, the political framework of AUKUS was to secure a "forever partnership" and a "forever responsibility" between Australia and the United States (Tillett 2021).

Before announcing his government's commitment to AUKUS, Morrison gave a two-hour briefing to the Leader of the Opposition, Anthony Albanese, and his deputy Richard Marles in the company of Penny Wong, Shadow Minister for Foreign Affairs, and Brendan O'Connor, the shadow Defence minister. According to journalist and historian Andrew Fowler:

> Morrison had lured Labor into a trap, confronting Albanese with an agonizing choice: the status quo, where Labor maintained its sixty years of opposition to nuclear power in Australia and rejected a deeper US alliance, or embrace nuclear power and risk a loss of sovereignty that many of the left of his party would bitterly oppose. (Fowler 2024:123)

After a meeting of the shadow Cabinet, Albanese swiftly announced that the Labor Opposition was offering bipartisan support to AUKUS on the conditions that no nuclear weapons would be acquired and no civilian nuclear energy industry created, and that Australia's non-proliferation obligations would be maintained. There was no consultation with the rest of the front bench, parliamentary caucus or the wider party (K. Carr 2024).

Albanese's acceptance of AUKUS prevented Labor being wedged as it had been by its equivocation on establishment of the US base at North West Cape, Western Australia, before the 1963 election. Following the 2022 election, Albanese became Prime Minister, Penny Wong the Minister for Foreign Affairs and Richard Marles, Deputy Prime Minister and Minister for Defence. As the Liberal and National parties needed to win 20 seats to form a majority government after the next election, there seemed good prospects for the Albanese Government to put its own stamp on defence policy after nine years out of office (Black 2024).

Implementation without review

Even Albanese's sternest critics in the Labor Party sympathised with his decision to give conditional support to AUKUS before the 2022 election (Curran 2024e). Once Labor was elected, however, it did not review AUKUS as the Hawke Labor Government had reviewed the ANZUS treaty after winning office in 1983 but moved to implement Morrison's plan without further ado.[1] This proved to be a critical error. Less than a year after the election, in March 2023, Marles announced the "optimal pathway" to Australia's acquisition of nuclear-powered submarines under the AUKUS arrangement. The three key elements of the pathway were, first, increased visits of US submarines commencing in 2023 and British submarines in 2027 and then rotations of British and American submarines, beginning in 2027, to HMAS Stirling under the Submarine Rotational Force West (SRF-West) initiative. The rotational force was to be maintained and sustained with the support of Australian military personnel and facilities. In the second phase, from as early as the 2030s, the plan was for the United States to sell Australia three and up to five Virginia-class submarines thus ensuring that there would be no capability gap in Australia. Finally, the pathway envisaged that, by the 2040s, the United Kingdom would deliver British-designed SSN-AUKUS submarines to Australia that would be based on a UK design and incorporate cutting-edge Australian UK and US technologies (Marles 2023).

Within the ALP, acceptance of AUKUS was smoothed by an alliance between the national left faction, of which Albanese and Wong were leading members, and a group that was still known as the "Cons", after (Stephen) Conroy, right and whose leader was Marles, the Member for Corio since 2007 (Rundle: 2023). The Conroy/Marles faction supported AUKUS because of its fervent ideological support for the Australian–US alliance. In earlier times, left and centre-left factions moderated the pro-American fervour of the Labor right. But in the 2020s the national left, which normally would have been expected to be critical of the AUKUS project, compromised with the Conroy/Marles group to defend Albanese from any attack from the right of the party as being soft on national security. At the ALP Conference in August 2023, the parliamentary party's national security team, led by Albanese and Marles, suppressed anti-AUKUS dissent welling in some branches. They also sealed deals with factional leaders and unions to deliver what was described as "the most important revolution in Labor's approach to defence in 60 years" (Dean and Beazley 2023). After the conference, former ALP leader Kim Beazley claimed that, because of Albanese's defence revolution, nuclear-powered submarines were a "core Labor value" and a "critical part of the party's platform for regional peace and stability" (Dean and Beazley 2023).

The Albanese Government gained considerable political advantage in implementing its defence policy from the continued support that the coalition parties gave to AUKUS. The project was supported by the mainstream media, defence contractors and prominent national security academics, including the Australian National University's Professor John Blaxland and Professor Rory Medcalf. Defence correspondents at major newspapers were generally supportive with the notable exception of the *Australian Financial Review's* James Curran. Also providing stalwart support to AUKUS was the Australian Strategic Policy Institute (ASPI). ASPI is a defence think tank headed by former coalition staffer and AUKUS backer Justin Bassi and funded by the Australian Department of Defence, some overseas governments and defence and technology companies (Parker 2024).

Losing the Public Debate

AUKUS was, however, sharply criticised by some strategists, notably Emeritus Professor Hugh White of the Australian National University and the Lowy Institute's Sam Roggeveen, and by former senior Labor policymakers from the right of the party (Roggeveen 2023 and White 2023). The latter category included the former Labor prime minister, Paul Keating and former foreign ministers, Gareth Evans and Bob Carr. Despite their support in the mainstream media, Albanese and Marles were unable to combat the arguments of these AUKUS critics by offering a convincing public explanation for the AUKUS project and particularly the purpose of nuclear-powered submarines (Curran 2024a).

Rather than offering a coherent strategic rationale, Albanese simply talked about the job opportunities AUKUS would create domestically (Olbrycht-Palmer 2024). Marles was unconvincing in his emphasis on the role that the submarines would play in protecting trade routes in the Indian Ocean and the South China Sea while Wong assured her Southeast Asian counterparts that AUKUS would create a new equilibrium, or balance of power, in Asia (Galloway 2023 and Argall 2023). The difficulty with Wong's argument was the contradiction between Labor's foreign policy supporting a multipolar order where no one power was dominant, and a defence policy based on using military power to maintain the primacy of the United States (Varghese 2023).

Although few, the former senior Labor policymakers made powerful arguments against AUKUS. In March 2023, Keating blasted the "incompetence" of his party for backing AUKUS which he labelled as the "worst deal in history" and the "worst international decision" by a Labor government since W. M. (Billy) Hughes tried to introduce conscription in the First World War (Karp 2023). Keating singled out Marles and Wong as "seriously unwise" ministers and chided the latter for running a "small target" political strategy by allowing defence interests to trump diplomacy. Keating maintained that the Chinese were "not going to attack us and have never threatened to attack us" and suggested that AUKUS was about preserving US hegemony in east Asia by seeking to contain China (Karp 2023). In a private email to members of the cabinet, Keating also warned of the growing "political dysfunction" in the US political system. For the first time in 70 years, he predicted, Australia "can't be confident that the general direction of US grand strategy will remain unchanged over the next eight years" (Hurst 2023). For his part, Bob Carr, speaking at a New Zealand Foreign Policy symposium in Wellington in August 2024, described Pillar Two of AUKUS as "fragrant methane-wrapped bullshit" (B. Carr 2024).

Multiple points of failure were built into the AUKUS project from its inception. The first, was the improbability of the United States ever delivering three or more of its Virginia class submarines to Australia. The United States already had fewer submarines than it needed so the more that international tensions increased, particularly between the United States and China, the less likely it seemed that the United States would be prepared to reduce its own fleet to help Australia's (Honrada 2024). The next problem was that the UK-Australia AUKUS design might not be ready to take over from the Virginia submarines if they were ever delivered to Australia. Third, the whole project depended on three governments maintaining commitment to the project over three decades and across many election cycles and whatever crises might occur over that time (White 2023). For White, the deeper lesson of the "AUKUS debacle" was the vast gulf between "commit[ment] to major defence capability investments without careful analysis of the outcome we want to achieve, and the most cost-effective ways of achieving it" (Curran: 2024 a). Defence expert Elizabeth Buchanan, writing for the *Sydney Morning Herald* in 2024, described the AUKUS plan as "unhinged from reality". In her view, "the closest Australia will ever get to nuclear-powered submarines, or SSNs, under the AUKUS initiative is the rotational basing of US and British subs out of Western Australia" (Buchanan 2024).

"National Defence" replaces "Defence of Australia"

As he was putting flesh on the bones of the AUKUS idea, Marles commissioned a Defence Strategic Review (DSR) to be led by the former Labor Defence Minister Stephen Smith and former Chief of the Defence Force, Sir Angus Houston. Professor Peter Dean, Director of Foreign Policy at the United States Studies Centre, University of Sydney, served as senior adviser and principal author to for the Independent Leads. Normally such strategic reviews would have preceded decisions on major acquisitions such as nuclear-powered submarines. Marles made clear, however, that AUKUS should be taken as a given by the project Leads (Toohey 2023).

At the time that the review was commissioned, Marles had introduced a new description for Australia's defence relationship with the United States. No longer, Marles declared, would Australian and US personnel just be interoperable, where the services worked alongside each other, they would be interchangeable, "creating in effect a large single military entity" (Fowler 2024 134). In December 2023, after the Australia–United States Ministerial Consultations (AUSMIN), Marles announced the establishment of a combined Australian–United Stated intelligence centre within the Australian Department of Defence. Intelligence cooperation between the five eyes partners was nothing new, but this Australia–United States intelligence organisation provided opportunities for the United States to skew the focus of intelligence gathering and shape its construction, in turn influencing Australian strategic policy. It was a further sign of the Albanese Government's ceding sovereignty in defence matters to the United States (Scrafton 2023).

Smith and Houston concluded that Australia and the world were entering a new "missile age" and that Australia was no longer protected by its geography as strategist Paul Dibb had concluded in his 1986 defence review for the Hawke Government (Dibb 1986). In the view of Smith and Houston: "China's military build-up is now the largest and most ambitious of any country since the Second World War ... this build-up is occurring without transparency or reassurance to the Indo-Pacific region of China's strategic intent" (Department of Defence 2023: 23). The DSR also repeated the contention first raised in the Morrison Government's Defence Strategic Update of 2020 that there would no longer be a ten-year warning time for Australia to detect and respond to a high-level military threat. Although Smith and Houston considered that there was "only a remote possibility" of a direct threat of invasion, they identified risks to Australia's trade and supply routes (Department of Defence 2023: 25).

The DSR proposed to confront the risks by adopting a "new strategy of denial" (Department of Defence 2023). This focused on developing the Australian Defence Force's (ADF's) anti-access/area denial (A2/AD) by accelerating and expanding investments into long-range missiles. The "strategy of denial" was tied to a broader concept misleadingly called "collective security" in the Indo-Pacific and aligned with the US framework for "integrated deterrence" of China (Rudd 2024). Even the Morrison Government's 2020 Strategic Update had defined Australia's strategic environment as falling short of China (Gilligan 2022). But the incoming brief for Marles as Defence Minister had urged his acceptance of the "transformation of the ADF from a primarily defensive force into one with much more potent deterrent capabilities" (Gilligan 2022). What the DSR proposed as "National Defence" a year later amounted to the militarisation of a significant sector of the Australian economy, under AUKUS and other arrangements, to supply, maintain and facilitate American forces in the north and west of Australia.

The DSR and the subsequent National Defence Strategy of 2024 satisfied neither the Albanese Government's critics nor its supporters. For White, the documents were muddled, sometimes talking about co-operating more closely with the United States to uphold the "global rules-based order"—a euphemism for projecting power to maintain US primacy in Asia—and at other times about increased self-reliance and the independent defence of Australia from direct threats to a narrowly defined "primary area of military interest" (White 2024). Although Marles hoped that what he called "impactful projection" would cover both priorities, they pulled in opposite directions (Davis 2023). For White the central unanswered question was whether Australia should support Washington to sustain US primacy or prepare to defend Australia when US primacy had passed. On the other hand, for John Blaxland, a supporter of AUKUS, there was a "jarring dissonance" between the DSR's rhetoric on the deterioration of Australia's strategic position and the lack of any provision by the Government of additional money for defence to meet the enhanced threat (Middleton 2023).

AUKUS did not involve plans to acquire nuclear-armed submarines or the stationing of US nuclear weapons on Australian soil. But viewed from a wider lens, AUKUS epitomised Australia's rapidly evolving nuclear posture within the US alliance. This was reflected by the fact that Australia was poised to become "the only ally in the world to host and support military operations by forward-deployed US strategic bombers and attack submarines" (Townsend 2023).

Under the Albanese Government, the US militarisation of northern and western Australia continued apace on a trajectory begun by Barack Obama's "pivot to Asia" under the Gillard Labor Government (Curran 2021).

This included a high technology cluster the length of the Exmouth Peninsula on the North West Cape of Western Australia, the Darwin-based US Marine Air-Ground Task Force and US Air Force Bomber Task Force of six B-52-H long-range bombers based on "permanent rotation" at the Royal Australian Air Force (RAAF) Base Tindal outside Katherine in the Northern Territory. About half of the fleet of modernised B-52-H bombers could carry nuclear weapons and all of them, whether nuclear capable or not, carried cruise and other missiles to be launched against enemy targets from a safe distance. When Michael McCaul, Chairman of the House Foreign Affairs Committee, visited Australia in September 2024, he declared that Australia had become "the central base of operations" in the region for the US strategic plan to "counter the [China] threat" (Curran 2024f). If ever there should be war between the United States and China, Washington's expectations might include Australia's direct support of nuclear operations "including potentially nuclear strikes by US strategic bombers forward deployed to northern Australia" (Scappatura 2024 and Bristow 2024).

The Trump victory and the absence of a defence 'Plan B'

By the middle of 2024, the progress of AUKUS was causing serious concern among defence experts. In early May, an expert group comprising navy commanders, submarine officers, industry veterans and senior defence officials, attended a confidential meeting in the Department of the Prime Minister and Cabinet in Canberra with Glyn Davis, the Secretary of the Department, and Graham Fletcher, a deputy secretary in charge of national security. The expert group warned that Australia was on course for a financial and strategic disaster. The group forecast that Australia could be left in the late 2030s and 2040s with no submarines at all, conventional or nuclear, if the current "optimal pathway" were followed (Curran 2024b and 2024c).

A few months later, Gareth Evans entered the AUKUS fray when he characterised his fellow Victorian Richard Marles's "love for the US" as so "dewy-eyed as to defy parody" and observed that Albanese, "still preoccupied with avoiding being wedged as weak on security" had " never given great attention to the complexities of foreign and defence policy and that seems unlikely to change" (Curran 2024e and Hurst 2024a). In Evans's assessment AUKUS was likely to "prove one of the worst foreign and defence policy decisions our country has made, not only putting at profound risk our sovereign independence, but generating more risk than reward for the very national security it promises to protect" (Curran 2024e).

By August 2024, James Curran was observing that the Albanese Government was at serious risk of losing the public debate over AUKUS. In his assessment, this arose from "a persistent failure in communication, an unwillingness to take the public into their confidence and the inability to explain the basic strategic purpose of why Australia seeks to acquire nuclear-powered submarines" (Curran 2024e). Curran's observations followed an announcement by Biden to Congress that a new AUKUS agreement had included "undisclosed commitments" (Greene 2024a). This left the Cabinet rushing to assure the public that Australian sovereignty and agency were uncompromised.

In December of 2024 came further problems, this time with the Australian Submarine Agency (ASA). Since its establishment under Vice Admiral Jonathan Mead, the ASA had grown to almost 700 full-time staff, including a dozen military officers holding a 1-star rank or higher and an annual budget of $330 million (Greene: 2024b). In September 2024, ASA staff were stunned to learn that one of its most senior technical directors was leaving the organisation. This news accompanied reports of rapidly deteriorating staff morale. Marles was forced to appoint the former Secretary of the Department of Defence, Dennis Richardson, to examine how to improve the ASA's performance. Richardson's appointment gave the Government some breathing space but would do nothing to address the fundamental and fatal flaws with AUKUS: that the submarines were unlikely to be delivered; that Australia did not have the sailors to crew them if they did; and that their strategic purpose had never been adequately explained.

Meanwhile, in November 2024, Donald J. Trump had been re-elected President of the United States, and his Republican Party had won control of both houses United States Congress (Curran 2024h). Before even assuming the presidency, Trump alarmed allies by discussing the possibility of US annexation of the Panama Canal and Denmark's autonomous territory, Greenland (Wintour, Willsher, Bryant and Cole 2025). In February 2025, when questioned about AUKUS at a conference with United Kingdom Prime Minister, Sir Keir Starmer, Trump, seemingly puzzled by the reference, asked "What does that mean?" (Vyas 2025) Trump has yet to announce a clear position on AUKUS, an initiative of the Biden Administration. But even if he were to support AUKUS in principle, his imprimatur would have to be given before there could be any sale of Virginia Class submarines to Australia.

In October 2024, the Congressional Research Service (CRS) had warned of the risk of a blowout in the project's costs and cast doubt on whether any rigorous cost-benefit analysis had ever been done for the project. Although Marles optimistically described AUKUS as a project "too big to fail", the CRS found it necessary to offer a "Plan B" for AUKUS. According to this plan B, the US Navy would not sell Virginia Class submarines to Australia but operate them from an Australian base (Hurst: 2024 b). In 2025, Elbridge Colby, Trump's pick for Undersecretary for Defense, made clear the unlikelihood of Australia getting Virginia-class submarines from the United States. In testimony before Congress in 2025, Colby pointed out that the United States was not producing enough attack submarines for its own needs. As Colby observed:

> So, if we can produce the attack submarines in sufficient number and sufficient speed, then great. But if we can't, [supplying Australia] becomes a very difficult problem because we don't want our servicemen and women to be in a weaker position and more vulnerable and, God forbid, worse because they are not in the right place in the right time. (Doherty 2025)

The concerns raised by Colby later prompted Trump to order Elon Musk, the leader of the White House's Department of Government Efficiency, to review the vessel procurement process and deliver a proposal to Trump to "improve the efficiency and effectiveness of these processes" (Koziol 2025).

The advent of the second Trump Administration brought with it serious questions about how the United States would treat its allies and what this might mean for Australia. Early in his second term, Trump made overtures to Russian President, Vladimir Putin, to bring an end to the Russo-Ukraine War. To that end, Trump and his Vice President, J.D. Vance, met with Volodymyr Zelenskyy, President of the Ukraine, in the Oval Office in February 2025. The conversation produced an unprecedented public confrontation between Trump and Vance and the leader of an American ally that had been staunchly supported by the United States and its European allies since the beginning of the Russo-Ukraine War in 2021. At the same time, the Trump White House also indicated that it would no longer be the primary guarantor of European security, and that European nations should be responsible for their own defence. Trump's apparent siding with Russia against Ukraine and his later imposition of tariffs on friends and foes alike helped to precipitate a rupture in the post-1945 "rules-based international order" as key European allies, such as Germany, resolved to achieve "independence" from the United States and warned that the North Atlantic Treaty Organisation (NATO) might soon be a dead letter (Ross and Nöstlinger 2025).

In the context of the turmoil in international relations instigated by Trump, the British parliament's defence committee launched an inquiry to examine whether the AUKUS partnership was on track under "the impact of geopolitical shifts" (Li 2025). Malcolm Turnbull followed suit by gathering a conference of experts in Australia in April to discuss the implications for Australia of Trump's foreign policy, the future of AUKUS and how best Australia should defend itself (Keane 2025). All these developments prompted the *Sydney Morning Herald* to call on 10 April 2025 for an Australian review of AUKUS, arguing that

Trump has distanced his nation from European NATO allies, which complicates the AUKUS arrangement with Great Britain and by implication, Australia. And his conflation of tariffs with defence has not only confused us, but his fellow Americans as well .... When such a once-reliable ally as the US no longer seems reliable, it is surely worth following the common sense of the House of Commons and taking a look at AUKUS. Given the huge amount of money involved and the implications of Trump's rancid patrimonialialism, there is nothing wrong with a renewed oversight (*Sydney Morning Herald* 2025).

Whither ALP defence policy after the 2025 election?

As 2025 approached, came fears that the electoral tide was perhaps turning enough for the coalition parties to win majority government. A more likely prospect in the election called by Albanese for 3 May 2025 was a hung parliament in which Greens, independents and other minor party representatives determine which of the ALP or the coalition parties would form a minority government. Whether in opposition to a Peter Dutton-led government or governing in minority or majority, the ALP would have to confront the problem that AUKUS now loomed over every aspect of Australian defence policy and was the ultimate expression of Australian support for the United States against China. As Hugh White has put it, "[u]ntil [AUKUS] is repudiated, no government will be able to articulate a realistic prospect of Australia's strategic priorities in the new Asia" (Curran 2024a).

An alternative agenda for ALP defence policy that is consistent with the party's traditions, more in harmony with its foreign policy and the foreign policies of countries in the region and potentially attractive to the Greens and some independents might follow the 2025 election. This would involve the ALP cutting its losses with AUKUS and returning to the defensive DoA strategy and a more balanced defence force that included acquisition of air-independent propulsion (AIP) submarines. The party could also develop a simple policy position that prohibited all Australian defence facilities and personnel from directly or indirectly supporting US nuclear operations. Such a position would also be consistent with the ALP's proclaimed ambition of signing the Treaty on the Prohibition of

Nuclear Weapons and with other treaties already ratified by Labor governments, the Treaty on the Non-Proliferation of Nuclear Weapons and the South Pacific Nuclear Free Zone Treaty. The Trump presidency has fortuitously provided an opportunity for the ALP to rescue itself from the AUKUS if it is re-elected on 3 May. As Allan Behm has argued:

> For perhaps the first time since 1942, we can now set our own strategic direction, unencumbered by the imminent threat of war or the dominance of a great and powerful friend, As we recover from our infatuation with ANZUS, we can now look at Asia and the Pacific as a region in which we can make our own way, in partnership with our neighbours instead of being a willing cats paw for America's narrowly defined contest with China (Behm 2025).

References

Argall, D., (2023), "To justify nuclear submarines as protecting trade routes is nonsense", *Pearls and Irritations*, 22 March

Behm, A., (2025), "The Russians aren't coming: Peter Dutton's poor judgment distracts from Australia's rare geopolitical opportunity", *The Guardian*, 16 April

Black, J., (2024), "Labor's chances look wafer thin", *Australian Financial Review*, 19 October

Briggs, P., (2024), "AUKUS risks are piling up. Australia must prepare to build French SSNs instead", *The Strategist*, 5 December

Bristow, A., (2024), "Australia could soon be hosting nuclear-armed submarines", *The Strategist*, 23 August

Buchanan, E., (2024), "Unhinged from reality: we're only a pitstop for nuclear subs", *Sydney Morning Herald*, 16 August

Buckley, C., (2021), "Nuclear-powered Submarines for Australia? Maybe No So Fast, *New York Times*, 29 October

Carr, B., (2024), "Fragrant, methane-wrapped bullshit": NZ should steer clear of AUKUS", *Pearls and Irritations*, 20 August

Carr, K., (2024), "Inside Labor's angst over AUKUS", *Australian Financial Review*, 25 October

Curran J., (2021), "Obama's pivot to Asia reminded Australia where its loyalties lay", *Australian Financial Review,* 7 November

Curran, J., (2024a), "AUKUS in the dock", *Australian Book Review*, No. 465, June

Curran, J., 2024b, "A 'cruel joke': Why AUKUS might leave Australia stranded", *Australian Financial Review*, 2 July

Curran, J., (2024c), " 'Miracle Needed': the big dangers of our subs deal", *Australian Financial Review*, 2 July

Curran, J., (2024d), "Albanese losing the AUKUS debate: Questioning AUKUS", *Australian Financial Review*, 12 August

Curran, J., (2024e), "Evans torpedoes Marles, Albanese over AUKUS", *Australian Financial Review,* 16 August 2024

Curran, J., (2024f), "Our forked tongue foreign policy", *Australian Financial Review*, 9 September

Curran, J., (2024g), "Trump 2.0 is the reckoning for Australia–US Alliance", *Australian Financial Review,* 11 November

Davis, M., (2023), "'Impactful projection'—from land and sea", *The Strategist,* 17 August

Dean, P., and Beazley, C., (2023), "AUKUS sparks a revolution in Labor defence policy", *The Strategist*, 6 September

Department of Defence, (2023), *National Defence: Defence Strategic Review*, Canberra: Department of Defence

Dibb, P., (1986), *Review of Australia's Defence Capabilities*, Canberra: Australian Government Publishing Service

Doherty, B., "Trump Pick for Pentagon says selling submarines would be 'crazy' if Taiwan tensions flare", *The Guardian*, 9 March

Evans, J., (2023), "Defence force shifts posture to ready Australia for "missile age", and combat threats further from sure", ABC, 24 March

Galloway, A., (2023), "New submarines will deter blockades that cut us off from the world: Marles", *Sydney Morning Herald*, 19 March

Gilligan, M., (2022), "Defence Strategic Review—Is Defending Australia Dead?", *Pearls and Irritations*, 30 September

Greene, A., (2024a), "Australia makes undisclosed 'political commitments' in new AUKUS deal on transfer of naval nuclear technology", ABC, 8 August

Greene, A., (2024b), "AUKUS boss insists project remains on track despite frustrations and staff upheaval within submarine agency", ABC, 20 September

Honrada, G., (2024), "Australia's nuclear plan sinking on multiple fronts", *Asia Times*, 7 December

Hurst, D., (2023), "Paul Keating sent explosive email to Labor cabinet two hours before attack on Aukus", *The Guardian*, 7 June

Hurst, D., (2024a), "Former Labor foreign minister Gareth Evans says Australia won't have sovereignty over Aukus submarines", *The Guardian*, 17 September

Hurst, D., (2024b), "US Congress research warns of risk of cost blowouts for Australia in Aukus submarine program", *The Guardian*, 17 October

Karp, P., (2023,) "Paul Keating labels Aukus submarine pact 'worst deal in all history' in attack on Albanese government'", *The Guardian*, 15 March

Keane, B., (2024) "Marles promised a better, more accountable Defence. It's worse and more secretive", *Crikey*, 12 February

Keane, B., (2025), "The who's who of Australian security sector are saying the quiet part out loud", *Crikey*, 1 April

Koziol, M., (2025), "Musk to review US subs as Australia warned tariffs could raise their cost", *Sydney Morning Herald*, 11 April

Lee, D., (1997), "Defence Policy, 1945-1994", in Malik. M., (ed), *Australia's Security in the 21st Century*, Sydney: Allen and Unwin, 8-31

Lee, D., (2023), "AUKUS and the Labor Tradition: Has Albanese Completed or Betrayed the Curtin Legacy?", *Arena*, June, 43-8

Li, Yiying., (2025), "UK's Inquiry is Unlikely to Suggest the Government Pull Out, Expert Says", ABC, 4 April

Marles, R., (2023), "AUKUS nuclear-powers submarine pathway", *Media Release*, 14 March

Middleton, K., (2023), "Inside Australia's Defence Strategy", *Saturday Paper*, April 29-May 5

Middleton, K., (2024), "Agency in charge of Australia's $368bn submarine program faces staff morale crisis", *The Guardian*, 5 December

Olbrycht-Palmer, J., (2024), "PM dodges China question, spruiks 'jobs for subs'", *News*, 2 September

Parker, J., (2024), "There is no catastrophic failure of AUKUS Plan A", *Australian Financial Review*, 4 July

Roggeveen, S., (2023), *The Echidna Strategy: Australia's Search for Power and Peace*, Collingwood: Black Inc Books

Ross, T., and Nöstlinger, N., "Germany's Merz vows 'independence' from Trump's America, warning NATO may soon be dead", *Politico*, 23 February.

Rudd, K., 2024, "The Complex Challenges of Integrated Deterrence, China, and Taiwan", Address, Annnapolis, Maryland, United States, 10 April

Rundle, G., (2023), "AUKUS: Labor goes to war – against itself", *Crikey,* 19 April

Scappatura, V., (2023), "National Defence' takes Australia closer to war with China", *Pearls and Irritations*, 2 May

Scappatura, V., (2024), "Australia's evolving nuclear posture: avoiding a fait accompli. Part 2", *Pearls and Irritations*, 14 October 2024

Scrafton, M., (2023), "Abandoned sovereignty: Australia's intelligence function colonized by US", *Pearls and Irritations*, 31 December

Sydney Morning Herald, (2025), "Inquiry into AUKUS is now common sense: The Herald's View", 10 April

Toohey, B., (2023), "The DSR's desultory treatment of nuclear submarines", *Pearls and Irritations*, 28 April

Tillet, A., (2021), "PM hails new subs deal as 'forever partnership'", *Australian Financial Review*, 16 September

Townsend, A., (2023), "The AUKUS Submarine Deal Highlights a Tectonic Shift in the U.S.-Australia Alliance", *Carnegie Endowment*, 27 March

Varghese, P., (2023), "The balance sheet of the nuclear subs deal", *Australian Financial Review*, 16 March

Vyas, H., (2025), "Donald Trump's 'what does that mean? AUKUS remark played down as a Verbal Slip", ABC, 28 February

White, H., (2023), "The AUKUS submarines will never happen", *Saturday Paper,* March 11-17

White, H., 2024, "Marles's 2024 National Defence Strategy another failed response to the China Threat", *Saturday Paper*, April 27 – May 3

Wintour, P., (2021), "What is the Aukus alliance and what are its implications?", *The Guardian*, 17 September

Wintour, P., Willsher, K., Bryant, M, and Cole, D., (2025), "Germany and France warn Trump against use of force over Greenland", *The Guardian*, 9 January

Endnotes

1. Gordon Scholes and Bill Hayden, "Review of ANZUS", 24 May 1983 and Report of the Defence Committee, National Archives of Australia: A13977, 170

18

The Albanese Government Record on Government Services and Digital Transformation

Mike Kelly

Digital transformation is the use of information and communication technology, not when trivial automation is performed, but in the case where fundamentally new capabilities are created in business, public government, and the lives of people and society. (Martin 2008: 130)

Introduction

The point made above by Allan Martin is critical to the following comments and to an understanding of what is genuine digital transformation. The technologies that are arriving in the marketplace and research have the potential to be transformational if applied to the right use cases, subject to an informed cost benefit analysis, sound evaluation of product, address real areas of human need and are properly regulated. The stars of the show in recent discourse around this subject are generative Artificial Intelligence (AI), Machine Learning (ML) and Large Language Models (LLM). The future also holds the vastly amplified transformation prospect of Quantum Computing (QC), but this is still several years away. LLM is little understood as part of this galaxy but consists of the "training" of vast scales of text data to enable generative AI to get closer to human capability. It is still subject to pitfalls such as what are known as "hallucinations" and "glitch tokens" requiring great care to be taken with how the LLM is curated and interrogated. AI in general raises the ethical questions of the point of critical decision making that ought to be performed by a human and how AI should be regulated in both the private and public spheres (Stewart-Weeks 2023; Sakkal 2023). The prospect is massive savings of labour, significant acceleration of decision making, production and administrative efficiency and cost savings, truncated research cycles and greatly enhanced security. Services such as health, aged care, disability support and the social safety net can be made sustainable and significantly more effective. The flip side is the uses that can be made of advanced tech by state, non-state and hybrid malign actors. It can be tremendously challenging and isolating for many who struggle with technology and automated interaction, which is often flawed and unsupported by human fall back. Commercial providers may over promise and under deliver at unacceptable cost, create unhealthy dependency or are not sufficiently secure in the handling of sensitive and private data.

The context

When the Albanese Government took power on 23 May 2022 it was coming into office at a time of highly significant technological developments and in the wake of serious failures in this aspect of government service delivery. The highest profile issue was the "Robodebt" scandal. This was a scheme launched by the preceding Coalition Government in 2016 that was designed to automatically identify overpayments made to welfare recipients through the Centrelink system, managed by the Australian Department of Human Services. The scheme used income averaging, cross-referencing income data from the Australian Taxation Office (ATO) with welfare claims, to calculate alleged overpayments.

The system automatically issued debt notices to recipients without verifying whether the debts were valid. Many welfare recipients were accused of owing money due to incorrectly calculated debts, based on a flawed method that assumed irregular income patterns. The scheme was criticized for being inaccurate, leading to significant distress for vulnerable Australians, many of whom were elderly, disabled, or living in poverty. It was revealed that the government did not have proper oversight or manual checks in place to prevent mistakes. The Robodebt Scheme was halted in 2019 after a Federal Court ruling found the method of calculating debts was unlawful. The Morrison Government later reimbursed victims, and the scandal led to widespread public outrage and calls for reforms in welfare administration. These matters were described and dealt with in detail by the *Royal Commission into the Robodebt Scheme* chaired by former Queensland Supreme Court judge, Catherine Holmes that was established in 2022 by Bill Shorten, Minister for the National Disability Insurance Scheme (NDIS). The Royal Commission reported a year later (see Holmes 2023; see also Chapters 5 and 7).

Another major service failure over an extended period of time was the operation of the Department of Veterans Affairs (DVA), as detailed in successive Australian National Audit Office (ANAO) reports (ANAO 2002; 2004; 2018; 2021), and the *Royal Commission into Defence and Veteran Suicides* (Kaldas 2024), which highlighted significant system failures, particularly in the management of veteran services and claims processing. DVA was found to have inefficient and slow processing systems for veterans' claims, leading to long wait times for services and assistance. The backlog of claims left many veterans without timely access to critical support, including healthcare, pensions, and compensation.

The Department's IT infrastructure was identified as outdated and ill-equipped to handle modern demands. This contributed to slow service delivery and difficulty in tracking and managing claims effectively. Communication between DVA staff, veterans, and service providers was inadequate. Veterans often face confusion and frustration due to lack of transparency about claim statuses. Case management was inconsistent, and the system failed to provide sufficient support for veterans through the complex claims process.

It was highlighted that DVA lacked a clear, cohesive strategy for managing its responsibilities and ensuring accountability. The absence of regular audits and performance assessments contributed to operational inefficiencies. Veterans often experienced dissatisfaction due to delays in services, with many reports pointing to a lack of empathy and understanding from staff, further aggravating the veterans' sense of neglect. DVA efficiency suffered from the fact that their operation is dependent on data sharing among Services Australia,

Defence and the ATO. It also has a wide range of medical issues to deal with in terms of causation, latest research data and treatment. Often the legacy data (including physical documents in poor condition) relating to service over previous decades is incomplete and deficient.

Another example of a major public controversy was the Census of 2016 (Dudley-Nicholson 2016a), (Dudley-Nicholson 2016b). This involved a significant technical failure during the national Census, conducted by the Australian Bureau of Statistics (ABS). The Census, held on 9 August 2016, was the first to be conducted primarily online, but the website experienced a massive crash on the night of the Census, rendering it inaccessible for several hours. The failure was attributed to a distributed denial of service attack (DDoS) followed by a hardware failure of one of the supplier's routers during an attempt to restore the system, which compounded the network issues. An error also occurred in the network performance monitoring system falsely showing unusual outbound traffic from the ABS system. This also caused concerns over the security of the data being collected, although no evidence of data theft was found.

This crisis was exacerbated by a lack of contingency plans and poor communication between the ABS and the public. The ABS initially downplayed the severity of the issue and did not provide a clear timeline for when the system would be back online. As a result, many people were unable to complete the Census on time, leading to calls for a paper-based alternative, which was eventually provided. The fallout included public outrage, criticism of the ABS's handling of the crisis, and concerns about the future of digital government services. The crisis also raised broader questions about the reliability and security of online government platforms. (Senate Economics References Committee Inquiry 2016).

During the life of the Albanese Government, it not only faced the challenge of learning the lessons from these experiences and digital transformation policy in government services generally, but the exponential escalation in technical capabilities and cyber threats. AI and the potential of QC would be the signature opportunities and threats forcing close policy focus and decisions across the spectrum of health and social services, national security, privacy, human control and coherent enterprise systems (Alhosani and Alhashmi 2024).

The promise of technology

For governments and large commercial entities new technology is highly relevant due to particular evolving dynamics. Right across the developed and developing world the growth of digital information has been exponential. This has presented challenges relating to the storage, organisation, protection and the effective exploitation of this data. The storage and management of data drove the development of Data Centre infrastructure and so-called "cloud storage". These massive data facilities are energy hungry, a hunger that is escalating with the development and deployment of AI Platforms (Galarza 2025).

Government organisations with large amounts of data are presented with regulatory requirements relating to privacy and may also be driven by the need to prevent disclosure of information that may compromise Defence or policing operational security. The information obtained by law enforcement agencies and intelligence agencies are obtained for different purposes that are the nexus to, on the one hand, successful arrests and prosecutions and, on the other, the management of external state and non-state-based threats. This challenge becomes even more complicated when these two regimes face the hybrid dynamic of integrated criminal enterprise and state-based actors.

The promise of evolving technology against these challenges is that game changing cost and labour efficiencies can be realised and the effectiveness of an organisation exponentially amplified. Good technology can enable the large amount of data an entity owns to be organised in a way that makes full exploitation possible. Data can be interrogated for accuracy and reliability. Theme tracking and linkages can be established that allow for rapid surfacing through alerts or interrogation of data to provide quick answers.

The next level beyond this is where organisations can create a "digital twin" and engage in powerful simulation and modelling. This can help drive accurate budget forecasting, trend prediction and test solutions to the most pressing challenges. In a defence context the "Military Appreciation Process" can be a very time consuming "handrolic" exercise where the selected outcome may not in fact be the optimal solution or the circumstantial underpinning may be highly fluid. Quality technology offers the possibility of distilling the vast amounts of data available to the Defence Department to be analysed and worked through multiple courses of action in a highly accelerated and iterative way. It can also be a powerful tool for management of the multidimensional battle space and accurate, efficient targeting. In the military sphere in the coalition setting this is referred to as Combined Joint All Domain Command and Control (CJADC2) (Clarke 2024).

Within the government galaxy the sharing of information can be facilitated by effective permissions regimes and access controls that protect the probity of processes. This can be through the anonymisation of data that ensures privacy, allowing one agency to manage an individual citizen's needs, the efficacy of payments and policing fraud while another can be surfacing significant trends for planning purposes, or understanding critical linkages and dynamics to shape government responses or policy development.

A good example is the DVA case study referred to above. The military operational environment can be very complex from a health perspective. Past and current issues have presented major assessment challenges including the "Agent Orange" situation from the Vietnam War[1], depleted uranium from the Gulf Wars, burn pit toxins from all recent deployments, extreme dehydration effects and exposure to environmental hazards such as diseases and asbestos, even during exercises in Australia. Often Australian service personnel have served singly or in small numbers and their situation does not present a cohort of scale from which research data and conclusions could be easily drawn. In contrast, the allies with whom Australians serve such as the US, often have large volumes of data and research. The potential of technology is that all this information and research can be shared in an anonymised format among allied nation's veterans services. DVA staff could also rapidly access an analysis of past DVA and Allied service determinations to see the percentage of clams of a particular nature that have been approved or denied, including a summary of the factors driving the determinations. This can give an assessor an excellent start point and save a great deal of labour and time. Fraud and over-servicing can be better detected and general efficiencies gained that will save crucial and often substantial funds.

Similarly challenged has been the National Disability Insurance Scheme (NDIS) which has bled billions of dollars through, fraud, overservicing and organised crime exploitation, whereby $8 billion worth of funding intended for people with disability is allegedly being abused by crime syndicates (NDIS 2024 and 2025; Edwards 2024; Evans 2024). There are available technology solutions to this issue that would obviously stem this bleeding and put the scheme on a sustainable budgetary footing, which includes improving the overall efficiency of the organisation as with the DVA.

A practical example of what can be achieved along these lines is the acceleration that was driven by the Covid pandemic. For the first time during that pandemic 67 separate medical research organisations were networked on a collaborative platform that protected their Intellectual Property (IP) but also enabled effective sharing of information. The anonymised data of millions of patients was ingested and shaped for analytic exploitation. These advances led to the most rapid development and deployment of new vaccines in history (Olawade et al 2024; Park 2021; Solis-Moreira 2021). This also resulted in other accelerated solutions in the US and UK that addressed hospital logistics and systems to address patient prioritisation, theatre bed and staff management, among other things. Australia has yet to embrace the full array of these opportunities and, most importantly, in a nationally integrated and standardised manner.

What should be of major interest to the Albanese Government in pursuit of its "net zero emissions" policy, is the creation of platforms that can provide veracity to claims of emissions reduction. Large multinational enterprises who care about the climate change issue and their "social licence" can now deploy capabilities that will allow them to capture the true picture of the carbon emissions they are associated with, right across their supply chain and production. They can use this data to model options for emissions reduction, budgetary impacts and potential savings. The Albanese Government could embrace this kind of tech in partnership with industry as part of a regulatory, verification and funding regime to avoid deceptive or fraudulent "green washing", So far there is no sign of any initiative in exploring this possibility (Trafigura 2023).

The Albanese Government's policy response

The Albanese Government adopted several policies designed to advance Australia's digital transformation across various sectors:

Data and Digital Government Strategy

In 2023, the government introduced this strategy, with the aim of delivering simple, secure, and connected public services by 2030. This strategy also outlined the key missions to guide the Australian Public Service's data and digital transformation (Department of Finance 2023).

Digital Identity and AI Initiatives

The government announced that digital identity systems and AI capabilities would be prioritised. Plans included legislating for Digital ID, establishing regulatory frameworks, and expanding its use across government services. The initiative was intended to be structured in four phases, aiming for a secure, convenient, and inclusive system. This has particularly been advanced through adaptation of the MyGov service (Gallagher 2023).

Government Website and Digital Service Standards

New standards and guidance were issued intending to improve digital government services. These standards set benchmarks for the performance of digital services, with the intention of supporting agencies in delivering better experiences by considering the broader digital service ecosystem (Gallagher 2024).

Aged Care Digital Strategy

The government released its first Aged Care Data and Digital Strategy, outlining an intention to embrace digital technologies to enhance aged care services (Wells 2024).

National Broadband Network (NBN) upgrade

A $3.8 billion investment is planned to upgrade the NBN from copper to fibre, aiming to provide 95% of Australians with fiber access by 2030. This initiative seeks to improve service reliability and reduce dependence on foreign providers such as Elon Musk's Starlink (Lewis 2025).

Quantum computing

The government has developed a quantum computing strategy that is directed at investing in, connecting and growing Australia's quantum research and industry. It aims to drive commercialisation through new programs to incentivise the continued growth of quantum use cases and create pipelines for investment in industry-ready quantum technologies through the National Reconstruction Fund. It also flags an intent to support new quantum infrastructure for Australian industry and attract research talent in this field. It looks outward to build on our international partnerships, influence and opportunities for Australian quantum companies (Whitson 2024).

NDIS remedial measures

Having appreciated the scale of the problem at the NDIS as discussed above, Minister Shorten has instituted a range of measures to crack down on fraud and organised criminal activity. This includes the *Getting it Back on Track Bill* and the National Disability Insurance Agency's (NDIA) enhanced capability to detect and prevent fraud through the $83.9 million Crack Down on Fraud program. This also includes the work of the Fraud Fusion Taskforce (FFT) in identifying criminals (NDIS Website 2024) (NDIS Website 2025). It remains to be seen whether the agency is able to acquire the necessary tools and forge the cross-silo government cooperation that will render these ambitions truly effective. The government record in this respect provides little basis for optimism.

The Albanese Government's implementation of Digital Transformation

The Digital Transformation Agency (DTA) in Australia has asserted a strong commitment to advancing the nation's digital government services. In its Annual Report for 2023–24, the DTA reported substantial progress in several key areas:

- *Service Improvement:* The introduction of the Digital Service Standard 2.0, following extensive consultations, has streamlined guidance and provided new resources to improve the design and delivery of digital services.

- *Policy Development*: The development of the Digital Experience Policy, released in July 2025, accompanied by four standards, aims to unify the approach to designing and delivering digital services across government agencies. This at least recognises the fundamental flaw of the siloed government landscape but to date there has been no real progress on achieving this outcome

- *Innovation Facilitation:* The DTA conducted a hands-on trial to assist government agencies in experimenting with generative AI, fostering innovation and understanding of its potential applications. True transformational AI implementation is yet to be demonstrated.

- *Digital Sourcing and Contracting*: Enhancements in digital sourcing and contracting have enabled government agencies to access essential digital resources, ensuring in some cases the availability of appropriate solutions, services, and expertise. This has been a positive step forward but is evident in only a very limited application to date and is vulnerable to flawed procurement processes.

In its Performance Statement, the DTA asserted that it "substantially achieved" its performance measures for 2023-24. The agency focused on improving its capability to deliver its mandate, enhancing the framework for managing digital and ICT-enabled investments, and refining standards and guidance. Employee satisfaction and well-being increased, and the DTA claimed to have strengthened relationships with stakeholders, thereby ensuring better outcomes and refining its advice on digital investments and assurance. Additionally, the DTA identified the need to revisit its performance measures to ensure they reflect its purpose, strategic objectives, and key activities (Fechner 2024).

Overall, the DTA's performance in 2023–24 was claimed to reflect a "proactive approach" to digital transformation, with a focus on strategic planning, policy development, innovation, and continuous improvement. On one level a measure of DTA effectiveness could be suggested by the fact that Australia has risen to be ranked fifth in the OECD Digital Government Index in 2023. The ANAO reports that 56 public sector entities claim to have been deploying AI tools across their business (ANAO 2024). This claim should be closely contested, however, as I have found many departmental personnel mistake ML for AI. The OECD definition of AI, which the Australian Government has adopted is that:

> An AI system is a machine-based system that for explicit or implicit objectives, infers, from the input it receives, how to generate outputs such as predictions, content, recommendations, or decisions that can influence physical or virtual environments. Different AI systems vary in their levels of autonomy and adaptiveness after deployment. (OECD 2024).

Returning to the premise set out by Allan Martin at the head of this chapter, digital transformation is "where fundamentally new capabilities are created" that genuinely transform an agency. We have seen nothing that graduates to this level in initiatives taken to date in the true exploitation of the potential of AI. The claims made regarding the adoption of AI also disguises the key significant deficiencies in deploying solutions to address integration, interoperability and procurement fault lines in government systems.

One of the critical factors in delivering effective policy outcomes is whether the machinery of government (MOG) is geared to properly implement initiatives. The DTA under the Albanese Government sits under the Minister for Finance, Katy Gallagher. The DTA was established on 14 October 2016 with a mission to increase awareness and digital literacy among agencies. Since its establishment it has gone from a stand-alone office to being placed under PM&C in 2021, to Finance Department in July 2022. It was intended to provide an Investment Oversight Framework to ensure alignment with Cabinet agreed policy standards and contestable procurement through the Digital Capability Assessment Process (DCAP). It was also intended to ensure alignment with whole-of-government platforms to reduce cost and duplication. It was also tasked to monitor the adoption of AI for responsible and ethical usage.

The DTA should be given a much higher priority within the MOG construct. Having it sit within the realm of the Minister for Finance is unsatisfactory. The focus of the Minister and the Department is on a range of critical policy areas that dominate its bandwidth. DTA to be more directly relevant to Ministerial policy focus should sit within the Department of Social Services as the key nexus in the data management challenge. An alternative would be the Special Minister of State, if ministerial appointments to this portfolio were sufficiently technology literate and the allocation of this responsibility was accompanied by sufficient staffing and input on funding determinations.

The DTA has not been successful in gripping up the management of technology procurement and deployment, or in driving the understanding and acceptance of the key infrastructure investment required to take government service delivery to the next level, exploiting the art of the possible. Artificial Intelligence Platforms (AIP) tied to Large Language Models (LLM) are not only hungry for storage space and energy but advanced computational processing capacity. A higher level of policy literacy is required here to comprehend that investing in infrastructure for enhanced government service delivery will not only achieve better support outcomes for Australian citizens but better security for the nation and substantial savings.

An example of that type of literacy was conveyed in a speech by the Minister at the centre of the government services vortex, former Minister for the NDIS Bill Shorten. In his speech (Shorten 2024) he was direct in delivering some home truths and announcing some coal face initiatives. He highlighted the scale of the challenge Services Australia faces and its significant data scale, noting that for FY 23/24 the agency:

- administered \$240 billion in payments;
- handled 1.1 billion transactions online;
- had 10.7 million face-to-face contacts; and
- took 53.9 million calls through the biggest call centre network in the southern hemisphere.

This workflow has cross referencing implications with the ATO, Finance, DVA, and law enforcement agencies with all the competing privacy and prosecutorial tensions mentioned above. Associated with this Shorten singled out what in his view is the major impediment to better service delivery:

> And I'll be blunt, the biggest barrier to Australia having the convenience of seamless government services is what I refer to as a plague of fiefdoms. The siloed thinking across departments and agencies has to stop. The world has moved on. But government has not. I recall reading years ago about a futurist who visited Australia and lamented what he called a clay layer in some public service department's upper management who were not digital natives and refused to learn, stunting the digital uptake of the whole organisation.

Minister Shorten also commented on the subject that dominated tech discussion over the last two years relating to AI. He asserted:

> But we need to look beyond the current hype on generative AI to more fundamental and structured AI, which can be used to look for efficiencies in back of house processes searching for information, for example, so staff can use their time on higher value tasks. It is about how we harness AI to give humans back the thing we have not been able to replicate - time. And it is about keeping the human decision making at the heart of human services.

This statement summarised well the practical opportunities of AI as well as the key ethical underpinning. The ANAO report into AI policy at the ATO highlighted the lag between moves to deploy AI tools and the establishment of effective governance arrangements, an issue that is reflected right across the public sector where such measures were described as "evolving". The ATO was found to lack effective arrangements for the design, development, deployment and monitoring of its AI models. The ANAO also stated that the ATO has not:

> established fit-for-purpose implementation arrangements for this strategy; clearly defined enterprise-wide roles and responsibilities; established AI-specific risk management arrangements; and implemented its data ethics framework sufficiently for AI. The ATO's data ethics framework aims to support the ATO to deliver ethical data activities, including AI. For its AI models, the ATO has not complied with the requirements of this framework (74 per cent of AI models in production did not have completed data ethics assessments). (ANAO Report 2025).

This analysis could presently apply right across the public sector.

In the speech Shorten also announced the development of a new government digital services capability in the form of the "Trust Exchange – or TEx". This initiative seeks to game change personal identity verification across government and in support of commercial operators. The key to the capability will be verification without the exchange of personal information.

This is also part of the "tell-us-once" policy where the organisations within the Services Australia orbit are demonstrating the practical advantages across a range of use cases affecting the daily lives of Australians. The case study cited by Shorten to illustrate the benefits of this approach relates to childcare in the ACT. The trial started with the details relating to newborn children provided by parents at the birthing hospital, registering the baby for federal government services. Shorten highlighted that the result is quicker access to health services, such as enrolling the baby in Medicare, the Medicare Safety Net, My Health Record, the Australian Immunisation Register and confirming the birth of the baby for the purposes of Centrelink Family Assistance claims.

There has been a level of criticism regarding the Government's Digital ID and Identity Verification measures including in relation to "data localisation" (Pane 2024), with concerns about privacy, security, efficiency, sovereign control and economic impact. There were also complaints about the rushed Parliamentary process and lack of sufficient safeguards and limitations (Daily Telegraph NZ 2025). The Human Rights Council also raised issues regarding the lawful basis of the policy but in the end the legislation passed with amendments by the Coalition. These amendments included that express consent be required for the use of someone's identity documents, there be alignment with the data breach scheme and the use of information captured for data profiling, online tracking, or marketing all be banned. The Coalition also succeeded in requiring that the operative provisions be delayed for six months and a review of the laws be carried out after one year (Australian Government: Department of Finance,2023) (Hendry 2023) (Sadler 2023) (Taylor 2023).

Harking back to Shorten's earlier comment regarding the twin evils of government siloes and the absence of tech literacy at management level Shorten concluded that, "We just need other departments and agencies to get onboard so we can offer tell-us-once across key events in people's lives." This "holy grail" is a very long way from being achieved and constitutes the biggest deficiency in the Albanese Government record on advancing tech solutions in government, a deficiency that has been shared across the last few Federal administrations on both sides of the political divide.

On the Albanese Government record regarding Quantum Computing there have been some questions raised about the decision to award a large research and implementation contract to a US company, including aspects of probity (Sakkal 2024). This is now the subject of an Audit Office inquiry (ANAO 2024). Questions have also been raised about placing all the quantum research investment eggs in one basket. The outcomes aspect of the government policy in this respect won't be possible to properly evaluate until around 2029 but as a general proposition it is absolutely vital to invest in this area, as a positive outcome will have wide ranging consequences for our security, government services and efficiency and for Australian industry.

Domestic Security Services

For our National Intelligence Community (NIC) and operational agencies the lack of state-of-the-art capability is a serious risk to our national security, particularly at a time of exponentially increasing technical threats from both state and non-state sources, including traditional and industrially related espionage challenges; now amplified by cyber warfare threats to our institutions and infrastructure and advances in AI (Kelly 2025). Added to this workload has been the evolution in the last 10 years of the sophisticated information warfare deployed collaboratively by Russia, Iran, China, North Korea and their willing autocratic partners, that has played into and helped feed the domestic social cohesion challenge (Applebaum 2024) (Rid 2020) (Allen 2023) (Singer 2018) (Buchanan 2020). This last threat is insidious in poisoning minds, particularly but not exclusively of the young, through the amplifying effect of bias confirming algorithms. This has included organised crime exploitation of the antisemitic dimension of this threat, promoted through paid violence and arson. We are also experiencing the increasing intersection of state-based threats and organised crime activity that requires a hybrid agency approach (Thorley 2025).

We have not empowered all our agencies to fight back in these circumstances. While there has been a significant investment in increased ASD capability and the cyber security issue has drawn much attention, other civil agencies have suffered from a lack of investment in the capabilities they need. There are extraordinarily effective technology tools available now with the AI revolution, but this requires an investment in infrastructure upgrades to take full advantage of them. All of the civil agencies who need to play a part in fighting the above-described threats are not properly funded to undertake this modernisation rapidly.

Confirming the observations of Minister Shorten, nor are these agencies properly funded, organised and equipped to more effectively cut across the silos that impede their cooperation domestically and internationally. This relates particularly to how classified material can be shared rapidly while still safeguarding the aspects that require protection, even in some respects in relation to other domestic and closely allied international agencies. The information must also be managed in a way that does not detract from the probity and admissibility of evidence. The way information is collected and shared must comply with different regulatory requirements which could be effectively managed through the deployment of built in access controls and permissions regimes.

Some agencies have resorted to in-house attempts to develop technical tools, but this has often been a blind ally and a financial black hole. In-house solutions have been plagued by delay and inadequate delivery. They are also vulnerable to dependence on the individuals who developed them and compatibility issues with other institutional tools or collaborative agencies. With the exception of ASD most government agencies and departments suffer from a dearth of top technology talent as they can't compete with the commercial sector for these highly sought after personnel. This also compounds in the difficulty departments have assessing commercial technology options in procurement. The number and cost of IT procurement mistakes or sub-standard delivery in Australian Government is appalling (Coade 2023) (Burton 2024).

In relation to the enhanced AI cyber threat former US President Biden issued Executive Order 14028 establishing a 'Zero Trust' regime to protect federal government networks. The US National Institute of Standards and Technology (NIST) has published several guidelines for implementing Zero Trust in organisations and the US Department of Defence (DoD have released a Zero Trust Strategy and Reference Architecture (Sherman 2022). There are DoD gateways set out for this policy which are focused on achieving a threshold level of security

by 2027 and an advanced level by 2032. US DoD have set up a rigorous program of testing capability against their Strategy and Reference
Architecture. The process is intensely rigorous involving skilled and
aggressive "red teaming" and "insider threat" analysis that is well re-
sourced and staffed and is extremely intrusive for the solutions under
test. We have nothing like it here in Australia and would struggle to
create it. Australia is also not approaching this Zero Trust issue with
anything like the comprehension and urgency that is needed as a priority national security measure. We must move quickly to initiate close
collaboration with NIST and US DoD to glean the benefit of their
resources and work, and this should be included in our AUKUS Pillar
II framework and refrain from deploying systems that have not passed
the US assessment regime.

The US Defence Advanced Research Project Agency (DARPA) has
initiated three efforts that seek to address the information warfare
threat. These are the Influence Campaign Awareness and Sensemaking, Modelling Influence Pathways and Deepfake Defense Tech Ready
for Commercialisation Transition Initiative projects (DARPA INCAS)
(DARPA MIP) (DARPA Deepfake). Recent studies have also surfaced
the potential of LLMs, which can interpret the context of text and au-
tomate foreign propaganda detection. A recent report found that,

> When prompted to label text according to a set of classical
> propaganda techniques, LLMs can provide indicators (i.e., yes
> or no) of whether the text employs each technique, thereby
> partially mitigating subjectivity. A fine-tuned model, trained
> on foreign propaganda manually coded for the presence of
> classical propaganda techniques, was shown to have effective
> performance in detecting the use of propaganda devices. This
> suggests that LLMs are a potentially useful detection method
> of foreign adversaries attempts to exploit other nations for their
> own objectives (Mouton 2025).

Again, we should look to include collaboration on this effort within
AUKUS Pillar II.

Beyond this we need a rigorous standardised approach to the national
education curriculum that equips our kids to navigate the world of

social media, promoting critical thinking, the evaluation of sources and how to do reliable research. At the school level we need to invest more in preventative education to ensure kids are not vulnerable to the othering, grooming and radicalising that is being pursued by malevolent actors, and to enable intervention regarding vulnerable individuals. This needs to be addressed through a standardising national policy led by the Federal Government, which has not happened to date.

We need to better police the domestic social threat by properly enforcing the law and requiring offenders to undertake remedial education activities. The urgency and multi-dimensional nature of the problem could be addressed by better cross-silo mechanisms such as the establishment of an Inter-Departmental Task Force (IDTF) headed up ideally by a person with appropriate experience such as an ASIO background. This IDTF could be mandated to engage with civil society and community organisations to enhance human intelligence (HUMINT) input that assists in the prevention of radicalisation and obtain information on potential illegal conduct and terror. This coordination role could alternatively be under the purview of a reinstituted National Security Adviser (NSA) office or assigned to the Office of National Intelligence (ONI). It requires the government to prioritise urgent funding to address agency technical deficiencies so that the extensive information relevant to this effort, with applied enhanced synthesising and analytical tools, across the HUMINT and TECHINT spectrum and data lakes can be effectively shared and acted on in a timely manner.

Procurement

A major question for government is how it can answer the challenge of procuring platforms that will enable full spectrum digital exploitation. How do they evaluate the promises made by commercial offerings and cost benefit analysis? How do they avoid pitfalls such as cost blow out from inadequate or over-ambitious scoping and failures in oversight? How do they avoid "lock-in" to a provider that may be overtaken by innovation and retain control and protection of sovereign data? How do they ensure interoperability across our government agencies and essential international partners? How does government deal with the impact of posting cycles and personnel changes through the life of a project?

In discussions I have had with a number of Departmental personal I have regularly heard a high level of dissatisfaction regarding over-promising and under-delivering Primes, with associated cost blow outs. This seems to have particularly been the case with Enterprise Resource Planning (ERP) and integration systems. One of the cultural impediments to sound procurement has been the attitudes prevalent in those sections of the bureaucracy tasked with managing procurement. Apart from suffering from a deficiency in expertise there has historically been an unwillingness to find a probative means of engaging closely with industry to avoid poor scoping and uncertainty over capability.

The DTA itself was the subject of a scathing Auditor's report in 2022, which covered activities before the Albanese Government came to office (ANAO Report 2022-23). The report stated that, "The DTA's procurement of ICT-related services has been ineffective for the nine ICT-related procurements examined by the ANAO...", "its implementation and oversight has been weak..." It also stated that "DTA has not been following its internal policies and procedures, and there are weaknesses in its governance, oversight and probity arrangements for procurements." The DTA was found not to have conducted procurements efficaciously, and it fell short of ethical requirements, with the procurements not complying with Commonwealth Procurement Rules. It failed to conduct market or tender evaluation processes effectively or provide sound advice to decision-makers. It was also found not to have managed contracts effectively to achieve value for money. There has not been an ANAO update to this report as yet so it is difficult to assess whether improvements have been made but procurement decision making in software deployment is still significantly deficient.

While procurement experience in the US has had some notable scandals from time to time, their approach to engagement with industry and the deployment of cutting-edge technology is certainly vastly superior to the Australian experience. The Zero Trust regime described above is one example. Another is the structures for collaboration between industry and government. US Space Command for example has four cells dedicated to industry engagement whereby uniformed and Department personnel will often be found helping commercial operators build algorithms.

One particularly compelling example is how the US Defence Advanced Research Agency (DARPA) conducts the through life procurement process from innovation to deployment and deprecation. To begin with this involves DARPA either setting an industry goal or going out to research and market places to deeply understand the art of the possible and over the horizon tech prospects. Off the back of this tracking and understanding there will be a better-informed project scoping and request for tender (RFT). That RFT itself will characteristically involve a "competitive bake off" amongst a range of companies that are assessed as at least being gateway competitive.

This involves simulated production environments to determine which tech solutions best meet their needs. This involves rigorous testing and evaluation of different vendor systems in a customised and simulated production environment that mirrors the buyer's use case processes and systems. In the case of the US Arm's Vantage program 15 vendors were involved in the "bake off" and the contract recently again went to a multi-vendor recompete. Typically, a contract will be limited to around 3 years and be awarded to a vendor that offers the potential for evolution during that contract term. If that relationship does not offer that direction or technology options have become available from another vendor, they have no trouble moving on at the completion of the contract, having catered for that eventuality, ensuring ease of deprecation, and kept a close eye on of R&D dynamics and the market (Nicastro 2024).

A helpful addition to the framework has been the Defense Innovation Unit (DIU) to accelerate the innovation journey for companies. This is additionally supplemented by a galaxy of programs, government owned laboratories and agencies that straddle innovation, research and the financing of startups. All of this industry engagement is directly subject to rigorous Congressional oversight.

Australia has nothing like this structured rigour although there have been recent additions to Defence seeking tech acceleration in the form of the Advanced Strategic Capabilities Accelerator (ASCA). ASCA was envisaged to perhaps take on board some of the functions performed by DARPA, but this has not transpired. Two things in particular hold ASCA back. The continuing attitude amongst some involved with ASCA, particularly from the Defence Science and Technology Group (DSTG) who believe in 'pure science' and feel morally reluctant to engage with industry. Secondly ASCA simply hasn't got the funding or institutional capacity to do what DARPA does. Wisely ASCA is exploring and has utilised some lower cost consultancy support to assist with project evaluation, but this clearly needs to be widened.

It seems clear that there is not much prospect of Australia having the ability to replicate the US approach, architecture and access to skills. The Albanese government and DTA have not found the answers to this procurement challenge. It is, nevertheless, possible for Australian governments to achieve similar results commensurate with our scale. There has been much recent controversy over the role of consultants providing support to government. Without question there has been an over reliance and inappropriate level of expenditure and out-sourcing to consultants. This includes effectively labour hire support replacing public servants at substantially increased cost, with the loss of public service capability, compensated by the inclusion of necessary labour in project contracts for a net financial loss, failing the cost benefit test.

There is however a role for consultancy to assist with the genuine lack of particular capabilities in Defence that is unlikely to ever be filled. Appropriate roles could be in scoping the research and market landscape, designing RFT and evaluating bids for Departmental decision. Some degree of 'competitive bake off' should certainly be attempted whenever possible. Technical uplift could allow agencies to take advantage of a digital twin to create a curated and sanitised data package that could be used for this purpose. It has to be said that there has been no appreciable advance by the Albanese Government in addressing these higher-level issues, a failure shared with previous governments.

Once again, the AUKUS Pillar II construct also offers a mechanism to create a coordinated effort drawing on the greater US resources to assist our procurement design and evaluation, providing quality input in connecting Australian innovation and research.

Accessing Digital Services for Older Australians

Senior Australians often face significant challenges in dealing with online government services due to digital literacy gaps, age-related physical limitations, and the complexities of digital interfaces. Many struggle with the pervasive reliance on digital platforms for essential services like Medicare, managing finances, and even basic tasks like paying bills. The levels of stress, anxiety, frustration, humiliation, vulnerability and anger that our seniors face in this respect cannot be ignored.

This is underpinned by a lack of experience with technology, making it difficult to learn new platforms. Physical limitations like reduced vision, hearing loss, and declining motor skills can make this even more of a challenge in engaging with interfaces designed for younger users. Government websites and apps can be poorly designed, with confusing layouts, jargon, and navigation systems that are not intuitive.

Seniors can fear making mistakes, becoming victims of online scams, or being seen as incompetent and vulnerable when they need help. The increasing reliance on online services exacerbates social isolation, those who are not technically literate struggle to connect with family and friends digitally or participate in online communities. The older migrant generation from diverse backgrounds may face additional barriers due to language differences and cultural expectations regarding technology use.

Seniors are disproportionately targeted by online scams and this adds to their apprehension and hesitancy to engage. While initiatives like the online learning offering, Be Connected, offers digital literacy training, many older Australians lack the support they need to navigate the online world independently. Government services delivery for this cohort of Australians has largely failed to prioritize user-friendly design, with clear and simple navigation, accessible fonts, and alternative formats like large print and audio. All these customer interface issues have recently been highlighted in research commissioned by TechnologyOne, in the Australian Digital Citizens 2025 report (Kitney 2025).

More accessible and localized digital literacy programs are needed to equip older Australians with the skills and confidence to use online services. The Government has failed to ensure readily available and crucial human support channels, such as phone lines and in-person service centres. Governments and service providers have also failed to keep this digital divide in the forefront of design, rollout and management. They are also not ensuring that all Australians, regardless of age, have access to affordable internet and digital devices. Raising awareness about the importance of digital inclusion and promoting digital literacy among older Australians is essential and this test has not been met (see Kollmorgen 2023; McCosker 2020; Thom 2024;).

Conclusion

The Albanese Government came into office on the back of some notable failures in the use of technology to deliver services. The "Robodebt" experience was particularly salient for a range of reasons. The grief and trauma to the thousands of affected Australians, some of whom took their own lives as a consequence, was unconscionable, but this also resulted in a public crisis of confidence, threatening the social licence for technology solutions, innovation, trust and protections delivered by government. At the same time the global surge in interest around the evolution of AI, LLM, automation and ML raised the prospect of untangling many policy, administrative and budgetary Gordian Knots.

It should be stressed that we are only assessing a 3 year sample size and new government performance must take into account the need to establish itself, deal with urgent demands and events and address legacy issues. The Albanese Government inherited a construct within the bureaucracy that was not geared, and did not lend itself, to efficient, cost-effective procurement and the proper evaluation of commercial and in-house options. The great challenge of recruiting and retaining expertise in the technology space for the public service renders government delivery of technology enhanced outcomes subject to significant vulnerabilities. The absence of tech literacy amongst senior management and the political sphere is also a major impediment to sound decision making on investment and truly transformational use case targets.

Clearly also a key element in assessing Australia's advanced tech deployment in government is the role the ANAO plays. In its recent report on AI adoption in the ATO it flagged that:

> The ANAO will continue to focus on governance of AI while it develops the capability to undertake more technical auditing of the AI tools and processes used in the public sector. Building this capability will require investment in knowledge, methodology and skills to enable the ANAO to test more deeply how AI tools operate in practice.

> Like audit offices around the world, the ANAO will seek to examine how AI can improve the audit process itself, in a profession where human judgement and scepticism are foundations in auditing standards. This work will progress through our relationships within the international public sector audit community over coming years. (ANAO Report 2025)

It is absolutely essential that the Albanese Government vigorously supports the ANAO in this ambition.

There have been some solid steps forward by the Albanese Government on what might be called "tactical" tech solutions in an array of use cases that directly impact on the lives of Australians depending on these services, and these have been a real advance on previous governments. There has, however, been no real progress on addressing the strategic issues across "whole of government" outlined above. In terms of national security, the requisite comprehension of the gravity and urgency of the need to step forward on the next level technologies, associated at the same time with securing our systems in a way compatible with our alliance relationships, is deeply disturbing and must be addressed in the next term of parliament.

Following Labor's resounding win on 3 May 2025 the Treasurer Jim Chalmers flagged what the next term priorities would be about: "Our agenda is really clear. We have to build more homes, we have to get this energy transformation right. We have to do more to embrace technology, particularly the AI opportunity. There's a huge agenda there for us" (ABC TV *Insiders*). In his first "Headland" speech of the new term, delivered the Prime Minister added the government intention is, "Ensuring all Australians are better prepared to capitalise on the opportunities of Artificial Intelligence while making sure we secure ourselves against its risks. And continuing the work we've done through Services Australia to make it easier for people to access and navigate the government services they rely on" (Albanese 2025). It is clear that this was a neglected policy area in the last term and the changes in the Industry and Science portfolio may be flagging the recognition of that. The proof will be in the flesh the government puts on these, as yet, vague bones.

References

Albanese, A., (2025) Address, *National Press Club*, 10 June https://www.pm.gov.au/media/address-national-press-club-0

"Albanese's Digital ID Bill 'shocking and disgusting' – Hansen", *Daily Telegraph New Zealand*, 28 March[3] https://dailytelegraph.co.nz/world/albanese-governments-digital-id-bill-shocking-and-disgusting-hansen/

Alhosani, K., and Alhashmi, S., (2024), "Opportunities, challenges, and benefits of AI innovation in government services: a review", *Discover Artificial Intelligence*, 4(18), 4 Marchhttps://doi.org/10.1007/s44163-024-00111-w

ANAO, (2002), *Information Technology in the Department of Veterans' Affairs*, Canberra: Commonwealth Government, Report No 44, Performance Audit

ANAO, (2004), *Information Technology in the Department of Veterans'*

Affairs-Follow-up Audit, Canberra: Commonwealth Government, Report No 52, Performance Audit

ANAO, (2018), *Efficiency of Veterans Service Delivery by the Department of Veterans' Affairs*, Canberra: Report No 52, Performance Audit

ANAO, (2021), *Effectiveness of the Planning and Management of Veteran Centric Reforms*, Canberra: Commonwealth Government, Report No 30, Performance Audit

ANAO, (2022), *Digital Transformation Agency's Procurement of ICT-Related Services*, Canberra; Commonwealth Government, Report No 5 https://www.anao.gov.au/sites/default/files/2022-10/Auditor-General_Report5.pdf.

ANAO, (2024), *Investigation into the investment in PsiQuantum announced by the Australian and Queensland governments*, Canberra: Commonwealth Government, 26 August https://www.anao.gov.au/work/request/investigation-the-investment-psiquantum-announced-the-australian-and-queensland-governments

Applebaum, A., (2024), *Autocracy Inc*, London: Allen Lan

Buchanan, B., (2020), *The Hacker and the State: Cyber Attacks and the New Normal of Geopolitics*, Cambridge M.A.: *Harvard University Press*

Burton, T., (2024), "$2.2b lost in federal IT fails after fifth project abandoned", *Australian Financial Review*, 19 August https://www.afr.com/politics/federal/2-2b-lost-in-federal-it-fails-after-fifth-project-abandoned-20240819-p5k3ko.

Chalmers, J., ABC TV, *Insiders*, 4 May 2025

Clark, J., Hicks Announces Delivery of Initial CJADC2 Capability, *DOD News*, 21 February 2024.

Coade, M., (2023), "Government contracts face 'major changes' with inquiry slamming APS failures", *The Mandarin*, 9 August

Department of Finance, (2023), *Data and Digital Government Strategy*, Camberral Commonwealth Government , https://www.dataanddigital.gov.au/

Defense Advanced Research Project Agency (DARPA), (2024), *INCAS: Influence Campaign Awareness and Sensemaking* https://www.darpa.mil/research/programs/influence-campaign-awareness-and-sensemaking.

DARPA, (2024), *MIP: Modelling Influence Pathways* https://www.darpa.mil/research/programs/modeling-influence-pathways

DARPA, (2024), Deepfake Defense Tech Ready for Commercialization, Transition, 14 March 2024. https://www.darpa.mil/news/2024/deepfake-defense.

Department of Finance, (2023), "Digital ID Bill introduced into Parliament", Canberra: Commonwealth Government https://www.finance.gov.au/digital-id-bill-introduced-parliament

Dudley-Nicholson, J., (2016a), "Census 2016: Australia has become a global joke", *The Daily Telegraph*, 11 August

Dudley-Nicholson, J. and Bickers, C., (2016b), "Australia's 2016 Census had 'significant and obvious oversights,' report finds", *News.com.au*, 25 November

Edwards, E., (2024), "Disability provider accused of billing $1 million in fraudulent NDIS claims in a month", *Nine.com.au*, 9 March

Evans, J., (2024), "NDIS rorting by criminal syndicates worse than feared, says scheme's watchdog", *ABC News*, 24 May

Fechner, C., (2024), Chief Executive Officer Digital Transformation Agency, *DTA's Annual Report*, 2023-24, 31 October 2024, https://www.dta.gov.au/blogs/dtas-annual-report-2023-24?utm.

Galarza, M., (2025), "To power AI, data centers need more and more energy", *The Current (UC Santa Barbara)*, 15 April

Gallagher, K., (2023), Minister for Finance, "Digital ID and AI insights: How the Albanese Government is leading the digital evolution", Speech, 19 September https://ministers.pmc.gov.au/gallagher/2023/digital-id-and-ai-insights-how-albanese-government-leading-digital-evolution?

Gallagher, K., (2024), "New standards for Government websites and digital services", *Media Release*, 25 July

Governance of Artificial Intelligence at the Australian Taxation Office, *Auditor-General Report No.26 of 2024–25*, 24 February 2025. https://www.anao.gov.au/work/performance-audit/governance-of-artificial-intelligence-the-australian-taxation-office.

Hansen, H., et al, (2024), *AI trends for healthcare,* Canberra: CSIRO Commonwealth Government, March https://aehrc.csiro.au/wp-content/uploads/2024/03/AI-Trends-for-Healthcare.pdf

Hendry, J., (2023), "Far from perfect' face matching laws pass Parliament, *Innovation Aus*, 7 December 2023. https://www.innovationaus.com/far-from-perfect-face-matching-laws-pass-parliament/

Holmes, C., (2023), (Chair), Royal Commission into the Robodebt Scheme, *Report*, Canberra: Commonwealth of Australia

How might artificial intelligence affect the trustworthiness of public service delivery? *PM&C Report*, 2023. https://www.pmc.gov.au/sites/default/files/resource/download/ltib-report-how-might-ai-affect-trust-ps-delivery.pdf.

How the NHS Federated Data Platform work? *NHS England Website.* https://www.england.nhs.uk/digitaltechnology/nhs-federated-data-platform/how-does-the-nhs-federated-data-platform-work/.

Hunt, S., (2024), "Artificial intelligence 'facing barriers' in our health system", *InSight*. Issue 1, 15 January

Kaldas, N., (2024), (Chair), Royal Commission into Defence and Veteran Suicide, *Final Report,* Canberra: Commonwealth Government

Kelly, M., (2025), "We need better tech to combat terrorism", *The Australian,* 31 January

Kitney, D., (2025), "Government digital services in need of overhaul", *The Australian*, 1 July

Kollmorgen, A., (2023), " Access still difficult for many older and elderly Australians", *Choice*, 6 January

Lewis, R., and Lam, J., (2025), "Communications Minister says Labor's $3.8bn to 'finish' NBN will mean Aussies don't have to rely on Elon Musk's Starlink", *The Australian*, 16 April

Lv, C., Guo, W., Yin, X., Liu, Liu., Huang, X., Li, S., Zhang, L., (2024), "Innovative Applications of Artificial Intelligence During the COVID-19 pandemic", *ScienceDirect, Infectious Medicine*, 3(1), March

McCosker, B., et al, (2020), *Improving the digital inclusion of older Australian: The Social Impact of Be Connected,* Social Innovation Research Institute and the Centre for Social Impact, Swinburne University, June 2020 https://www.dss.gov.au/system/files/resources/improving-digital-inclusion-older-australians-social-impact-be-connected-16-june-2020.pdf

Mailey, J., (2024), "Iran's criminal statecraft: How Tehran weaponizes illicit markets", *Global Initiative Against Transnational Organised Crime*, 30 October

Martin, A., (2008), "Digital literacy and the "digital society", *Digital Literacies Concepts Policies Practices*, 30, 151-76.

Mehta, N., Shukla, S., (2021), "Pandemic Analytics: How Countries are Leveraging Big Data Analytics and Artificial Intelligence to Fight COVID-19? – PMC", *National Library for Medicine, National Centre for Biotechnology Information*, 9 November https://pmc.ncbi.nlm.nih.gov/articles/PMC8577168/

Mouton, C., Lucas, C., and Ee, S., (2025), "Defending American Interests Abroad: Information campaign, election interference, Russia, China, Iran", *Homeland Security Newswire*, 11 April. Department of Industry Science and Resources, (2023*), National Quantum Strategy: Building a thriving future with Australia's quantum advantage,* Canberra: Commonwealth Government https://www.industry.gov.au/sites/default/files/2023-05/national-quantum-strategy.pdf

NDIS, (2024), *Criminals jailed as crackdown on multi-million dollar NDIS rorting continues,* 1 November 2024.https://www.ndis.gov.

au/news/10480-criminals-jailed-crackdown-multi-million-dollar-ndis-rorting-continues,

NDIS (2025), *Crack Down on Fraud,* 17 January https://www.ndis.gov.au/about-us/improving-integrity-and-preventing-fraud/crack-down-fraud

Nicastro, L., Analyst in U.S. Defense Infrastructure Policy, (2024), The U.S. Defense Industrial Base: Background and Issues for Congress, *Library of Congress,* 23 September

OECD, (2024), "Explanatory memorandum on the updated OECD definition of an AI system", *Report,* March https://www.oecd-ilibrary.org/science-and-technology/explanatory-memorandum-on-the-updated-oecd-definition-of-an-ai-system_623da898-en.

Olawade, D., Teke, J., Fapohunda, O., Weerasinghe, K., Usman, S., Ige, A., and David-Olawade, A.C., (2024), "Leveraging artificial intelligence in vaccine development: A narrative review", *Journal of Microbiological Methods,* 224, September

Orthia L., Maccora J., and McCallum J., (2022), *"I am trying to keep up to date…but it is moving so fast": Older Australians' Digital Engagement in Turbulent Times,* Canberra: National Seniors Australia

Palantir for Hospitals, *Palantir Website,* https://www.palantir.com/offerings/palantir-for-hospitals/.

Pane, J., (2024), "Chair of EFA, Albanese Government caves (again) to Big Banks and Big Tech", *Electronic Frontiers Australia,* 12 July https://efa.org.au/albanese-government-caves-again-to-big-banks-and-big-tech/.

Park, T., (2021), "Behind Covid-19 vaccine development, MIT Schwarzman College of Computing", *MIT News,* 18 May

Rid, T., (2020), *Active Measures: The Secret History of Disinformation and Political Warfare,* Profile Books

Sadler, D., (2023), "Identity verification bill passes with 38 changes: Senate squeezed in privacy enhancements", *Information Age,* 7 December https://ia.acs.org.au/article/2023/identity-verification-bill-passes-with-38-changes-.html

Sakkal, P., (2023), "The trouble with transparency when it comes to AI", *Sydney Morning Herald,* 28 September

Sakkal, P., (2024), "Probe flagged for Labor's $1b showcase quantum computing deal", *Sydney Morning Herald,* 27 August

Sakkal, P., and Swan, D., (2024), "Albanese defends $1b start-up bet as Queensland support wavers", *Sydney Morning Herald,* 12 November

Senate Economics References Committee Inquiry, (2016), *Census: Issues of trust,* Canberra: Commonwealth Government, Novem-

ber   https://www.aph.gov.au/Parliamentary_Business/Committees/
Senate/Economics/2016Census/~/media/Committees/economics_
ctte/2016Census/report.pdfof trust

Sherman, J., (2022), *DoD Zero Trust Strategy*, US Department of Defense, 7 November https://dodcio.defense.gov/Portals/0/Documents/Library/DoD-ZTStrategy.pdf.

Shorten, B., (2024), "Government Services in Australia: The Next Decade", *Address:* National Press Club, 13 August https://ministers.dss.gov.au/speeches/15616

Singer, P.W., and Brooking, E.T., (2018), *Like War: The Weaponization of Social Media*, Boston: *Houghton Mifflin Harcourt*

Solis-Moreira, J., (2021), "How did we develop a COVID-19 vaccine so quickly?", *Medical News Today*, 13 November https://www.medicalnewstoday.com/articles/how-did-we-develop-a-covid-19-vaccine-so-quickly.

Stewart-Weeks, M., Cooper, S., and Burton, T., (2023), "How government can safely embrace AI", *Australian Financial Review*, 20 July

Taylor, J., (2023), "Hundreds of millions of Australian identity checks may have been illegally conducted, Senate hears", *The Guardian*, 31 October https://www.theguardian.com/australia-news/2023/oct/31/hundreds-of-millions-of-australian-identity-checks-may-have-been-illegally-conducted-senate-hears.

The Future of Healthcare and AI: Oracle Health Summit 2024, https://www.youtube.com/watch?v=gYxLwnYqex0uture of Healthcare and AI: Oracle Health Summit 2024

Thom, G., (2024), "Research reveals elderly multicultural Australians falling through the digital divide", Institute of Community Directors Australia, 17 September *https://www.communitydirectors.com.au/articles/research-reveals-elderly-multicultural-australians-falling-through-the-digital-divide*

Thorley, M., (2025), "Of kingdoms and crooks: The rise of geocriminality", *Global Initiative Against Transnational Organised Crime*, 17 March

Trafigura (2023), Supply chain carbon emissions platform Agora is announced for the energy sector during APPEC 2023 in Singapore with first users bp, Ecopetrol and Trafigura, *Press Release*, 6 September 2023 https://www.trafigura.com/news-and-insights/press-releases/2023/supply-chain-carbon-emissions-platform-agora-is-announced-for-the-energy-sector-during-appec-2023-in-singapore-with-first-users-bp-ecopetrol-and-trafigura/

Transforming NHS Inventory Management – A Blueprint for Success, *NHS Supply Chain Website*, 21 January 2025.

Wells, A., (2024), "Minister for Aged Care, Minister for Sport, Government delivers first aged care digital plan", *Media Release*, 4 July

What you need to know about fraud, (2024), *NDIS Website*, https://www.ndis.gov.au/participants/working-providers/what-you-need-know-about-fraud, 20 November 2024

Whitson, R., (2024), "The Government's bold $1 billion gamble on quantum computing technology", ABC TV *7.30 Report*, 29 May

Endnotes

1   The Agent Orange issue was reviewed by the 1983 Hawke Government appointed *Royal Commission on the Use and Effects of Chemical Agents on Australian Personnel in Vietnam.*

2   This is the *National Disability Insurance Scheme Amendment (Getting the NDIS Back on Track No. 1) Bill 2024* (Cth)

3   This New Zealand article was referring to One Nation Senator, Pauline Hanson, although it spelt her name incorrectly, as "Hansen" in the headline and text.

19

Religious Freedom: Always the Bridesmaid, Never the Bride

Mark Spencer[1]

Introduction

Those who have had any significant experience with politicians will recognise the feeling. You come out of a meeting knowing you have been "handled", in the preceding days you have been "played" and you know that in the days and weeks ahead that the outcome will be "spun" as a win for all concerned. It is all part of the "sport" of politics, the "cut and thrust" of the democratic process. The greatest frustration arises when the meeting in question was with a purported ally. The most profound disappointment is reserved for when the subject matter is a fundamental and inalienable human right, such as religious freedom.

Like the Morrison Coalition Government before it, the Albanese Labor Government failed in its first term to deliver its promised protections for religious freedom. Spoken of reverentially in the abstract, religious freedom was once again unable to find any concrete expression under a prime minister focussed very early in that first term on the next election. Following a pre-parliamentary process that seemed destined to result in failure, the final confirmation of the Albanese Government's decision to abandon legislation came in a clumsy set up question at a press conference as the Prime Minister slipped into election mode. The reformist zeal of the Hawke-Keating era subsumed in a blunt political calculus.

Background

The history of attempts to provide religious freedom protections under the Morrison Government is covered extensively in Chapter 9: "Religious Freedom was left at the Altar" in *Tragedy without Triumph: The Coalition in Office 2013-222* (Prasser 2024). That chapter outlines the genesis of the need for legislative protections arising from the passage of the *Marriage Amendment (Definition and Religious Freedoms) Act 2017* (Cth) in December 2017, and prior to that the *Discrimination Amendment (Sexual Orientation, Gender Identity and Intersex Status) Act 2013* (Cth) under the Gillard Labor Government. This act inserted "sexual orientation" and "gender identity" into the *Sex Discrimination Act 1984* (Cth) as protected characteristics.[2]

As noted in that chapter, at the time of the insertion of additional protected characteristics into the *Sex Discrimination Act 1984* (Cth), exemptions, or balancing clauses, were also included as the means of protecting religious freedoms. This was, and remains, a fundamental means of protecting religious freedom in Australia.[3] These exemptions, in both Commonwealth and State and Territory laws, determine how issues arising from the interaction of rights are resolved, however as Parkinson identified, "in recent years there have been strong attacks on this method of balancing anti-discrimination norms with religious freedom rights" (Parkinson 2019).

The Morrison Government took policies to the 2019 federal election to introduce a religious discrimination bill, if re-elected, and refer the amendment of the exemptions in the *Sex Discrimination Act 1984* (Cth) to the Australian Law Reform Commission. As canvassed in that earlier chapter, many faith groups valued these clear commitments and a wide range of commentors, including key ALP figures (Vistonay 2019) recognised the impact of religious voters on the outcome of the May 2019 election.

Having felt the electoral pain of not supporting protections for religious freedom in the 2019 Federal election, the ALP ensured that it committed to introducing religious freedom protections at the subsequent 2022 Federal election (Crowe 2022; Visentin 2022). At the same time the Coalition was reported to be vacillating on its commitment to such legislation (Brown and Kelly 2022) and some Christian groups actively campaigned against Liberals who had "crossed the floor" to vote with the Opposition in the debate of the Morrison government's legislation (Murphy, 2022). Major Christian school groups proposed a positive plan to parties in the run up to the election seeking to find a solution to the long running legislative impasse (Christian Schools Australia 2022a).

The New Albanese Government

While the newly elected Albanese government did not rush to introduce legislation, the intersection of religion and Australia's other "religion", football, served to keep attention on the lack of Federal legislation. The sacking of the Essendon Football Club's CEO prompted calls from religious groups for the government to "urgently" reintroduce legislation (AAP/SBS, 2022). The urgency for comprehensive Commonwealth protections was exacerbated by developments at a State and Territory level. The *Equal Opportunity (Religious Exceptions) Amendment Bill 2021* (Vic) which it has been argued "failed to conform with important principles of international human rights law" (Fowler 2023) and contributed to elements of the failed 2022 Morrison bill, had been followed up by the Australian Law Reform Commission (ALRC) reviews in a number of states that recommended, for example, that "already very narrow protections of the freedom of religious schools to preference staff that share their religious ethos be narrowed further still" (Aroney 2023).

Christian school groups had earlier called for the recommencement of the ALRC review into religious exemptions, conscious that the term of the then ALRC President, Hon Justice Sarah Derrington, was due to conclude in January 2023 (Christian Schools Australia 2022b). Given the extensive work already undertaken by Justice Derrington looking at religious exemptions for faith-based schools, it was disappointing to many groups that there was insufficient urgency to address this issue by the Albanese Government which would have allowed her to continue.

Instead, on 4 November 2022 Attorney-General Mark Dreyfus announced the appointment of Justice Stephen Rothman to lead a newly constituted review with amended terms of reference and only a short timeframe before reporting. While the Opposition raised questions about Justice Rothman's long-term involvement with the ALP[4], his appointment was generally warmly welcomed. Initial meetings between Justice Rothman and a range of groups were all very positive with his grasp of the issues impressive. Faith groups ended 2022 with considerable hope that a sensible and balanced solution to protect religious freedom was achievable. Then in January 2023 the ALRC released its radical consultation paper.

The ALRC Review

The bombshell consultation paper released by the ALRC as the initial stage of its review process shocked faith groups across the country. In purporting to consider how to "balance" freedom of religion with other human rights such as freedom from discrimination under the *Sex Discrimination Act 1984* (Cth) the consultation paper put forward extreme options well beyond anything ever previously proposed.

In response to the consultation paper the National Catholic Education Commission's executive director, Jacinta Collins, said the proposed reforms failed to provide real protections for religious schools to effectively operate and teach according to their religious beliefs and ethos (Karp 2023). More than more than 30 leaders from the Christian, Jewish and Islamic faiths wrote a letter to Attorney-General Mark Dreyfus sounding the alarm on the controversial reform proposals (Kelly 2023). Perhaps most tellingly, in an unprecedented move, two major Christian schooling associations pulled out of the consultation process with the ALRC, claiming to have "lost faith" in the commission remaining "balanced" in tackling the issue (Dudley 2023).

Despite these concerns, the ALRC continued with review process, with some insiders reporting a very hands-on role being taken by the newly appointed ALRC President, the "[c]ontroversial Federal Court judge Mordy Bromberg" (Pelly 2023) also described as the "most radical, hard-left activist the Federal Court bench has yet seen" (Stoker 2023).

The resulting final report lived up to expectations.

The final report, *Maximising the Realisation of Human Rights: Religious Educational Institutions and Anti-Discrimination Laws* (ALRC Report 142), was tabled in Parliament by the Attorney-General on the last day possible to meet legislative timeframes, 21 March 2024. The report recommended the repeal of all existing protections for religious educational institutions in the *Sex Discrimination Act 1984* (Cth) and the *Fair Work Act 2009* (Cth) and forcing these institutions to rely upon the notoriously difficult to establish "Indirect discrimination: reasonableness test" for protection.

The response from Christian schools and other faith groups was swift. The National Catholic Education Commission said it was "at odds with religious freedom and the high regard parents place in faith-based schools", three Christian schools associations called it "a direct attack on faith and freedom of belief in Australia", suggesting "Christian education as we know it will cease to exist" if the ALRC's suggestions were adopted (Crowley 2024). One of Australia's most senior Catholic leaders described the recommendations as "a most serious threat to the existence" of religious schools (Shanahan and Kelly 2024). The President of the Islamic Schools Association of Australia also agreed the recommendations were a "blatant attack on religious freedom and faith-based education" (Crowley 2024). Legal academics described how the recommendations constituted a "breach of faith" with religious communities (Fowler 2024).

Less than a month after the tabling of the ALRC report its purported author, Justice Rothman, came out strongly promoting a very different approach. In a speech to a legal conference Justice Rothman spoke of the constraints within the terms of reference set by Attorney-General Mark Dreyfus and promoted an alternative approach of a "positive right" for religious freedom (Brown and Down 2024). This echoed the preliminary thinking of the former ALRC President, Justice Derrington, in her 2019 speech on these issues (Derrington, 2019). Faith leaders quickly expressed their support, with the author of this chapter opining that Justice Rothman's comments took away "any moral authority that report has" (Brown 2024).

Possibly anticipating such a negative response to such controversial recommendations, when announcing the tabling of the ALRC report in Parliament the Attorney-General was at pains to point out that "[t] he Australian Law Reform Commission's report tabled today is not a report from the Government. It is advice to the Government, and we will continue to consider it" (Dreyfus 2024). While this remains the Albanese government's public position, their actions in secret draft legislation paint a very different picture.

Secret consultations about a fundamental human right

While the ALRC review process was underway, the Albanese government was busy working on a legislative package that included a religious discrimination bill and amendments to the *Sex Discrimination Act 1984* (Cth) and the *Fair Work Act 2009* (Cth).

As early as April 2023 faith leaders began to express concerns about the prospects of religious discrimination protections being introduced during the first term of the Albanese government (Ison, 2023). This was in response to the government's perceived unwillingness to effectively progress such legislation despite extensive work being undertaken by faith communities to develop a consensus proposal for such legislation. This consensus was reached the previous year and conveyed to the Attorney-General in a June 2022 letter signed by about 20 leaders from varied faith groups including Anglican, Catholic, Presbyterian, Greek Orthodox, Baptist and Pentecostal churches, as well as Christian Schools Australia, the Australian National Council of Imams and the Executive Council of Australian Jewry (Visentin 2024). The consensus position was based on the Morrison Government's *Religious Discrimination Bill 2022*, as passed overwhelmingly by the House of Representatives, 91 votes to 6, adjusted to incorporate several of the proposed amendments sought at that time by the then ALP Opposition.[5]

It was not until early February 2024 that the Attorney-General started to sound out the positions of faith groups. These meetings were conducted under conditions of strict confidentiality, which severely limited the scope of the discussions and the ability of these groups to canvass the views of their constituents (Knott 2024). In private discussions on a flight to Canberra on the Monday prior to the release of the ALRC report on Thursday of that week, the Prime Minister claimed to have briefed the Opposition Leader on their proposals, but the Opposition Leader said the two had a "cordial conversation" but no "meaningful engagement" on the details of the proposed changes (Basford Canales 2024).

The Prime Minister then publicly indicating the following day, once again prior to the release of the ALRC report, that he would not be introducing religious discrimination legislation without first having bi-partisan support (Gould 2024). This announcement "sparked a political firestorm" with the Opposition Leader accusing the Prime Minister of trying to dump their election promise (Crowe 2024). In the words of Mr Dutton, which proved particularly prescient, "[h]e's looking for a way to crash this before the legislation has already been released" (Lewis and Kelly 2024).

On the Friday of that week, the day after the ARLC Report had been publicly released, the Prime Minister indicated that Cabinet had seen copies of the two pieces of legislation which had been drafted for the government, one that would amend the *Sex Discrimination Act* and another that would create a religious discrimination act, although this was reported to be "at odds with what other senior members of the government have told the ABC" (Worthington and Borys 2024). Despite requesting bipartisan support on the issue, it wasn't until Wednesday afternoon that Attorney-General Mark Dreyfus handed a hard copy of the draft legislation to Shadow Attorney-General Michaelia Cash (Worthington and Borys 2024), once again under strict confidentiality requirements.

After a brief dalliance with the idea of negotiating with the Greens, a proposal roundly condemned by faith leaders given the establish positions of the Greens (Borys 2024), the Albanese Government continued its process of confidential and constrained briefings.

With the Government refusing to rule out the adoption of the ALRC recommendations, Christian school groups joined together to organise

"Town Hall" style meetings in Brisbane, Sydney, Perth, Launceston, Melbourne and Adelaide to oppose the proposals and share some of the positive stories about the impact of Christian schools on students, parents and families. Over 4,200 supporters turned out to these events at relatively short notice on weeknights in Autum and early winter, in some case travelling over 7 hours each way (AACS et al 2024a). Over 3,700 postcards from attendees were subsequently delivered to the Prime Minister calling for his support (AACS et al 2024b and AACS et al 2024c).

At the same time, public support was clearly behind religious schools. National polling indicated that nearly 80 per cent of Australians supported the right of a religious school to employ teachers and other staff who support the clearly stated values and beliefs of the school, with 57 per cent backing a religious school's right to sack staff who no longer support those values and beliefs (Bita 2024).

It was during these consultations, in a meeting between the Prime Minister, Attorney-General, and a small group of faith leaders including Christian school representatives, that the Prime Minister make his commitment that religious freedom protections for faith groups "[w]ill not go backwards while I'm Prime Minister of Australia" (Christian Schools Australia 2024). In response to a request from the Prime Minister, faith leaders continued to work hard to find a solution, providing a detailed line by line analysis by legal experts of the Government's draft legislation (Lewis 2024a).

Meanwhile, the behind closed doors discussions between the Attorney-General and Shadow Attorney-General broke down, allegedly in a spectacular fashion with Coalition sources reported as claiming that "in her 16 years in parliament Senator Cash has never been spoken to or treated in such a demeaning way by anyone else" (Lewis and Down 2024). Despite these reports, faith groups continued to push the Albanese Government to work towards a solution, seeking the direct intervention of the Prime Minister to break through the deadlock (Lewis 2024b).

Instead, in a coldly calculated political move, the Prime Minister "took out the trash" at a Friday afternoon press conference (Albanese 2024):

JOURNALIST: Prime Minister, I believe you also had an update on religious discrimination laws. Can you provide an update on where they are at?

PRIME MINISTER: Well, we provided legislation to the Coalition a long time ago now, months ago. We provided them with that on the basis that we wanted to see if we could get some bipartisan support, because that's an issue that requires that. One of the things I've spoken about is the need for greater social cohesion. And the last thing that Australia needs is any divisive debate relating to religion and people's faith. I respect people's faith and I think that they should be able to engage free of discrimination. And so it's quite clear, the timing I said, had to be that we would introduce legislation during the Budget session if agreement could be reached. Agreement hasn't been able to be reached because there's been no suggestions from the Coalition of amendments of the legislation. So I don't intend to engage in a partisan debate when it comes to religious discrimination, and I think that that is unfortunate.

"Prime Minister, I believe you also had an update on religious discrimination laws …", with that set up question, slipped in towards the end of a media briefing on other issues, the prospect of religious freedom legislation in the term of the 47th Federal Parliament was buried, without the secret draft legislation even being tabled in Parliament.

The "worst PM since Whitlam"?

This was the epithet that Dennis Shanahan indicated was a risk for Anthony Albanese in the weeks after the tabling of the ALRC report and in the midst of the debate on religious freedom, "[t]oo often, politics is being put ahead of policy" being his claim (Shanahan 2024). Later in the year, after the religious discrimination legislation was dropped and the Voice referendum lost, the ABC's Brett Worthington described Prime Minister Albanese as leading "a risk-averse party humbled by its own fumblings" (Worthington 2024). All of this a long way from the promises on the morning of his first day in Parliament as Prime Minister, as pointed out by Nick Cater (Cater 2024):

He began the day in the front pew of St Andrews Presbyterian Church in Canberra for an ecumenical service seeking God's blessing on parliamentary session.

As Albanese left the church with his partner Jodie Haydon, he removed his facemask and stopped briefly to talk to the press.

"Given we're outside a church today, what is your message to religious communities?" asked one journalist.

"What will you do for them in this term?"

Albanese promised he'd deliver religious discrimination legislation in his first term.

Much was expected of the Albanese Government. When it came to people of faith it was said that the lessons of 2019 had been learned, trust had to be rebuilt, promises had to be kept. Yet the dominant calculus remained once of politics not principle, re-election not reform. The promise that religious freedom protections for faith groups "[w]ill not go backwards while I'm Prime Minister of Australia" was accompanied by a hard politically driven deadline for achieving "bipartisan support" that faith groups were expected to deliver. The words of the Opposition Leader will long ring in the ears of faith leaders, "[h]e's looking for a way to crash this before the legislation has already been released" (Lewis and Kelly 2024).

What hope now for religious freedom?

The failure of the Albanese Government in its first term to deliver on its promise of religious freedom protections casts an even longer shadow than the tragedy of the Morrison Government. Failings of people and personalities in the former have been magnified in failings, deliberate or otherwise, of process and politics in the latter. A clear pathway forward was provided by a broad ranging and united coalition of faith groups. The proposals reflected a considerable compromise of their position and preferences in order to find an enduring and reasonable accommodation for all stakeholders. Despite this extraordinary unity amongst faith leaders, the antithesis of a "divisive debate", the political will for such an outcome was lacking. It is almost as if a solution is not the desired outcome, and the lacklustre promises by both parties at the recent Federal election gives no confidence of any sudden reformist zeal in this area.

It is hard not to be reminded of the curse uttered by the dying Mercutio "A pox on both your houses!".[6]

References

AAP/SBS, (2022), "'Pushed out': Anglican bishop calls for religious freedom bill to be implemented after Essendon CEO's exit" https://www.sbs.com.au/news/article/pushed-out-anglican-bishop-calls-for-religious-freedom-bill-to-be-implemented-after-essendon-ceos-exit/rhkczn15a, 5 October 2022

Albanese, A., (2024), "Press conference–Perth: Transcript", Prime Minister's Office, 9 August *https://www.pm.gov.au/media/press-conference-perth-6,*

Aroney, N., (2023), "Cherry Picking Human Rights", *Australian Journal of Law and Religion*, 95-100

Australian Association of Christian Schools, Associated Christian Schools and Christian Schools Australia, (2024a), "Joint Media Release: 4,200 Mums and Dads Unite for the Future of Faith in Christian Schools", 13 June https://www.csa.edu.au/CSA/Resources-and-Media/Media-Centre/Media-Release/2024/4200_Mums_and_Dads_Unite_for_Future,

Australian Association of Christian Schools, Associated Christian Schools and Christian Schools Australia, (2024b), "Joint Media Release: A 'Positive Right' For Christian Schools", 24 June https://www.csa.edu.au/CSA/Resources-and-Media/Media-Centre/Media-Release/2024/A_Positive_Right_for_Christian_Schools,

Australian Association of Christian Schools, Associated Christian Schools and Christian Schools Australia, (2024c), "Joint Media Release: 1,556 Signed Postcards Delivered to the Prime Minister", 16 May https://www.csa.edu.au/CSA/Resources-and-Media/Media-Centre/Media-Release/2024/1556_Signed_Postcards_Delivered_to_the_PM,

Basford Canales, S., (2024), "Peter Dutton refuses to support religious discrimination law changes without seeing details", *The Guardian Australia*, 19 March

Bita, N., (2024), "Parents back the right of religious schools to hire and fire on grounds of faith", *The Australian*, 24 March

Borys, S., (2024), "Faith groups warn Albanese a deal with Greens on religious discrimination would be a 'betrayal'", *ABC News*, 28 March

Brown, G., (2024), "Labor urged to revisit religious freedom laws", *The Australian*, 14 April

Brown, G., and Down, R., (2024), "NSW Supreme Court judge Stephen Rothman urges Anthony Albanese to grant 'positive rights' to faith schools", *The Australian*, 12 April

Brown, G., and Kelly, J., (2022), "Election 2022: Scott Morrison refuses to commit to religious freedom laws", *The Australian*, 12 April

Cater, N., (2024), "'Dark days for people of faith': Drafted version of Labor's religious discrimination bill gives Australian faith groups every right to feel betrayed", *Sky News Australia*, 1 April

Christian Schools Australia, (2022a), "Media Release: Our Plan for Freedom and Equality", 10 May https://www.csa.edu.au/CSA/Resources-and-Media/Media-Centre/Media-Release/2022/Our_Plan_Freedom_Equality,

Christian Schools Australia, (2022b), "Media Release: It Is Time to Protect Students and Protect Schools", 19 July https://www.csa.edu.au/CSA/Resources-and-Media/Media-Centre/Media-Release/2022/Time_Protect_Students_Protect_Schools,

Christian Schools Australia, (2024), "Media Release: Christian Schools Welcome Prime Minister's Commitment To Protecting Religious Freedom", 14 April https://www.csa.edu.au/CSA/Resources-and-Media/Media-Centre/Media-Release/2024/Christian_Schools_Welcome_PMs_Commitment,

Crowe, D., (2022), "Scott Morrison, Anthony Albanese tell MPs to get ready for 2022 election campaign", *Sydney Morning Herald*, 15 February

Crowe, D., (2024), "Albanese's sudden retreat on religious discrimination sparks Dutton fury", *Sydney Morning Herald*, 19 March

Crowley, T., (2024), "Government hears back on religious schools review, but its own plans are still unclear", *ABC News*, 21 March

Derrington, S., (2019), "Of shields and swords – let the jousting begin!", *Speech to Freedom19 Conference, NSW Parliament House, Sydney*, 4 September

Dreyfus, M., (2024), "Statement on the tabling of the Australian Law Reform Commission's report on religious educational institutions and anti-discrimination laws", *Media Release*, 21 March

Dudley, E., (2023), "Religious schools 'lose faith' in law reform", *The Australian*, 14 February

Fowler, M., (2024), "Sex Discrimination Act reform proposal a breach of faith", *The Australian*, 13 April

Gould, C., (2024), "Anthony Albanese says he's prepared to shelve religious discrimination reform", *NCA Newswire*, 19 March 2024

Ison, S., (2023), "Fears religious discrimination bill could be delayed beyond next federal election", *The Australian*, 26 April

Karp, P., (2023), "Catholic schools to oppose LGBTQ+ teacher and student law reform proposal", *The Guardian Australia*, 31 January

Kelly, J., (2023), "Churches versus state to save faith school rights", *The Australian*, 13 February

Lewis, R., (2024a), "Catholic Church leaders say faith laws 'going backwards'", *The Australian*, 30 May

Lewis, R., (2024b), "'We're fast losing faith,' community groups warn Anthony Albanese", *The Australian*, 3 July

Lewis, R., and Down, R., (2024), "Mark Dreyfus and Michaelia Cash fail to reach agreement on religious discrimination reforms", *The Australian*, 28 May

Lewis, R., and Kelly, J., (2024), "Anthony Albanese says no religious freedoms changes without bipartisan support", *The Australian*, 19 March

Murphy, K., (2022), "Australian Christian Lobby targets Liberal MPs who voted against religious discrimination laws", *The Guardian*, 20 April

Parkinson, P., (2019) "The Future of Religious Freedom", *Australian Law Journal*, September 2019

Pelly, M.J., (2023), "Controversial judge to head law reform commission", *The Australian Financial Review*, 20 June

Shanahan, D., (2024), "'Anthony Albanese risks epithet of 'worst PM since Whitlam'", *The Australian*, 29 March

Shanahan, D., and Kelly, J., (2024), "Catholics warn the existence of religious schools is at threat", *The Australian*, 18 March

Stoker, A., (2023), "Labor appoints the most 'radical' hard-left activist as president of the ALRC", *Sky News Australia*, 25 June

Visentin, L., (2022), "Labor commits to religious freedom and LGBTQ protections but no timeline", *Sydney Morning Herald*, 9 May

Visentin, L., (2024), "Christian groups back Labor's plan to tackle hate speech", *Sydney Morning Herald*, 21 January

Worthington, B., (2024), "Inside Anthony Albanese's first-term inertia", *ABC News*, 29 September

Worthington, B., and Borys, S., (2024), "Anthony Albanese comments on religious discrimination draft legislation cast into doubt", *ABC News*, 22 March

Endnotes

1   The views and observations in this chapter reflect the author's personal perspectives and analysis, they are not necessarily the views of Christian schools or the many faith leaders, legal scholars and academics and advocates the author had the privilege to work alongside during this period. Many, many hours of work, often unpaid, was contributed by those people into seeking to improve government proposals and make them better aligned with international protections. Whether religious freedom legislation ever sees the light of day, their contribution to public policy in this area is worthy of recognition. Most are still actively involved in this work and thus they must remain nameless.

2   As indicated in that chapter, the act also inserted into the *Sex Discrimination Act 1984* (Cth) protections against discrimination on the basis of "intersex status". No exemption for discrimination on this basis was sought by religious groups in relation to this ground as outlined in the explanatory

memorandum to the bill.

3   It is beyond the scope of this chapter to outline the important legal
     and human rights issues associated with this discussion. For a more
     comprehensive legal analysis see, for example, the many articles in the
     special issue of the *Australian Law Journal,* Vol 9, Issue 9, on religious
     freedom and the law published September 2019 or the many high-quality
     articles made freely available in the *Australian Journal of Law and
     Religion* or the excellent Law and Religion Australia blog by Associate
     Professor Neil Foster.

4   See the questions raised by Senator Scarr of the *Senate Legal and
     Constitutional Affairs Legislation Committee Estimates,* Tuesday, 14
     February 2023.

5   *The Religious Discrimination Bill 2022* (Cth) was part of a legislative
     package that also included the *Religious Discrimination (Consequential
     Amendments) Bill 2021* (Cth) and *Human Rights Legislation Amendment
     Bill 2022* (Cth). *The Human Rights Legislation Amendment Bill 2022*
     (Cth) contained important amendments to the: *Age Discrimination Act
     2004, Disability Discrimination Act 1992, Sex Discrimination Act 1984
     and Racial Discrimination Act 1975* to amend or insert objects clauses to
     provide that, in giving effect to the objects of each Act, regard must be had
     to the indivisibility and universality of human rights and their equal status
     in international law, and the principle that every person is free and equal
     in their dignity and rights; *Charities Act 2013* to provide that otherwise
     charitable entities that engage in lawful activities promoting a traditional
     view of marriage are undertaking those activities for the public benefit and
     not contrary to public policy; and *Marriage Act 1961* to allow religious
     educational institutions to refuse to provide facilities, goods or services
     in relation to the solemnisation of a marriage in accordance with their
     religious beliefs. These also formed an important part of the consensus
     position.

6   Or "A plague o' both your houses!", from William Shakespeare's *Romeo
     and Juliet,* Act III, Scene 1.

408

20

Anyone for Footy? A Policy in Search of a Goal: The Albanese Government's PNG NRL Initiative

Andrea Wallace

Introduction

The chapter examines the Albanese Government's decision to fund a National Rugby League (NRL) team for Papua New Guinea (PNG), to counter growing Chinese influence in the Indo-Pacific region. It interrogates whether sporting franchises can meaningfully contribute to nation-building and stability in ways that traditional overseas aid cannot. Can Rugby League replace, or even complement, the essential work of institution-building and ethical governance in PNG? If regional stability and countering China's influence in the Indo-Pacific remain Australia's primary objectives, was Albanese's pivot toward sporting diplomacy a strategic innovation or a misalignment of resources? What does this initiative reveal about Labor's broader foreign policy vision under the Albanese Government, and to what extent does it represent continuity or departure from Australia's historical approach to providing support to nations in the Pacific region?

Prior to the election of the Albanese Government in 2022, concern was mounting about an increased Chinese presence in the Indo-Pacific region, particularly considering the Solomon Island's decision to participate in China's Belt and Road initiative in 2019. Framed as a way counter growing Chinese influence in the region, the Albanese Government decided to fund a national NRL team for PNG in 2024. This chapter examines the provision of overseas aid through the Albanese Government's decision to fund a national NRL team for PNG. Governments provide overseas aid to achieve specific outcomes, such as building human capital or enhancing regional security. The Albanese Government's decision to fund a NRL team in PNG raises several questions, such as whether overseas aid through the mechanism of NRL can replace, or even complement the essential work of institution-building, nation-building and stability so necessary in PNG? If regional stability and countering China's influence in the Indo-Pacific remain Australia's primary objectives, was Albanese's pivot toward sporting diplomacy a strategic innovation or a misalignment of resources? What does this initiative reveal about Labor's broader foreign policy vision under Albanese's Government, and to what extent does it represent continuity or departure from Australia's historical approach to the Pacific?

Understanding overseas aid

At its most basic, overseas aid is when one country transfers money, goods, or services to another country to benefit the recipient country's population. The aims can be humanitarian, or economic, or even militaristic. The most common form of foreign aid is Official Development Assistance (ODA), a type of assistance that endeavours to alleviate poverty whilst simultaneously promoting economic development. Modern overseas aid, of the type that we are most familiar with these days began with Prussia providing military assistance to its allies that were of strategic importance to enhance regional security. Security is but one aim for a donor country to provide aid. Economic assistance can help countries to become stronger and resist maleficent foreign influences, such as the Marshall Plan, where the United States (US) provided overseas aid to Europe after the Second World War, to build human capital and provide a counter against the growing threat of Communism.

Overseas aid is not always an altruistic endeavour but is often a strategic tool that serves two purposes. First, it fulfils the moral and ethical imperative of alleviating poverty and fostering development in countries where assistance is required. Second, such aid advances the donor country's strategic goal of enhancing regional stability. Within the milieu of international relations, particularly for countries like Australia, the benefits of having stable, functioning neighbours are obvious: conflict is reduced, there are lower migration pressures, trade is more predictable, and the opportunity for rival powers to intervene is lessened.

PNG – the Australian connection

Australia's relationship with Papua New Guinea (PNG), its closest geographical neighbour, exemplifies the need to have politically stable neighbours. At its nearest point, PNG lies just 6 kilometres from Australian territory, with approximately 150 kilometres separating Cape York from PNG's mainland, however Australia's relationship with PNG is more than geographic, the histories of both countries have been intertwined over the last century. For Australia, ensuring stability in PNG transcends moral obligation, as foreign aid to PNG represents a pragmatic decision vested in national self-interest.

In an increasingly volatile world marked by challenges to the rules-based global order and intensifying strategic competition, Australia has identified PNG and other Pacific countries as potential focal points for China's growing regional ambitions in the Indo-Pacific region. The logic underwriting Australia's aid missions in the Indo-Pacific region appears relatively straightforward; stable countries with robust democratic institutions, functioning infrastructure, and economic opportunities for citizens rarely fall prey to stronger countries wishing to assert their dominance. Overseas aid, alongside security pacts and regional cooperation, serves as a mechanism through which Australia can potentially diffuse China's influence while ensuring its closest neighbour remains a reliable ally.

How governments pursue regional stability matters. Traditional approaches to achieving stability, such as building infrastructure, strengthening healthcare systems, or investing in education might seem conventional but have been proven effective. In 2024, however, the Albanese Government committed approximately $600 million over ten years toward a surprising, and most unconventional goal: supporting PNG's entry into the NRL competition. This initiative, framed as "sports diplomacy", raises profound questions about the evolution of foreign policy tools and the relative value of cultural engagement versus institution-building. The mythologising of foreign aid as an exercise in moral generosity often obscures its function as a vehicle for strategic self-interest.

Papua New Guinea, Australia's former mandate, remains the largest recipient of Australian aid. Since 2019, Australia has provided over $2.4 billion in concessional loans to PNG, and the projected amount for 2024-25 is $650 million in Official Development Assistance grants (see, for instance, Australian Government 2022). In 2024, however, the Albanese Government made headlines with a new form of support: a $600 million soft-diplomacy package to fund PNG's participation in the NRL over ten years (Papua New Guinea Post-Courier, n.d.).

Political stability and overseas aid

Political stability refers to the capacity of a state to maintain a functioning government, uphold law and order, and avoid large-scale internal conflict or regime collapse. Steinwand (Steinwand 2015) presents a framework, theoretically economic, that shows stability is primarily concerned with the absence of violent conflict that are the result of tensions stemming from the redistribution of resources. His model is built upon the premise that a government retains sufficient authority to deter rebellion and can manage domestic dissent without resorting to repression or provoking societal upheaval. Political stability, as per Steinwand, is a condition that is especially valued by Western donors, who fear that political instability may lead to civil conflict, terrorism, or perhaps even external interference. However, foreign aid is often replete with a shadow side. Aid intended to alleviate poverty or promote domestic political stability can inadvertently create a moral hazard. Recipient governments, aware of donors' fears, may exploit this by entrenching themselves in power, diverting funds, and encouraging rent-seeking behaviours. Ironically, this undermines the very stability donors aim to support. Stability in development terms refers to the presence of functional institutions, basic public service delivery, economic opportunity, and a reasonably peaceful social fabric. It does not mean the absence of poverty, but the absence of chaos. It means that governance exists, systems function, and violence or collapse is not imminent. Stability is built through investment in education, healthcare, infrastructure, sound governance, and economic growth. It is curious that Albanese chose to pursue security and stability in PNG through sport, rather than the more traditional means of ODA.

As a developed Western country, Australia has a complex system of how it distributes overseas aid. Overseas aid is both bilateral and multilateral. Bilateral assistance refers to money given directly to another country or government, and includes financial grants for infrastructure, education projects, and health initiatives. Bilateral aid may also include technical assistance, where Australian experts work with local organisations to train and support workers in governance, education, or health systems. In times of crisis, such as natural disasters or conflicts, bilateral humanitarian relief includes essentials like food, water, shelter, and medical supplies. Multilateral aid is funding contributed to international organisations that then distribute it according to thematic goals, such as gender equality, human rights, or disaster relief, for example. These efforts are often described as 'grassroots' aid because they target vulnerable communities directly. Australia also uses private sector partnerships, such as the Emerging Markets Impact Investment Fund (EMIIF), to mobilise both public and private funds for sustainable development projects like renewable energy in Southeast Asia (DFAT 2023/24).

Australia's aid framework is coordinated through the Department of Foreign Affairs and Trade (DFAT), which ensures that funding aligns with Australia's diplomatic and development goals. Since taking office in 2022, the Albanese Government has adjusted these priorities to reflect its stated values: a greater emphasis on climate change, inclusion, and regional stability. Climate change now features prominently in Australia's foreign aid framework, with increased funding for mitigation and adaptation projects in the Pacific and Southeast Asia. In addition, LGBTQ+ rights have emerged as a symbolic focus. In 2022, the Pacific Islands Forum reaffirmed support for LGBTQ+ inclusion, and Australian overseas aid now contributes to HIV prevention strategies and sexual health education, among other initiatives. Australia also advocated for the inclusion of LGBTQ+ rights in all Commonwealth commitments at the 2022 CHOGM.

Sport aid as foreign policy

While sports can contribute to national cohesion in very limited ways, sport is unable to address the root causes of instability. Using sport to paper over serious systemic deficiencies risks mistaking theatre for transformation. Stuart Murray (Murray 2012) aptly observes that while sports diplomacy is often celebrated as a clever modern innovation, it can just as easily become "a Trojan horse for soft propaganda", or a pretext for doing less of the hard work foreign aid is supposed to accomplish. Steinwand (2014) also challenges the presumption that foreign aid inherently fosters stability, suggesting that aid, especially when framed as a stability mechanism, may inadvertently increase the risk of conflict. This happens when governments, aware of donor anxieties about instability, exploit those concerns to extract rents, suppress dissent, or avoid governance reforms. Ironically, then, aid designed to preserve order may end up subsidising dysfunction. Whether sport-as-aid escapes this same trap is unclear, but the risk remains.

The nature of Papua New Guinea

With a landmass of 462,840 square kilometres, over 5,000 kilometres of coastline, and its only land border shared with Indonesia, PNG is a resource-rich country has experienced a patchwork of colonial influence throughout its modern history. Germany declared the northern region a protectorate in 1884, with Great Britain soon claiming the south, before Australia assumed administrative control in 1902. The former German and British territories were unified under Australian administration until PNG finally gained independence in 1975 and joined the British Commonwealth, entering a challenging phase of state-building and self-governance.

Despite PNG's political evolution, tribal tensions have remained a constant feature of PNG society, most notably during the violent secessionist conflict in Bougainville from 1988 to 1994, which ended with a ceasefire in 1997 and a formal peace agreement in 2001, though the legacy of tribal loyalties and inter-group mistrust remains deeply embedded in the national psyche. Although blessed with considerable natural wealth, including gold, copper, silver, and oil, PNG has struggled to translate these resources into broad-based economic development for its more than 10 million people; as of 2023, GDP per capita was estimated at just USD $4,200, with China now receiving 28 per cent of the country's exports, surpassing Australia at 17 per cent while much of the population remains outside the reach of a functioning economy (CIA 2025).

The challenges facing PNG are multifaceted: only 13.7 per cent of the population lives in urban areas; the mountainous terrain makes infrastructure development slow and prohibitively expensive; roads are often impassable during the rainy season; electricity is unreliable in many regions; and basic services are inconsistent or entirely absent, with the World Bank's most recent assessment in 2023 flagging a continuing decline in public service delivery (World Bank 2023). Healthcare spending represents a mere 2.3 per cent of GDP, resulting in life expectancy of only 63 years for men and 67 for women, dangerously high maternal mortality rates estimated between 192 and 500 deaths per 100,000 live births, half of all children under five suffering from stunting due to chronic malnutrition and recurring infections, low immunization coverage, and high rates of tuberculosis, often antibiotic-resistant, and HIV. Education receives just 1.3 per cent of GDP, contributing to widespread teacher absenteeism, poor school infrastructure in rural areas, and literacy rates of only 65.9 per cent for men and 62.8 per cent for women aged 15 and over, while the country's extraordinary linguistic diversity; 839 living languages exist in PNG, and with English spoken fluently by only 1-2 per cent of the population, despite being an official language, service delivery and national cohesion is complicated (CIA 2025).

Compounding these challenges are deeply rooted social tensions; PNG's tribal structure underpins frequent inter-group violence, often sparked by land disputes, and gender-based and sorcery-based violence. LGBTQ+ individuals also face discrimination; while male homosexual acts are illegal and punishable by up to three years in prison, the law is rarely enforced, though social stigma remains widespread, especially in health services and community participation. Corruption further compounds the dysfunction, with the New Guinea Independent Commission Against Corruption (ICACPNG) estimating that around four billion kinas, which is approximately AUD $1.5 billion, is lost to corruption each year, evidenced by cases like that of Elizabeth Genia, the acting head of PNG's central bank who was investigated for money laundering in 2024 but retained her position, underscoring the weakness of institutional accountability (OCCRP 2025).

Australia's Department of Foreign Affairs and Trade (DFAT 2022) classifies PNG as politically unstable, and the Asian Development Bank (cited in DFAT 2022) describes it as a fragile, conflict-affected state with limited government capacity and chronic difficulty achieving sustained development, while the country's Defence Force remains small and under-equipped with only around 3,000 personnel, insufficient to manage a state that is vast, fractured, and facing persistent internal insecurity, creating a fundamentally fragile state where efforts to govern, build, or reform are continually undermined by geography, history, tribal allegiance, administrative weakness, and economic distortion. PNG, Australia's closest neighbour, became part of China's *Belt and Road Initiative* in 2018, complicating Australia's relationship with, and influence on PNG (Belt and Road Portal 2024).

The NRL for PNG: How was it funded and from whence it came?

When Prime Minister Albanese addressed Australians on election night in 2022, his rhetoric was carefully tuned to the concerns of the ordinary person. Drawing, as usual, upon his formative years, he assured the electorate that he would never forget his roots. As the son of a single mother who had not had an easy life on a disability pension, he would govern with compassion and a clear-eyed commitment to those "doing it tough". Albanese's pledge to prioritise the disadvantaged struck a moral chord with many voters. Labor campaigned as the party of ordinary Australians: those navigating mortgage stress, rising fuel prices, underfunded schools, and overstretched hospitals (McKay 2024).

However, subsequent policy decisions have cast doubt on the sincerity of these declarations. Few moves have more starkly highlighted Labor's divergence between rhetoric and reality than the Australian Government's commitment of $600 million to establish a professional rugby league team in Papua New Guinea (PNG). Presented under the banner of "Pacific diplomacy", this initiative has been described as a strategic gesture to counter China's growing influence in the region. Yet, at its core, the project resembles a sports vanity exercise underwritten by Australian taxpayers, with negligible direct benefit to the very constituents Labor claimed to represent (The Strategist 2024).

The Albanese Government formally announced the NRL funding commitment in December 2024, announcing that Australia would support PNG's entry into the National Rugby League (NRL) by 2028. This ten-year, $600 million package was unveiled at a press event featuring Albanese, PNG Prime Minister James Marape, and Australian Rugby League Commission (ARLC) chairman, Peter V'landys. Whilst heralded as a vehicle for "soft power", the arrangement merits serious scrutiny. The funds are to be drawn from Australia's foreign aid budget, specifically, the development assistance program, and are additional to Australia's existing $500 million annual aid to PNG, effectively doubling the country's financial exposure in the region.

Freedom of Information disclosures have since revealed that early in 2024, DFAT officials raised concerns about both the transparency and policy rationale for such a large grant for this purpose (Capital Brief 2025). Despite these internal warnings, the initiative proceeded. The structure of the funding is atypical: a capped, non-competitive government grant, disbursed over a decade, and divided into three components. The largest share, $290 million, is allocated to establishing and the operation of the PNG franchise: staff salaries, training, facilities, and administration. Another $250 million is earmarked for rugby league development across PNG and neighbouring Pacific countries, including Fiji, Samoa, and Tonga. The final $60 million covers the expansion licence fee payable to the ARLC (Capital Brief 2025). The PNG Government, for its part, has promised to provide land, undertake a significant upgrade of the Sir Hubert Murray Stadium in Port Moresby, and offer tax concessions to attract foreign players. The team is expected to become commercially viable after 2034, at which point taxpayer support would ostensibly cease, replaced by sponsorship and NRL revenue streams.

The decision to fund PNG's NRL team began shortly after Labor's 2022 victory, when Pacific Minister Pat Conroy initiated conversations with ARLC and PNG stakeholders. The project quickly gained favour within government as part of the so-called "Pacific Step-up", a strategic campaign to reinforce Australia's regional influence. By late 2023, Cabinet had signed off in principle on the $600 million commitment. Minister Conroy was reportedly unambiguous in negotiations, warning that Australia could redirect its funding if suitable terms were not reached. The agreement appears to have been endorsed by the National Security Committee of Cabinet, which shielded it from standard public expenditure scrutiny under the justification of strategic necessity. In May 2024, a final agreement was reached during Brisbane's Magic Round, and formally announced followed in December. Government messaging framed the project as a win on multiple fronts: regional security, cultural ties, grassroots sports development, and economic diplomacy. But this narrative was met with scepticism in Parliament. Senator Pauline Hanson criticised the government's priorities, questioning why Australians facing soaring living costs were being asked to subsidise a "foreign footy team". Hanson's petition to overturn the decision (One Nation 2024), whilst unsuccessful, struck a chord with a public increasingly weary of expensive international gestures amidst domestic hardship (National Broadcasting Corporation 2024). Foreign Minister Penny Wong and Minister Conroy defended the deal as an investment in regional stability (Guardian 2024). Their public statements conspicuously avoided any discussion of the opportunity cost: what $600 million could have delivered to struggling Australian communities. Whether in terms of upgrading crumbling regional hospitals, reversing the attrition in public school sport programs, or assisting families priced out of organised sport, the alternatives remain pointed and poignant.

Responsibility for the delivery of the funds is divided among DFAT, as the funding agency, the ARLC, as the implementing partner, and the PNG Government, as host and facilitator. Unusually, this funding is routed outside conventional aid mechanisms and is governed by a bespoke Australia–PNG–ARLC Partnership Agreement. Due to the size and structure of the grant, DFAT flagged the need for "robust governance," including performance benchmarks, phased funding, and stringent auditing protocols. These safeguards reflect the recognised risks of operating in PNG's complex governance environment. One feature of the agreement that has attracted considerable attention is its "escape clause," allowing the Australian government to withdraw support at any time, unilaterally, and without explanation. Less publicly discussed aspects of the NRL deal to PNG, but geopolitically significant, is a purported side agreement in which PNG agreed not to enter any security arrangements with China for the duration of the NRL deal. If accurate, this provision underscores the underlying strategic calculus: the fusion of sport and security in Australia's Pacific diplomacy.

The NRL initiative complements the 2023 Australia–PNG Bilateral Security Agreement, which expanded cooperation in defence, policing, and cyber-security. In that context, a sports franchise becomes a vehicle for cultural entrenchment, an unconventional soft power play. Rugby League is deeply embedded in PNG's national identity, and few instruments of Australian influence carry such emotive resonance. Nonetheless, the divergence between foreign largesse and domestic neglect is difficult to ignore. Whilst Albanese's government was making this arrangement with PNG, public schools in Australia were outsourcing physical education to third parties due to budgetary constraints. Participation in community sport was in decline, particularly among children from low-income households. Maintenance backlogs plagued local sporting facilities across regional Australia (Guardian 2024).

Sports-diplomacy has been tried by Australian Governments before; however it was started in 2015 and ten years is insufficient time to ascertain its long-term efficacy (DFAT 2015). It is prudent to ask whether the $600 million allocated to rugby in Port Moresby might have had a more immediate and equitable impact if invested in sport, health, or infrastructure at home. The Albanese Government may well believe that securing influence in the Pacific is worth the price tag. But for a government elected on promises of empathy and pragmatism, the symbolism of this decision is both telling and troubling. It is also questionable as to whether funding sports will secure regional security as the Albanese Government hopes it will (see McKay 2024).

Conclusions

The Albanese Government provided a symbolic gesture to PNG in the form of sporting diplomacy. Whether this decision to fund a NRL team for one of the world's most disadvantaged, and undeveloped countries will prove helpful remains to be seen. Whilst funding an NRL team was framed by Albanese and his Ministers as a masterstroke of soft power, the shadow side of the initiative could also be viewed as an exercise in hubris, ignorance, and geopolitical short-sightedness. On the surface, Labor's policy to create geopolitical stability and deter further Chinese influence in the region appears benign and noble, is rugby league able to create necessary institutions in a country plagued by problems? Is it able to immunise children against common diseases, or create judicial independence? Is political fragility solved by scoring NRL tries, and will a NRL team be sufficient to counter Chinese influence?

The human cost of this policy could be severe; as the glamour of footy arrives in PNG, how will society cope the associated phenomenon of gambling, or economic distortion? Will Labor's policy create a veneer of unity in PNG that could descend into resentment when promises are not kept?

The opportunity cost of funding a footy team raises the question of whether Australia is subsidising entertainment, or whether the Albanese Labor Government is providing favours for the NRL. Had

Australia spent $600 million over the next ten years increasing its defence capabilities, or even in conventional aid arrangements to PNG building institutions and infrastructure is worth questioning. Given PNG's 2018 entry into China's *Belt and Road Initiative*, and Australia's response six years later, of funding a footy team rather than any concrete infrastructure assistance, raises questions; does Albanese's government understand the nature of strategic competition in the Indo-Pacific? It appears the Labor Government, under the leadership of Albanese, has established a new model for regional engagement in the Pacific, and a model that perhaps is either too optimistic about the efficacy of soft power through footy, or is reluctant to make the harder choices regarding military deterrence in the Indo-Pacific.

PNG's existing status as a signatory to China's *Belt and Road Initiative* further complicates Australia's strategy of trying to use footy as soft diplomacy. The case of the Solomon Islands serves as a cautionary tale: Australia relied on its role of regional peacekeeper and its historic ties with the Solomon Islands, thus becoming complacent. Australia neglected to see that the Solomon Islands could become receptive to alternative arrangements. Thus far, China has built much needed infrastructure, and initiated a number of healthcare programmes. Can the NRL offer the same of assistance to stabilise PNG and counter Chinese influence in the Pacific?

At this stage, it is too early to tell, but given that Albanese put a new, and untested form of diplomacy into action, it is difficult to ascertain what the result of this policy will be. What is clear, however, is that whilst Albanese told Aussie battlers that he could do all could for them to make their lives easier, his legacy will be of the politician who prioritised political symbolism over substantive policy outcomes, effectively trading PNG's development needs for a footy team.

References

Australian Government, (2022), *National Interest Statement: Loan Agreement between the Commonwealth of Australia and the Independent State of Papua New Guinea*, Treasury, Canberra: Commonwealth of Australia https://treasury.gov.au/sites/default/

files/2022-02/p2022-247810.pdf.

Capital Brief, (2025), "DFAT officials raised alarms over NRL's $500m PNG deal', *Capital Brief* https://www.capitalbrief.com/article/dfat-officials-raised-alarms-over-nrls-600m-deal-for-png-expansion-db2706cb-a5c2-4da2-9755-5a3fa8b86c6c/preview/.

Central Intelligence Agency (CIA), (2025), *The World Factbook: Papua New Guinea*, , Washington DC: CIA https://www.cia.gov/the-world-factbook/countries/papua-new-guinea/.

Department of Foreign Affairs and Trade, (2015), *Australian Sports Diplomacy Strategy 2015-18*, Canberra: Commonwealth of Australia   https://www.dfat.gov.au/sites/default/files/aus-sports-diplomacy-strategy-2015-18.pdf.

Department of Foreign Affairs and Trade, (2022), *DFAT Country Report on Papua New Guinea*. Canberra: Commonwealth of Australia https://www.dfat.gov.au/sites/default/files/country-information-report-papua-new-guinea.pdf.

Department of Foreign Affairs and Trade, (2023), *Australia's Official Development Assistance Budget Summary 2023-24*, Canberra: Commonwealth of Australia   https://www.dfat.gov.au/about-us/corporate/portfolio-budget-statements/australias-official-development-assistance-budget-summary-2023-24.

McKay, J., (2024), "Albanese drops the ball on rugby league diplomacy with PNG", *Pearls and Irritations*, 12 December https://johnmenadue.com/post/2024/12/albanese-drops-the-ball-on-rugby-league-diplomacy-with-png/.

Murray, S., (2012), "The two halves of sports-diplomacy", *Diplomacy and Statecraft*, 23(3), 576-92.

National Broadcasting Corporation, (2024), "Attorney General rebuts Australia's One National Senator Pauline Hanson's NRL bid remarks" *NBC Papua New Guinea* https://www.nbc.com.pg/post/13675/attorney-general-rebuts-australias-one-nation-senator-pauline-hansons-nrl-bid-remarks

Organized Crime and Corruption Reporting Project (OCCRP), (2025), "PNG's central bank chief appointed amid money laundering investigation" https://www.occrp.org/en/scoop/pngs-central-bank-chief-appointed-amid-money-laundering-investigation

One Nation, (2024), *Oppose the Allocation of the $600 Million to the NRL for an 18th team in Papua New Guinea*, One Nation Australia https://www.onenation.org.au/oppose-the-allocation-of-600-million-to-the-nrl-for-an-18th-team-in-papua-new-guinea

Papua New Guinea Post-Courier n.d., "PNG is Australia's largest development partner budget reveals", *Post-Courier* https://www.postcourier.com.pg/png-is-australias-largest-development-partner-budget-reveals/

Steinwand, M.C., (2015), "Foreign aid and political stability", *Conflict Management and Peace Science*, 32(4), 395-424

The Guardian, (2024a), "Inside PNG's NRL deal: how the licence was won and what comes next", *The Guardian*, 12 December https://www.theguardian.com/sport/2024/dec/12/explainer-inside-png-nrl-deal-how-the-licence-was-won-and-what-comes-next

The Guardian, (2024b), "Papua New Guinea to join NRL under historic deal with a China 'escape clause' ", *The Guardian*, 12 December https://www.theguardian.com/sport/2024/dec/12/png-nrl-team-rugby-league-papua-new-guinea-2028-expansion-licence

The Strategist, (2024), "Game-planning national security and the PNG NRL team", *The Strategist*, https://www.aspistrategist.org.au/game-planning-national-security-and-the-png-nrl-team/

World Bank, (2023), *Papua New Guinea Country Economic Memorandum: Pathways to Faster and More Inclusive Growth*, Washington DC: World Bank https://openknowledge.worldbank.org/entities/publication/169d105d-7560-485c-b6f3-b59827612b80

Part 4
Aftermath: Lessons for the Future?

21

Lessons for the Future

Scott Prasser

Introduction

What a difference an election makes – the 2025 election that is. The results make assessing the first Albanese Government, of drawing any lessons, completely different now. It is both the size of the Albanese Government's 2025 election win and its very unexpectedness that require us all to reconsider just how to evaluate this government's first term.

All this means that when coming to draw lessons from the Albanese Government's first term it needs to be seen not just in terms of policies initiated or legislation passed, important as these are, but also in terms of a government's electoral success or failure. It is that success or failure that really affects how any democratic government is perceived and what lessons can be drawn from its preceding term in office. If a government or opposition wins an election, then surely it must be doing something right. So, what is it with the Albanese Government? If a government loses, then its policies were wrong, its governing misplaced and lastly, its campaigning poor. Of course, the Labor Party has a particular way of viewing failure – for the Whitlam Government the cause was noble, but its reforms were too fast and the electorate was not ready for so much change. For many, Howard lost office in 2007 for the single reason of the "poisoned chalice" of WorkChoices – forgetting about Howard's age, length of time in office, scandals, controversies and sheer voter weariness – and Rudd.

Reviewing the size of the Albanese Government's 2025 win, the government has not just secured a second term but has succeeded so spectacularly that it may have even gained a third term. As things now stand Albanese has secured a bigger two-party preferred vote than several previous Labor leaders including its heroes – Whitlam, Hawke, Keating and Rudd. Hawke's Labor never won more than 86 of 148 seats of the House of Representatives whereas Albanese has won 94 of 150 – a larger proportion than Hawke. That the Labor primary vote is still low at 34.6 per cent (see Table 9, **Chapter 1**) is neither here nor there. Albanese now has the numbers in the House of Representatives and given the extra seats Labor has won in the Senate, can, with Greens support, secure its left of centre policy agenda. It is, however, all over for the Coalition as their combined House of Representatives seat losses in the 2022 and 2025 elections total of 34 is huge. Further, their diminution of the Senate (down five seats) is significant. They cannot think of blocking anything in the Senate or even being at the negotiating table. They are now more sidelined politically and in parliamentary terms than at any time they have been in opposition since the 1970s. It is all largely over too for the motley crew of independents, minor and micro party crossbenchers in the Senate for reasons explained. Their relationship with the government will not be the same in this coming second term as it was in the first.

When you combine these results with their unexpectedness, then the Albanese Government's 2025 election win deserves even more attention. Remember, almost all the pundits were saying in the twelve months prior to the election and even as late as January 2025, that it was either all over for the Albanese Government, or at best it was going to be a minority government (Black 2024a; Black 2024b; Carney 2025; Samaras 2025; Williams 2025 – see also **Chapter 1** for other examples). After all, only once before, have governments seeking a second term gained seats.[1]

So, as the Australian political landscape has changed, what then are the lessons we can take from the Albanese Government's first term? What's happened?

Lessons

The first lesson is in the future not to underestimate Anthony Albanese's political skills, campaigning abilities, judgements and connectiveness with the electorate. He has seen off two Coalition leaders. He has secured a second and even possibly a third term.

The second lesson, closely related to the first, is that Labor, if not Albanese himself, are far better campaigners than the Coalition parties, notwithstanding Labor's low primary vote, but both major parties suffer in that regard. The issue is that in a changing political environment with voters less attached to the major parties, Labor's ability to garner votes and turn them into the landslide of the 2025 election deserves attention. It partly reflects how better networked the Labor Party is, the skills their party structure and links with trade unions and other community organisations, affords them compared to the Coalition parties.

The third lesson is that leadership stability and party unity matter – that is not new, but it is worth reiterating. Treasurer Chalmers may be the emerging heir apparent but there was never any countenance to a possible coup against Albanese, even when the polls were dipping. Dutton did secure unity in the Coalition but there were frequent outbreaks of "conservatives" versus "progressives" warfare especially across the state branches. This infected the federal Coalition's policies and electoral competitiveness. On nuclear power and the Voice state coalition party backing was lacking or only lukewarm. Labor practised unity across all levels of government. Winning federal office was always the greater cause. Labor was able to do so because there was a unity of policy and purpose.

Fourth, there is the political narrative lesson. Melleuish lays this out loud and clear (**Chapter 2**). Labor had a cohesive narrative that encompassed their policies and was further reinforced by them. You may not agree with the Albanese's mantra that more government is needed, that more spending is warranted or that we turn back the clock on industrial relations and the redefining of what "reform" means – but it worked as the election shows (see **Chapters 8-11**). Labor's narrative has become the new conventional wisdom for Australian politics and policy development. That the Coalition lacked a comparable narrative to counter this, made Labor's look acceptable and compelling. The Coalition's policy responses were ad hoc, disconnected, reactive and opportunistic, too often taking their cue from the government rather than projecting their own. The Coalition failed to counter head on Labor's political and thus policy agenda (**Chapter 4**).

Fifth, there are lessons about governance. Certainly, Labor handled the transition to office with less friction than previous Coalition administrations (**Chapter 5**). There was, for instance, unlike for the Abbott Administration, no external National Commission of Audit established with its impending report of budget cuts, departmental restructures, or re-federalisation. Nor was there any parade of exiting department secretaries and numerous personnel changes (Wettenhall and Gourley 2016). And of course, during the 2025 election the Coalition made matters worse by their attacks on the public service concerning the working from home arrangements and proposed public sector staff cuts.

Sixth, portraying itself as open, consultative and corrupt free was easy for the Albanese Government given its predecessor's tarnished reputation over a host of issues. This concerned: matters emanating from the Robodebt scandal; workplace culture in Parliament: political appointments to the Administrative Appeals Tribunal: delays in forming an anticorruption commission: and Morrisons's pandemic multi-ministerial roles. Labor exploited these with further reviews, royal commissions, and legal opinions (**Chapter 7**). The Liberal Party, once the party of propriety and respectability has looked increasingly as the party of backroom deals, support for mates and being generally untrustworthy.

Seventh, the political environment has changed, perhaps irrevocably, so that what used to be certainty of where Australia was heading no longer applies. What used to be accepted as good policy and economic argument no longer does. What policies we ought to follow, we no longer strive to do (Kelly, 2024). What concerns we should have, we seem too numb to feel. Public policy is no longer what the late Reserve Bank economist Austin Holmes (1981: 1) called the "good fight" which was "the struggle to get good sense (economic rationality if you like) into our economic affairs and, more specifically, into the economic policies which influence those affairs". There was a time when that was the policy game, and the politics was gaining support for it by evidence, debate, negotiations and persistent determination. Now we are more captured by: the electoral cycle; outdated ideologies; vested narrow rent seeking interest groups with some especially attached to political parties; a lack of understanding of the interdependencies of policy; and as good money goes after bad policy and projects, a disregard of efficiency.

Conclusion

The Albanese Government is probably one of Australia's most left of centre national governments. Its "reform" agenda is very different to that of the Hawke-Keating and Howard governments. It is even different to that of the Whitlam Government, which despite its flaws, introduced some important, needed and overdue reforms including several for the economy. By contrast, most contributors to this volume and other commentators, see the Albanese Government's narrative, and its reset of the national agenda and policy settings made during its first term very negatively across the economy, energy, living standards, defence and for certain freedoms. Its 2025 electoral success and continual good polling will give greater impetus to those very same policies in its second term.

The key lesson is that a party with clear goals, a commitment to achieve them, the strategies to implement them, and most importantly in a modern democracy, the personnel with the skills to argue them, can change a nation's agenda. By so doing the Albanese Government has rendered the previous criteria for judging "good" policy redundant and sidelined not just its political opposition, but all those who disagree. Michael Sexton got it right. Previously, he highlighted how the non-Labor parties have been disestablished from our key institutions – the media, the universities, the legal profession, schools, community and cultural groups and even the corporate sector (Sexton 2024). Now, those trends combined with Labor's 2025 election win and with a third term possible, means Labor has replaced the Liberals as the "natural party of government" (Sexton 2025). Consequently, it is now Labor who sets the political agenda, defines the problems and priorities and thus what the policies should be. This is what American political scientist E.E. Schattschneider called the "mobilization of bias" which through a range of activities, processes, and techniques, determines what gets talked about and what gets ignored. It involves "the organizing into politics of certain issues and the organizing out of others" and "whoever decides what the game is about decides also who can get into the game" and ultimately who wins the politics and gains office (Schattschneider 1960 [1983]: 69, 102). This is exactly what most chapters in this volume have sought to highlight – issues have been redefined to a narrower range in tune with the Albanese Government's ideological objectives, institutions re-missioned to support and implement the agenda, and language and community values and myths, manipulated to control the public discourse. The "fix" is in but how is it ever going to be undone and by whom is the challenge. It has been observed (Mair 1997: 953) that:

> Party competition is not just about the competition between one set of demands, ideologies or even leaderships ... It is about a competition between contested terms of reference, and about the ground on which the game will actually be played.

The Labor Party has long appreciated this and now under Albanese has reached its zenith in giving it a practical application with resulting lasting political success. The non-Labor parties have never really understood the game being played hence their surprise at the situation in which they now find themselves. Given their current, depleted, fragmented and confused state, it seems they may be unable to respond, if at all, unless they completely reconfigure themselves organisationally, ideologically, and in terms of fundamental political skills. The political environment has fundamentally changed. The challenge for all the non-Labor forces, but especially the Coalition, is how they are going to fit into this new landscape. They need to distinguish themselves from Labor politically while developing policies that address the nation's problems more effectively than is presently the case under the Albanese Government, while garnering voter support to project them back into office.

References

Black, J., (2024a), "Labor's chance of holding on to power was slim. Now it's wafer thin". Australian Financial Review, 18 October

Black, J., (2024b), "Federal election 2025: Anthony Albanese will need that Copacabana beach house next year", 27 December

Carney, S., (2025), "Albanese now realises he is on a rescue mission to save a sinking ship", *Sydney Morning Herald*, 23 January

Holmes, A.S., (1981), "The Good Fight", *The Economic Record*, March, 1-11

Kelly, P., (2024), "2024: The Year Australia Lost its Way", *The Australian*, 28 December

Samaras, K., (2025), "Dutton is riding the backlash against woke capitalism", *Australian Financial Review*, 4 February

Schattschneider, E.E., (1960) [1983], *The Semi-Sovereign People,* New York: Holt, Rinehart and Winston

Sexton, M., (2024), "The Disestablishment of the Liberal Party", in Prasser, S., (ed), *Tragedy without Triumph: The Coalition in Office 2013-2022,* Redland Bay: Connor Court Publishing, 224-33

Sexton, M., (2025), "Has Labor finally become the natural party of government?", *The Spectator,* 24 July

Wettenhall, R., and Gourley, P., (2016), "The public sector", in Aulich, C., (eds), *From Abbott to Turnbull: Australian Commonwealth Administration, 2013-2016,* West Geelong: Echo Books, 69-94

Williams, P., (2025), "Like Jimmy, history will be kind to Albo's legacy", *Courier-Mail*, 3 January

Endnote

1   Curtin gained office in 1941 when the UAP-Country Party coalition loss the confidence of the House. At the later 1943 election the ALP won 13 additional seats and received 58.2 per cent of the two-party preferred vote.

Contributors

Gary Banks AO, is an independent economist who has published widely on economic reform issues. He recently stepped down as Professorial Fellow at the Melbourne Institute and as a Senior Fellow at the Centre for Independent Studies. He was Chairman of the Productivity Commission from its inception in 1998 to 2012, after which he was appointed Dean of the Australia and New Zealand School of Government (ANZSOG). During this period he also chaired the OECD's Regulatory Policy Committee and the Australian Statistics and Advisory Council. He has been an advisor to foreign governments and international agencies.

Salvatore Babones is a quantitative comparative sociologist at the University of Sydney. His current research focuses on the political sociology of democracy. In the past he has also published on economic development in post-socialist transition economies and quantitative methods for cross-national comparisons. He writes extensively on public policy issues and is a widely cited commentator on Australian higher education.

Richard Calver is an employment lawyer working in Canberra in his own private practice. Richard has had 50 years experience in the law, having previously conducted his own legal practice in the state of Victoria, taught law at the Faculty of Law Monash University, the RMIT University and the University of Canberra as well as having had roles in government and industry. He has had experience as a director of not-for-profit organisations as well as private and public companies. Richard is also the wine writer for the *Canberra City News* and has published a novel entitled *Blinded,* available on Amazon KDP.

Michael Easson AM, is a businessman, company director, former union leader, and Labor historian. Michael was Secretary of the Labor Council of NSW, 1989-94, and Senior Vice President of the NSW ALP. Michael holds a MSc with distinction from the University of Oxford, and a PhD in history from the ADFA at the UNSW, and a PhD in transport planning from the University of Melbourne. Michael was awarded Member of the Order of Australia in 1997.

Saul Eslake is an independent economist based in Hobart. He previously worked as an economist in Australia's financial markets for more than 25 years, including as Chief Economist for the ANZ Bank, and Chief Economist (Australia & New Zealand) for Bank of America-Merrill Lynch. He was Chief Executive Officer of the Victorian Commission of Audit in 1992-93, and in 2024 conducted an Independent Review of Tasmania's State Finances. He is a member of the Australian Parliamentary Budget Office's expert advisory panel.

Peter Forsyth was Professor of Economics at Monash University until recently. His research has been on transport economics and the economics of aviation, He recently published *Aviation and Climate Change: Economic Perspectives on Greenhouse Gas Reduction Polices* (with F. Fichert and H-M, Niemeier, Routledge, 2020).

Gary Johns was a Minister in the Keating Government and was the Commissioner of the Australian Charities and Not-for-profits Commission. He has served on the Productivity Commission, received the Centenary Medal and the Fulbright Award, and is the author of ten books, the most recent being *The Burden of Culture* (2022).

Paddy Gourley spent 30 years in the Commonwealth Public Service after which he became a director of two big private sector companies and a journalistic commentator on public administration. He has written chapters on the Whitlam Government's Coombs Royal Commission on Australian Government Administration and the more recent Thodey Review of the Public Service appointed by the Turnbull Government.

Aynsley Kellow (PhD) is Professor Emeritus of Government, University of Tasmania. Recent research is focused on international climate change negotiations, the OECD, global governance on these and similar areas. Aynsley is particularly interested in the processes by which more effective multilateral environmental agreements can be developed.

Mike Kelly is Adjunct Professor of Business, Government and Law, University of Canberra. He served for 20 years in the Australian Army, 13 years in the Australian Parliament as Member for Eden Monaro, National Security Adviser to the Leader of the Opposition and Minister for Defence Materiel along with Assistant Minister roles. He was also President of Palantir Technologies Australia from 2020-2024. He has written two books emerging from his PhD and multiple articles in books and journals.

David Lee is Associate Professor in History in the School of Humanities and Social Sciences, University of New South Wales, Canberra. His publications include: *Iron Country: Unlocking the Pilbara (*2015); *The Second Rush: Mining and the Transformation of Australia* (2016) and *John Curtin* (2022). He is Cabinet Historian of the National Archives of Australia.

Maria Maley is Senior Lecturer in the School of Politics and International Relations at the Australian National University. She has published widely on the work of ministerial staff and political advisers and on the culture of parliamentary workplaces. Her publications include *Toxic Parliaments And what can be done about them* (with Marian Sawer, 2024). In 2021 she worked as a consultant to the Human Rights Commission's *Independent Review into Commonwealth Parliamentary Workplaces.* In 2022 Maria was awarded the *Marian Simms Policy Engagement Award* by the Australian Political Studies Association "in recognition of outstanding achievement, innovation and creativity in research impact and policy engagement in the discipline of Political Science".

Malcolm Mackerras AO, is Visiting Fellow at the Australian Catholic University and was previously Associate Professor at the Australian Defence Force Academy. Malcolm has been writing and commenting on Australian elections and politics for decades and developed the now widely used electoral pendulum. In 2006 Malcolm was made an Officer of the Order of Australia (AO).

Greg Melleuish is an honorary research fellow with Campion College in NSW. He has written widely on Australian politics and history. His books include *Cultural Liberalism in Australia* (1995), *The Packaging of Australia (1998), Despotic State or Free Individual (2014)* and with Stephen Chavura, *The Forgotten Menzies* (2021).

John Mickel was a Queensland State Labor parliamentarian representing the seat of Logan from 1998 to 2012. He held several senior portfolios in the Beattie and the Bligh governments and from 2009 until the 2012 election when he retired he was Speaker of the Legislative Assembly. John is currently an Adjunct Associate Professor in the School of Justice at QUT. He holds a Bachelor of Teaching from Griffith University, as well as a Bachelor of Arts, Bachelor of Educational Studies, and Master of Literary Studies from the University of Queensland. John recently gained his PhD from Queensland University of Technology.

Scott Prasser has worked in senior policy and research position in federal and state governments including secondments to ministerial offices and held academic roles, the last at professorial level. His recent publications include: *Royal Commissions and Public Inquiries in Australia* (2021) and *Tragedy without Triumph: The Coalition in Office 2013-2022* Scott is a graduate of Queensland and Griffith universities.

Mark Spencer spent nearly 34 years serving Christian schools, including responsibility for public policy and advocacy on behalf of over 200 member schools. During that time, he advocated tirelessly in areas including religious freedom and discrimination law and school funding, appearing before multiple committees and inquiries and across a wide range of media. Mark has qualifications in accounting, governance and law, and has been involved in party politics in a variety of roles. He is married to Melanie, a Christian school principal, and they have three adult children.

Gene Tunny is a former Commonwealth Treasury official who has managed teams in department's Industry and Budget Policy divisions and is now Director of Adept Economics, a Brisbane-based economic consulting firm. Gene is a regular economics commentator in the national media. His book *Beautiful One Day, Broke the Next: Queensland's Public Finances Since Sir Joh and Sir Leo* was published in 2018. He is also an Adjunct Fellow at the Centre for Independent Studies.

Peter van Onselen is Professor of Politics and Public Policy at the University of Western Australia and a regular commentator on Australian politics in the national media. His books on the Liberal side of politics include: *John Howard: The Biography* (2007); *Battleground: Why the Liberal Party Shirtfronted Tony Abbott* (2015); *The Turnbull Gamble* (2017); and *How Good is Scott Morrison?* (2020).

Andrea Wallace is a Lecturer at the School of Business, University of New England, Anderea holds an undergraduate and postgraduate qualifications in politics, history, and economics from the University of Canterbury, New Zealand. In 2019 she completed her PhD focusing on local government structural reform. In addition to her ongoing research in local government, other research interests include public policy and social and economic issues.

Index

Aboriginal issues – see 'Voice', Ch 15

Administrative Appeals Tribunal (AAT), appointments to, 106-7

Albanese, A., as prime minster, 9-12, promises 13-15, legacy 18, Narrative 53-6, on productivity 203, vote getter and campaigner 27-34, 429; assessment, 432-4

AUKUS, see Ch 16 and Ch 17

Australian Building and Construction Commission, abolition of, 227-8

Aviation policy, Ch 13: assessment of, 278-80; COVID-19 impact, 272-4; Domestic aviation policy,270-71; Qatar Airways issue, 262-7; White Paper on Aviation, 267-70

Bell, Virginia, (Bell Inquiry) see Ch 7, 140,151-2, 157

Bowen, Chris, Minister for Energy, see Ch 12, energy policy, 243, 244, 247-8.

Briggs, Lynelle, Report on public employment diversity, 115-16

Calma-Langton Indigenous Voice Co-design Process Final Report, 309-10

CFMEU – see industrial relations, Ch 11

Chalmers, J , Treasurer, Chs 2, 8, 9 10; Narrative speech 56-60

Coalition (parties) see Chapter 4: federal election campaign strategy 87-90; failure 95-96

COVID-19 Response Inquiry (Kruk Inquiry), see Ch 7, 140,153-57

Craven, Greg, views on the 'Voice', 307, 308

Davis, Glyn, Head of Department of Prime Minister and Cabinet, 109, 111, 113-14

de Brouwer, Gordon, Australian Public Service Commission, 111-13, 114, 120

Defence policy, Ch 17: A UKUS partnership, 344, 355; China. 343-4; 348-51; 352; 356-7; Defence of Australia (DoA), White Paper, 343; Defence Strategic Review (DSR). 349-5; Forward defence, 343, 351-2; nuclear-powered submarines, 344, 346, 348-9, 351-4, 356

Digital services, see Ch 18: initiatives, 370ff; Service failures: Veterans' affairs, 363-4, 366Census 2016, 364; NDIS, 367-69; Data and Digital Government Strategy, 369

Dreyfus, Mark, Attorney-General, religious freedom legislation, 396, 398

Dutton Coalition Opposition see Chapter 4: assessment of 96-9, campaign 2025, lack of alternatives 93-6; negative, disruptive strategy, 87-90

Economy under Albanese, Ch 8: assessment of 179-80; cost of living, 167-70;

employment, 173-6; immigration and housing, 176-78; productivity, wages and living standards, 170-73'decline in productivity, see also Ch 10

Education (universities) see Ch 14: assessment of 297-300; attainment rates, 288-90, Australian Universities Accord. 285-88; election 2022 promises, 284-5; Higher Education Loan Program (HELP), 285; international students numbers, 284; Indigenous student deficit, 291-3

Elections, federal results, two party preferred 1980-2025 37, seats won 2007-2025 38-4

Energy, Chs 10, 12, crisis, 205-6; energy and climate policy, 242-49; net zero, lower productivity, 206-08

Environment policy – see Ch 12

Fair Work Act and related legislation – see industrial relations Ch 11

Fiscal policy, see Ch 9; election promises, 184-5; Budget results, 185-9

GST distribution, 209-10; Assessment of government, 199-201

Foreign policy, see Ch 16: assessment of, 316-29, 333-6;

ASEAN, 328-9; AUKUS policy. 325-7; Blue Pacific, 329-30;

China, 332; Isael-Gaza, 331-2; SE Asia, 327-9; Ukraine, 330; USA, 324-5, 332

Fraser, Malcolm, Prime Minister, 146

Future Made in Australia (FMIA), 172, 218

Gaetjens, Philip, Secretary, Department of Prime Minister and Cabinet, 108-9, 114, 124

Gallagher, Katy, Senator (Minister for Finance)Chair, Senate COVID-19 Committee, support for royal commission, 154; Minister for Finance, 111-2, 116, 185

Higher education, see Universities, Ch 14

Holmes, Catherine, The Hon, chair, Royal Commission into Robodebt Scheme, see Ch 7, 139-40, 147-51

Indigenous issues, see Voice', Ch15, foreign policy representative, 33;

university education, 291-3

Industrial relations, Ch 11:promises, 225-7;Australian Building and Construction Commission, 227-8;

Fair Work Act 2009, CFMEU, 228-30;Review of Secure Jobs Act, 230-3;assessment 233-6

Inquiry into the Appointment of the Former Prime Minister to Administer Multiple Departments (Bell Inquiry), see Ch 7, 150-2, 157

Jenkins Report, see Ch 6, implementation of, 133-5

Keating, Paul, attack on Wong and

Marles, 348; economic policies of Albanese government, 166-7,179, 209

Kruk Inquiry, see COVID-19 Response Inquiry, Ch 7, 152-7

Ministerial staff, uses and accountability, 123

Morrison, Scott, 9, 15, 17, 35,85, 81,106 (public service), 146-50 (robodebt),150-2 (ministerial posts), 316,325,344,395 (AUKUS)

Nature Repair Market Bill 2023, 249-52

Narratives, Labor's, see Chapter 2, Albanese, 53-56; Chalmers, 56-63

National Anti-Corruption Commission (NACC), 120-21, 118-121

National Rugby League (NRL), see Overseas Aid Chapter 20

Net Zero see Chs, 10, 12, 206,-08 254 254-5

NDIS (National Disability Insurance Scheme), see Ch 18 and Digital Services

Overseas aid, see Ch 20, 410-11 (definition), 412-14 (funding), 420-21m 414-16 (PNG), sport and overseas aid, 414-15

Parliament, see Ch 6

-   Independent Parliamentary Standards Commission (IPSC), 133-4
-   Jenkins Report, see Ch6,
-   Joint Select Committee on Parliamentary Standards, 131-2
-   Office of Staff Support, 136
-   Parliamentary Workplace

Support Service, 133

Plibersek, Tanya, Minister for Environment, see Ch 12, 242-3

Politicisation of, public service, 123, 125; ALRC, 396

Price, Jacinta, Senator, see Ch 15, 304

Productivity, see Ch 10, Albanese's promise, 202; assessment of, 221-2

declining performance, 203-05; labour market rigidities, 208-10; net zero and productivity, 206-08

reform failures, 221-22

Productivity Commission, see Ch 10

Public inquiries, see Ch 7

Public service (Australian), see Ch 5: consultants, use of, 116: secretaries appointments, 123-5

integrity, 118-21; Robodebt Scheme, 107, 114, 118-21; Thodey Review -108, 111-12, 117, 119

Public Service Commissio1, 11-14, 120

Queensland Labor Party

-   Labor's Queensland federal election results:
    -   federation to 1929, 68
    -   1929-1961, 68-70
    -   1961-1993, 70
    -   1996-2022, 72
    -   2015 results, 77-80
-   Drivers of Labor's election results, 73-6

Referendum, 2023 see The Voice, Ch 15

Religious freedom, Ch 19

- Albanese's broken promises, 401-3
- ALRC review of religious freedom legislation, 395-98
- Equal Opportunity (Religious Exceptions) Amendment Bill 2021 (Vic), 395
- Secret consultations and draft legislation, 398-401
- Assessment, 402-3

Reserve Bank of Australia (RBA)

- inflation target, 180
- interest rates, 226

Religious freedom legislation see Ch 19 and entry

Robodebt royal commission see Royal Commission into Robodebt Scheme

Robodebt Scheme, see Chs 5, 7, 18

Royal Commission into the Robodebt Scheme see Ch 7 and 107, 109-10, 118-20, 124, 362-3, 384

Rothman, Justice Stephen, review of religious freedom legislation, 396-8

Shorten, Bill, Minister, see Ch 18 reforms to NDIS

Taxation policy, 216-18, 222

Thodey Review into Australian Public Service, see Ch 5, 108-11, 112, 117, 119

Uluru Statement from the Heart – see Voice, Ch 15, 305-07

Universities, see education and Chapter 14

Veterans' affairs, Ch 18, service failure, 363

Voice, referendum, see Ch 15,

White elephant projects, 215-16

Wong, Senator, Minister for Foreign Affairs see Ch 16: AUKUS, 345-6, 328; speech 'Securing our future, 320; strategic vision, 316-17, 322; on China, 323; US relation, 324, 332; SE Asia, 325; Quad, 326' Blue Pacific, 329

www.ingramcontent.com/pod-product-compliance
Lightning Source LLC
Chambersburg PA
CBHW051947270326
41929CB00015B/2559